the stranglers

LIVE (EXCERPTS)

SPENWOOD BOOKS

A catalogue record for this book is available from the British Library.

ISBN: 978-1-915858-31-3

The authors and publisher gratefully acknowledge the permission granted to reproduce the copyright material in this book. Every effort has been made to trace the copyright holders of the photographs in this book but one or two were unreachable. We would be grateful if the photographers concerned would contact us.

Spenwood Books Limited, 2 College Street, Higham Ferrers, NN10 8DZ, United Kingdom

SPENWOOD BOOKS

Email: richard@spenwoodbooks.com

The Stranglers September 1977, left to right Jet Black, Hugh Cornwell, JJ Burnel and Dave Greenfield. Alamy Stock Photo

FOREWORD

As the Stranglers approach fifty years of gigging and touring, we take a fond look back at the people, places and situations that we've encountered.

We have met so many people over those years, some we still recognise today, some with whom we are on first name terms and others who have become friends. Some have fallen by the wayside, others have passed away and yet others have met, married and been brought together through a shared passion.

The thing that binds us together through all is the Stranglers.

I am so grateful for the richness that this has brought to my life and I know that many have their own anecdotes and stories that they would like to share with us in this book.

JJ Burnel
September 2022

JJ: THINGS STARTED TO BUILD UP AROUND THE END OF '75. WE STARTED GETTING A FEW PEOPLE INTERESTED IN US LIKE THE GUYS AT THE HOPE AND ANCHOR. THEY'D HAVE BANDS IN EVERY NIGHT APART FROM SUNDAYS BUT THEY DECIDED TO OPEN UP ON SUNDAY NIGHTS AS OUR RESIDENCY. THE FIRST TIME WE PLAYED I REMEMBER THERE WAS NO ONE THERE AND WE HEARD SOME FOOTSTEPS COME DOWN THE STAIRS AND THIS GUY TOOK A SEAT IN THIS EMPTY CELLAR AND WE PLAYED OUR SET TO HIM. THE FOLLOWING WEEK HE CAME DOWN WITH A DOZEN PEOPLE AND IT PICKED UP FROM THERE.

HOPE & ANCHOR

15 MARCH 1976, LONDON, UK

PAUL MASON

Paul Mason walked into the Hope & Anchor and discovered the Stranglers (and son Luke is also a fan)

Many years ago, my friend Peter Jones and I were two young lads who had gone down to London from Staffordshire for a great adventure. Purely by chance, we walked past the Hope & Anchor and went in. There was a band playing and it turned out to be the Stranglers. What I didn't know at the time was that this would be the first of almost 400 times I would go on to see them. I've seen them on every tour and purchased everything they've released.

Sadly, Peter was killed about five years later. While he was in hospital, he asked me that, if he didn't survive, to make sure he was buried in a Stranglers t-shirt. Obviously, I carried out his wishes.

I'm so glad I went into the pub that day. My 30-year-old son Luke, who is now a sergeant major, has been to see the Stranglers with me about 15 times and loves the band. My wife and I went to see them when she was eight and a half months pregnant with Luke, so he heard them before he was born! I'm still part of the familyinblack to this day.

JJ: IT WAS A VERY SMALL VENUE. IT WAS RAMMED, STICKY AND HOT. IT WAS A GREAT EDUCATION FOR US…

FRIARS

11 DECEMBER 1976, AYLESBURY, UK

NICK FORSHAW, AGE 13

They were due to support Deaf School, who pulled out of the gig at the last minute so the Stranglers headlined. The Friars crowd were - and had always been - a picky crowd and the Stranglers didn't go down too well, probably because the expected three chord punk thrash from a 'punk' band never materialised. I recall Jet being hit on the head by a bottle and JJ having verbal and possibly physical altercations with members of the audience. They never played Friars again, which is a shame as it was a cracking venue that hosted many great acts. Personally, I thought the band was slightly out of tune as well as (understandably) grumpy. I didn't give them much attention for a couple of years as a result but something stuck. It wasn't until *Black and White* was released that I really got into the band, and I've since seen them over a hundred times.

Nick Forshaw has seen the Stranglers over 100 times

1st SHALFORD SCOUT HUT

LATE 1970s, SHALFORD, UK

JOHN PAGE

John Page recalls hearing the Stranglers practising at Shalford Scout Hut – photo Malcolm Wyatt

I've lived in Cornwall since early 1998 but had a great upbringing in rural Surrey, and on a trip back in my late twenties, I wanted to pay a visit to the River Wey at Shalford, where I spent time fishing with friends, looking around the village where I grew up. I'd been coming back down since 1978 to see my girlfriend (now my wife) in Crawley, just over the Sussex border in Crawley from Warwickshire. I parked my Honda 550F1 motorcycle by the scout hut I had attended as a cub and then a scout back in the day. I took a wander to the river when, coming from the hut, I heard loud music. My ears pricked up to a rather good rendition of one of the Stranglers' early chart successes, 'Peaches'.

I remember thinking they were good for a local band and stopped to listen for a while, hearing another recognisable song. I'm pretty sure I also heard 'No More Heroes'. After a while I decided to... erm, walk on by, but passed by again about an hour and a half later, and they were still playing. This time there was more stopping and starting, and voices could be heard between.

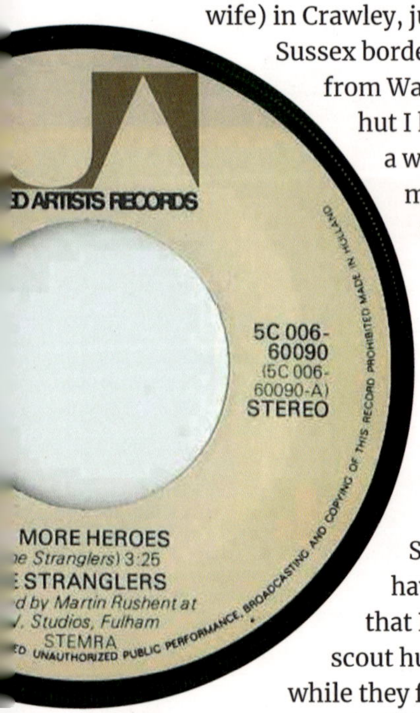

This was sometime in the late Seventies, and looking at the Stranglers discography and my activities around then, it could have been anytime between '77 and '80. It was only in later years that I came across an article about the band and discovered the scout hut was one of the places the Stranglers used to practise. And while they first rehearsed there in the mid-Seventies, I'm convinced it was them that I heard.

HOPE & ANCHOR

14 FEBRUARY 1977, LONDON, UK

TONY FITZGERALD

I was a 15-year-old tearaway from Palmers Green in North London. My mate Dale was a few years older than me and had just passed his driving test. His dad would lend him the family Austin Allegro to 'practise his driving' and so one night we piled into the car and ended up somewhere in Islington. He was 18 and was legally allowed to drink so we parked the car and found a pub.

The pub we found that night I now know to be the Hope & Anchor, and playing that night were the Stranglers. There was nobody on the door so we just walked in without having to pay. Dale got his pint, I got half of lager... and what followed was what I would call an 'Elvis Moment'.

The first time kids in the 1950s saw Elvis must have been magical, and the very same thing happened to me in the Hope & Anchor that night. It was totally unexpected, especially as I had already experienced one Elvis moment fairly recently after seeing the Sex Pistols for the first time on the Bill Grundy's *Today* programme.

I have been a massive Stranglers fan ever since. I bought my first album on the strength of hearing them in Islington that night, when they played 'Go Buddy Go' and 'Down in the Sewer', totally blowing me away. Over the years I have seen them many times, and Baz has proved an excellent replacement for Hugh. The band has lost none of its punch. And it was brilliant to see Hugh's *Hi Fi* tour along with 40 other people in the Army & Navy in Chelmsford. The first set was just him on an acoustic guitar, while the second set left no track unturned with his three-piece band.

Tony Fitzgerald saw the then unknown Stranglers at the Hope & Anchor

CITY HALL, GLASGOW

Outlaw in association with
Albion Management presents

THE STRANGLERS

Plus Special Guests
LONDON

Wednesday, 22nd June, 1977
at 7.30 p.m. Doors open 7 p.m.

STALLS
PROMENADE AREA

MUSIC WEEK DECEMBER 24, 1977

NEW WAVE Chart

(**) Denotes entry or re-entry into charts

This Week	Last Week	
1	(2)	JET BRONX + FORBIDDEN – Ain't Doin' Nothin'
2	(**)	DAMNED – Don't Cry Wolf
3	(3)	ELECTRIC CHAIRS – Fuck Off
4	(12)	JERKS – Get your Woofin' Dog off Me
5	(7)	J. C. CLARK – Psycle Sluts
6	(26)	BANNED – Little Girl
7	(17)	A. T. V. – 'Ow Much Longer
8	(4)	GENERATION X – Wild Youth
9	(13)	IAN DURY – Sweet Gene Vincent
10	(9)	MENACE – Screwed Up
11	(10)	WIRE – Mannequin
12	(15)	CANNIBALS – Good Guys
13	(**)	SOFT BOYS – Give it to the Soft Boys
14	(11)	STOAT – Office Girl
15	(**)	TALKING HEADS – Psycho Killer (12")
16	(18)	NEW HEARTS – Just another Teenage Anthem
17	(19)	KILBURN + HIGH ROADS – The Best of .. (EP)
18	(29)	ALBERTOS + PARANOIAS – Old Trust
19	(14)	ADVERTISING – Lipstick
20	(6)	MINK DE-VILLE – Cadillac Walk
21	(8)	MOTORS – Be what you wanna be
22	(21)	MICK FARREN + DEVIANTS – Screwed Up
23	(22)	FLIES – Bunch of Five (EP)
24	(24)	WASPS – Teenage Threats
25	(20)	STRANGLERS – Something better Change (EP)
26	(28)	PENETRATION – Don't Dictate
27	(23)	PIGS – Youthanasia (U.S. Import)
28	(**)	PORK DUKES – Makin' Bacon (12")
29	(25)	LONDON – Animal Games
30	(**)	BLITZKREIG BOP – Let's Go

BARBEQUE GRILL NOW OPEN UPSTAIRS

HOPE & ANCHOR

UPPER STREET ISLINGTON, N.1

Thursday Nov. 17th	PLUMMET AIRLINES	£1.00
Friday Nov. 18th	DIRE STRAITS	£1.00
Saturday Nov. 19th	THE YACHTS	75p
Monday Nov. 21st	MICHAEL CHAPMAN "FRONT ROW FESTIVAL"	75p
Tuesday Nov. 22nd	THE STRANGLERS	£1.00
Wednesday Nov. 23rd	THE PIRATES	£1.00

BRUNEL UNIVERSITY S.U.
Kingston Lane, Uxbridge, Middlesex
Tel. Uxbridge 39125

Thursday, September 29th

THE STRANGLERS
+ Support
In The Sports Centre
Members Bar

Tickets: £1.60 in advance, £1.80 on door
2 miles from M4. Nearest tube: Uxbridge

MBER 24, 1977

OP ALBUMS 1977

JANUARY 1 — DECEMBER 9 1977

	○	Abba	B. Anderson/B. Ulvaeus	Epic EPC 86018
REATS	○	Shadows	—	EMI EMTV 3
REATS	○	Diana Ross & The Supremes	—	Motown EMTV 5
ORN	●	Soundtrack	Phil Ramone	CBS 86021
	○	Fleetwood Mac	Fleetwood Mac/Dashut/Caillat	Warner Brothers K 56344
FORNIA	○	Eagles	Bill Szymczyk	Asylum K 53051
OF BREAD	●	Bread	David Gates	Elektra K 52062
LIGHT	○	Leo Sayer	Richard Perry	Chrysalis CHR 1125
HITS	○	Abba	B. Andersson/B. Ulvaeus	Epic EPC 69218
ATHIS COLLECTION	●	Johnny Mathis	—	CBS 10003
	●	Pink Floyd	Pink Floyd	
ND THE BOLLOCKS, HERE'S THE SEX PISTOLS	●	Sex Pistols	Chris Thomas/Bill Wright	
OF SINATRA	○	Frank Sinatra	—	
ER		Various	—	
ORLD RECORD	●	Electric Light Orchestra	Jeff Lynne	
R THE ONE	●	Yes	Yes	
ME GREATS	●	Connie Francis	—	
R VALLEY	●	Slim Whitman	—	
THE KEY OF LIFE	○	Stevie Wonder	Stevie Wonder	
E	●	Jean Michel Jarre	Jean Michel Jarre	
NORVEGICUS	●	Stranglers	Martin Rushent	
PET SHOW	●	Muppets	Jim Henson	
REATEST HITS 71-75	○	Eagles	—	Asylum K 53017
		Various	—	K-Tel NE 954

T.C.D.
Ents. presents...
STRANGLERS
plus
THE RADIO STARS
on SAT. 12th NOV. 1977
in The Tivoli Theatre, Francis Street,
at 8 p.m. (Doors open 7.30)
Ticket : : £1.80

PRIORY HOTEL

19 FEBRUARY 1977, SCUNTHORPE, UK

STEVE DRAYTON

Steve Drayton in 1977

In the history of music, Lincolnshire is very rarely credited at being a gob-face of punk, however on the 19th of February 1977 it most certainly was. Following the release of their debut single 'Grip/London Lady' the Stranglers came to play the Scunthorpe Priory Hotel. The Saturday night disco at the Priory was the place to be. It was a house of denim, patchouli oil and ton-up boys revving their Garelli Tigers and Fizzi 125s, marking their territory with the great smell of Brut and oil spills.

This audience was still in thrall to the rock sound and without fail, the last three songs of the night would be 'Smoke on the Water', 'Stairway to Heaven' and 'Freebird'.

With it being 1977, in the audience were six fledgling punk rockers keeping themselves at the edges of the crowd trying to be seen, and also, not seen as there was a considerable amount of animosity from the bike boys.

Support band The Hammersmith Gorillas were fantastic, mutton chopped front man Jessie Hector lead the band through a good humoured 20 minutes of pub rock fury, their drummer playing so hard his kit kept sliding forward to the edge of the stage. A couple of nervous looking punks would run forward between songs to help shove his kit back.

The Stranglers were loud and angry and changed the mood, being scarily aggressive towards us all. Understandably, we were all standing well away just in case the band puked on us.

Following some half-hearted spitting, a couple of punks did the pogo, enraging one daft lad to hurtle across the dance floor and to lamp the upstarts with his skid lid. Rather than make the rest of us punks cower, it ennobled us and a short amount of jerky dancing ensued. At one point it looked as though Hugh Cornwell was going to vomit, but he was only scratching his neck.

My abiding memories of the gig were: The Punks were the kids and The Stranglers looked old. They were hard men who were very loud, like fairground roustabouts.

They were very good, the bass and the keyboards being particularly pleasing. Oh, and I got punched into a hedge on the way home by a Hairy by the name of Dids Ancliffe. He said it was for being a punk, but I knew deep down it was because his girlfriend had ditched him to go to the gig with me.

Some thirty years later Hugh Cornwell visited the radio station I worked at and I regaled him with this sad story of punk rock urban violence. He said, without a hint of irony that I'd probably deserved the beating for being a soft cunt.

GREEN BAR, NEWCASTLE POLYTECHNIC

23 FEBRUARY 1977, NEWCASTLE, UK

DAVID HOWARTH

I have fond memories of this gig as I was already in the building early on. The Green Bar had a line of pinball machines along the back wall and the 'stage' was to the right of them. I had Jean Jacques Burnell playing on a machine next to me on the left, and Hugh Cornwell playing next to me on my right. I am also pretty sure that this wasn't the first Stranglers gig at the Poly.

Just before Christmas they had been booked as a support band in the main hall. The main band cried off so they ended up headlining and I remember them playing stuff then that appeared on their second album, so much of their material must have been written long before they were signed up to a label. The Entertainments Officer at the time told me that most punk was shit but the Stranglers were different because they could play and were reminiscent of the Doors.

PETER SMITH

I first saw the Stranglers in the Green Bar of Newcastle Poly in February 1977, and have a natty little ticket from the event which shows a victim of (I think) the Boston Strangler.

The bar was completely packed. The audience was a mix of students, and locals with a smattering of people starting to wear punk gear. A group of fashion students were into the punk scene and would dress in Vivienne Westwood gear which they must have bought from Seditionaries in London.

The Stranglers played a blistering performance featuring early songs, many of which were to appear on the soon to be released first album, *Rattus Norvegicus*. Their only release at the time of the Poly gig was the first single 'Grip' which was probably my favourite song of theirs at the time.

MARK TAYLOR

The Stranglers originally asked for more money than we had in the bank. But they made us an offer... if we put them up for the night, they would reduce their fee by £50, which made the gig possible. They were a great bunch of guys, very interesting to talk to. And they gave my bother a lift in their old rover car to the gig at the Rock Garden in Middlesbrough which was the next day. I recorded the Middlesbrough gig and is available amongst collectors. I also recorded the Newcastle Poly gig, but the sound on the recording was no good, so I didn't keep it (the sound at the gig itself was great).

All the posters had the same design, except different colours. The Stranglers sent publicity stuff, which I used for the tickets. But I designed my own poster, because I didn't want people copying the poster to forge tickets. At that time, the Stranglers were the best-known punk band after the Pistols.

THE PENTHOUSE

25 FEBRUARY 1977, SCARBOROUGH, UK

TERRIERS FAN

Now then, here's a question: the Stranglers – punk or not? For me it's always been 'no.' Cornwell's snarling and the racy lyrics aside they were simply too - ahem! - talented, with way too much melody and ability to be classed as punk. That said, I certainly didn't enjoy the evening when I saw them. They were promoting their debut album, which wouldn't be released until 15th April and the band had already built up a huge following and reputation based on their January released single 'Grip' and their energetic stage show.

The place was packed to the rafters and there was a significant number of pogo-ing punks filling the dance floor. I remember Cornwell's crass masturbation mime where he frantically rubbed his throat before spitting on the assembled throng as he 'climaxed'. That said, his acolytes loved every second, but not me, I'm afraid. I really hated everything punk back then as it attacked all aspects of the music that I loved; now I quite like elements of it and I'm listening to my Stranglers compilation LP as I type this, but back then I had no time whatsoever for them.

'So why did you go'? I hear you ask... I suppose it was a combination of it being Friday night, which was always band night and curiosity getting the better of me. Mind you, I never bowed to curiosity when Sex Pistols came to town because I simply never bothered.

History tells us that the Stranglers would go on to achieve world stardom (and are still touring now) and that punk was clearly what the music world of the mid to late 70s was crying out for, a burning of the dead wood, if you will. But at the time to me, as fully paid-up member of classic rock's fan club, it was awful. I suppose that I should now count myself quite fortunate to have caught the band on the up, before it had actually released an LP, but at the time it really didn't feel like that. Another box ticked I suppose...

RIF REGAN

Our band London had only just started gigging when Hugh and Jean-Jacques offered us the support slot on their lengthy *Rattus Norvegicus* tour in 1977. Suddenly we were traveling the country and playing to these huge audiences.

For many people we were the first punk band they had ever seen. I think real punk fans were in isolated pockets around the country just as it had been in central London during 1976/77. It didn't matter though; you just felt you were part of an exclusive club.

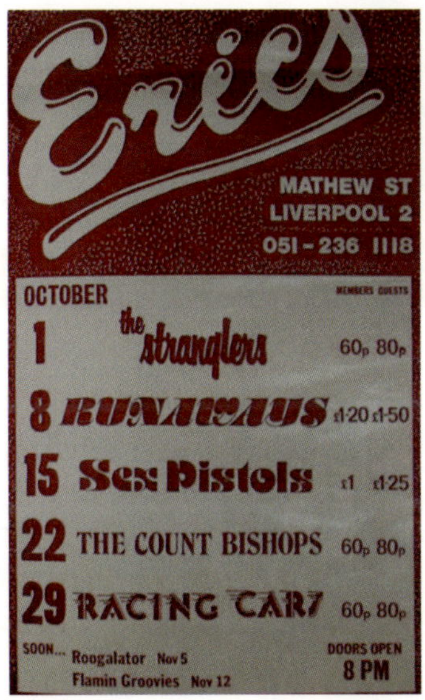

I remember playing Erics, Liverpool on the Stranglers tour. We did two gigs but I can't remember whether they were on consecutive nights or both on the same day. One thing that stands out in my mind was how hot it was. I remember Jet Black sweating like anything when the Stranglers were on, and that was despite a huge film studio size electric fan being bought in on the side of the stage.

The other thing that stands out was that although the Stranglers were high in the charts with 'Peaches', they rarely played it live. We found that most odd.

We played the Roundhouse for two shows at the end of the tour. That was good, playing on the stage where we had watched so many of our favourite bands perform.

STUDENTS UNION, HUDDERSFIELD POLYTECHNIC

3 MARCH 1977, HUDDERSFIELD, UK

PROF ALISTAIR

I saw them first in early 1976 in the Students Union small hall at Huddersfield Poly just before their first album came out. Awesome gig. Wouldn't call them punk. I remember Hugh Cornwall saying if there was any 'gobbing' (dreadful habit) they'd walk off. Too many shades of the Doors, the Pirates and some very clever informed lyrics to be called punk. Excellent stuff.

ELECTRIC CIRCUS

5 MARCH 1977, MANCHESTER, UK

DUNCAN ROUND

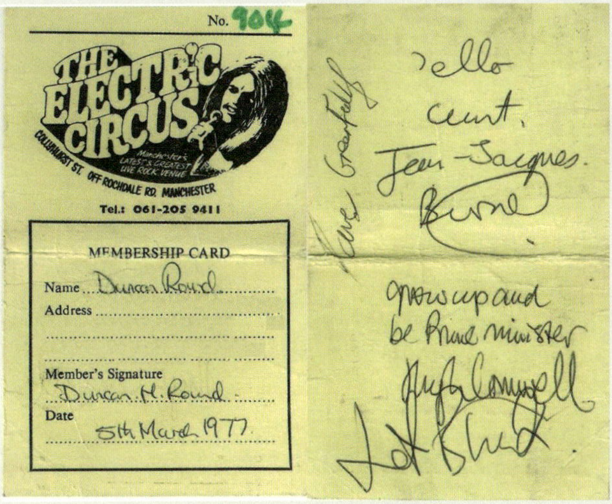

Duncan Round scored a couple of posters on the Grip tour and still has his membership card for the Electric Circus

'And that was the single by the Stranglers, '(Get a) Grip (on Yourself)'. And what's more you can see them on Saturday night coming to Manchester,' came blasting out of my transistor radio on Piccadilly Radio 261.

Next morning at school, I talked to my mates and we decided we had to go. The single had been on the radio quite a bit and already we were hooked. I was 17 and had come back from a life-changing moment, having seen the Stranglers the previous Saturday night at the Electric Circus in Manchester with three mates.

The band had talked about the John Peel session after the gig and how things were really moving for them. I'd only ever seen bands up to then who were stars, out of reach and inaccessible. To see the Stranglers play literally in front of me at full tilt, as Manchester was dealing with the gutter press punk headlines predicting anarchy and the end of life as we knew it, was just was one of those moments.

To get to meet them was great, slipping past what security there was; after all, they had only released a single at that stage, 'Grip'. They were just cool blokes full of attitude and front and what a chemistry there was between them. Yet they talked for ages to the four of us about life and the wave they were rolling on. Can you imagine how they felt at that time, to be listened to and watched after two and a half years of nothing? That night they were stunning and the crowd was mental. I have no idea how we made it home in one piece, and my mum's old Renault car still had all its tyres on.

We went to school on the Monday and were full of it. The other lads were green with envy. I put two posters on the sixth form common room wall - a Pistols poster and an AC/DC one of Angus in those shorts - which we had grabbed from the venue. They were ripped down by the school and we got it in the ear. It's a shame because if I still had the Pistols one, it's worth a bit. But I still have the priceless ones of the 'Grip' tour promo and 'Coming Your Way'. They were never going to school.

John Peel broadcast the first Stranglers session that night, the one we'd been talking to the band about only a few nights earlier. My microphone set, I captured it forever on a C60 and played it to death, full low fi with radio noise and fade off Radio 1 on 247AM. But that was how it was with John Peel, ad libbing as he went. He was pretty on side with the band in those days. A 'proper' version came out, but this was my tape and I still have it, with this tracklisting:

'Goodbye Toulouse'
'Hanging Around'
'I Feel Like a Wog'
'Something Better Change'

...and it did.

LEEDS POLYTECHNIC

1 APRIL 1977, LEEDS, UK

RAYMOND HUNTER

I once went to Leeds Poly to see the Stranglers with support from The Jam and got backstage with the lads. They asked what the atmosphere was like 'out there' and I said it was banging. There had been a bit of bother in the mosh during the Jam set. They said 'cheers' and gave me some badges with 'Get a Grip of Yourself 1977' written on them. Top night and a top band.

RICK BUCKLER, THE JAM

There were a lot of very interesting acts that came out of what was the pub scene in London. The Stranglers were a lot older than us, or seemed very much older, as they were probably four or five years older than the average age of The Jam at that time.

When punk started to grab the headlines with the Bill Grundy incident (when the Sex Pistols swore on TV, attracting lots of headlines), a lot of bands justifiably said, 'Well, we are part of this young band movement as well.' They were not necessarily punk, but there were bands like Ian Dury and the Blockheads, the Stranglers and ourselves - because we weren't really a punk band - a lot of really good acts and great songs songwriters around at that time. Mostly this was because a great live scene was happening, which gave people the opportunity to be in bands and to play and to find their own audience. Like The Jam, the Stranglers gained a lot of attention because of the punk scene and on a national level rather than just in London.

London was where it really started for us. We used to keep an eye on everything that was going on in and around the London area. You'd see these other bands and where they were playing and the sort of gigs they were doing. But when you're doing gigs you very rarely bump into other people, unless you're on the same bill or playing a festival or something. So you miss out on seeing some of the bands that are playing around because you're usually working in a completely different place to where they're working.

The only time we ever came across the Stranglers was at Leeds, when we supported them at Leeds Polytechnic (1 April 1977). They were extremely late turning up, which was causing problems for the audience. We'd been on and done our set and we were keen to wait around and see them. We'd heard a lot about them and they were obviously a name that was on the scene.

I remember the audience were getting really quite pissed off. Tension at those sort of gigs was quite high to start with. And you were thinking, 'Oh crikey, things are going to kick off in a minute if the main act doesn't turn up.' They did turn up eventually - we weren't quite sure if they were being fashionably late or being popstars - but they were very good. It was worth the wait.

Iain Ferguson was pissed off that his parents bought him an ABBA record

IAIN FERGUSON

In 1977 I was 13 and in hospital for a minor operation. My parents visited me and asked me if I'd like a record. 'Yes please, the new Stranglers' album *Rattus* please.' Upon their return later that day, I could see the HMV bag in my dad's hand. 'Here you go, son. Something you'll like.' Opening the bag excitedly, I thrust my hand in, expecting to pull out said album. But – no! – these bastards had decided I wanted *ABBA's Greatest Hits* more. I have never forgiven them, the idiots!

JIMMY WILLIAMS

When I met JJ, I showed him my arse. I've got the *Rattus Norvegicus* album tattooed on it! He told me the story of when the Stranglers, the Ramones and the Clash had a ding-dong in the lane. He shook my hand to say goodbye and said, 'Anyway, what is your name?' I said, 'Jimmy Williams,' and he said, 'I'll never forget you.' I was well chuffed.

PAUL WESTCOTT

It wasn't until the summer of '77 that I decided to check out this punk music that the media were obsessed with. Not having heard any of it before I just blindly bought *Rattus Norvegicus* and the first Clash album. Both were so different to what I had listened to before, but also the difference between these two albums was stark. the Clash album (one of my favourite ever albums but that's another story) was more like how I thought punk would sound after reading about it. *Rattus Norvegicus* was more unexpected, with the exception of 'London Lady'. Despite the hype and feigned outrage about punk, the media did get one thing right. The Stranglers were a cut above the other punk bands when it came to talent. And the keyboards and bass set the Stranglers apart from the other bands musically. I particularly loved the bass. I hadn't heard the bass so prominent in the songs before, and so brilliantly played. From that first Stranglers album, JJ has always been my favourite bass player in any band by a country mile.

In July and August of that year the Sex Pistols released 'Pretty Vacant', their third great single in a row, and The Adverts brought out their classic single 'Gary Gilmore's Eyes'. But, best of all, the Stranglers released 'Something Better Change'/'Straighten Out'. I now abandoned all the old established bands I had been listening to up to this time. I regularly fed the juke box in the pub we went to in those days to hear 'Something Better Change', 'Straighten Out', 'No More Heroes' and 'In the Shadows' all evening.

No More Heroes came out in the autumn. I liked this even more than *Rattus Norvegicus*. But *Black and White* surpassed even that. They really nailed it with that third album. It's one of those very rare albums. There's not a mediocre track on it, let alone a rubbish one. The mid-late-Seventies produced some great bands, but the Stranglers topped them all. The black clothing, the dark menacing image, and most importantly some fantastic rock music. What's not to like?

'PEACHES'

RELEASED 21 MAY 1977

GARY HESOM

I first heard the Stranglers on Radio Luxembourg, aged 14. I was listening to it on my small transistor radio under the blankets in bed. 'Peaches' came on and I thought, 'Wow, I have to buy this record,' but hearing the band name and song title was difficult because of the reception – the Luxembourg signal was often weak and would keep fading in and out. The next day, and armed with my school dinner money, I went off to Virgin Records in Birmingham during lunch break and asked for 'Beaches' by 'the Wranglers'. The guy in the shop gave me a strange look and said, 'Do you mean this?' He put 'Peaches' on the turntable. 'Yes, that's the one,' I said. 'I think you mean 'Peaches' by the Stranglers.' I was hooked from then on.

UNIVERSITY OF ESSEX

25 MAY 1977, COLCHESTER, UK

JON MURFIN

The Stranglers arrived by helicopter to play at Essex University because they had appeared on *Top of the Pops* the same afternoon (performing 'Go, Buddy, Go'). The light was very poor, and when the helicopter arrived, a guy on the ground was struggling to catch the pilot's attention and signal to the pilot that he was about to land in a deep lake. Luckily, the pilot steered the helicopter away.

Someone else recalls, 'The Stranglers were late and it was getting dark. We had a large white cross set out. The helicopter came through the dusk with its lights on coming to us and started to descend over the lake. It got very low indeed before, with a lot of screaming engine noise, it climbed and circled around before landing. We got the band into the minibus and on the way to the dance hall. They didn't seem aware of what had happened. I asked one of the 'copter crew about it and he said they thought they could see us waving torches and only at the very last minute did they realise it was their own landing lights reflecting in the ripples of the water. It was a great gig which nearly went very wrong indeed.'

ST. ANDREWS HALL

26 MAY 1977, NORWICH, UK

KARL TROSCLAIR

My second ever gig. I had been there to see AC/DC in 1976. But this was something else entirely. The support was a long forgotten band called London. Their drummer was Jon Moss later of Culture Club.

ODEON THEATRE

28 MAY 1977, CANTERBURY, UK

ANDREW ROBINSON

Recently, my older brother asked me when I first saw the Stranglers live. It was a curious question because he actually took me to see them. The answer was 28th May 1977 at Canterbury Odeon. He didn't believe me, because that would have meant he was only 16 years old and me only 13. But those were different times, even at the 'height' of punk rock. Today, we'd probably not get through the front door.

I remember very clearly the first time I heard the Stranglers. I was listening to Annie Nightingale's Sunday radio show. I didn't hear her introduce the song but within a few seconds I got out my cassette player and recorded it. I couldn't believe what I was hearing. At the end she said, 'And that was the Stranglers with '(Get a) Grip (on Yourself)' and I think that's going to be the first big punk hit.' Move on to a few weeks later and the Stranglers came on stage and Dave hit us with that famous intro to 'Grip'! It's the first Stranglers record I ever heard and the first Stranglers song I heard live. It's still my favourite track.

There have been quite a few highlights along the way. My brother borrowed *Rattus* off a friend so we could tape it. I didn't have the money to buy my own copy. The problem was, we could only record it whilst it was playing loud. There we were, having tea and taping the album for the third time, when 'Ugly' came on. To this day, I've no idea how I hadn't heard the word 'fuck' on the previous times I'd taped the album, but my dad certainly heard it. He went ballistic. He made it very clear that that sort of language was not acceptable in his house. Again, this was 1977, times were different. The Stranglers didn't get to go on the children's television programme *Magpie* because of the Sex Pistols...

At school, I was always going on about how great the Stranglers were and one day someone replied, 'The Stranglers? Bloody brilliant'. That was Paul, now a lifelong friend.

When I was at college, I was very fortunate to be able to pay a visit to the Stranglers Information Service where I met Saz and Paul Roderick. Jet turned up, which I thought was amazing, but I'd been asked to a little job to get some t-shirts out and to Saz's surprise, I did it quickly with no fuss. She said to me that most fans that pop in didn't bother helping but just hung around. I went a few more times and even went with them to look at new premises in Kingston. I don't know how Saz swung it for me, but when the next UK tour was scheduled, I was asked if I wanted to join the SIS crew in selling the merchandise. I obviously jumped at the chance. My partners in crime were Nik Yeomans and Chris Twomey; infamous company indeed. Three weeks' touring did take its toll on me, especially the food poisoning in Liverpool. We went out for some Chinese food with Jet and almost instantly I regretted it.

It was on this tour that the band's minder, Dino, was arrested for trying to get into the hotel's casino. Dino was a huge guy and one of the policemen, who just happened to be in the hotel kitchen that evening, was perplexed to find that the handcuffs wouldn't fit around Dino's wrists. I remember Hugh being very unhappy about the whole thing, as he knew it would be the Stranglers that got the blame.

When I finished college, the previously mentioned Nik, who I first met at the recording of the Stranglers for TVS, persuaded me to move to the Midlands, where I joined Paul and a friend of his called Michael. Nik dragged me along to a 'youth' club where all the guys seemed to be into the Stranglers. Long story short, I met my wife there. She used to come with me to see the Stranglers and was at Hugh's final gig, but she doesn't bother anymore. A few years later, a friend of my wife got married to an ex-policeman from Liverpool and he turned out to be the same policeman I had seen arresting Dino. It's a small world. A small Stranglers world and the conventions and the gigs have been a great way to catch up with old friends from school and new friends, waiting for the door to open so we can get to the front.

I've no idea how many times I've seen the Stranglers live. I wish I'd kept a record because I have an appalling memory for these things. If you ask my wife, she'll tell you it's 300 but I don't think it's quite that many. And I don't think it matters how many times you've seen them as long as you get to see them.

Now we have Toby as the newest Strangler. I count my blessings that I am coming up to the 45th anniversary of seeing them live. If anything, my enthusiasm for seeing them in concert has increased over the years, and I thank every Strangler there has ever been, and every fan I've met and reminisced with, for the unadulterated pleasure that the Stranglers have brought into my life.

CASTAWAYS

8 JUNE 1977, PLYMOUTH, UK

STEVE POTTER

It was the Queen's Silver Jubilee Week. The nation was gripped with monarchy mania, with street parties and celebrations of Her Majesty's 25 years on the throne. Rod Stewart was number one for the fourth week with 'I Don't Wanna Talk About It'. But I do want to talk about the hot evening of Wednesday 8th June. On my own, and wearing my dad's leather motorcycle jacket and a pair of Jet jeans that had been let out into flares and then returned to their original skinny style, I joined the queue in Plymouth Castaways for the Stranglers. No punks, all flares.

The place was absolutely heaving. I was about 15 feet from the stage on Dave's side. To this day, having attended hundreds of gigs since, I have never felt such a change in the atmosphere generated by a band simply walking on stage. Their sense of purposeful menace was electric. They entered stage right, so Dave had to cross to the keys in his green flying suit and went into 'Grip'. Unbelievable. There was brooding tension in the intro of 'Hanging Around'. I can remember Hugh wanking his throat and spitting on the ceiling at the climax of 'School Mam' and the blistering encore of 'Something Better Change', which in the context of the time felt so absolutely on the money. It still does.

I saw them again in October of the same year and, like so many of us, have seen dozens of times since, including twice on the last tour, one of which was the final night. But that first gig remains the best gig I have ever witnessed. By any band.

CITY HALL

15 JUNE 1977, NEWCASTLE, UK

PETRA JAGGARD

'Peaches' was in the charts. JJ played the first notes. Cue the first few rows storming the stage and the bouncers catapulting people back into the crowd. Seemingly, the tiring bouncers left a few fans, one of these being my boyfriend who was the last person to be chucked off after he had pogoed next to JJ until the end of the song. I now know (because he is my husband) that he had purposely headed for the back of the stage. First on, last off.

Petra Jaggard was at Newcastle City Hall

PETER SMITH

I first saw the Stranglers in the bar of Newcastle Poly in February 1977, and have a natty little ticket from the event (pictured here) which shows a victim of (I think) the Boston Strangler. The gig was in a small upstairs bar, rather than the usual venue of the main ballroom, and completely packed. The audience was a mix of students and locals with a smattering of people starting to wear punk gear. A group of fashion students were into the punk scene and would dress in Vivienne Westwood gear which they must have bought from Seditionaries in London. The Stranglers played a blistering performance featuring early songs. Their only release at the time of the Poly gig was the first single 'Grip'/'London Lady'. 'London Lady' was probably my favourite song of theirs at the time. I found a bootleg listed for a performance at Middlesbrough Rock Garden, also on 23rd February 1977. The Rock Garden gig was in fact the night after, on 24th February 1977.

Come June 1977 and the Stranglers were back and headlining at Newcastle City Hall. I remember being surprised that they could contemplate playing such a large venue only a few months after I had seen them play in a student's union bar. But by June, punk was making news everywhere, the Stranglers had released 'Peaches' which was climbing up the charts, and the gig sold out. The venue was packed with a mix of rock fans, those curious to see what this new 'punk' phenomenon was all about, and several sporting their own home-made t-shirts, complete with zips, safety pins, chains, locks etc. This was probably the first big punk gig that the north east had seen, and certainly the first in a public venue that was accessible to all (ie not in a student's union or in a bar or club with an over 18 entry). The crowd made the most of it. The Stranglers played an amazing, challenging set: Hugh Cornwell very non-PC spitting and growling lots of apparently sexist and racist innuendo, Jean-Jacques Burnel looking moody, dark and dangerous and driving the band with his lumbering, thundering bass guitar, Dave Greenfield providing the melody with some swirling Hammond organ that could just as easily have come from Deep Purple, and Jet Black, the grumpy looking man in black at the back on drums. The Stranglers were one of the hardest working, and most consistent, live acts at the time. They made it through a set of great songs, and through hard graft, playing up and down the country throughout 1976 and 1977.

It can be argued that The Stranglers were not punk, but more classic rock. But the kids at the City Hall in June 1977 didn't care either way. As far as they were concerned, they were getting their first slice of the action, and were seeing a real live punk rock band. And, of course they were meant to go totally crazy and spit at the band, and that is exactly what they did. This was a manic gig, and the first of many that the City Hall and other venues would host in the months to come.

Support at the City Hall came from London, who were a four piece punk band formed in London in 1976, and were well known for their wild stage act. The original line-up was Riff Regan (vocals), Steve Voice (bass), Jon Moss (drums, later of the Damned and then Culture Club) and Dave Wight (guitar). I'm sure that somewhere I have a flyer for London which I picked up at the gig.

LUDOVIC MALCOVICH

I saw the Stranglers play the City Hall. I had seen quite a few groups by now, aged 18, mainly punk and new wave, Eddy and the Hot Rods, Iggy Pop, Devo, Blondie, the

Clash but this gig stood out, for one reason, the quality of the musicianship.

I don't know if they are particularly gifted musicians or if it was one of those nights when it all falls into place, but I left thinking they are more than just another punk group, and they went on to prove that.

Hugh did kind of ask for people to spit on him which is something I never did understand, the bass was powerful and driven, the keyboards memorizing and the drumming metronome-like, it all just worked very well and sounded great.

Hugh's singing and clever lyrics made it special, the PA must take some credit as the guys in the mixing desk got the balance of volume (lots of it) and clarity spot on. a nod to the support band that night, London (not London SS). I bought their cut price single ('Everyone's a Winner') from the merchandise stall for 50p (I think) they did give away some copies of it, hidden under random seats.

JOHN DOWNING

I remember London were great and really warmed the crowd who were electric with anticipation awaiting the Stranglers. The room was hot and sweaty and so was the audience. The set was mostly Rattus but although unknown then some tunes from the second album. Spit was flying everywhere, Hugh Cornwall masturbating his neck and the gobbing the most enormous piece of spit I've ever seen over the crowd.

I think the encore was 'Go Buddy Go'and most of the front row clambered on stage and pogoed with the band!

CHAS DE WALLEY, *SOUNDS*, 1977

I couldn't care what anybody else says, the Stranglers are still one of the finest rock 'n' roll bands this country has spawned in years. Old wave, New Wave, fart, new fart, what do the labels matter, eh? Electric music is electric music. It either hits you where it should or else it apologises and passes by on the other side. And since when did the Stranglers ever apologise for anything?

GAUMONT

17 JUNE 1977, DONCASTER, UK

NIGEL LOCKWOOD

The Gaumont has an orchestra pit separating the stage from the audience and a barrier getting savagely sat upon by the throngs of the enthusiastic overreacting kids. JJ and Hugh didn't take too kindly to the space between them and the audience but the bouncers were trying to make sure nobody attempted to leap over. But of course it was all in vain. One very drunken sod clambered over and started dancing to which he was greeted by a nice thump from one of the bouncers.

JJ spotted this and lept off the stage to give the bouncer some of his own medicine. That was it. All the kids went to the front much to the bands relief.

The final encore 'Go Buddy Go' is worth a mention. They started the number and suddenly a kid appeared on stage jumping up and down nobody stopped him so everybody else thought likewise joining him. It was amazing all those kids including me pogoing along right next to the band with no resistance from the bouncers!

BOB GREEN

In 1977 my band supported the Stranglers a couple of times. I had the great privilege of getting my ears permanently damaged while on stage dancing right next to JJ's bass rig. I still love that sound.

CITY HALLS

22 JUNE 1977, GLASGOW, UK

DAVID BOYD

David Boyd wondered if there'd be any punks at the City Halls

Myself and a friend were walking towards the City Halls discussing whether there would be any punks at the concert. We had over the past six months or so been listening to John Peel's radio show where he would regularly feature punk bands new music and I had a copy of the recently-released *Rattus* and had been playing it non-stop.

As we approached the venue, our questions were answered. Torn t-shirts and safety pins in flesh were everywhere. We were very conservative in our dress and behaviour. However, we loved the taste of rebellion in the air. The City Halls were small inside, with a low stage and not many bouncers on hand. The support band, London, came and went. The atmosphere was electric and the noise deafening as the Stranglers took the stage. There was mass pogoing at the front and sweaty bodies everywhere. There was some spitting too, which the band immediately stopped.

'Grip' was the opener and it was chaos. A stage invasion occurred early on and bouncers somewhat aggressively cleared the stage. The band continued playing. However, a second invasion materialised which forced the band offstage. The concert was abandoned after about half an hour but to say it was eventful would be an understatement. It was sheer excitement from the beginning to (the early) end.

The next morning, I came down to breakfast and my father said, 'Were you at that concert at the City Halls last night? It's been on the news that there was a riot and police were called.' I said, 'Yeah, but I didn't see any police.' He said, 'I don't think attending concerts like this is a very good career move for you at the bank.' Perhaps Glasgow Council agreed with my father, as they banned the Stranglers from playing in the city again.

However, following appeals (largely from the fan base) it was negotiated that the band would be able to play at the Glasgow Apollo on 16 October 1977, not long after *No More Heroes* was released. This concert was phenomenal and an absolute game changer, concreting my support for the band. Only recently, I read that JJ commented that this concert was one of his favourites.

By the way, my father was also wrong. I went on to a long career in banking whilst also enjoying watching the boys play over 120 concerts around the world, including several in my new home Sydney, Australia.

WINTER GARDENS

23 JUNE 1977, CLEETHORPES, UK

JACK RAWLINSON

I was at some of the early gigs, including a memorable night at Cleethorpes Winter Gardens where things, shall we say, really kicked off. It was written up in that week's *NME*, if I recall correctly, under a headline something like, 'This Sure as Hell Ain't the Summer of Love,' referencing the Blue Öyster Cult track'.

ROUNDHOUSE

26 JUNE 1977, LONDON, UK

STUART HERKES

Although I've followed the Stranglers since 1977, the only time I have (briefly) managed to get to meet them was at the

Stuart Herkes got a £1 note autographed

Roundhouse in 1977. It was a 4pm start and afterwards I got a few autographs. I had no paper, only a one pound note. London were the support act and I got a couple of them to sign it too, including Jon Moss - who went on to better things!

EILEEN GREEN, AGE 14

Eileen was immovable when it came to the school photo

I was 14 years old and immensely proud to be a Stranglers fan. The photographer was determined the badge was coming off.

'Look, it's really going to spoil the photo.'
'Don't care.'
'Could you just take it off for a second?'
'Nope, it's staying on.'
'Could somebody get a teacher in here to talk sense to her?'
'Not going to make any difference.'
'Look sweetheart, I know you told me they are your favourite band and you are proud of your badge but it is really going to draw attention from you and dominate the photo.'
Me, beaming, 'Aye, that's about right.'
Photographer, under his breath, 'Fukkit.'
CLICK!

PAUL MCGUIGAN

Wig owns a keyboard which belonged to Dave

My journey following the Stranglers started with a dare to buy a punk single. I was twelve years old. The woman in the record shop handed me 'No More Heroes' and we took it home, stuck it on the turntable and I was hooked. I have travelled all over the UK and Europe and made lifelong friends from following the Stranglers. I even got to train with JJ Burnel at his London dojo. I own a keyboard which belonged to Dave Greenfield and which I bought at the first Stranglers convention in Peterborough in 1992, for the princely sum of £30.

EXHIBITION CENTRE

15 SEPTEMBER 1977, BRISTOL, UK

DARRELL SMITH

Darrell Smith saw the Stranglers back in '76

I first went to see the Stranglers in Bristol in September 1976, and much more recently in Reading. I can remember 57 occasions on which I've seen them altogether. I lived in Tetbury and I met Jet Black in a chip shop and asked if he would autograph my albums and he told me to drop them off at his local, the Trouble House. A few weeks later, after seeing them in the Colston Hall in Bristol, I was hitching a lift from Cirencester to Tetbury and he came along in his ice cream van – registration number GVA 279K. He duly stopped and picked me up, drove to his place and then gave me a lift all the way home in his brown Ford Cortina. I cheekily asked for a t-shirt and he gave me one.

On my 19th birthday, I invited Jet for drinks to which he said to come over to the Trouble House. My mate Simon gave me a lift and we spent two hours drinking with him and he wouldn't let me pay for any of the drinks.

In August 1981, word had gotten around that the Stranglers were rehearsing at Jet's place. I cycled over and spent 40 minutes waiting outside to pluck up the courage to meet them. They were playing 'Tramp' and when they stopped, I knocked on the door. Jet answered and let me in. I was shaking terribly and blurted out, 'Can you sign my albums please?' Hugh said, 'Do they think there's a gig going on here?'

I said, 'Would you be able to get Robert Williams to sign my *Nosferatu*?' and Jet said, 'Do you know where he lives?' I shook my head and Jet said, 'He lives in Los Angeles,' to which Hugh sneered and said, 'Yeah, I'll go on my bike, shall I?' They duly signed my albums, Hugh with a broken pencil, but it was the rare 'Uncle Hugh' scrawl. On my limited-edition 3D copy of *The Raven*, JJ drew a comedy cock.

Over the years I have seen them all over the country and also was on the first Wonky Bus tour to Paris and Ghent. When JJ got his signature bass, I was at a gig and asked Mikey, his then guitar tech, to ask JJ if I could buy one of his old Shukers. I said to Mikey, 'Tell him I'll give him £500.' JJ came onstage, looked me in the eye and said, 'Fuck off!' I took that as a no!

For many years I thought I was the inspiration for the songs 'Punch and Judy' and 'Mad Hatter'. I was in the RAF at Brize Norton and was in the Theatre Club. The local town, Carterton, put on a gala in 1984 and we staged a live Punch and Judy show. I played the part of Punch, and during a break between shows and whilst still dressed as Punch, I literally bumped into Jet Black. He remembered me and we chatted for a while, with me saying I had not heard anything recently.

When *Aural Sculpture* came out, I was convinced that the lyric in 'Mad Hatter' – 'It was getting late when I went through the gate, but I'd seen a happy chap - was me, and the song 'Punch and Judy' for obvious reasons, but when I read Hugh's book, *Song by Song*, it seems that the inspiration lay elsewhere!

BRACKNELL SPORTS CENTRE

17 SEPTEMBER 1977, BRACKNELL, UK

STEVE BIZLEY

Strangulation!

35 DATES IN MAJOR TOUR

THE STRANGLERS' autumn tour, for which dates and venues were announced this week, is one of the most comprehensive itineraries ever undetaken in Britain — and certainly THE most extensive by a new-wave band. It also marks the acceptance of new-wave by some of the country's leading venues. The schedule takes in 35 dates, including four at London Roundhouse, and more may be slotted in later. And it's followed by a five-date Irish tour.

A feature of the tour is that it is not restricted to the same support act throughout. In fact there are ten different supports, the idea being to give exposure to as many upcoming bands as possible. Heading the list of guest acts are critically-acclaimed U.S. band the Dictators, who were recruited after Hugh Cornwell saw them play in New York. Also involved on various dates are the Only Ones, Wire, Johnny Curious, Steel Pulse, Krypton Tunes, the Drones, Pop Group, Penetration and the Rezillos.

The first four gigs feature the Only Ones — at Cambridge Corn Exchange (September 23), Bracknell Sports Centre (24), Canterbury Odeon (25) and Norwich St. Andrew's Hall (27). Johnny Curious is so far set for just one date at Dunstable Queensway Hall on October 2, and Krypton Tunes support at Carmarthen St. Peter's Hall on October 5.

Steel Pulse play with the Stranglers at Leicester De Montfort Hall (October 3), Coventry Locarno (4), Birmingham Mayfair (20) and Hanley Victoria Hall (21). Wire guest on the gigs at Uxbridge Brunel University (September 29) and Crawley Sports Centre (30). And the Drones are at Malvern Winter Gardens (October 6), Bangor University (8), Manchester Belle Vue Elizabethan (13 and 14), Leeds Queens Hall (15) and Sheffield Top rank (19).

Pop Group play Plymouth Fiesta (October 9) and Exeter University (10), while Penetration guest at Newcastle City Hall (12). Scottish band the Rezillos appear at Glasgow Apollo (16) and Carlisle Market Hall (17).

The Dictators are featured on the final 12 dates — at Cardiff Top Rank (October 23), Swansea Top Rank (24), Brighton Top Rank (26), Bournemouth The Village (27), Guildford Surrey University (28), Hastings Pier Pavilion (29), Reading Top Rank (30), Southampton Top Rank (31) and London Chalk Farm Roundhouse (November 3, 4, 5 and 6).

Tickets for the four Roundhouse shows are £2 each; at Leicester, Glasgow and Newcastle they are £1.75, £1.50 and £1.25; and at most other venues there is just the one price of £1.60 in advance (also obtainable on the night, if any remain, at £1.80). Promoters are Straight Music and Albion.

The Stranglers' Irish mini-tour, with Radio Stars supporting on all five gigs, takes in Belfast Ulster Hall (November 8), Coleraine Ulster University (9), Galway Leisure Lands (11), Dublin Stadium (12) and Cork City Hall (13).

As reported last week, the band's new album "No More Heroes" is released by United Artists on September 16, and it has now been decided to issue the title track the same day as their new single. Their current album "Rattus Norvegicus" is now rapidly approaching the quarter-million mark, after 19 weeks in the charts.

Steve Bizley saw the 1977 tour

I left school in 1977. Having failed the eleven plus, I attended a Secondary Modern. Most kids at the school were into progressive rock – bands like Yes and Genesis. I didn't get it, and during the previous three or so years had played safe – listening to glam rock and whatever was popular. I lived on a small council estate in one of the shires about 20 miles outside London. I missed the 1976 punk rock scene totally and like most people became aware of something happening after the 'scandalous' Bill Grundy interview with the Sex Pistols. However, my live music experience up to this point was seeing Showaddywaddy and Darts. I was quite a shy and naive kid with little knowledge of the world. All that was about to change...

During the summer of 1977, I got a part time job in a factory, printing Christmas cards. The radio was constantly on and I got chatting to people about what was playing. Bands like the Stranglers became a topic of conversation. I started buying the *New Musical Express* and *Sounds*. And turning the page – there was the headline 'Strangulation' – advertising the *No More Heroes* tour of late '77. 'Fuck Showaddywaddy,' I thought - I'm off to see the Stranglers! Little did I know that over 40 years later, I would still be seeing them live.

My first concert was the now infamous Bracknell Sports Centre gig. It was exciting, loud and dangerous. What an initiation to new music. I wasn't even 17 yet. I'd got *No More Heroes* by this point and added *Rattus* and the singles quickly. Not only was the music different and addictive but it was educational. I became interested in the lyrics. Who was Leon Trotsky? Why the reference to the ice pick? Where was Toulouse? Who was Dagenham Dave? Remember, this was a time before the internet!

Black and White followed but I had to wait until the Battersea Park gig to see them again. Years later, I spotted myself in the crowd on the video at the start of 'Hanging Around'. A friend at the time knew a photographer who had a stage pass and I managed to get some rare photographs of the gig.

Once the *Raven* LP was released, I started attending as many gigs as possible, including when Hugh was in prison – the Stranglers and Friends concert. The band were well and truly part of my life – I even remember wearing Stranglers boxer shorts (featuring a cartoon by Stephen Beaumont). It's amazing to look back and see ticket prices were as cheap as £3.00. One of the most memorable concerts in the earlier years was the London gig after the band had been released from a Nice prison. There was real energy and an incredible atmosphere.

I met the band briefly a few times over the years. Sadly, some of those early photos mistakenly got thrown away by a third party. I do remember attending the 'My Young Dreams' promo event and meeting Dave and Jet, who signed my black leather jacket and various merchandise. I bored everyone about that for years!

DRILL HALL

19 SEPTEMBER 1977, LINCOLN, UK

IAN HODGKINSON

Ian Hodgkinson with JJ. Ian's first gig was at Lincoln Drill Hall in 1977

I was still at school in 1977 and starting to hear about this new music called punk. All my mates were talking about it. My father had a building business and I found a tape in one of the work vans one day from one of his tradesmen - that tape was *Rattus*. I listened and it is still the only album ever where I loved every track.

I thought the music was fantastic, an unbelievable sound that I had never heard of before. Then *No More Heroes* came along and that was just as good. From that point onwards I was hooked, a total fan, and I started following the band and collecting every record and album. I remember rushing home from school to listen to the Top 20 on Radio 1 every Tuesday, eagerly waiting for the new chart to hear at what number the Stranglers were going to come in at that particular week.

My first gig was at Lincoln Drill Hall. I bunked off school and got two buses from Ilkeston to Lincoln. It was an odious journey to say the least. The Stranglers on that particular night were being supported by the Skids, so in theory the first band I ever saw live was the Skids, who I still love to this day. The Stranglers came on stage and their performance and presence were dark, intimating, electrifying and downright menacing. It was an unbelievable gig and has stayed with me all my life.

To have seen the original line up at the height of the punk scene is something that I really treasure. It was 30 years before the Stranglers returned to Lincoln, and I was there when they played the Engine Shed. By coincidence, I booked the same hotel as the band and sat drinking with them in the hotel bar until 4am, telling Dave the last time they'd played there and having the privilege of buying him a drink. In return he gave me a triple of brandy from a bottle he had in his bag.

I've seen the band 100 times or more, including overseas and in a wood in Holt in Norfolk. I've lost count as to exactly how many, but I always made sure I attended at least one of the gigs on every tour in the early years. These days, I might go to three or four gigs per tour, simply because nothing is forever and I want to get in as many gigs in as possible before the Stranglers do finally call it a day. I've been to a couple of conventions - the 2001 Pontins one where I met the band and played football, and the Camden one in 2011 to witness the band doing some cooking. That was bizarre!

TOP OF THE POPS

22 SEPTEMBER 1977, LONDON, UK

ROGER KASPER

My life changed forever on 22 September 1977 – the day of the Stranglers' second appearance on *Top of the Pops*. They played 'No More Heroes', and although I had heard *Rattus Norvegicus* played at the youth club by neighbour Phil Franklin – some years my senior – for whatever reason, the band hadn't landed in my consciousness yet. I was a very young 12-year-old, more interested in racing around the hall, playing table tennis and generally being, well... a 12-year-old than dwelling on Ozymandias, Nostradamus and the other even more nefarious themes which inhabit *Rattus*. Probably the *No More Heroes* themes of Shakespeare, Sancho Panza and Lenny Bruce passed me by as well, although, I like to assure my 12-year-old self that I did chuckle at the 'ice pick' making 'his ears burn' lyric.

What did stick was Hugh Cornwell's air guitar solo on *Top of the Pops*. In double English at school the following day – sitting near the front with

Nicholas Kidd because we'd previously been naughty! – I leant back on my chair and mimicked the guitar solo. The next day, I raced into town in Gravesend to purchase 'No More Heroes' from OK! Records. I can't recall the price but I do remember that the B-side, the studio jam 'In the Shadows', blew me away. I knew then I was in the presence of a very special band.

I began collecting the back catalogue, purchasing the aforementioned *Rattus* (obviously the first 10,000 copies with the free single had long since gone – I probably have a fourth pressing of the LP) and then all the singles (again, the 'Peaches' 'Blackmail' sleeve was well out of reach).

When *Black and White* came along, I bought it on the day of release and, being 13 now, naturally gave a childish chuckle to 'Toiler on the Sea'. (Come on, who else sang 'Toilet on the Seat'? Oh… just me.) The obsession was well under way. I read everything about the band, collected everything I could and listened on the radio in vain to hear them – why were they so underplayed?

Among my collectables were the *Strangled* magazines which had been started by Tony Moon, who had featured the fab four on his *Sideburns* fanzine, which then morphed into *Strangled*. I eagerly became a subscriber.

Fanzines were an integral part of the punk movement and reinforced the DIY attitude and the fact that, if he could do it, so could I. At school, my classmates had formed a band called RPM, so I produced a fanzine to sell at their gigs called *Revved Up*. It featured articles on the band, pieces by school friends and cartoons I'd pinch from student mags my older brother Nick would bring back from Leicester. It was a much smaller world those days, and I could get away with recycling them without anyone knowing.

I talked the receptionist into letting me use the school's printing facilities – an old Ditto machine later to be replaced by photocopier – and I stapled all the editions together and sold them for 50p a pop. It always sold out.

Come the summer of 1983, my life was about to make another major change. My A-Level exams were in the bag, my Saturday job as a shop assistant at Dickins and Jones in London's Regent Street had become full time whilst I sorted out a career, and I'd long since forgotten about a job application I've made to my local paper, the *Gravesend Reporter*. The phone rang at home and, before I knew it, I was in front of the chain-smoking editor Ken Addison, showing him copies of *Revved Up*. After a spelling test – ten out of ten, by the way – I was on my way to Hastings for six months on a journalism training college.

And it's all thanks to the Stranglers for inspiring me with their thought-provoking and educational lyrics, and Tony Moon for giving me the visual inspiration which put me on the road to a 33-year career in journalism. Now I'm on the dark side – public relations – but I still write for punk website punktuationmag.com now and again, and fly the flag for the band that changed my life.

KARL KAY

Karl Kay heard 'I Feel Like a Wog' and instantly fell in love

I'm not a punk. I don't even identify with any particular genre of music. However... the Stranglers sound 'found' me and I wasn't even looking. I was sitting at home one day in early 1978. My friend Tim lived in the next street to me, a mere two minute walk away, yet we still phoned each other. On this particular day, he called me and, rather than the usual back and forth he just said, 'Get round here... now!' So I ran.

I had no idea what was occurring. It sounded important. He lived with his mother and brother. He had the middle bedroom and I had freedom to come and go, so I let myself in and went to his room. He was just sitting on his bed, with his record player next to him, top open with an album on the turntable. He looked up, grinned and then said, 'Listen to this...'

He dropped the needle on the *No More Heroes* album. The opening keyboard swirls to 'I Feel Like a Wog' rang out and all I recall thinking was, 'What is this?' followed by, 'I love this.' We sat and stared at the inner sleeve, with the photos of the band, and could only imagine who these people were. Needless to say, since that very moment, my life changed course. Some music simply changes or influences you. The Stranglers are that impactful to me.

ODEON THEATRE

25 SEPTEMBER 1977, CANTERBURY, UK

CHRIS PRITCHETT

I first heard 'London Lady' on Stuart Henry's Radio Luxembourg show, Street Heat, in early 1977 and that was me hooked. I first saw them at Canterbury Odeon after climbing though a toilet window to get in – I couldn't afford a ticket. I've seen them many times over the years in some great locations - a country house garden, Rochester Castle grounds, outside the Royal Palace in Brussels.

I saw Hugh get his arse caned by a young lady he brought up on stage in Folkestone, Jet singing 'Old Codger' and I saw some fantastic gigs during the Paul Roberts' years. At a Folkestone gig, stagehand Andy did a striptease to 'Nice 'n' Sleazy' – I've seen way too much of Andy, including him showing his new bum tattoo off at a gig in Lille. My wife and son were on the barrier in front of JJ (as usual) and she said to JJ that he should have done it. At the encore he came out minus his shirt and my wife ended up with a smile and his plectrum. It made her night.

I went to Stranglers gigs for my 30th, 40th and 50th birthdays, and am planning a gig for my 60th. I count myself very lucky that my favourite teenage band are still in my life all these years later. Long live the MiB.

BRUNEL UNIVERSITY

29 SEPTEMBER 1977, UXBRIDGE, UK

JOHN ALLARD

I first saw the Stranglers live at Brunel University in 1977. *Rattus Norvegicus* was already very popular, but *No More Heroes* had not yet been released, either as a single or an album. I had been drawn to their irreverence, and distinctly remember my dad arriving home saying he had just heard a record on the radio with the lyric that he was going to stick his finger 'right up your nose'! It was very tame by today's standards, but at a time when disco was at its height, songs didn't challenge the status quo, and the Sex Pistols and the punk/new wave movement was changing everything.

John Allard saw the Stranglers at Brunel Uni

And the Stranglers didn't disappoint. Their music was loud and aggressive, but with a melodic keyboard keeping things together. The words were challenging but also amusing, and Hugh Cornwell was a vocalist with a huge attitude, seeming to be annoyed by everything and not afraid to say so. He particularly didn't like the fact that fans showed their appreciation by spitting onto the stage and the band!

At the time, it was really odd for the lead singer of a band to verbally abuse the audience and complain about our behaviour, but we got used to this from Hugh.

My recollection is that the set was entirely from the *Rattus* album. I do remember hearing and being blown away by '5 Minutes' for the first time - which wasn't released as a single until the following year. The finale was the 'Down in the Sewer' trilogy, which they extended so that it went on for ages, which was awesome. As they played it, someone from the crowd jumped onto the stage and started dancing. The band seemed okay with it, so someone else jumped up, and then another... until the stage was heaving with members of the crowd. I so wanted to join them, but didn't have the guts... and then was relieved afterwards, when I found out my dad had arrived early to pick me up, and was watching from the back of the theatre.

The support act was Wire, who were okay - I have since enjoyed their music - but at the time, I and the majority of the rest of the crowd just wanted the main act, so they didn't stay on stage for long.

A few days after the concert, I caught the train into London after school to buy tickets to see them at the Roundhouse on successive nights. I'm not sure how I intended to get there or back again, just that I desperately wanted to see the band again. However, my parents had a different idea, and refused to let me go to either concert, mainly because it was in what they considered to be a very rough part of London - Chalk Farm. I had to sell the tickets to a friend's older brother, who subsequently told me I'd missed two superb concerts - and that he had left on both nights drenched in sweat and spit and, rather bizarrely, banana in his hair!

CRAWLEY LEISURE CENTRE

30 SEPTEMBER 1977, CRAWLEY, UK

RICHARD MURPHY, AGE 14

I discovered the Stranglers as a 14-year-old in 1977. I remember that we were driving back from a family holiday in the West Country when 'Peaches' came on the radio. I just thought, 'Wow, who is

this band?' Back off holiday I rushed out to buy the single and *Rattus Norvegicus* – I absolutely loved that album!

I found out that the Stranglers were appearing that year on tour in my home town of Crawley. The whole punk scene was just emerging, with some bad publicity, so it took a lot of persuading of my parents to allow me to attend. But attend I did, with two school friends – my first ever concert and it was brilliant. On the night, I wanted to fit in so remember half-freezing my ear with a lump of ice and sticking a safety pin through it! As a 14-year-old, it was an amazing experience. I was goggle-eyed seeing a female punk in fishnet stockings and a corset, with one breast exposed and a safety pin through the nipple!

Richard Murphy saw the Stranglers in Crawley in 1977 but not again until 40 years later – Brighton

UNIVERSITY OF BANGOR

8 OCTOBER 1977, BANGOR, UK

GEORGE MUD

Dave Greenfield was in a green Renault. He stopped by me and asked for directions. I asked the band to sign my ticket and Hugh said if he did it would make him a hero and 'there's no more heroes'. Only Hugh could do that. The Vibrators were the warm up act. I can remember the lead singer putting his jacket on the floor in front of me and he caught me trying to grab it. It was a great gig, and the first time the Stranglers played '5 Minutes.'

APOLLO THEATRE

13 OCTOBER 1977, MANCHESTER, UK

SANDRA JONES

Sandra Jones fell in love with the bass on 'Peaches', and with JJ

It started with the bass on 'Peaches' in 1977. I had to hear more. I was 14, a very young and naïve child who was soon to become a Stranglers fan. I was wishing I was old enough to be a groupie but too young to understand what that meant! My older sister had a radiogram and every Sunday the family went to church and left me with her empty bedroom where said equipment was, as was my album, *Rattus Norvegicus*. Next came the poster of JJB on Trotsky's grave... naked but for a stapler across the centre. I was smitten.

That summer a friend said she had two tickets to see the band at the Apollo in Manchester. It was a really hot summer and I waited for her to pick me up but she never arrived. I was so upset. Life happened and I started work, then got married had two children and then divorced. Finally, my time had come – the Stranglers and me. I went to as many gigs as I could, some in Manchester, some in London.

In July 1994, I went to the corner shop for a loaf of bread and ended up getting on the back of my friend's Harley and we went from Felixstowe to Matlock and a festival where the Stranglers were playing. In 1995, JJ was messing about at the front of the stage when he stepped onto the barrier in front of me and kicked me in the mouth. He fell into the pit and the bouncers quickly threw him back on stage, where he apologised several times. I wrote to him and he wrote back, inviting me to meet them at the Stranglers Convention in London's Kings Cross. It was the best thick lip ever.

APOLLO THEATRE

16 OCTOBER 1977, GLASGOW, UK

SOAPY DEE

Soapy Dee rates the Stranglers as 'the best band I have ever seen live'

Growing up in Glasgow, there was no music to excite a 15-year-old kid until I heard my brother playing 'Grip' on his record player. My world changed. My first gig was October 1977 and I went to as many gigs in Glasgow as I could afford. But the Stranglers are still the best band I have ever seen live. My all-time favourite gig was my last, in Adelaide, Australia. It was so small it felt like a personal gig and the band were just perfect. My favourite song has always

been 'Bitching'. It has the perfect amount of angst needed for a 15-year-old kid whose sisters were playing David Cassidy at the time.

I grew up in the same street in Glasgow as my mate Allan. We lost touch in our late twenties when he moved to Australia. 15 years later, I moved to Australia and we finally caught up. As usual, the talk was all about the Stranglers. A few years later, we both moved into the same area and started catching up some more. One boozy night, Allan was playing 'Bitching' on the guitar and I blurted out that I could sing it better. I was totally pissed at the time, and to be honest I had forgotten some of the words. A few more beers later and he was filming us.

There began the birth of The Old Codgers. We would get pissed once a week and try to play some Stranglers songs. We would then post them on *YouTube*. We did this for about six years, covering about 150 Stranglers songs.

During that time, I received a poster from Ava Rave, Jet's wife, that Jet had signed. I opened it at work and was delighted at Jet's personal message. That afternoon, I had a heart attack and, while in hospital, sent a jokey message to Ava asking her to tell Jet that the poster had caused it. Ava replied that she had mentioned it to Jet and he had replied, 'Well, whatever you do, don't send the poor bastard a get well card. It might finish him off.' I cherish that more than the photos I have of me with the band.

I have built a pub in my back garden called The Raven. It houses my Stranglers posters and other memorabilia. On the last tour of Australia, my wife and I followed the band to every Australian gig. We used it as our wedding anniversary trip. We even got an anniversary card from the band on the last night. The Stranglers are not just a band, they're a family. The following, no matter where in the world you go, is immense.

TOP RANK

19 OCTOBER 1977, SHEFFIELD, UK

NEIL MOORE

Neil Moore with JJ

I first saw the band at Sheffield Top Rank. I was aged 14 and went with my mate Spaceman from school. Only a handful of us in the whole school had discovered punk and new wave. The rest of the yoons were still wearing flares and denim jackets covered in Status Quo patches. My dad took us on the 20 mile trip and dropped us off. The tour bus was parked outside and as we drove past, I recall that Jet looked menacingly at us through the window.

The gig was amazing and brought to life all the music I had listened to endlessly on vinyl. We caught the last bus home and I remember there were a few Mods in the bus station. One of them threw a glass tankard at us as we boarded the bus, which hit a poor guy next to us on the head. He was left bleeding as the bus drove off. I couldn't understand the hatred just based on what music you liked, as though it was bloody football.

I am a lifelong fan with too many gigs to count them all up throughout the years and the line up changes. They always deliver on stage, and who would have thought they would still be thrilling audiences 45 years later? One of my favourite gigs was when they played the Other Stage at Glastonbury in 2010. The band appeared to be taken back by the huge crowd that had gathered for them (bearing in mind there are over 100 stages for festival goers to choose from).

Another favourite was when they headlined *Bearded Theory Festival* in 2014. We were on the front row and a bloke had passed an urn with his dad's ashes in it to a security guy. The security guy just put it down and didn't realise that the bloke wanted it handing to the band for the ashes to be spread on stage. The bloke ended up crying all the way through the set, and frustrated at not being understood. After the gig finished, after constant tears, he said to the guard, 'Can I have my dad back please?' and wandered off into the crowd.

I've met all the band members and they always have time for fans. I met JJ at Nottingham's Rock City in 2015. I had recently treated myself to his Shuker signature bass but I was too ashamed to admit that I could barely play 'Peaches'.

I am proud to be a Stranglers fan. My hobby is music and as I have got older, my taste has become very eclectic. I'm always on the look out for new music and new bands. But I always revert back to the Stranglers and the early records still sound like they were made yesterday.

I was deeply saddened by the untimely death of Dave. I was laid in the bath when I heard the news and decided there and then to get my first and only tattoo, which I did as soon as possible. So now I'm branded with the band's name and rat logo on my arm. Proud.

MAYFAIR SUITE

20 OCTOBER 1977, BIRMINGHAM, UK

IAN EMERY

I first heard of the Stranglers on Alan Freeman's *Saturday Rockshow* on a Saturday afternoon in January 1977 when he played 'London Lady', the B-side of 'Grip', the first single. It blew my mind and I got the single and waited eagerly for the album.

I first saw them at the Mayfair Suite in Birmingham in early 1977. It was a tiny venue. They were supported by Steel Pulse who had a terrible time with missiles, etc. being thrown at them. The Stranglers came on and Hugh Cornwell said, 'We didn't like the way you treated our friends,' staring at me as he said it because the mob had moved back. I looked older (I still do) but I was 16 - and terrified. It was a great gig, with lots of pogoing, heat and sweat. I bought *Rattus Norvegicus* from Boots the Chemists in Walsall and it came with a free single. It was the best album ever for a 16-year-old. It just hit the spot; this lot were my band!

In 1981 I saw them at the Birmingham Odeon on the *Meninblack* tour. At the time I was unconvinced by the album, *The Gospel According to the Meninblack*. It was a sparse stage with strobe lighting and the audience shouted, 'Oh no!' every time a track from the *Meninblack* album was played. I remember JJ beating some audience members with his bass who had attacked a roadie rescuing JJ's microphone. Later the same year saw the *La Folie* tour and album. I liked the new direction. It was a return to form and I saw the tour – a great gig with a different atmosphere.

JJ in action 1981 - photo Takahashi Yuka

TOP RANK

24 OCTOBER 1977, SWANSEA, UK

STEVE MALONEY

My first Stranglers gig was in a very wet and windy Swansea. The atmosphere was dark from the start, with the locals settling their disputes with the aggression expected. After the Stranglers arrived onstage, it didn't take long for it all to kick off; JJ Burnel's boot flying past my left ear, running punch ups everywhere, and then my introduction to the Finchley Boys, who more than earned their stripes and got JJ back onstage. Over 45 years later, I write and record with Finchley Boy original Steve Hillier. Who'd have thought it possible?

HOPE & ANCHOR

17 NOVEMBER 1977, ISLINGTON, LONDON, UK

SARAH CHAPMAN

One of the first bands I really got into back in the day, (I saw the Clash not long after seeing the Stranglers). The first three albums are classics, they helped develop punk. The Stranglers were way ahead of anybody else musically at the time. I saw them lots of times around this time period at the Hope & Anchor and in various locations in London (along with The Pirates and Dr Feelgood) and the energy was incredible. I seem to remember they opened up the Hope & Anchor Festival which ran over three weeks and was recorded for a double album.

I thought they were fairly old blokes at the time but on reflection I was wrong! Without question JJ is up there with some of the best bassists ever.

COLIN FOSTER

I saw loads of bands at the Hope & Anchor. As for the Stranglers I saw then live from the outset, and they were always great live and think they played at the Hope & Anchor around 20 times.

Dr Feelgood, were brilliant when I saw them at the venue. Their *Stupidity* (live) album is a classic. I saw them a few times, but the last time I went to see Wilko a few years back he didn't turn up on stage! The story goes that he arrived, collected some cash in advance, headed towards a local pub and never came back!

PARADISO

28 NOVEMBER 1977, AMSTERDAM, THE NETHERLANDS

BARRY CAIN

Pass me the aphrodisiac honey, we're in Amsterdam. And all the cutie canal streets of this cold Indonesian restaurant night lead to the Paradiso.

The Paradiso reminds me of the Roundhouse only dirtier – a huge filter tip after the cigarette has gone, the death-brown fusing of nicotine, tar and spit. Then you look up, way above the stage, at the stained-glass windows that provide the only clue that this was once a church. Now there's a dope bar where the font used to be, kids snort in the shadow of the altar and the Stranglers have replaced Christ. Hey, is that a tear on the multi-coloured cheek of Mary up there?

Christ he told his mother, Christ he told her not to bother

There's a thousand punters inside, another thousand outside and a Dutch TV film unit recording the lot for posterity.

The Stranglers – high-rise exponents of the kind of devout decadence inherent in pre-war Berlin. They always remind me of a scene in the old Alexander Korda movie *The Thief Of Baghdad*, when a wealthy Indian merchant falls in love with a life-size mechanical doll that has eight arms. He pays a fortune for it and in the privacy of his cavernous marble clad bedroom he begins to caress the doll. It has huge fingernails proceeds to dig them into the merchant's back. Gently at first, then harder, until the blood starts to gush and he collapses dead to the floor.

There's something very unclean about the Stranglers. I always feel like taking a shower after seeing them.

Their phenomenal success among the pre-pubes baffles me – what 13-year-old has ever heard of Trotsky? They're not glamorous. Their clothes are straight out of a Black Sabbath wardrobe. But the far-out, bombed-out, bleached-out fallout that is the Stranglers somehow gets across to them. Like dirty old men offering sweets...

The Paradiso show is their usual sex act without taking their boots off. One new song, '5 Minutes', indicates a variation but the tried-and- trusted format is retained. Why change success? If that's what the proles want, give it to 'em and give it to 'em good.

I enjoy their shows, their records, their pose. It may be real cool to slag them for writing anti-feminist songs (though I thought most songs professing to be 'love' songs were anti-feminist anyway – writers from Porter to Lennon have regarded women as merely love objects, gossamer fantasies) or for making money, but their desirability rating is high amongst the record buying public.

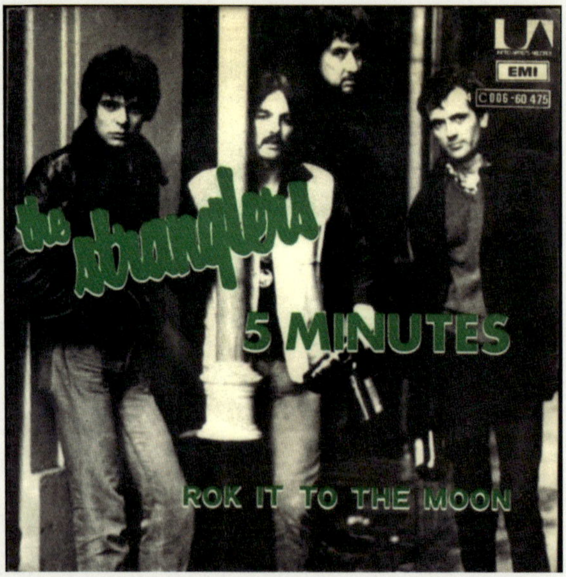

They bring out the prurience in people – and that can't be all bad.

Now we get to the meat of the story. Half-way through 'Ugly', just before Jean-Jacques Burnel screams, 'It's only the children of the fucking wealthy that tend to be good-looking,' a kid jumps on stage and dances.

A security guard hurls the kid off the stage. Nothing out of the ordinary you might say. But the guard is a Hell's Angel, built like a brick shithouse, and the stage happens to be eight feet off the ground. Jean stops playing and tells the Angel to cool it. But that's all he can do. The Angel grudgingly nods. A taste of things to come...

Barry Cain with The Stranglers

The band finish the number and the rest of the show runs relatively smoothly, with only the slightest hint of Angel cakewalking side-stage. The kids have taken the hint and limit their enthusiasm to soccer sways while sitting on the stage in front of the band.

The Dutch Angels have muscled their way into the Stranglers' camp. Whenever they play Holland, the Angels are there offering friendly advice and five-star service. The band like them, there's no doubting that. But it wouldn't much matter if they didn't.

The Hell's Angels of Amsterdam are different from their counterparts in Britain, America or Timbuktu. They're government approved! No kidding. The Dutch Government allocated a £150,000 grant to enable the Amsterdam Hell's Angels Society, as it's officially known, to set up shop. With that money the society built a complex on the city outskirts. It includes a large clubhouse complete with disco and bar, sleeping quarters, a garage to house their 1000cc steeds and a makeshift shooting range. And, wait for it, each of the society's 25 members receives an annual grant of £2,000.

Altogether now – why? Fear appears to be the prime motivation for such a bizarre policy. It seems the government are afraid of this happy band of men, and the money is merely a ruse to keep them quiet. A DIY protection racket only it's not forced upon any little speakeasy owner. It's on the government, maaaan!

Backstage after the show, The Stranglers enjoy a spot of quiet relaxation with their new-found buddies. I get a long, ludicrous, electric-drill-in-the-kneecaps stare from one of the Angels as I walk into the dressing room.

'He's all right,' Hugh assures me. His timing's perfect. The Indonesian meal I had earlier is ready to make an unscheduled appearance.

'They took us back to their clubhouse after we played last night,' Hugh continues. 'I stayed until 6am. They gave us anything we wanted and treated us like kings.' Hugh is clearly loving every Evel Knievel moment of it. Dave sits nearby cuddling his missus. Jet surveys the scene and Jean-Jacques is AWOL. Apparently, he's gone to collect a motorbike.

By this time the dressing room is crowded and one of the roadies locks the door. 'Let me in,' shouts someone outside. 'It's me, Pedro.' He's one of the Angel clan.

'Sorry, we're too full.' says one of the roadies

'Let me fucking in. It's fucking me,' says Pedro who starts punching the door.

'Piss off.'

Pedro kicks the door in frustration before pissing off. A few minutes later after two hefty blows on the wall by the door, Pedro emerges through a pile of masonry carrying a sledgehammer. 'Which one of you said 'piss off'?' Nobody was gonna own up to that one.

'We're all going back to their club tonight,' Hugh tells me.

Oh, great.

Suddenly, the loudest banger I've ever heard explodes at my feet. A group of three bearded Angels with dirty faces chuckle in the corner. 'You come with us, yah?' says, yeah, you guessed it, Pedro.

'Er, well, if it's all the same to you I'll go in the van with the band.'

The last time the Stranglers played here, the Angels took them to a pleasant little bar slap-bang in the middle of the red-light district. Their girlfriends are the girls in the windows who pop in between grovelling clients for a sociable drink.

But this time it's da bizness... the Angel Club.

The building is well away from residents' areas, one of the government's stipulations. A prison is under construction nearby.

'They'll never finish building that jail,' a visiting Angel from Brighton informs me. 'The Communists don't want it, so they keep bombing the place every now and then.'

There's another reason why the prison won't be completed for some time. In the back garden of the club a large machine gun is mounted on a tripod. When an Angel fancies some fun, he strolls out, loads up the gun and shoots off a shitload of bullets at the construction site.

'Can't get the workers.'

The clubhouse is tastefully lit, probably because most of the light bulbs have been smashed. Hugh plays pool with a guy affectionately referred to as 'Loser'. His face is heavily scarred, the result of an acid attack.

Half-way through the game, the barman turns down the lights and starts showing 'home' movies. The pool table Hugh was just using appears on a screen against the wall and a naked woman climbs on top of it. Someone giggles at the bar. 'Look, that's me, haha-hahahaha,' says an Angel. And sure enough, it is. He walks onto the screen holding a milk bottle, which he inserts into the woman as she reclines on the pool table.

'She was a German girl who wanted to be shown round,' whispers Loser in my ear.

That's followed by a film of two German Angels who had, 'Stepped out of line'. They're dragged to the club, searched at gunpoint and their weapons confiscated. Big Al, the president of the society, tells them to get out of Amsterdam, never to return.

An Angel with a bushy red beard and wearing a Stetson, acts the fool in one film. Loser says the guy was in a lunatic asylum after beating up three men and putting them in hospital. When the barman turns the few remaining lights back on, I spot the Stetson guy drinking at the bar.

Get the picture?

At that moment, Jean-Jacques roars into the clubhouse on his Triumph T160 Trident Cardinal along with an Angel on a Harley Davidson. They motor round the pool table, along the bar and then out into the backyard where they spin round the machine gun. JJ's stage mascara is a little smudged, but he still retains his cucumber cool.

I'm sitting at a table near the backyard with Alan Edwards, the band's publicist, and we both can't quite believe what we've just seen. A guy in a balaclava wanders over to our table.

'Look at this, ja.' He pulls out a small revolver and places it against Alan's head. 'You like Russian Roulette?' He pulls the trigger. It clicks.

'Good, ja? It's a .22 calibre. Powerful for such a little gun, ja?'

'Oh, ja, ja!' says Alan, who looks totally stunned.

Balaclava Billy wanders off. 'Bet it wasn't loaded,' I say.

Billy then shoots the gun at the prison...

I ask president Big Al if they have problems with the police. 'The police? Hahahahaha! They never come here. They're too scared.'

What about licences for their shooters? 'Hahahahaha!' He gives me his card: 'Amsterdam Society of Hell's Angels. President Big Al. Vice-President Stanley'.

Someone places a joint in my hand and I take several substantial hits.

As we leave, the Angels shake our hands and tell us we're welcome back any time. With every shake I keep thinking a knife will be plunged into my back. That ice-cream soft entry, comb-like parting of the flesh, the rose-red spill, the thump-thump of the heart, the dirty steel caressing the bone, the cool call of death.

I get to thinking about newspaper headlines 'Pop Group And Friends Slaughtered By Hell's Angels'. Of only the good-die-young. Of bright-future epitaphs, of Mum and Dad, Dina.

SLAP!

A hand hits me on the back. 'Goodnight. Safe journey.' Phew! That's some smoke.

While the Stranglers keep insisting on playing smaller venues, there will always be the danger of violence. Playing a place the size of the Paradiso is not fair on the fans or the band. Christ, they could pack out the Empire Pool two nights in a row, maybe even three. Slapdash security just won't work anymore. Nice gesture, sure, but something better change, quick.

Whatever happened to the Finchley Boys?

A week later Jean Jacques sends me a letter about my Amsterdam article. It feels like some kind of honour. Our conversations lengthen considerably in 1978 and I develop a tremendous respect for him. He has a lot of bad press, some of which is warranted, but I have a sneaky regard for his fists of fury attitude. This is punk rock after all, it has to have an edge, and JJ is on hand to push you over it, if necessary...

CLOUDS

10 FEBRUARY 1978, EDINBURGH, UK

NEIL MCCORMICK

My first time was February 1978 at Clouds in Edinburgh. It was one of those 'secret' gigs but the queue went all the way round the block and a freezing cold night. I remember Jet coming to the front of the stage and saying, 'Scotland? More like fucking Iceland.'

Neil McCormick with JJ

REYKJAVIK

2-4 MAY 1978, ICELAND

BARRY CAIN

This is a weird one. It's the tail end of winter 1978 and I've just made one of those career swerves that some of us do from time to time with varying results. I find myself working out of a cold, damp room in a Covent Garden squat as the Stranglers publicist.

I've teamed up with the now legendary PR Alan Edwards to help run his Modern Publicity company. The client list is impressive and also includes Blondie, the Buzzcocks, Generation X, and 999.

One of my first tasks is to organise a press trip to publicise the Stranglers third album release in a year, *Black and White*, and their forthcoming tour which opens in Iceland.

In these heady days when money is no object, the record company decide to fly the band and their entourage, plus a mob of media and management, to Reykjavik for a couple of serious nights in white satin. Turns out, nights don't exist in Iceland. It was the leave-the-light-off season, daylight 22/7.

I'm charged with the task of promoting the album and tour to the national and music press and persuading journos to come on the trip. It wasn't difficult, although for a not so plucky few, the thought of sharing a plane with the Stranglers scared the shit out of them and one says he'll only consider going if he can wear a parachute.

I write the invitations on pieces of rags and insert them into empty bottles of Black and White scotch that I collected from a distillery in London. Each bottle is delivered by hand...

Reykjavik, Iceland.

HELP!

Anarchic Arctic alcoholics slashing their wrists and 20-hour days. Blood streams in the white. Ice 'n' sleazy in Reykjavik. No night, no black, just a northern light frostbitten whiteness. Follow the instructions in the bottle and all this (and more, much more) can be yours. And you can even get to bring home a dead husky, if you play your cards right.

I know this won't end well when I'm mistaken for Jet Black upon our arrival at Keflavik Airport. An Icelandic reporter is convinced I'm the bearded drummer because I'm the only other person on board sporting a beard. Everybody at the airport is excited – it's the first time a major band had played there since Slade three years earlier.

The next 48 hours are the strangest I've had without dropping acid. Not seeing darkness for that length of time does something to a man. I crave the night life like a vampire or Alicia Bridges. These few endless days are full of thrills and spills and danger that all belong big time to the night-time, and make everything disarmingly surreal. Great if you're a journalist but not so hot for PRs who have to *organise* while they're day trippin'.

And Iceland isn't the best place to trip in. Outside the city the landscape is comic book Martian; the sky is flecked with red and never-ending streams of volcanic hot water po

Inside the city there's a thousand things I wanna say to you. Like the time I'm bitten by a dead shark...

On the night of our arrival, a special Icelandic buffet had been arranged for us all by the hotel whose manager insists I try, 'Iceland's most expensive delicacy,' and hands me a plate containing what appears to be a small white, saturated flannel. I place it gingerly into my mouth and I can honestly say, hand on heart, it's the worst thing I'd ever tasted and believe you me, I'd tasted some pretty shitty things. My immediate reaction is to spit it out, but the manager is awaiting my praise.

'What is it?' I ask after forcing this foul, fiendish thing down my throat and draining a glass of red wine to kill the taste.

'Well, it's raw shark marinated in cow's urine and buried underground for three months. Very nice. Have some more.'

'Er, no, thank you.'

Of course! That's the taste I couldn't place - old fish soaked in cow's piss. Shit, you wouldn't want to pick a fight with an Icelander.

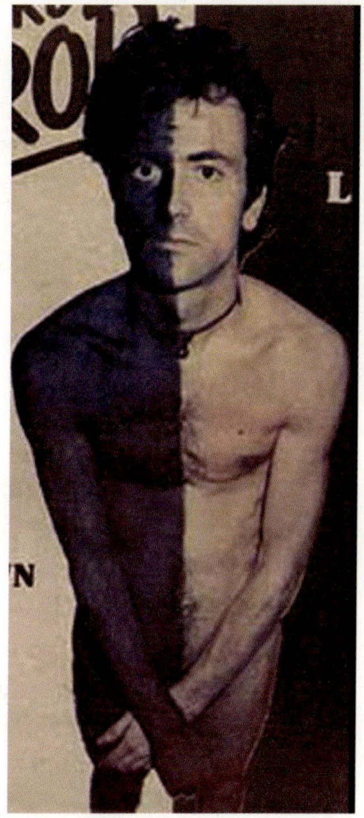

Cover photo of Record Mirror after the Iceland gig

That evening I find myself standing in the middle of a hotel room with a naked Hugh Cornwell as I paint half of his body black and the other half white for a Record Mirror cover shoot. Painting his knob is a fairly sobering experience but I would do anything for love and seven column inches. Or eight.

When I complete the paint job, I have to arrange a few interviews with the band in one of the rooms. The journalist from the *New Musical Express* looks a little apprehensive as we wait for the elevator. The Stranglers are universally feared by journalists and with good reason. Reports of kidnappings and violence against writers reverberate around the industry. It's all really heavy duty, so the *NME* guy's obvious agitation is only to be expected as the lift finally arrives.

I become a proper PR in that eight-floor ride.

'I've never seen them so laid back,' I say convincingly as we get in the lift.

'Really?'

'Yeah, Jean has assured me' (and he did too) 'that they've stopped all their antics. This album means a lot to them and they really want people to appreciate it.'

'Great,' he looks relieved. 'I really like the album.'

We hit floor eight.

'You'll have a great interview. I know it. Like I said, I've never seem them so relaxed.'

Jean opens the door of his room. 'Hi.' He smiles warmly. 'Come in.'

I make the introductions and Jean invites the writer to take a seat.

As he goes to sit down, Jean pulls the chair from under him and he falls flat on his arse in the most ignominious fashion. I quickly help him to his feet and kinda remonstrate with the band who apologise profusely. But the damage has been done and I don't know whether to laugh or cry. So I leave, and laugh. Out loud.

As we all make our way to Reykjavik Exhibition Hall where the band will be playing, I'm a little disconcerted by the number of ambulances parked outside. It didn't take long to figure out while they were there. The thousands of Icelandic young blades who have gathered for the show may be deprived of beer (it's not available anywhere on the island) but they more than make up for it by downing industrial amounts of whisky, vodka, gin and local brew Brennivin made from potato mash and herbs. They proceed to smash the shit out of each other throughout the entire concert. The blood gets on your shoes as broken bottles hit vacant faces and life suddenly seems cheap. I'd seen London dancehalls erupt but not like this, not with such hatred. This is drunkenness blinded by the light; all reason extinguished by a 50 per cent proof flood and some hard-assed Stranglers sounds.

It must be the raw shark.

On the final morning of our stay – or was it night? – a pony trek has been arranged for the whole party. A small band of pissheads and myself opt for some extra hours in our luxury hotel rooms followed by a long, slow comfortable swim up against the pool. Besides, horse-riding seems far too hazardous a pursuit after a night – or was it day? – of skulldruggery.

However, I badly sprain my ankle after treading awkwardly on one of the stairs leading down to the hotel pool, at least, that's what the doctor tells me three hours later after checking my x-rays in Reykjavik General.

What a klutz. I'm supposed to be looking after everyone, getting them on the coach to the airport, checking them in, attempting to prevent any of them from getting too pissed in the airport bar. And now, here I am, a cripple who can't walk without assistance. They even radio Heathrow on the flight back to ensure there's a wheelchair waiting for me.

Jean pushes me in the wheelchair when we get to Heathrow. I'm surprised and a little flattered, but also have a vague fear that he'll whip it away as I try to sit down. That would've been stretching the boundaries of taste way too far.

But I'd have laughed. Out loud.

One of the reporters is pissed morning, noon and night, and becomes the unintentional clown of the party because he's a bit of a toff who works on a national gossip column, carries a silver-topped cane and is too drunk to care. On that plane journey home, JJ bets that nobody can drink the full bottle of whisky he has in his bag in half an hour and the Toff volunteers, pouring the lot down his throat in 15 minutes, with a little help from his friends. He immediately enters a catatonic Hades and also requires a wheelchair at the other end.

The perfect end to the perfect day – or was it night...?

BLACK AND WHITE

RELEASED 12 MAY 1978

SIMON SMITH

It's early 1978 and I'm standing in the horrible brutalist Ryemarket Shopping Centre, a copy of *Sounds* in my hands (well, all over my hands, such was the nature of ink in those days) and the proceeds of my paper round in my pocket. I was thirteen and deeply in the thrall of punk which had begun thrillingly for me the year before.

I had jumped at the chance to get into all these new bands that seemed to be springing up and sneered at the vast majority of my classmates who seemed to be constantly arguing about who the best guitarist was (Page, Blackmore, Howe, blah, blah...). As now, music then was primarily about how it made me feel, what it evoked in me, and punk bands appealed to something very basic. They spoke of rebellion in a way that I was only just coming to appreciate.

The first 'punk' record that I bought was the Stranglers' double A-side 'Peaches'/'Go Buddy Go', which appealed to an immature teenager in its inherent rudeness, something which these days seems to be a very English seaside postcard sort of filth. Two albums had followed, and the Stranglers were pretty much my band at the time. Sure, I liked the Pistols but there was something about them that seemed what I would now describe as ephemeral (and actually Public Image Ltd would be far more interesting), and the Clash were beyond my experience somehow.

Two days earlier I had seen the Stranglers video for '5 Minutes' on *Top of the Pops*, a thrilling track played against a clock counting down, which seemed to give fresh impetus and urgency to a band who clearly sets out its state of mind in the very first verse: *I need a dream where I can live what I said I need a place where I can make my bed I need a hole where I'll find darkness now And if you hassle me mister, I might just lose my head.*

The Stranglers were angry, they had a chip on their collective shoulders. They were on the edge and were seeking an outlet for all this pent-up frustration and resentment at being ostracised by the music press and other bands, something with which the band had itself colluded. My 13-year-old self didn't pick all of this up, but by the same token I did have a sense that '5 Minutes' was a special record for me, and one of the few where I can remember exactly where and when I bought it.

I played that single to death, along with B-side 'Rok it to the Moon', and it remains a track that I turn to when I want to shed some aggression. Then, when the band's third album, *Black and White*, appeared I took it very much in my stride and did not at the time think it to be anything out of the ordinary. However, *Black and White* is one of those records that has developed with me over time, and I have never become tired of it.

If '5 Minutes' set out the Stranglers psychology at the time, *Black and White* is a full realisation of it. Setting out to reflect how the band had polarised opinions they really went for it and broke out of their pub rock past, creating an album that is a lost classic despite being a commercial success (listen to it and then imagine that it charted at number two).

There can be very few albums that start with a statement of intent as powerful as 'Tank', a track that sounds just as it's named: the sound of a band piledriving its way through its critics and emoting a massive 'fuck you!' 'Nice 'n' Sleazy' is a track that at the time got caught up with the Battersea Park gig, during which the band had strippers on stage. This has somewhat distracted us from the song itself which is far from a re-hash of 'Peaches', as was seen at the time. This is a track in which we begin to see changes to the Stranglers' sound with JJ Burnel's bass playing in the foreground and Dave Greenfield's keyboards alternating between the sinister and the fairground, while Hugh Cornwell's vocals have a new focus and urgency to them. Underpinning all of this are Jet Black's drums which at the same time as being solid – holding everything together – also have a certain liquidity to them which help give the track its squalid nature.

With the band's trademark preoccupation with violence and feculence established, the Stranglers now seem to be freed to explore some very dark places and, although the album is split into the 'white' and 'black' sides, the overall narrative is of the latter, with a focus on what goes on at the edges of society. 'Outside Tokyo' is a case in point with its deep and short bass riff and off-kilter rhythm: a meditation on time and existence every bit as profound as that of *Dark Side of the Moon*, but not one that is dwelt upon.

Next up is the dystopian 'Hey! (Rise of the Robots)' which on the face of it looks like a prescient view of the encroachment of technology on society but can also stand as a sense of foreboding about the rise of Thatcherism. Here the addition of X-Ray Spex's Laura Logic on saxophone gives the track a suitably otherworldly feel that takes the band further away from previous expectations. 'Sweden (All Quiet on the Eastern Front)' is arguably Cornwell's mordant and biting lyrics at their most effective. Based on his time in Sweden prior to the Stranglers, in which he was drifting and isolated, he finds just the right balance between humour and attitude.

Ending the so-called 'white side', 'Toiler on the Sea' is a great example of what makes this album different from its contemporaries; it shows how the band did not adhere to hitherto accepted rock structures. This was a group of four people who musically had an equal voice; four strong characters that were all fighting their corner, while at the same time fighting the Stranglers' corner. The internal tension is what gives this album a unique sound. This was after the punk tsunami, but now re-building and creating something new and different.

The 'black side' of the album kicks off with 'Curfew', setting out the bleakness to come, but also reflecting an insecurity that is every bit as relevant today as it was under the threat of nuclear annihilation in the 1970s. When you listen to 'Curfew', and the rest of this side, you have to remind yourself that this was made before anything by Magazine ('Real Life' came out the following month), Gang of Four, the Pop Group, Joy Division or Wire. Indeed, Peter Hook has declared that the Stranglers, and Burnel in particular, were a huge influence.

'Threatened' is about our rights and abilities to be offended and the extent to which we should feel vulnerable from verbal aggression, and how on the other hand we have the right to say what we think. Like 'Tank' it is a track that sounds as it reads, placing the onus on the threatened. The real threat for me comes in the spareness of the music, it's not what *is* said, but what is *not*. It's the Stranglers at their most aggressive while at the same time showing that force and stupidity are not the same. This might be a forthright album, but it is also an intelligent one.

By the time 'In the Shadows' starts, you already get the impression that the record has been playing for ages. This is one of the centrepieces of the album with its dark and sinister bass and synth beginning; this is where the band truly begin to go off-piste. It's hard to imagine now, but there was nothing like this at the time and while the lyrics have been dismissed as simplistic in some places, the atmosphere that is created here is redolent of violence and discomfort. We are really being taken outside our comfort zones and it ain't gonna be pleasant.

The Stranglers come up with a far more biting attack on the establishment and the prevailing values of the time than the Pistols, and didn't need to get onto a boat to prove their point; they did it intelligently and wittily with 'Do You Wanna?'

'Death and Night and Blood (Yukio)', is possibly the clearest congruence between Burnel's two passions of music and martial arts. He has described this as a warrior's song and the bass is front and centre driving the track, not as part of a rhythm section but almost as a second vocalist; you get the feeling that it is his weapon of choice. This is like a duet, with the rest of the band consistently and menacingly backing him before Greenfield's keyboards emerge near the end like a rallying cry.

Returning to the nature of existence for the final track, 'Enough Time', which is as disorienting as anything on the album. This is a track that is extremely unsettling with its irregular beat and piercing Morse code halfway through. It's a track that seems to signal the later 'Meninblack' theme as the vocals are sped up while the instrumentation is slowed down. Is this the end? The final moments for our species as we move even faster towards destruction? Have we got enough time? Probably not.

This is a suitably apocalyptic end to an extraordinary album which has not only stood the test of time musically, but philosophically too. It is an album that has something to say on the major issues that affect our lives today, in a world that politically is once again becoming increasingly black and white.

Buying '5 Minutes' as a 13-year-old, I would not have imagined that some 38 years later I would still be finding meaning in that song and the album that followed it. *Black and White* continues to amaze me to this day and, if anything, I have become more convinced that it is a stone-cold psychedelic classic, an album that is of its time and out of time. Whether or not it was the first 'post-punk' album I neither know nor care; for me it was the moment that both punk and my musical taste began to grow up.

'SVERIGE'

12 MAY 1978

ROB OCKFORD

I was in Stockholm around 1990 staying with family friends who are Swedish, and I noticed there was a small write up on the Stranglers in a local paper. I asked if they could help me read it. After they translated it for me, it appeared the journalist was not a fan of the band, as he didn't like their music and he claimed that trouble always followed them.

My friend's dad does not speak very good English, and he asked why did I like the band as they were trouble makers and they had such a bad reputation, but he admitted that he had not listened to any of their music. I explained that the press always gave them a bad time and they were not as bad as they were made out to be, and I told him that they had even written a song about Sweden. Before I realised what I was saying, I said I had my Walkman with me and would he like to listen to the track. To this day, I don't understand why I said it.

He appeared really chuffed to think that someone had written a song about his country, but I failed to tell him that the song was not very complimentary. Both he and his wife shared the headphones and I played the track to them in Swedish. It didn't take long for his face to change, and he started to mutter and moan about what he was listening to and at one point I thought he was going to blow a gasket! He did not like the track and he decided that the bad press the band got was justified. I gathered from his expression, that he was not going to rush out and purchase any of the band's records.

NEW BINGLEY HALL

30 MAY 1978, STAFFORD, UK

MARK OWEN

Mark Owen with Hugh

In early February 1977 and, as a change from listening to Noel Edmonds' *Breakfast Show* on Radio 1, I tuned into 261 Piccadilly Radio, Manchester's independent radio station. One morning, I heard 'Grip' by the Stranglers. A couple of days later, they played it again and I was hooked. I needed to know a lot more about this band...

I was 16, living in rural Cheshire and didn't know a great deal about the punk scene that had emerged over the previous twelve months, other than seeing some clips on TV and a few articles in the music press about the bands who later were to be recognised as the pioneers of punk and new wave. I remember buying *Rattus* in Chester one Saturday afternoon, playing it over and over again and even staying in instead of cycling to see my girlfriend at the time.

Next came 'Peaches' and 'Something Better Change' and the Stranglers seemed to be all over the news, good and bad, and *No More Heroes*, both album and single, were released. I remember John Peel playing all of *Black and White* on one of his shows in 1978.

The *Black and White* tour was announced and they were playing at Stafford's New Bingley Hall. My friends and I bought tickets and were so excited about seeing the band for the first time that we even drove the 70 mile round trip to Stafford to check the place out beforehand. On the day of the gig, we finished work early and arrived at the venue around six o'clock. There were coaches everywhere. We parked the car and joined a long queue to get in. Once inside, we watched the support band Steel Pulse, which I enjoyed, even though they had lots of stuff thrown at them whilst on stage.

The moment we had waited for soon arrived, and the four Meninblack were on stage. The first song I heard live was 'Burning Up Time'. The first part of the show was material from *Rattus* and *Heroes* and then all the lights went out and the venue was plunged into complete darkness. Two search lights came on and the band went into 'Curfew'. They played most of the *Black and White* album, finishing with '5 Minutes'.

Just before the encore, I had a nosebleed due to being too hot and I went into the First Aid area, expecting just to grab some tissue to shove up my nose so that I could get back into the crowd. But I had to sit down with my head back, much to my frustration as I could hear 'Toiler on the Sea' starting up. I just managed to get back to hear the end of it. For the next week, I was buzzing and couldn't stop thinking about the gig.

I've remained a Stranglers fan. A craze in the late Seventies was to put you and your girlfriend's names across your car windscreen, or the name of your favourite band. I had the Stranglers across the windscreen of my red Ford Escort Mark I. My wife Diane's first of many times watching the Meninblack was in October 1986 at Liverpool University, closely followed by a trip to Manchester Apollo the following week. Our son, Alex, first saw them when he was three years old, at *Dracfest* in Whitby back in 1997. Whilst walking along the lane to get to the gig, I overheard a little girl saying, 'Dad, why do we have to go and see the Stranglers again?' We never had that trouble with Alex, who has now seen them 99 times.

I was very disappointed when Hugh left. I thought that would be the end of the Stranglers. How wrong I was, and I have carried on watching them through their various line ups up to the present day. I have followed the band all over the United Kingdom, including just three miles down the road from where I live at an acoustic festival in Nantwich. I've seen them playing in a record shop and watched Baz playing in a barn in North Yorkshire. I've been soaked through on the beach in Looe and sweltered in Fibbers in York. I've seen them in Europe, the USA and Australia. And I've made lots of friends along the way.

ANCIENNE BELGIQUE

13 JUNE 1978, BRUSSELS, BELGIUM

CHRIS ACHER

It all started with a riff back in 1977. I was finishing my studies in Brussels and going to some punk gigs. I had seen quite a few rock bands on stage, including in France and Manchester where I had been a student, as glam rock was on *Top of the Pops* and Elton John and David Bowie were rising stars.

I heard those three notes on the radio that are still so easy to spot today when the man who created their sound plays them. 'Peaches' did it forever for Jean-Jacques Burnel and the band he had co-founded with a Hugh Cornwell, a 'Jet Black' and a Dave Greenfield. As a long-time fan of the Doors, my ear also caught right away the most appealing sound of the keyboards.

I was already hooked when their third album, *Black and White*, was released and had been playing it constantly when they appeared at Ancienne Belgique. It was my first

Stranglers gig. JJ was still 'John' and wearing his famous black knitted top under the leather jacket. On the photos, he looked (and looks) very sexy but I was not interested in him as a sexy man, I swear! I was totally bluffed by him being (originally) French but having found his way into a British band. That night, and because of his talented bass-playing, 'Nice 'n' Sleazy' became my favourite track. Still does it, does it every time.

My favourite album of the Stranglers, though, was to be the next one, *The Raven*. That may be something to do with my own Viking ancestry. 'Genetix' is a piece of art and they are all so good at playing it. I've been listening to it many times since Dave has been 'wandering among the stars...'.

ULSTER HALL

7 SEPTEMBER 1978, BELFAST, UK

STEPHEN FLEMING

Because of the troubles in Northern Ireland very few bands played in Belfast. Me and a friend went to the gig and we were not disappointed - what a night. While the support band, a local band called Starjets, were on stage, we noticed a lot of the crowd spitting at them. Unfortunately for me and my mate, we were mistakenly judged to be doing this and the bouncers ejected us from the building via the back door. Fortunately for me and my mate, the Stranglers were entering the hall via the back door and the band stopped the doormen from ejecting us by refusing to play if we weren't allowed back into the gig. JJ was drinking a bottle of QC sherry, which he allowed me to hold and drink while he was talking to the doormen. We got back into the gig, and what a gig it was.

ARCADIA

8 SEPTEMBER 1978, PORTRUSH, UK

MICKEY BRADLEY, BASS GUITAR, THE UNDERTONES & BBC RADIO ULSTER PRESENTER

We supported them in 1978 in Ireland, before 'Teenage Kicks' came out. And they were very considerate, made sure we got a soundcheck and all that, made sure the doors were kept closed until we had our

Mickey Bradley tells it as it is at Derry's Central Library - photo Vinny Cunningham

soundcheck. They were really encouraging and we had a bona fide Jean-Jacques jumping into the crowd to beat up somebody who was spitting all night! I still remember seeing that. He just jumped off and... 'boom!'... and then jumped back up on stage and just carried on.

UNIVERSITY OF LANCASTER

11 SEPTEMBER 1978, LANCASTER, UK

IAN WILLIAMSON

I remember two Lancaster Uni gigs: singing 'Tits' in front of the speakers whilst waiting for an encore on the *Black and White* tour, and a stage invasion - an act of love, not aggression - on the *Raven* tour. I've seen them many times since and will again.

BATTERSEA PARK

16 SEPTEMBER 1978, LONDON, UK

DAVE CARROLL

Dave Carroll heard there was going to be a concert in Battersea Park

I don't know how it came about, but we heard there was a concert in Battersea Park, so two friends and I went. We saw all these punk rockers heading up to the park and they all looked absolutely incredible. We followed them and got to where the concert was in the park, but you had to pay to get in. We tried bunking in there, but there was no way you could get in, so we all actually walked back home to get the money, went back up there, and paid to get in.

Appearing were the Stranglers, supported by Peter Gabriel from the band Genesis, The Skids and a comedian called Johnny Rubbish. Johnny Rubbish got absolutely bottled and ended up in an ambulance. I don't remember the crowd liking Peter Gabriel too much either because he was an old hippy. It was a boiling hot day and pretty full on, with an army tank parked on the field. It was pretty far out.

As the day went on the Stranglers came on. I wasn't that interested in the Stranglers beforehand, but they were absolutely fantastic. More and more people turned up as their set went on, and the punks there were very cool. There was a group of punk girls in the crowd wearing white shirts with school ties, their hair dyed multi-coloured and spiked up, black knickers, fishnet stockings, suspenders and high-heels. Wow! It was lingerie in a public place, worn by girls who truly didn't give a fuck what anyone thought of them. It was pure rebellion; fantastic and absolutely mind-blowing.

A guy with them had one side of his head dyed black and the other side bleached white, which I thought was quite good because the Stranglers album was called *Black and White*. One of the punk girls was stood behind him, with her arms around his shoulders, whilst he reached around with his hand down the front of her knickers. I was like, 'Wow, fuck the music, I just want to be a punk rocker!'

Then, all of a sudden, the Stranglers started playing their song 'Nice 'n' Sleazy' and strippers ran onto the stage wearing stockings, suspender belts, bras, open bras, no bras and no knickers! I was 13 years old and couldn't get into a bar to see strippers. I couldn't believe it. The one that stood out for me was wearing a green leather outfit, with leather stockings and pink around her bra. They were the best dancers I've seen in my life. They were amazing.

This was my first ever gig and the most eye-opening thing for a young adolescent teenage boy to see. It was the moment I fell in love with punk rock. The police raided the gig and arrested the band and the strippers. What a fantastic way to begin your teenage years.

NIGE CRANFIELD

It's a date and a day I'll never forget. I was a 15-year-old schoolboy and a huge Stranglers fan, but had yet to witness the band live - or any band for that matter.

I was living in Southend at the time, and the Stranglers had been subject to a year-long ban from performing in London by the now defunct GLC, so getting to see my heroes was a tricky task. Suddenly the announcement came that the ban was lifted and the Stranglers would be performing at Battersea Park. In the days before social media, we had to rely on the music press for snippets of information, and *Strangled* magazine.

I had a paper round at the time and borrowed some money from my dad to send off for the £4 ticket. Once my ticket arrived, the day couldn't come quick enough. My schoolmate, Warren Tall, and I set off ridiculously early, catching the 6.30am from Southend to London Fenchurch Street, eventually arriving at Battersea Park at 8.30am – just a little wait for the noon opening. But we were there and so full of excitement, if a little apprehensive.

When the gates opened, we ran to the stage to be at the front to be sure we could get a good look at our heroes. There was a tank, a huge Stranglers balloon and Jet's ice cream van. Thousands of fellow worshippers and I had a feeling inside like never before – this was it, Nige, everything you had been waiting for.

It was one of those beautifully warm September days and we patiently sat and stood through the various acts sent out to entertain us.

I quite enjoyed the Edge and the Skids, wasn't a fan of Peter Gabriel and was a little bemused by Johnny Rubbish (who was later to re-appear at the Albert Hall for *Friday the Thirteenth* – I'm sure he did the same set). Finally, after what had seemed like an eternity, the Stranglers took to the stage. Opening with 'Grip', I somehow found myself about ten feet further back from the stage as the masses began to surge and pogo like crazy around me.

I managed to find Warren and we found a spot facing Hugh that was a little calmer. The rest of the set seemed to fly by up until the introduction of the now infamous 'Nice 'n' Sleazy' strippers. What a treat! I was transfixed, not only my first ever Stranglers gig, but now my first ever strip show – 'These boys certainly know how to serve up a treat,' I thought. A small fight nearby during 'Peaches' couldn't spoil the day and I honestly can't remember the journey home. I had this feeling inside that I'd just witnessed something so magnificent, so uplifting and - like a drug - I needed it again.

And so began my love affair with the Stranglers. I've been lucky enough to travel the length and breadth of the UK, Europe and Australia to see them. I've met some fabulous people and made some great friends along the way. I've been through the difficult times and the good and have met the band on several occasions. I have so many fond memories but Battersea, from a live perspective, is the day where it all began.

JJ on stage at Battersea Park, London, 16 September 1978. Pictorial Press Ltd / Alamy Stock Photo

JOHN ALLARD

My next opportunity to see the Stranglers was an open-air concert at Battersea Park in London in 1978, and I was able to go with a friend from school. The support was Peter Gabriel, who was superb. As he sang 'Solsbury Hill', he dropped into the crowd and mingled among us, which seemed to be very unusual, and he passed within a few feet of where I was standing.

The Stranglers were a little less 'raw' than previously, and were also on a raised stage quite high above the crowd, so felt a little distant. They had a far larger repertoire to choose from by now, and it was a much more professional and polished performance. Hugh was again on good form. As they started to play 'Nice 'n' Sleazy', several dancers came onto the stage - from memory there was one guy and three women. As the band played, the dancers removed all their clothes and started simulating sex positions on the stage. I have to say that I was fairly close to the stage, but because it was so high, it was difficult to see much of what was going on! I think this was about the time the band had been arrested in Nice for some reason, so it was almost expected that they would stretch boundaries and break rules.

The other notable thing about that concert is that the band apparently had wanted to arrive on jet-packs. I have no clue why, but the story was that they weren't able to because they would have needed several weeks of training. However, there was a full-size tank at the back of the crowd area, which seemed to have had something to do with the jet-pack idea.

The next time I remember seeing them was at UEA, around 1985 and the time of the *Aural Sculpture* album, so many of the tracks featured a brass section. We were positioned quite close to the stage, so had a really good view of all four band members, and it was again a very professional performance - full of energy and Hugh's usual moaning between songs. Jean-Jacques had by this time developed a weird dance style, where he would put his weight on one leg and pivot in both directions while lifting the other leg up and down, and then switch to the other leg.

The most bizarre thing, though, was that there were three additional band members playing the brass parts, but they were completely hidden from view where we were stood, and I had had no idea they were there! Around this time, I had been to many concerts at this venue, and invariably went to the stage door afterwards to meet the musicians, but for some reason, I didn't at this one, so didn't get to meet the band.

This was the period when the band produced their best music. Obviously, 'Golden Brown' was their biggest hit single, but I always liked their songs which included brass instruments, from '(Get a) Grip' through 'No Mercy' to 'Big in America', and particularly the *Aural Sculpture* and *Dreamtime* albums.

I continued to follow the band's progress over the following years, through the album *10* and the departure of Hugh, and subsequent releases, but I didn't see them live again until 2010 - at a Triumph motorcycle festival at Mallory Park. The festival was interesting, although I hadn't yet developed an interest in motorbikes. I did

Battersea Park 1978 – photos Steve Bizley

brush shoulders with JJ Burnel over the bridge, and he was commenting to another of his group about a display where a rider was somehow pulling wheelies on a Triumph Rocket – an unfeasibly large motorbike which effectively has a three-litre car engine between the rider's legs!

The support act was Mumford and Sons, who I hadn't really heard of before the event. They were good, but the crowd were not there to see them, and they didn't stay around for long. The Stranglers came on, with their 'new' vocalist, and played a set which included their newer songs, but enough of the older ones to satisfy their older fans (like me!). The new guy is no Hugh - if only because he is too nice, and lacks Hugh's vitriol! JJ looked almost exactly the same, but Jet and Dave both looked noticeably older - particularly Dave, who had much shorter hair and seemed a little gaunt. And JJ was still doing that weird one-legged dance...

WIRRINA STADIUM

18 SEPTEMBER 1978, PETERBOROUGH, UK

IAN PITTS

Ian Pitts, Martin Blenco and Roger Denton were at Peterborough's Wirrina Stadium

I remember my first ever gig like it was yesterday. I was introduced to the Stranglers by my good mate, Gary, playing 'Go Buddy Go' and 'Peaches' non-stop on a juke box at a football tournament in the summer of '78. Then he let me borrow *Rattus Norvegicus* and I was hooked and we have going to Stranglers gigs ever since.

From the Wirrina Stadium (more like a gymnasium)
To Butlins Skegness (I would never have guessed).
Brighton, Brixton, Leeds and Manchester
The Rainbow, the Palais, De Montfort in Leicester.
Birmingham, Cambridge and Coventry
A civic centre in Corby for 35p.
A roundhouse, a bowl and even a racetrack
Rock City of course with a singing Jet Black.
Shepherds Bush Empire, the Royal Albert Hall
There's far too many to mention them all.
From the opening bars of 'Sometimes' on *Rattus*
To the final breath of the last track on *Dark Matters*.
Aged 16 to 60 from 78 to 22,
For this musical journey, I sincerely thank you.

MARTIN BLENCO

Having grown up on a diet of Slade and Gary Glitter, I was an 18-year-old heavy metal fan who'd seen Black Sabbath, Thin Lizzy and Status Quo in concert by this time. But I'd also seen the Clash, because in 1977 and 1978 you couldn't escape the sound of punk and the new wave if you had a pair of ears, and had a selection of 45s in these new-fangled picture sleeves. So my musical tastes were fairly broad, the Stranglers were all over the radio, and my mate Roger (who had arrived at the same musical destination via Queen and David Bowie) and I drove to Peterborough's Wirrina Stadium in my dad's yellow Bedford CF van. To be honest, I don't remember much about the gig, other than the sea of heaving, pogoing bodies when the Stranglers were on, and the Skids introducing themselves via Richard Jobson's thick brogue, 'We're the Skids from Scotland.'

Apparently, a pre-solo fame Billy Bragg was bottom of the bill with his band Riff-Raff, but Roger and I were sat in the van in the Wirrina's car park, necking Gaymer's Olde English cider from a two pint bottle. Roger knocked the bottle over and spilt cider all over the passenger seat. So, while the gig memories are faint, the memories of my dad's reaction to his van stinking of stale cider for weeks after the gig still linger, much like the smell of cider did.

ROGER DENTON

As a budding young punk in the late Seventies, I made the pilgrimage to see the Stranglers at Peterborough Ice Stadium (with the editor of this book). It was a memorable night, a storming performance from support act The Skids and a raise the roof show from the main act, JJ's bass and Dave Greenfield's epic organ (?) crushing our ear drums. .

My enduring memory from this gig though occurred just after the Skids set. Someone a few rows back kept shouting, 'I want a fag.' I was planning to give up ciggies, so I decided to let him have my last Rothman's. I threw the box up in the air behind me and it descended from the sky just in front of the fellow fan. 'Thank you God!' was his retort.

Thank you God for a cigarette and thank you God for the Stranglers.

PS. I almost certainly bought some more ciggies the next day.

TIFFANY'S BALLROOM

21 SEPTEMBER 1978, GREAT YARMOUTH, UK

NIGEL HOWES, AGE 13

My first big gig was when I was 13 in 1978. My brother and I together with a few friends were first in the queue as we travelled there straight from school. We had the pleasure of JJ coming out to have a quick chat. He did try to kick the door open... but it only swung the other way. He was telling us about his planned trip to Japan in early 1979 and declined my request for him to give me his black leather jacket. During the gig I sat on the edge of the stage next to Hugh's monitor, which is where the set list came from, along with the ticket for the night. It still has the gaffer tape on it. JJ kept sticking his tongue out at me throughout the evening. I suppose I was quite young. I've loved the band ever since.

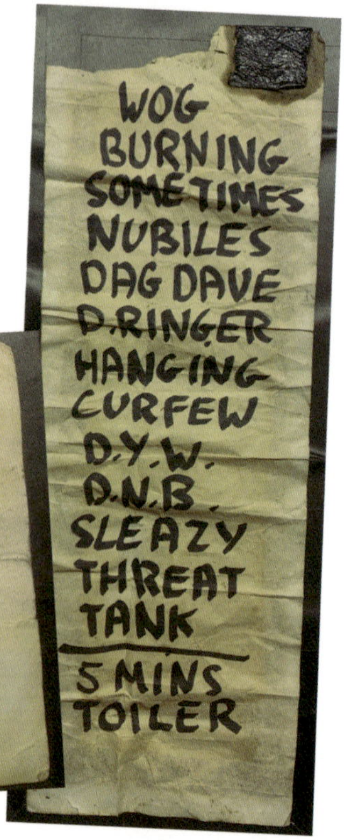

Nigel Howes still has a set list and his ticket

WINTER GARDENS

22 SEPTEMBER 1978, MALVERN, UK

SIMON ATKINS

I fell in love with the Stranglers and their music when I was 13 in 1977. As a very polite, well-mannered grammar school boy with an interest in drama, punk and new wave music appealed to my theatrical and dramatic instincts as well as providing me with a way to be a bit rebellious. What made the Stranglers so different was the quality of their musicianship and the strong, dark melodic character of their songs. The addition of keyboards to the usual instrumental line-up particularly appealed, as I was learning piano and aspired to play organ and other keyboards. Dave Greenfield's virtuoso keyboard solos on tracks such as 'No More Heroes' (I bought the single and the album) were what hooked me in. I purchased *Rattus Norvegicus* very soon after *No More Heroes*, and in 1978 remember excitedly listening to John Peel play the *Black and White* album in its entirety on his Radio 1 show on its release.

Later in 1978 I saw them play live for the first time on the *Black and White* tour. I was now 14 and it was one of the most exciting nights of my life to date. Before the Skids - who were supporting - had even appeared on stage, JJ suddenly ran on and began squirting the crowd with a CO_2 fire extinguisher he had presumably picked up backstage. The crowd chanted for 'Peaches', but it wasn't included in the set. Still, it was a brilliant and memorable night.

LOCARNO BALLROOM

24 SEPTEMBER 1978, PORTSMOUTH, UK

GORDON MACKENZIE

Gordon Mackenzie's love of the Stranglers live began 44 years ago

The Stranglers were due to appear at the Carisbrooke Arms, near Fareham, back in '75 or '76 but as a young-looking 14 or 15-year-old, there was no way I could get to see them there. So it was that I had to wait until they came to the Locarno in 1978. I had just turned 17. I went with my next-door neighbour, Kevin, a fair-haired best mate who dyed his hair green for the night, and a chap called Clint, who was known to Kev and who I've not seen since.

The energy outside the venue was electric. Some teddy boys decided to walk past - and then to run past as the abuse started. They were chased off in short time. Inside the venue, the excitement and tension was awesome. The Skids opened. I thought they were great and I went on to buy their first single, 'Sweet Suburbia', which I still have. The crowd seemed to feel rather different and the Skids were, effectively, spat off stage.

The Stranglers came on and were raw and powerful. This was the *Black and White* tour and we weren't that familiar with the album, so to hear it for the first time was fantastic. I cannot imagine that now, after spending 44 years seeing them and 46 or 47 years listening to them.

The rawness and energy were exhilarating and the crowd pogoed violently and spat as much as they could. This was not appreciated by the band, who stopped playing and politely (not) mentioned people might like to stop or they would just fuck off. One guy didn't stop and Hugh beckoned him to the stage. The chap happily did so and was rewarded with the end of a heavy guitar to the face, rendering him unconscious. The road crew then removed him from the venue by throwing him out of the fire door without opening it first. This seemed to stem the tide of spitting!

The set was awesome and the gig a blur. Many a fight started outside afterwards, but it was nothing serious. My mate Kev washed his hair off in the fountain at Gosport. Unfortunately, the green did not wash out and his Catholic and very strict father was less than impressed and took it out on his son in no uncertain way. I had a choke chain and padlock round my neck and my parents just thought I was odd. I cannot disagree.

This gig was the start of a lifelong love of all of the Stranglers stuff, with me eventually meeting Hugh on his *Totem and Taboo* tour. I've not been fortunate enough to meet the Stranglers themselves and remain upset at Dave's passing. I have a towel from Worthing that Baz used all through the gig and threw out into the crowd. This is in a sealed bag in the safe at home. And I was fortunate enough to receive a postcard from Jet when the chance to win one of those was running, which is also locked in the safe.

My ex-wife was nine months pregnant when we saw them in 1990 and my youngest was born less than a week after that concert. I started taking my son to concerts when he was old enough (bear in mind he grew up listening to them) and, at the most recent concert in 2022 at Portsmouth Guildhall, I managed to take my 10-year-old granddaughter too.

Whilst I am ashamed to say that I really couldn't get on with the Paul Roberts-era version of the band, I thank the Stranglers for the many years of enjoyment listening to their music and seeing them live. I've even stood outside a festival just to hear them as I couldn't get tickets.

BATH PAVILION

27 SEPTEMBER 1978, BATH, UK

ETHAN PRICTOR

Every year the family travelled to Scotland for our summer holiday. We would visit our cousins in Elgin and one day cousin Brian said to me, 'Come and listen to this.' I sat in his bedroom whilst he played 'Ugly' by the Stranglers. That was the moment it all started.

At Bath Pavilion in 1978, I was 15 years old and it was my first ever gig. I walked into what seemed this vast hall and I was hooked without a note being played. On came the Stranglers - snarling, aggressive and moody and just what a teenager in the Seventies wanted. I was transfixed by the angriest-looking person I had ever seen... Jean-Jacques Burnel. Who was this guy?

All I can remember about the show is that it was loud and brilliant. I have since spent the last 44 years admiring what they are about. The Hugh era was amazing. They have remained the Stranglers with great albums and a fantastic live show - no frills, no needless chit-chat; just great music time after time.

Two other concerts spring to mind. Firstly, in my home town of Chippenham in Wiltshire at the Golddiggers on 28th January 1983. The early evening was spent in the Rose and Crown, where we were proud patrons, so much so that the landlord allowed a scattering of Stranglers classics on the jukebox. Then, much to our joy, we were told the band were in the lounge so in my wisdom I put on 'Sverige', a rare recording of 'Sweden' in Swedish. However, I never found out if the band commented as we were jumping up and down in the bar!

The second gig was far more recent - July 2019 at Caerphilly Castle. It was a fantastic venue full of pissed up Taffies who really knew how to enjoy themselves. It was also the first gig for my stepson and he loved it. What a night and one memory I will take with me to my grave.

The Stranglers have made so many great tracks and they all mean something to me. But I want to mention two in particular. Firstly, 'Toiler on the Sea', which I think is the best opening track live. The whole song is magical but the first two seconds of JJ's bass is just amazing. The other song is 'The Last Men on the Moon' off *Dark Matters*. It has all the ingredients of Stranglers' brilliance over 40 plus years. The instruments come in one by one and it has great lyrics, great subject matter, fantastic keyboards (from the legendary Dave Greenfield) and a melodic tune that draws you in. It is, quite simply, fantastic.

When I look back on my life, the Stranglers have always been there like a heartbeat. Like many other people, I have seen them live more times than I can remember and in venues all across the UK. Controversial, resilient, talented and much adored by an incredible fan base, the Stranglers are unique and quirky, but legendary.

APOLLO THEATRE

28 SEPTEMBER 1978, MANCHESTER, UK

STUART EDWARDS

I was 15 years old. A few girls at the front started to strip off their tops so that gave me hours of fun. A punk tried to climb on stage and grab JJB and got a round house (karate kick) for his trouble. He was thrown out. I still think I was brave going to the Apollo on my own.

I remember waiting for mail from the SIS fanzine, *Black and White*. I had a few pints with Hugh Cornwell after a solo gig at the Witchwood in Ashton-under-Lyne. I was so star struck I'm sure I made a cock of myself, but we chatted for a good hour after the gig. Dave's keyboards always blow me away. The Stranglers are my true favourite band.

SEAN LYNCH

Sean Lynch and part of his collection

I first became obsessed with the Stranglers when I heard 'Hanging Around' on a John Peel session on 7th March 1977. I had never heard such a domineering bass sound before. I was still at school, and bored with the boring music being played on Radio 1, *Top of the Pops* and *Old Grey Whistle Test*, so I was instantly converted to any of the new sounds associated with punk. I could not get tickets for the *No More Heroes* tour, but did for the following year, at Manchester Apollo 1978, with the Skids and it is still my all-time favourite gig. They were as brilliant live as they were on record - the energy, excitement and aggression were a sight to behold.

COLIN NAYLOR

I first heard the Stranglers on Radio 1. I was leaving school at the time. 'Peaches' was the very first song I heard. My family at the time were, and still are, Elvis fans. I think that was what I enjoyed about the Stranglers, because it was totally the opposite to what my family liked. The Stranglers music was like a breath of fresh air. Listening to Dave Greenfield on the keyboard and Hugh Cornwell's voice was very raw and powerful. I went out and bought *Rattus Norvegicus* on the strength of 'Peaches'. I purchased the album with a free single (which I've still got) from Javelin Records in Heywood, Lancashire. I've bought one copy of every single, album, twelve inch or picture disc that's become available.

The first time I ever saw the Stranglers was at the Manchester Apollo and then it was every concert after that, 17 times in total. They all have a special meaning so the first concert is probably my favourite, because that was when I could put names to real faces for the first time and not have to rely on paper clippings or magazines. The Stranglers have become part of my DNA.

SPA

29 SEPTEMBER 1978, BRIDLINGTON, UK

AJAY SAGGAR, PRODUCTION MANAGER, MUSICIAN (BHAJAN BHOY, KING CHAMPION SOUNDS, DANDELION ADVENTURE, DEUTSCHE ASHRAM, DONKEY)

Ajay Saggar's mum with the copy of Black and White she bought him all those years ago

My family emigrated from the wilds of Kenya to the concrete jungle of Glasgow in the spring of 1976. It was a culture shock to say the least. To appease the giant step we made from one continent to another, my parents presented my brother and I with a National transistor radio, possibly with the idea that it would open our horizons and minds to the brave new world we had entered. There were medium wave, long wave and three short wave bandwidths we could scour. And within those bandwidths lay a voyage of discovery, and ultimately something that changed and defined my life forever.

I discovered the John Peel show by chance in the summer of 1976. Listening to the radio very quietly, deep in the night, next to my bed, I stumbled on a clatter of noise and aggressive vocals that was nothing like I'd ever heard before. Utterly intrigued,

I listened to something that had just exploded the mind of a young teenager. I didn't know anything of this phenomenon that would later be termed 'punk rock', but I did know that I wanted to learn more about it.

The John Peel show became my secret friend, a place I could escape to and be in my own newly discovered world. In the winter of 1976, we moved to England and a new chapter in my life began. The transistor radio also made the move, so I took my secret other world with me.

It was after the summer of 1977, granted admission to a grammar school in Pocklington in the East Riding of Yorkshire, that I met people who also knew about the John Peel show and the world there within. It wasn't a secret anymore, but I knew I belonged in a small secret club with a few fellow students.

Visiting my uncle and aunt in Nelson, Lancashire proved a huge turning point for the start of my love affair with the Meninblack. My cousin happened to have a huge record collection in his bedroom, and that was the first time that I became utterly enchanted by the world of vinyl. His record collection came as a revelation, and it mirrored the spuzz I'd been listening to and loving on the John Peel show. My mind was blown. He'd play me stuff I already knew and loved, and then played me new stuff I'd previously never heard and turned me onto a whole bunch of new stuff. He totally saw that I was in love with the music and offered to make me recordings of some of the records onto cassette. I giddily accepted his offer, and he duly made me a number of tapes. There was so much to hear and discover, but one tape more than the rest made the deepest impression.

The Stranglers' debut album, *Rattus Norvegicus*, was like nothing I'd heard before. The bluster and bravado that had been the hallmark of so many punk bands to date was brushed aside for something so much more enticing, smart, powerful and slightly off the beaten track. What was it that made it different? After all it was just four guys playing normal instruments. But it's what they did with those instruments and the sounds they got from them, mixed with lyrics that didn't have the nihilistic bent of other groups, but offered a dark, surreal, almost psychedelic tint to it all. The music lay somewhere within the punk realm, and yet drifted in its own unique universe. I was intrigued, and I was in love. Love at first (rat) bite.

That album – first heard while we were living in Hull, before we moved to Pocklington – made a huge impact on me. Do you remember when a particular band meant so much to you that they belonged to you only, that they took over and ruled your life? The Stranglers were such a band. The Stranglers were my band. They were my gang. They wrote brilliant songs that confounded critics, and they never compromised. I wanted to play the bass and make it sound like that of JJ Burnel. His was a killer demon sound that could flatten the Berlin Wall at a thousand paces. A sound that growled and was menacing and yet so sensual. And his riffs were to die for. I wanted the bass to be the lead instrument for many of the groups I played in throughout the years. I wanted to be able to write songs that weren't pinned down or defined by any genre. The Stranglers always led the way and were my group.

The first seven-inch single I bought was 'No More Heroes', and my first album was *Black and White.* I made my mum go to Boots on the morning it was released just so I would get the copy with the free single. And the first gig I attended? In September 1978, when I was 14, under the pretext of going on a school trip, my pal Owen Slater's brother in the sixth form, who was in Bridlington punk band Aerosol, took me to see the Stranglers at Bridlington Spa on the *Black and White* tour. His brother held me for the duration of that concert, and I saw every corner of that hall that night. It was Pogo Central, and remains such an incredibly vivid memory. My life was never the same again.

JAPAN

FEBRUARY 1979

BARRY CAIN

JJ, Hugh and Jet in Japan. Photo Barry Cain

They wait – in bullet train stations, in airports, in hotel lounges, in the shadows of afternoon corridors, in vain, in rain, armed with heart-shaped chocolates, flowers, love letters, sugar-sweet smiles, bird-wing eyes, all things feminine, for... the Stranglers.

It could've been any other band, any other full-cream hard-ons in Brylcreemed trousers, any other bunch of matinée idols with fake bollocks and painted smiles.

But the Stranglers?

As the bullet train pulls into Osaka station, they're waiting and when the band alight from a carriage onto the platform, they pounce. Much of the delightfully manicured mob's polite giggles and stiletto-heeled admiration are aimed at JJ and he is clearly enjoying the attention. It's impossible not to when the delirium is so respectfully restrained.

The band walk through the crowd like a hot knife butter through butter and climb into a couple of waiting cabs.

'They don't think of us as idols,' says Jean as we head to the hotel. 'They're really into what the band says. They understand.'

To back up his statement, he shows me some letters written in over-formal, shaky English. They'd been thrust into his hand at various points of his journey across Japan by girls anxious to identify with his admiration of the writer Yukio Mishima and maybe talk about the reasons why he committed suicide, seppuku. Not exactly love letters in the sand.

When we arrive at the hotel, they're waiting...

Osaka is around two hundred miles from Tokyo. Its modernity is kinda curvaceous and sparkly and clean. So clean. It's home to the second concert of the Stranglers' Japanese tour.

The opening night was in Fukuoka where the band went down so well, they were banned from ever playing there again. They were blamed for the unacceptable violent reaction of the fans, who had broken through the barriers in their eagerness to get upfront and personal with their idols.

And again tonight, the barriers at Mainchi Hall don't prevent the fans tumbling down to the front in desperation to celebrate being in the presence of sour-faced Jet, doe-eyed Dave, lecherous Hugh and jumping Jacques flash.

After years of heavy-metal conditioning in the shape of clapped-out, podgy, monolithic dross bands from far beyond the seas, it's not surprising they find the Stranglers fascinating. They're even starting to spit!

What other race of people would go berserk for an hour, kick stewards in the bollocks, mob the band and then politely bow to each other afterwards as they file out of the hall?

I expected order. I expected rules. I expected the Stranglers to be regarded as a novelty act whose only redeeming factor was Jean's romantic attachment to their country and his cutie-pie smile. But with a kind of indomitable elegance, the fans gratefully and gracefully accept the moribund flesh the band relish chewing before their very eyes.

They get it.

Back in the Osaka hotel basement bar, Jean intimates that he wants a fight. And he wants a fight with Judas Priest, who'd just played a concert of their own and sit like Madame Tussaud rejects in the corner surrounded by a dozen girls drenched in leopard skin.

Jean writes, 'Judas Priest R Fucking Women.' on the back of a menu and places it on a silver platter held by an unsuspecting waiter who proceeds to deliver the message to the Birmingham metalheads. No takers. Maybe they'd never heard of the Stranglers...

None of the band participate in on-the-road clot antics. They're parsimonious with their off-stage energy. Apart from Jean's occasional muscle flexing (he does tend to tread on your toes every so often, but I put that down to him being French an' all), they're more inclined to exercise the mind rather than the inebriated soul. I guess that's part of their attraction.

The following day we coach it to Kyoto, the ancient capital awash with Buddhist temples all made entirely of wood and without the merest hint of a nail. Despite the overbearing symbolism that pervades the ornamental parks in which these wonderful edifices are set, it's difficult not to snigger at the 'Get your souvenir Buddhas here' signs.

The venue tonight is Kyoto University where there are holes in the ceiling, holes in the walls, holes in the hearts. Even the fucking holes have holes. This black hole of Kyoto is tailor made for the band. No police are allowed on the campus. No chairs are allowed in the main hall. No holds barred.

But without the barriers, the red jacketed stewards and the cops, the element of anarchy is dispelled. Unfortunately, it becomes just another gig – unusual in Japan, maybe, but I've seen more exciting nights at the Palladium with Demis Roussos.

'No, I don't mind Jean getting all the attention at the moment. After all, he makes a prettier cover than me.'

Hugh, wearing the tongue-in-cheek sincere look he cultivates so well, pours another beer in his hotel room at the Nagoya Miyako Grand the day after the Roussos gig. Initially, he was the Strangler who grabbed the attention but in recent months he's taken a back seat.

'Last year I got pissed off with being pushed into situations. We've had a very depressing time on the business side, but things are looking up. I haven't got time for the pain.'

There's a knock on the door and the tour manager wanders in with a leather-jacketed girl. 'You said you wanted to talk to some fans,' he says to me. 'Here's one.' Hugh leaves.

Ayako is twenty-three, works for a bank and lives in the dormitory her company provides for its employees. She has a record player in her room, a boyfriend in LA and a thing about Jean. Or she did have.

'He was my favourite. I liked his playing, I liked his philosophy. I think he is very strong and very manly. More manly than Japanese men. But I was disappointed when a friend told me he had gone to bed with a Japanese girl while he was here. I was surprised. I didn't think he would be just another rock star.'

She leaves. Hugh returns and I tell him about the conversation.

'She's just like anybody else,' he says 'She can't cope with reality. She hasn't sussed out yet that there are no more heroes. You'd have thought the Zen way would have taught them to think otherwise.'

Before going to the soundcheck, I corner Jean and tell him what Ayako had said.

'Oh, really man? That's so frustrating. What her friend told her just isn't true. Pure gossip. No, I don't think we behave like other rock bands. No. Shit, man, that's a drag. I didn't expect to hear something like that. Ever.'

As he slips into his Doc Martens, I mention what Hugh had said.

'I always felt Hugh had a lot more going for him than me,' says Jean. 'He's got a regular place to live. He can concentrate on higher things. I've never had security, just the Stranglers.'

Nagoya lies sixty-seven miles outside Kyoto and is the fourth most populous city in the country. It's a little like Osaka but feels quainter, if, indeed anything Japanese can be regarded as quaint.

The show at the Nagoyashi Kokaido is a triumph. The stewards, up until now fairly tame by Japanese standards, start coming on strong about midway through the set. So strong in fact, that the band stop playing and point an accusing finger at one particularly venomous steward who is subsequently hounded out of the hall in a blaze of vitriol.

Backstage I meet up with Marl Takahashi, a bespectacled twenty-year-old, and the president of the Japanese Stranglers' Information Service. She, too, has been travelling with the band for the duration of the tour.

'At the moment there are seventy members,' she says, 'but I expect that to really increase after all this. The average age is 18 but we have a few 32-year-olds. We also have a fanzine.

'For me the Stranglers are so different from other bands. They have opinions and they point out all the wrong things in England. Other bands just sing and wear pretty clothes and I'm tired of all that.

'I realise the band look so wild, but after meeting them I know they are gentle. But all the girls that come to the hotel don't understand them. They just want to go to bed with them. I don't. I just want to be their friend. If I went to bed with Jean, I wouldn't be his friend anymore.'

And you thought the Stranglers were a boys' band.

'It's amazing,' says the normally diffident Jet Black the following day, on the bullet train to Tokyo. 'The girls are everywhere. We get off the train and they're there. We go to the hotel and they're there. We wake up in the morning and' (they're there?) 'they're sleeping outside the door in the corridor.

'Sure, that happens in England – but there it's not girls, it's the fucking police!'

I know what he means, not the police, the girls. I feel like an 18th century European sailor in the South Seas greeted by a bevy of lei-bearing beauties with Bali Hai's to die for.

Despite the obvious temptations, I never fool around home or away. I sussed out a while back that sex without love was intensely unsatisfactory and not worth the hassle. Hey, but if you're a rock star it's part of the nine to five.

I've been going out with Dina pretty solidly for nearly two and a half years. I love her madly, but I know she's unsure about me, about the kind of job I do, about the way I live my life.

She could hardly be described as a rock chick. She hates receptions, doesn't matter how glitzy, she doesn't care much for most of the music, and she definitely never bothers with people she hates. It's part of the attraction.

Dina is the most important thing in my life: why fuck it up?

So, what am I doing walking down this endless corridor to my room at the Nagoya Miyako Grand holding the hand of a girl called Haroko with oriental sex on my mind?

The foyer had been full of girls when I returned to the hotel with some of the band and their entourage after touring the city's hot spots straight after the gig. Many of the fans are staying at the hotel after booking double rooms months in advance and sneaking in some of their friends without the management's knowledge to keep costs down.

We went to the bar where the girls giggled at tables in corners. At around 3am we decided to call it a night and strolled to the elevator followed by a bunch of around eight girls, and we all squeezed in together.

I'd been drinking solidly since 6pm and I was pissed. Really pissed. And that's why, as the elevator stopped at my floor, I shouted, for a laugh and for the first time in my life, 'Right, who's coming back to my room, then?'

'Yes, please.' Softness is a thing called comfort. Her voice sounded miles away. And then, there she was, suddenly, magically, standing next to me in the corridor as the elevator door closed to the sound of applause from the roadies.

'Hi.'

'Hi.'

'What's your name?'

'Haroko.'

She wore shiny red boots with high heels, a shiny red mac over a shiny red mini skirt. Her shiny black Stranglers tee shirt was as shiny as her shiny black lipstick. Her eyes stretched into infinity and beyond, I was pissed. When she smiled my heart skipped a beat, I was pissed. She was gorgeous, I was pissed.

And now here I am, outside my door, fumbling for the key. I may be pissed but I'm as nervous as hell. What if she thinks I'm Jet Black? After all, we are the only two people with beards in this travelling show, maybe in this entire country. Do I play along?

When we get inside, I don't quite know what to do. Does she expect sex or is she just being polite?

Then she starts to cough. Shit, it's a nasty one. And it's persistent. And it's a bit wet. Knowing my luck, the only time this happens to me I get someone with some weird oriental flu for which there's no known cure for westerners. Why isn't she wearing a surgical mask like everyone else?

I convince myself she's okay. The gallon of sake I'd imbibed earlier has distorted my judgement. 'Bad cough,' I say, pointing to my throat, like a fucking jerk.

'Sorry. Very sorry.'

'That's okay.' I tell her I'm feeling tired and indicate by closing my eyes and resting the side of my face on my clasped hands, like a fucking jerk. I point to the bed and start to undress. Like a fucking jerk.

'Would you like to sleep here?' I ask. (altogether) like a fucking jerk.

'Yes, please.' She starts to undress and we both get into bed, my pants still firmly intact. We kiss. She coughs. We kiss again. She coughs again. I feel like Benny Hill.

'Sorry. Very sorry.'

'That's okay.' I tentatively touch one of her breasts and immediately feel a lump. She coughs. No! Japanese flu and fucking cancer! Maybe you get the cancer as a result of contracting the flu. Oh my God! Infectious cancer!!! You've got to be fucking kidding me.

Then she starts to cough again. I convince myself she's at death's door and whatever she's got, I've probably got now. I've just signed my own death warrant, and all I did was kiss a Japanese girl in the dark.

I have to get her out of here.

'Are you staying in the hotel?'

'Yes, with my friends.'

'Look, let me take you back to your room. You'll feel more comfortable.'

'Yes, please.'

We both dress and before we leave the room I give her a signed copy of the band's *X-Cert* live album. She starts to cry. 'Thank you so much. Sorry. Very sorry.' My heart breaks.

Her friends welcome her, and me, with open arms, and Haroko sniffs, and coughs, as she proudly flashes the signed album and they all go, 'Oooh!' None of them has a cough.

I'll never ask anyone back to my room again, and even think twice about asking myself, although I do request a hotel masseuse, on the record company, to come up to my room when we hit Tokyo, and walk all over me, literally, shaking liberal amounts of talcum powder on my body as she dances in the dark.

It's raining in Tokyo.

The city is straight out of *The Shape of Things to Come*. It's more advanced than any other major city on the planet. Wells envisaged the vertical aspects perfectly. He just didn't latch onto the eastern promise of it all. The sight of people walking around the coruscating streets wearing surgical face masks to prevent the spread of infection is bordering on the surreal.

This dripping, mesmerising metropolis is glistening in the glare of a billion neon lights while the Stranglers prepare for the show.

'You two keep playing,' Jean says to Jet and Dave in the dressing room backstage at the Korakuen Hall, like someone planning to break out of Colditz, 'while Hugh and I jump into the audience and start wrenching up the chairs. If that doesn't get them going, nothing fucking will.'

I gulp. I can see where this is going. I'll end up behind bars in a police cell with a samurai, a yakuza and a sumo wrestler all out of their bonces on hot sake and ketamine.

Hugh and Jean do manage to rip up the seats. The result? One of the most exciting Stranglers shows I've seen this side of the Nashville. The opener, '5 Minutes', has never sounded so menacing and sets the tone for the rest of a concert that has more edges than Benson. Their music has the soul of punk but is essentially beatnik blues on sulphate and it has the power to charm the most tempestuous heart.

'5 Minutes' is one of eight songs that make it onto every setlist during the tour. The others are, 'Dead Loss Angeles', 'Burning Up Time', 'Bring On The Nubiles', 'Curfew', 'Threatened', 'Tank' and, of course, 'Down In The Sewer'.

Later in the band's dressing room, I talk to the very glamorous Kato who is keen to ensure I know she's now a groupie. She's bright and sassy and 21 and, with the help of several of her laughing friends, during our conversation I found myself turning Japanese. I come away with a sizeable knowledge of the language. I discovered that oppai means tits, shakuhachi blow-job, senzuri wank, omeko vagina, ochinko penis, and omekoshiyo means fuck. That's all you really need to know to get by in any country.

'Before they came, Japanese girls thought the Stranglers would rape them,' Kato tells me. 'See, English bands often make fun of Japanese girls, but this band seem more friendly than most.

'Also, in general, English men have bigger ochinkos than Japanese men. It frightens the girls, y'know. They had to make a slightly smaller condom especially for the Japanese market.

'There's no doubt we are hampered by our lack of English. Usually the only thing a Japanese girl can say to a guy in a band is, 'Can I come to your room?' That doesn't give you much of a start! And the girls then get very sad because they know the guy will leave shortly.'

I find Haroko sitting outside my hotel-room door when I get back from the gig. She's followed me to Tokyo. I can't believe it. I start to worry that she's some kind of mad stalker. That she'll stab me repeatedly, mercilessly and tomorrow in the Tokyo Daily under the headline Coughing Killer Strikes Again, they'll report that Jet Black was found stabbed to death in his room.

So, I tell Haroko she can keep a-knockin, but she can't come in...

KORAKUEN HALL

17 – 19 FEBRUARY 1979, TOKYO, JAPAN

YUKA TAKAHASHI

I live in Japan. I can't remember exactly when it was but I was watching a music programme on TV alone one day when the Stranglers' release of their second album *No More Heroes* was announced, with 'Something Better Change' and 'Straighten Out' as a single. It was love at first sight, and sound. It all started there. The next day I went to a local record shop and bought the album.

The copy of *No More Heroes* I bought was a Japanese release and its insert had the record company's telephone number for the Stranglers fan club. I just loved the album and wanted to know more about the band, so I phoned up and Mr Katoh, who was the director in charge of the band, answered. When I asked him about the fan club, he said, 'We don't have it at the moment actually... would like to start one?' So I said, '...Yes' without thinking much and started the Stranglers Information Service in Japan (SIS Japan).

It was 1978 when JJ came to Japan for Karate training and I met him for the first time. Then the band came over for their first Japanese tour in February 1979. It was my first opportunity to experience a Stranglers gig, at Korakuen Hall in Tokyo. They played in other cities like Kyoto but I was still at school, so Tokyo was the only location I could go to. It was a memorable one as they played 'Something Better Change' three times as they thought that they were received as an idol band, saying, 'We are not the Bay City Rollers.' They were also the first so-called 'British punk band' to perform in Japan and were very popular by the time they arrived here.

I continued to run SIS Japan with new people for a while and went to the UK to study in 1982 for about two years. I was looking forward to seeing the band at Hammersmith Odeon one night but the gig was cancelled as the audience destroyed the seats the night before!

QUEENS HOTEL

27 FEBRUARY 1979, BRISBANE, AUSTRALIA

KIRSTY

I was on the front row and squashed up against the road case barrier, dodging spit and pogoing punks, when JJ came close to me and proceeded to straddle my head whilst still playing. He wore black leather pants and a white t-shirt, this guy and his huge cock. Hugh was in his long coat dodging spit and full beer cans and Jet was kicking the drum kit apart and finishing after 35 minutes. Luckily, I saw the two other gigs!

APOLLO THEATRE

16 APRIL 1979, MANCHESTER, UK

CHRIS ACHER

By autumn 1978, I was collaborating on a rock music magazine. News arrived that the British-Froggy, JJ, had recorded a solo album during the *Black and White* sessions with Europe and its music as a theme. My curiosity was piqued: I wanted to meet him

Chris Acher joined JJ on the Euroman Cometh tour

and have him explain his views on the matter, being a convinced European myself. I joined him in Manchester and then Brighton, on the *Euroman Cometh* tour. I found out he was less the sexist violent punk he was supposed to be than a shy intelligent, cultured, educated little-froggy having suffered from being ostracised for being French. From our talks grew the idea of a *Strangled* fanzine in French.

ERIC'S

17 APRIL 1979, LIVERPOOL, UK

LEE MURRAY

I was a 16-year-old Liverpool punk in 1979 who had earned the nickname Rat for my love of the Stranglers so was really excited when JJ added Eric's club to his *Euroman Cometh* tour. A bunch of us were hanging around (pun intended) outside a few hours before the gig, watching the roadies load the gear into the club. Sitting there on the road in all its glory was JJ's Triumph Bonneville.

One of my mates, knowing I was an idiot, dared me to sit on it. Well, I didn't need asking twice so duly jumped on... just as JJ walked out! Knowing his fearsome reputation as a martial arts expert, I really thought I was going to have every bone in my body broken, and from the look on the faces of my mates so did they!

But instead, JJ asked if I'd like a ride up and down the street. 'Er, let me think for a bit... Oh, go on then... ha ha!' The looks on my friends' faces changed from 'oh shit' to 'you lucky bastard' in seconds. After a couple of rides past my mates, with me giving them the finger every time, JJ parked the bike up again and then signed his name right down one leg of my jeans in thick marker pen. Unfortunately, my mother threw them away a few weeks later because they 'had holes in the knees'. Yes, Mum, I'm a punk!

Great days.

LOCH LOMOND ROCK FESTIVAL

26 MAY 1979, CAMERON BEAR PARK, ALEXANDRIA, UK

PHIL COXON

I set off for the *Loch Lomond Festival* from Derby on the Friday night, arriving at the venue late the following morning. It was a really good line up including The Dickies, UK Subs and The Skids. Sadly, the weather put a bit of a dampener on the occasion but it was all forgotten once the Stranglers appeared on stage, with Hugh wearing a pair of very baggy trousers. We were treated to a great set of tracks off the first three albums plus three tracks off the album to be released later in the year. It was the UK premiere of those tracks.

VINY PARKINSON

We were four squaddies heading up the M6 from Gloucestershire to Bonnie Scotland in our hired Hillman Avenger on a glorious day. Three of us were very excited as we'd waited two years to fulfil our dream of seeing the Stranglers, having missed out on the Battersea Park gig the previous year because it sold out. The fourth member of our crew didn't like punk, or anything relating to that period of music, but said he fancied the drive. This was Wally Dog.

We expected the festival to attract thousands heading north from England, but there was a football international at Wembley attracting thousands of Scots southwards, and the closer we got to Scotland the more of them we saw on the hard shoulder of the M6 thumbing a lift to London.

We got off the M6 and headed to Dunfermline. We drove through small villages plastered with the Saltire (the flag of St Andrew) and my first thoughts were, 'For God's sake, don't stop or break down.' Wally thought he'd be a clever twat and shout out the window of the car. 'Mate don't, come on,' we all said, but as sure as eggs is eggs, he let out a volley of abuse - and then put his foot down.

Arriving at the festival site, we drove around trying to find anything resembling a pub or chip shop but there was nothing. Some fans had lit fires and were just sat there looking bored. We parked up, pulled our coats over our heads and tried to get some shut eye. Being soldiers we had packed absolutely nothing, thinking, 'It's summer so we should be warm enough in the clothes we stand up in.' How wrong were we? It absolutely chucked it down throughout the night.

Next day it was lovely and sunny, so we shot off to look for food and found breakfast - a burger van parked in a big puddle. We queued up and heard a couple of young English punks get into conversation with the locals, who asked them if they were footy fans. The lads quickly said, 'No, we're into music and don't like football.' I was thinking, 'Correct answer,' and tried not to stare. The locals seemed to be ferreting through the queue to find the English who just might say the wrong thing.

The gates opened and we made our way up to the festival. It didn't take long for the park to start to fill up with the weird and wonderful. A big gang of Glaswegian punks were absolutely plastered; kids aged no more than twelve or 13 with bottles of Scotch slagging off everyone and anyone who looked their way.

When the bands started, it was a bit tame. Some were clearly at the wrong festival. I remember the bald black guy Mr Superbad in wraparound shades introducing the bands and getting some real abuse. He stood well back from the front of the stage, because things were being thrown at him but only lasted about ten minutes before disappearing.

Charlie Harper and his UK Subs did a set and threw coloured vinyl records into the crowd, only for them to come skimming back. Buzzcocks played next and Pete Shelley was really camping it up with the audience. The Skids did a really good set and at one point their lead singer, Richard Jobson, decided to ask if there were any English fans in the audience (over the PA, they'd just given the latest score as Scotland losing 3-0). Some were daft enough to say yes, where he quickly commented, 'There are some guys over here looking for yer!'

We found a stall doing JJ Burnel merchandise for his *Euroman Cometh* album and I bought a sweat shirt with the EU logo. But we never found the Stranglers merch stall, which was strange considering they were headlining.

After the Dickies played a great set, mainly of covers at 100 mph, we told Wally we were heading closer to the front as the Stranglers were due on. Like an old uncle, he said, 'I'll hang about here, so we don't get split up.'

We saw the Stranglers being ushered onto the stage from the side. 'This is it lads, this is what we've been waiting for the last two years.' The audience was packed at the front so we stayed back a bit in order to be able to see (I'm only a little lad). They broke into a song we didn't know (it was 'Genetix') and played it as an instrumental because Dave's keyboard was playing up and he normally would sing it. They carried on without him and played 'Dead Loss Angeles' and 'The Raven' from the forthcoming album of the same name, which I knew nowt about. After that it was all the classics. The cherry on the cake was 'Down in the Sewer', a monster of a track with the lads prowling round the stage looking all menacing and sounding immense. JJ decided to climb off the stage and 'did the rat' in front of the crowd. What an absolute geezer! Like all great gigs, it flew by. We found Wally, who was still waiting in the place he said he would be, bless him. We were still beaming and asked him what he thought of it. He said it sounded 'ok, but no more than that...'. Miserable get!

It was dark and there'd been a fireworks display, so after the day's events we trooped off to the old Hillman for another comfy night, me with my leather jacket over my head. As I was walking through the throng, I kicked something so picked it up. I waited until we got out of the site to have a good look at what it was and it was one of those hippy shoulder bags. I looked inside and I'd struck gold - a blanket!

WEMBLEY STADIUM

18 AUGUST 1979, LONDON, UK

ANDY MILLER

The Stranglers have been my band since 1977, when I saw them perform 'Go Buddy Go' on *Top of the Pops*. The first album I ever bought was *No More Heroes* and three days later *Rattus Norvegicus*. I first saw them on the supporting bill for The Who, where they premiered several tracks from the forthcoming album, *The Raven*.

I've seen them countless times in every incarnation of the band. I have several favourite gigs but the Hammersmith Palais gig on the *La Folie* tour in 1981 is up there as I was right at the front for the first time and in front of JJ Burnel in his red braces.

Another one that sticks in the mind is the Windsor Old Trout gig in 1991, which was Paul Roberts' first UK gig with the band, and more recently the Sub89 gig in Reading in 2014, an intimate venue at the height of summer where for the only time I can ever recall there was a vote off as to whether 'Golden Brown' or 'La Folie' should be played next and 'La Folie' won. The gig at Brighton Dome in February 2022 was very special too, with Toby Hounsham on keyboards after the sad passing of the legend that was Dave Greenfield.

I have met all the members of the various line ups, except Toby, and always found them all to be top people who have time for people like me and numerous other people in black. They're all very different personalities but each has been integral to the band I love. The Stranglers have been the soundtrack to my life for 45 years and long may that continue.

DAVID JOHNSON

Excitement spread amongst fans that the Stranglers had been announced as special guests to The Who at Wembley Stadium. The hallowed ground. AC/DC were on the bill as well. 'Yeah, we can blow them off stage.' It would be great seeing them there.

The t-shirts and jackets gradually filtered into the crowd as time came for the Stranglers to perform, slowly spreading amongst the fans at the front of the stage. 'This is gonna be good - three albums of classics.' ''You Won't Get Fooled Again'? My arse!' But the band took the huge risk of deciding to play most of the as-yet-unreased Raven. It was a brave move but in the end, it was a bit deflating. They were great songs but we didn't know them yet. We wanted the Wembley crowds shaken up with classic after classic.

I remember a member of the band's entourage moving across the rafters up in the roof. He was throwing down pin badges, white ones with, 'Who Are The Stranglers' and black ones saying, 'Who Are Themeninblack'. People scrabbled to grab one of each. They are now very collectable as a pair.

MARTIN KING

My mate wanted to see The Who at Wembley Stadium and persuaded me, a young 15-year-old who had been into the Stranglers for two years, to go along when they were added to a line up also featuring Nils Lofgren and AC/DC with Bon Scott. The cost was £8. Those were the days! I enjoyed the gig but as they played a lot of *The Raven*, which was yet to be released, I knew few songs in the set. I was blown away by both Hugh and JJ playing bass on 'Dead Loss Angeles' with no lead or rhythm guitar. I've never heard any band do that, before or since. Hugh made me laugh when the first thing he said to the crowd was, 'Any Brighton fans here today? Well, you just lost 4-0.' Very Hugh. I managed to get a 'Who are the Stranglers' badge thrown from the gantry down onto fans which was a nice memento. That gig cemented them being my band. They have always been there, the gigs and new albums helping me when I was going through a divorce.

Martin King got a badge thrown from the stage at Wembley – photo Martin King

THE STRANGLERS & FRIENDS VS THE MEDIA PADDINGTON RECREATION GROUND

16 SEPTEMBER 1979, LONDON, UK

PAUL JENNER

This was a cricket match promoting *The Raven* and to raise money for Capital Radio's charity *Help a London Child*, organised by publicist Alan Edwards. I saw the advert in *Sounds* and Tubed across to Maida Vale. The event was sandwiched between me seeing the Stranglers for the first time at The Rainbow on *The Raven* tour and seeing Buddy Holly's Crickets (with Paul Macca no less) at the Hammersmith Odeon - fate!

There was lots of buzz at the Padding Rec ground for the event, with the Stranglers team - in black kit - batting first. The team included Hugh, Jet, JJ, Philthy Animal Taylor and Fast Eddie (from

Paul Jenner witnessed the infamous Stranglers vs Media cricket match

Motörhead - Lemmy was on chemical duty only), Eddy and Rudolph Grant, John Watts (Fischer-Z), Rat Scabies and Captain Sensible (The Damned), Rudi Thompson (X-Ray Spex), Henry Priestman and Martin Dempsey (The Yachts), and David Cunningham (Flying Lizards). Kate Bush was rumoured to be there but - nope – 'twas Flying Lizards singer, Deborah Evans. Jet opened as first man pairing with a 'large Finchley Boy', followed by Hugh who had a spirited innings with the Captain; both cricket fans, the partnership scored the most runs for the home side.

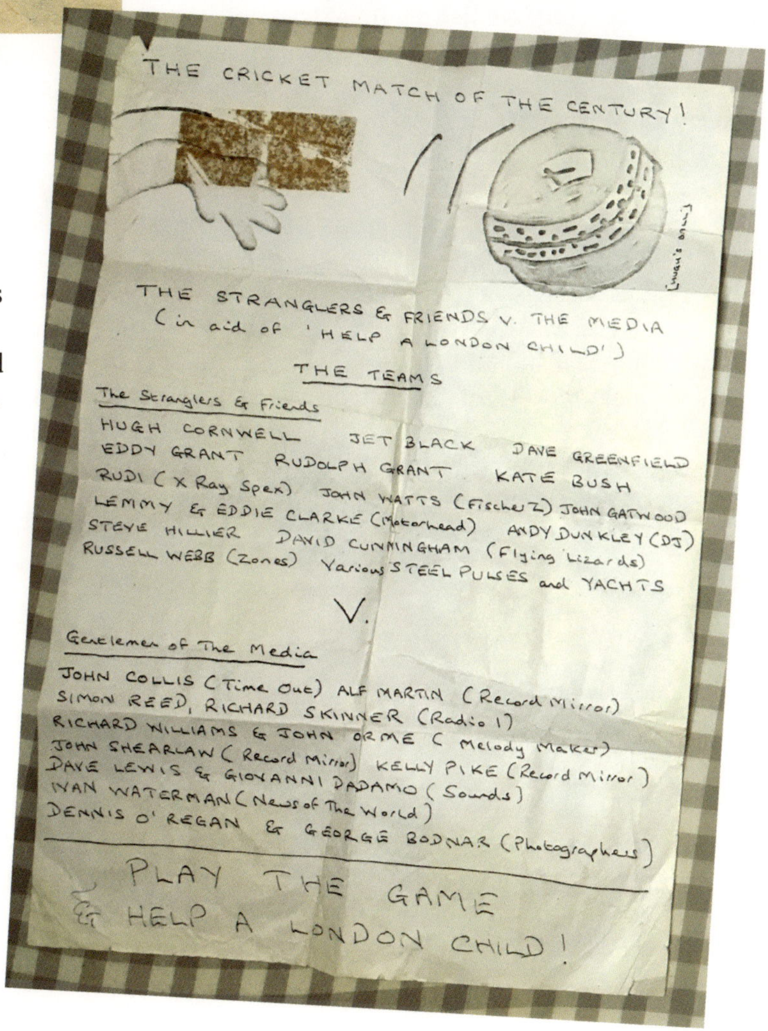
THE CRICKET MATCH OF THE CENTURY!

(Hugh's drawing)

THE STRANGLERS & FRIENDS V. THE MEDIA
(in aid of 'HELP A LONDON CHILD')

THE TEAMS

The Stranglers & Friends

HUGH CORNWELL JET BLACK DAVE GREENFIELD
EDDY GRANT RUDOLPH GRANT KATE BUSH
RUDI (X Ray Spex) JOHN WATTS (Fischer Z) JOHN GATWOOD
LEMMY & EDDIE CLARKE (Motorhead) ANDY DUNKLEY (DJ)
STEVE HILLIER DAVID CUNNINGHAM (Flying Lizards)
RUSSELL WEBB (Zones) Various STEEL PULSES and YACHTS

V.

Gentlemen of The Media

JOHN COLLIS (Time Out) ALF MARTIN (Record Mirror)
SIMON REED, RICHARD SKINNER (Radio 1)
RICHARD WILLIAMS & JOHN ORME (Melody Maker)
JOHN SHEARLAW (Record Mirror) KELLY PIKE (Record Mirror)
DAVE LEWIS & GIOVANNI DADAMO (Sounds)
IVAN WATERMAN (News of The World)
DENNIS O' REGAN & GEORGE BODNAR (Photographers)

PLAY THE GAME
& HELP A LONDON CHILD!

JJ smashed up his stumps and was chased around the ground by fans. The Stranglers chalked up 133 all out, apparently despite the poor efforts of Radio 1's Richard Skinner as scorer.

At the break we all rushed around getting autographs. I made the fatal mistake of getting Hugh and Jet's on the shrinkwrap photo accompanying 'Duchess' in *Smash Hits* (they were illegible) and, when asking the Captain, he saw I had a Stranglers badge on so scrawled his moniker on it. We also watched Philthy and Rat attempting an ill-advised three-legged innings which got as far as the boundary!

The media went into bat with Richard

Williams (*Melody Maker* editor), Giovanni Dadomo (*Sounds* editor), Kirsty MacColl and *Record Mirror*'s Alf Martin scoring something like 25 off the last over. Hugh bowled quite a bit but the home side lost by three wickets, although Hugh reckoned it was a tie 'because when the other team batted, we kept sneaking on extra fielders to stop 'the run flow'.

A great laugh and my first introduction to the Stranglers 'live'!

ODEON THEATRE

21 SEPTEMBER 1979, TAUNTON, UK

JEREMY DARE

My first gig was also my first Stranglers gig. It was three days before my 17th birthday and the first date of *The Raven* tour. None of my mates wanted to go but that wasn't going to stop me. I rode the 12 freezing miles to Taunton on my old Suzuki AP 50 moped. I remember parking up and seeing all the punks queuing up outside.

Deciding I didn't want to be gobbed on by all the punks down the front, I bought an upstairs ticket. It was a good view. *The Raven* had only just been released and I didn't have it, so I didn't know any of the new songs. I remember the big *Raven* backdrop with the eye lit up and the amazing lights shining out over the crowd from under Jet's drum riser. There were also lights surrounding Dave's keyboards which pointed upwards, so when they were turned on it looked like Dave was behind bars. Another thing that sticks in my mind is Hugh's massive baggy trousers! Oh, and the uncut strings on his guitar, which he was famous for. I bought a t-shirt after the gig. It was black with *The Raven* head in an orange velvet kind of material on the front. It looked great but after a few washes the orange came off, leaving *The Raven* head grey. I've still got it somewhere. Ahh... the memories.

'NUCLEAR DEVICE (THE WIZARD OF AUS)'

RELEASED 3 OCTOBER 1979

RUI DINIS

I've never seen the Stranglers live, but I remember seeing them on the telly with the video for 'Nuclear Device' when I was nine years old. They really amazed me with the extremely funny song and their performance. I loved the hats with corks, the outfits - and all the attitude. And then the moderator said the clip had been filmed in Costa da Caparica, here in Portugal, which I found very interesting. I've always found it strange that the Stranglers were considered a punk band... the melodies are far more complex.

ULSTER HALL

4 OCTOBER 1979, BELFAST, UK

MICHAEL MCCLUGHIN

This remains the only Stranglers gig I have ever taken a seat at.

It all began for me, as a young lad growing up in Belfast in the Seventies and Eighties, when I was chosen by St Anne's Cathedral as a 14-year-old to learn to become a choirboy. This chance to 'improve myself' was the only way that my parents would let me into Belfast city centre in 1977 given the unstable situation, so every Saturday morning I was dropped off for practice, which I would then skip in order to go to the nearest HMV to flick through the latest album covers, to see if I had heard of any of this new punk music... I still have my original copies of *Rattus* and *Heroes*. And no, I never did sing in the cathedral as a choirboy.

I can't remember which came first... the music or the album cover for *Rattus*, but I loved both and then came the art of having to play it as loud as I could get away with, especially given some of the language! I had many a battle with my younger sister, who only wanted to listen to ABBA.

After months of behaving and pleading with my poor parents (thank you, John and Eileen), they relented and bought me a ticket for my first ever gig, of any kind, one month short of my 16th birthday but on one condition; I had to actually sit in my seat in the balcony, on the left hand side, in the Ulster Hall... they just didn't trust these punks. The first band whose music I really liked were coming to Belfast, and remember, it's not like today; back then, no one came to Belfast that could be remotely called big or famou'.

When JJB first started with his bass I could feel the music run through the floor and up into the soles of my feet, even on the balcony. Boom! And from the balcony I had a perfect view of the heaving mass of sweaty humanity, from all sections of Northern Ireland's fractured society, pogoing away to their hearts' content to the music, with sectarian bullshit left with the bouncers on the door.

One cocky local thought he would make himself infamous by leaning over the barrier at the front, right in front of JJB, and trying to rip all the leads taped across the front of the stage off that stage. With perfect timing, JJB swung one of those martial kicks of his and landed his boot right on the header's hand, stopping him dead in his evil plan. Swiftly, I thought to myself, 'That is going to hurt', but as it turned out, that was nothing; JJB immediately transferred all of his weight onto that leg, and hand, and swung away with his other leg and I knew that was going to fucking hurt!

I loved the feel of that bass, the band's music and the ballsy attitude (for daring to come to Ulster at all, but then for not taking any shit). And I loved JJB in a 'I want to be him/man crush' sort of way, which I hope he is okay with.

APOLLO THEATRE

7 OCTOBER 1979, GLASGOW, UK

DAVID REID

I was filled with unbearable Beatlemania excitement to see my first ever Stranglers gig, at the Apollo in Glasgow. I went with my two cousins and my brother, who was wearing an identical *Black and White* t-shirt, that we found in a record shop in Sauchiehall Street. It was like stepping into another world. We were little boys in a carnival. Our eyes pinballed back and forward at all the different cool people, the likes of which we never saw on our street or at school but only on the news and in the newspaper. There were people with green hair, Dr Marten's boots, rowdy behaviour, safety pins on lapels, tartan trousers, Mohawks sticking out the crowd, and beautiful girls wearing leather, aggressive makeup and fishnets.

Everyone stood around politely before they appeared on stage, but as the light dimmed, we raced to the front because we had no choice. A wave of people pushed us towards the stage. We all screamed along to the words until hoarse, while confidently punching the air with our fists, while there was scuffling and thrown beer. It was great! I didn't want the gig to finish, and it felt like it was over in a shot.

When we piled out, the October breeze froze my sweaty t-shirt and while walking away from the Apollo we all spoke over each other, expressing how much we loved the gig. We sang as we walked, re-enacting JJ's poses and playing the air keyboard. I felt so high on life, exhausted with temporally hearing loss. I felt I had grown up more from the experience. It was more adult and dangerous and a million miles away from my mum and dad, sitting in the living room watching *Coronation Street* with a cup of tea and a biscuit.

LANCASTER UNIVERSITY

12 OCTOBER 1979, LANCASTER, UK

JONATHAN STUBLEY

My first Stranglers gig was my first 'real' gig by any band. I was 15 and they played at Lancaster University on *The Raven* tour. I loved the new single, 'Duchess', which had been released a few months earlier and so decided to fork out the princely sum of

£3.50 to see this song played live along with a few other Stranglers songs that I knew from the radio and *Top of the Pops*. After standing in the Great Hall for a couple of hours, not really knowing what to expect, the band finally took the stage and blasted out their 1978 hit '5 Minutes' and the place went crazy. I didn't own any Stranglers records at the time, so the rest of the gig is a bit of a blur but finally, towards the end of the set, they played 'Duchess', the song that I had come to hear, and I was absolutely blown away by it.

The gig was filmed by the BBC for their *Tomorrow's World* programme, with the featured item being a firework remote control device. To demonstrate this innovation in firework technology, there were fireworks going off inside the venue with some flying over our heads in the crowd. It was all very exciting but I'm not sure such a demonstration would pass the health and safety requirements of the 21st century! After the gig, there was another huge fireworks display outside the venue. When that had finished, my friend - a worldly-wise 16-year-old veteran of many gigs at Lancaster - assured me that he could get us backstage so we waited for what seemed like an eternity before we were finally - to my amazement - allowed in to the band's dressing room. Having been offered a can of lager by Dave Greenfield himself, I pulled the soggy tour programme from my jacket pocket and had it signed by all four Stranglers. I still have it somewhere in the loft but it has probably disintegrated by now. It was an amazing experience and inspired me to attend dozens of gigs over the next 40 years.

Years later, I found out that a friend had got a job with the BBC and was working on *Tomorrow's World*. I persuaded him to go in to the vaults and see if there was any surviving footage of the 1979 gig. He managed to find a tape containing the whole of the final song, 'Toiler on the Sea', and ran me off a VHS copy. For many years, I believe that this was the only copy in existence outside the BBC and I've sent copies to a few fellow fans. I've still not seen it appear anywhere on *YouTube*.

UNIVERSITY OF LEEDS

13 OCTOBER 1979, LEEDS, UK

JOHN SCRIVEN

They played for 35 minutes and off they went. They were clearly into their 'not liking students' phase.

TOP RANK

14 OCTOBER 1979, BIRMINGHAM, UK

PAUL WESTWOOD

Paul Westwood with JJ

Whenever the topic, 'What was the first record you ever bought?' came up, I was always too embarrassed to tell the truth. I would say I wasn't sure and that it must have been Slade or David Bowie, so this is partly a confession about something that's gnawed away at me for decades. The first record I ever bought was an Osmonds single. I was only ten and the song was 'Crazy Horses'. I guess it was the guitar riff that hooked me but I was most taken by the slide thing they did on the keyboard to create the effect of a manic horse. Even aged ten, I enjoyed things with a different edge. This is most probably why I got into the Stranglers six years later.

I was almost 16 when *Black and White* was released. My mates at school were beginning to get into music that was more alternative than Queen, ABBA and all that shit from *Saturday Night Fever*. We would spend evenings at each other's houses listening to records and drinking crap beer from those seven-pint bumper cans. A mate played *Black and White* one night and I was hooked as soon as the opening of 'Tank' came on. Like an artillery barrage, this track was a violent and visceral volley from all four musicians. No prima donna lead guitarist or egomaniacal vocalist; they were all lead instrument players in their own right making a statement of intent that their every note was an explosion of sound. Dave making his keys swirl into the final crescendo at the end of the track is simply a work of genius.

I went into town the next day and bought the album. I got it home and played it repeatedly for the next 15 hours. The free white vinyl single was a truly magnificent bonus, with a comedy introduction to the band members via 'Tits' and the brilliant version of 'Walk On By'. Mom wasn't impressed. Good. No Parental Advisory stickers back then.

The next Saturday I went back into town and purchased *Rattus Norvegicus* and *No More Heroes*. Being able to play the first three albums concurrently was overwhelmingly good. I fell in love with the band immediately. They were the only ones for me. This trio of albums sit so closely together chronologically and the sheer quality of this early output is one of the reasons why most of us in the familyinblack have stayed loyal to the band.

However, it is the individuality and subtle nuances of sounds in each subsequent track over the next 40 odd years that marks our band out as being uniquely brilliant. Over the years, the Stranglers never have ceased to impress and each new album release date is like waiting for Christmas. Okay, there are one or two tracks I don't like ('Mad Hatter'), but I can still play each of those albums again and hear and appreciate different things almost 45 years on.

JJ's bass sound is raw, powerful and gritty. I guess the 'Force 9 gale of bad breath' line from whatever critic it was emanates from his distinctive sound. But Dave's keyboard was the big point of difference between the Stranglers and other bands. Me and my mate Jones used to refer to the keyboard runs as 'the warbly bits'. We were too working class to have learned about scales and arpeggios. The Stranglers are interesting to us in the Family because they have always been more musically diverse and original. Me and Jones were right, and our other mates, who never quite appreciated them as much as us, were wrong.

The Top Rank gig we attended was my first ever live experience of any band. I remember the smell of weed and sweaty bodies. The heat generated by the energy of pogoing meant that my clothes were soaked within minutes of the opening number. I can't remember the set list but 'Tank' stands out as it was a personal favourite and the use of strobe lighting added an appropriate visual war-like effect.

I remember a fight breaking out and the band stopped playing. Hugh asked if the victim was dead or alive. The crowd shouted back 'dead!' in unison and Hugh asked if we wanted him buried or cremated? The preferred option was emphatically declared as a burning. This gig was an awesome experience for my impressionable young mind. An unconditional adolescent crush soon became a lifelong obsession.

I became so obsessed that I wanted to share the love with others. I managed to work 'Death and Night and Blood (Yukio)' into being played at our school assembly later that year. Being a Goody Two-Shoes girly swot, I was a sixth form prefect and I was asked to do the morning assembly for the junior kids. A big news story at the time was the mass killing in Jonestown, where a cult leader had induced his followers into committing suicide. I read aloud a news article about the carnage and explained what had happened and said that this Stranglers record was like a statement about this tragedy. I put the needle on the record and let go. The opening bars were loud and strident, 'And when I saw that Sparta in his eyes! Young death is good'. The teachers scowling at the side of the hall were not impressed. Eyeballs rolled.

I had to wait for the next album to be released but I was not disappointed by *The Raven*. I was one of the lucky ones who got the limited edition 3D cover. The album had a different feel to the previous three as the band's sound was evolving but this was still unmistakably a Stranglers record. This first-listen experience has been the case for me with all of the other new tracks and albums that have been released over the years. Stranglers definitively, but different. *Dark Matters* is unmistakably a Stranglers record but it is markedly different to what has gone before but it has clearly evolved from *Rattus*. From 'Sometimes' to 'Breathe', there is so much that is musically fascinating.

I have been really lucky to see a load of gigs, mostly in the Birmingham and Wolverhampton area, enduring mosh pits, sweat, cannabis, beer and partial deafness before going home on the late bus in a brand new (dry) tour t-shirt. My wife

Tracy carried at least two of our boys, Tom and Jack, to these gigs in her womb. (Jack is named after JJ.)

The first time I saw the Stranglers at an 'away' venue was at the Albert Hall. It stands out because of the nature and prestige of the place. The other fascinating aspect of this concert was the Electra Strings ensemble that accompanied the band. It made me appreciate the quality of the Stranglers canon, that their songs can be arranged and presented orchestrally. As audiences still listen to Mozart and Beethoven today, will future generations attend Stranglers concerts in the 24th century? Will the London Symphony Orchestra do a rendition of *Rattus*?

GAUMONT THEATRE

18 OCTOBER 1979, SOUTHAMPTON, UK

MARK GRIFFITHS

I was already a big fan when I and three other 14-year-olds went to see them. The management of the Gaumont stupidly left the theatre seats in and so the fans helped to 'remove' them, seat by seat and row by row. It was *The Raven* tour and the back drop graphics were amazing. I became a lifelong fan and have seen the band over 30 times since that first gig.

RAINBOW THEATRE

19 OCTOBER 1979, LONDON, UK

GARETH GORDON-WILKIN

I first heard and got into the Stranglers during the February half-term holiday 1977. I was 15 and not really into music at all. My mate Danny had an older brother called Lucas who was really into the new exciting music craze known as punk rock. He'd go to gigs and record them. He had recorded the Stranglers at the Nashville and Marquee and he played us a tape. The first song I heard was 'London Lady'. I thought, 'Wow, amazing.' Then hearing 'Peasant', 'Sewer', 'Goodbye Toulouse' and others, I just thought, 'This music is fantastic!' and I went and bought their first single, 'Grip', and never looked back. I later heard 'Hanging Around', and to this day I think it's the greatest song ever.

When the Stranglers played *Top of the Pops* singing 'Go Buddy Go', that song, their look and their 'bollocks to you and don't mess with us' attitude just blew my mind. From then on, I decided they were and are the greatest group of all time, both on record and as a live act.

Through them, I've been all over the UK and have many great memories from attending over 350 gigs. I've made some great friends, met several women and gained a hobby that is still strong today. I am astounded, yet delighted, that the Stranglers are still going despite personnel changes and the very sad death of keyboard legend and gentleman Dave Greenfield in 2020.

During the pandemic, many people were off work or working from home. I re-catalogued my Stranglers collection. I found so many badges, patches, gig flyers, set lists, cuttings, photos and stickers and many music papers, fanzines and magazines from all over the world. I counted 5,019 posters, 500 t-shirts (I stopped buying t-shirts in 2010) and videos, DVDs, records and tapes from all over the world.

I have many favourite Stranglers gigs. The Roundhouse in November 1977 is one – it was sold out but I managed to see half the set with mates after giving the bouncers £2 each. And Loch Lomond in 1979, the Rainbow in 1980 (Hugh was in prison and Jet gave a great speech), the Royal Albert Hall in 1997 with the Electra Strings and the 1980 benefit concert for steel workers in Corby.

But the Rainbow gig in October 1979 is a real stand out. I was just 18 and the superb *Raven* album had done very well. I remember rushing back home to change after my day release study at Croydon Technical College and then catching a bus to Brixton and the Tube to Finsbury Park, where I met my eight gigging mates in the Sir George Robey, opposite the Rainbow.

We all came from different parts of London. As we walked in and tickets were sorted, we joined in the mad rush to grab signed album covers that staff had put out on stands. My mate Ben lived just off the Holloway Road and pissed us off because he had purchased circle seats and we all wanted to pogo in the stalls as usual.

The Stranglers came on in complete darkness but you could just see the white safety curtain rise and then the unmistakable intro of '5 Minutes'. The song burst into life and orange and yellow lights lit up the theatre. It was absolutely fucking brilliant. We had a fantastic view and Ben was quickly forgiven for the terrible choice of seats.

Early on in the set, Hugh Cornwell remarked, 'Yeah, it's been two fucking years since we've been allowed to play here,' referring to the ban the band got because he wore a 'Fuck' t-shirt two years previously and the dislike of punk rock shown by the Greater London Council and other local authorities. Not much was played from *Rattus Norvegicus*, but 'Hanging Around' was perfect and during 'Sewer', Burnel was King Rat, walking around the stage and jumping on a balloon someone had thrown next to Hugh. 'The Raven', 'Ice' and 'Baroque Bordello' were by now firm live favourites just like 'Tank', 'No More Heroes' and 'Straighten Out', which were all played.

When the gig finished, we all said our goodbyes. Travelling back to Brixton, everyone was saying just how good the Stranglers were live. We had witnessed a band at their best.

COVENTRY THEATRE

27 OCTOBER 1979, COVENTRY, UK

STEPHEN CARR

I didn't really take much interest in music until starting sixth form in the autumn of 1977, where we had the luxury of our own common room and a record turntable. I ended up listening to a wide range of music, and although it was the punk bands that caught my imagination, it was another year or so before I started buying singles. Buying albums was another matter and this idea didn't start until after I'd spent New Year's Eve 1978 at a next-door neighbour's house with my family. I found myself leafing through her record collection and *Rattus Norvegicus* and *No More Heroes* quickly caught my eye. Having borrowed these for a few days, it wasn't long before I found my way to WHSmith in West Bromwich to buy my own copies, soon followed by *Black and White*.

What initially attracted me to the band was Dave Greenfield's unique keyboard sound, and he remained my hero until his untimely demise. Appreciating the parts played by the other band members came much later

By October 1979, I was a student at the University of Warwick, and very early on I saw my first Stranglers gig, at Coventry Theatre. The 1970s were a violent time, and as a football supporter I was already familiar with the perceived threat of 'aggro' seemingly everywhere I went. Waiting to get into the gig was no different, as this was the age of Doc Martins, spiked hair, safety pins and ripped clothes, and so a lot of very strange-looking people. By coincidence my football team, West Bromwich Albion, had thrashed Coventry City 4-1 earlier that day, and many Coventry fans were around me talking about the game, another reason to keep my head down.

Inside the venue there was heavy security and pockets had to be emptied before you were allowed in. The tension inside was almost unbearable – it hardly seemed feasible that was I actually going to see this great band live, and this wasn't helped by having no idea when the band would appear on stage. This was a feature of all Stranglers gigs for many years. I can't recall the set list after all this time, but 'Nuclear Device' (my favourite song) was definitely played. I can't put my finger on why this is my favourite song; it's just a brilliant piece of music, and unlike anything I've heard before or since.

NEW THEATRE

29 OCTOBER 1979, OXFORD, UK

BILL LEIGH

It was the summer of 1977 when I heard 'Something Better Change' at Butlin's Holiday Camp. It seemed to be played constantly, along with Donna Summer's 'I Feel Love' and 'Ma Baker' by Boney M. Being one month away from being a teen, I was still in disco mode. Disco went straight out of the window the following year when my older brother brought home *Black and White*. I was blown away by Dave's keyboards and JJ's bass. My brother already had *Rattus* and *No More Heroes*, so I gave my neighbours a good ear bashing. I saw the Stranglers on the *Raven* tour and was mesmerised by JJ's karate moves. I couldn't believe I was seeing my new favourite band live. With my brother, I managed to get the band's autographs.

Bill Leigh has a rare Stranglers acetate

I've been lucky enough to meet all the band members over the years but my favourite time was going to Nice with the bathtub race team and meeting up with JJ once we got there. I've been collecting Stranglers memorabilia since I left school in 1982. My favourite item has to be the *Rattus Norvegicus* orange sleeved acetate. I've been told there's only four in existence! I've missed so much out but that would fill up a whole book in itself lol. But what a journey I've had following this band for over 40 years!

God bless the Meninblack.

BRIGHTON CENTRE

30 OCTOBER 1979, BRIGHTON, UK

ANDREW PARKER

My first memory of the Stranglers, aged 13, was hearing 'No More Heroes' on Radio 1. It was the first seven-inch single I purchased with my paper round money and I soon collecting their back catalogue. I saw them on the *Raven* tour. When I turned up

Andrew Parker saw the Meninblack at the Brighton Centre

to work wearing a *Raven* tour t-shirt, my then boss who was a friend of Stranglers management gave me a rare 'Peaches' 'Blackmail' sleeve. I still have it and was pictured with it the 40th anniversary slideshow tour.

In 2022, I reached my half century of seeing the band on their final full tour, seeing them at Guildford, Portsmouth and Brighton. These shows are up there with some of my favourite Stranglers gigs, a list topped by the 2001 Weston-super-Mare convention show. That was an amazing weekend.

The only member I've ever met is Hugh, at a book signing in Exeter. He bought me a drink for my 40th birthday in the hotel we stayed in after he gigged that same evening. I would have liked to have met Dave, as it's because of him that I took up the keyboards. I enjoy playing Stranglers tracks, my favourite being 'Baroque Bordello'.

ERIC THULLIER

I had already been a fan for a year when, in June 1979, I found out they were in Paris to record a new album. After making inquiries, I went to the studio and waited for them to arrive. I was 15 and almost afraid to talk to them. I decided to speak to JJ in

French but with an English accent, so that people from the studio wouldn't take me for a fan. I talked for ten or 15 minutes with JJ and Hugh came over to see what was going on and to say 'hello'. I then asked if it would be possible for me to come and see them during the recording. The next day, I was in the studio with my friend Martin, discovering the birth of *The Raven*. I must have spent almost ten days with them, staying discreetly in a corner of the studio.

I remember asking Dave to show me how he played the 'Sweden' solo. Dave always had a shoulder bag that he never parted with... and Pamela was already at his side.

Jet grumbled sometimes, especially the day he was locked in the room where his battery was. Hugh, JJ and Dave sneaked into the studio section and completely taped off the cabin he was in. They came out turning off the light. Thanks to the microphone remaining open, we had a good laugh listening to him. Before leaving, we were given the gift of a tape with 'Don't Bring Harry' which didn't include a recording of Hugh's solo.

October and November 1979 saw the promotional tour for *The Raven*. I planned to visit the UK with my friends Magalie and Martin and attend the Brighton and London concerts. At the end of the Brighton concert, the sound engineer we had met in Paris directed us to the group backstage. The band invited us to come to Cardiff with them. It was obviously impossible to refuse this offer. Magalie and Martin went to stay with Dave at Jet's house in Bath while I went in the car with Hugh, JJ and Paul, the producer of the tour.

We arrived at Hugh's house and I spent part of the night listening to audio tapes of the group's old recordings. It was a bit surreal to be there, in this little house with Hugh and JJ. I don't know what happened, but when I turned off the light I think I blew the fuses in the house and it was impossible to turn the heating back on... When I woke up it was very cold.

TOP RANK

31 OCTOBER 1979, CARDIFF, UK

ROB PROSSER

I was 17 and it was the first gig I ever went to. The Stranglers were playing the Top Rank while the Boomtown Rats were playing in the venue across the street. The abuse that was hurled between the two sets of fans was quite scary so I was glad to get inside. 'Mothra', from Hugh's solo album *Nosferatu*, was playing just before the band came on. I

Rob Prosser was covered in sweat – and spit – after the Top Rank show

was pumped full of adrenalin and the gig was fantastic. I remember coming out after the gig, covered in sweat, spit and God knows what else into a freezing cold Febuary night. I was well and truly hooked.

STEVE OWENS

My first gig was Cardiff in '79 on the last date of *The Raven* tour. I was 16 and took the train from Tenby with two mates. We hadn't actually planned what we were going to do afterwards, which probably meant a night on the platform at Cardiff Central Station. We arrived at the venue at lunch time. There was no security back in those days and so we were able to wander through the open stage doors and watch the sound check. Joe Seabrook, the Stranglers' security manager, checked us out and told us to sit down and behave.

After the sound check, we found Dave on the Space Invaders machine. He didn't say much apart from asking for a loan of 20p, which I never got back. But I've let it go now. After that, we went down to Spillers Record Shop where the band were doing signings, and then hung around for the gig, which was brilliant. Then we spent a freezing cold night at the train station. I bet Hugh wishes he had hung out around with us instead of getting arrested on his way back to London.

Hugh was returning to London by car with four other people when they were stopped by police and searched for drugs. Hugh was found guilty of possessing cannabis, heroin and cocaine. He received a £300 fine and an eight week custodial sentence which he served at HMP Pentonville in London.

RAINBOW THEATRE

1 NOVEMBER 1979, LONDON, UK

MATTHEW ELVIS BROWN

JJ, Dave, Matthew and his nephew Will - photo Owen Carne

I first became aware of the Stranglers at 12 years old in 1977 and have fond memories of 'Peaches' being a summer hit. I started obsessively buying their singles and *No More*

Heroes was my first album. It filled me with fascination, awe and dread. The purchase of *Rattus* soon followed and I continued to collect everything up until around 1980...

A group of friends would regularly go into London on a Saturday to see what was happening and pick up gear and records. On one such Saturday in September 1978, we diverted to Battersea Park. I was excited to see the *Black and White* hoarding and the tank. We made our way round the side to watch Spizzoil through the chain link fencing, but we had to leave way before the main attraction. I was gutted. Near miss one.

For Christmas 1978, I convinced my parents to get me a bass guitar. The following February (1979) at a Stiff Little Fingers gig at The Lyceum with the gang, we spot Hugh and Joe Strummer and all make a beeline for them. Two Pint Pete and me went straight to Hugh. He was friendly and shared his beer with us. At this time, having already missed the band at Battersea and with no London gigs on the horizon, I was getting anxious about seeing the band and relayed this to Hugh, who did no more than invite me to Loch Lomond and said he'd get me in... I remember getting home from the gig, with Hugh's Heineken can in hand, really very excited and telling my mum why I needed to go to Scotland... Bless her, Mum did no more than get two tickets for the festival and standby flights to Scotland... The Saturday came around and we went down to Gatwick to get our flight, only to find that there was an international football game with Scotland and England and all the flights were fully booked – so no standby (Aarrgh – near miss two).

Fast forward to the autumn of that year and I finally got to see the boys at the Rainbow on *The Raven* tour – it was hugely awesome! And at Christmas 1979, I traded in the short-scale Satellite bass for a Japanese-made Precision copy by Columbus – that was more like it!

CITY HALL, Newcastle-upon-Tyne

Derek Block presents—

The Stranglers

AND GUESTS

Tuesday, 24th November 1981

Evenings 7-30

STALLS

£3.50

R 20

Retain this portion

A. B. Cooper (Printers) Ltd. MANCHESTER

JJ – photo Trevor Aindow

Hugh Cornwell – photo Chris Acher

ASSEMBLY ROOMS, GREAT HALL
MARKET PLACE, DERBY

HARVEY GOLDSMITH/PAUL LOASBY by arrangement with BLACK AND WHITE MANAGEMENT present

THE STRANGLERS

PLUS GUESTS

11 THURSDAY OCTOBER at 7.30 p.m.

UNRESERVED STALLS

Ticket £3

Tickets cannot be exchanged or money refunded

№ 733

Photos Steve Bizley

LE PALACE

13 NOVEMBER 1979, PARIS, FRANCE

MICHEL GARCIN

Michel Garcin has many Stranglers milestones

My milestone events with the Stranglers? Concerts at the Palace in Paris in 1979, in June 2009 at the Le Mans 24 Hour Race and November 2009 at the Rock School Barbey in Bordeaux. I am the architect of that building and had a long discussion with the band and Jean-Jacques in particular about wine and architecture.

I have been to dozens of Stranglers gigs around the world over more than 40 years and had magnificent exchanges with JJ, Baz, Dave, Jet and the Fansinblack. And I'm proud to have seen Jean-Jacques and the Purple Helmets play in May 1988 at La Locomotive in Moulin Rouge, Paris and Le Truck in Lyon in 1989. I am the architect who designed both schemes!

PALAIS D'HIVER

14 NOVEMBER 1979, LYON, FRANCE

HUGO HIGGINS

I had been collecting articles and pictures about punk for about six months before actually hearing my first punk tune in January 1978 at the age of twelve. It was 'Holidays in the Sun' by the Sex Pistols. I remember looking at pictures and reading about that weird-looking band the Stranglers in French music magazines, thinking that their bass player had a great punk look. But those two moustached-bearded old men? Not so much. The fact that their bass player was French made me more curious, since my cheese-eating country didn't have much to offer me, musically speaking.

And that ad from a national French rock mag that read:

« Stranglers, les plus punks des punks, votre mère ne les aimera pas »

which translates as, 'The punkest of the punks, your mother won't like them,' seemed promising, but I had yet to hear what their music sounded like.

In the autumn of 1978, I finally found a copy of *No More Heroes* at the Bruit Bleu record shop in Lyon, France. I'd spend all my Wednesdays and Saturdays there listening to every new record that seemed punk or new wave-related (before that category turned into awful synthesized crap). It was there that I fell in love, not with a beautiful French mademoiselle. (At 13, I was only interested in football and punk rock!) No, within ten seconds I fell in love with 'I Feel Like a Wog', with that huge bass sound and that pissed-off voice, even if the keyboard/organ sounded a bit strange and un-punk. That was probably a teenage reaction to my dad's prog-rock band sound of the time.

I already had a small collection of punk LPs by the Pistols, Damned, Dead Boys, Clash, Devo and Suicide, so adding the *No More Heroes* LP to my collection totally made sense, especially with all the kick-ass songs like 'Nubiles', 'Bitching', 'Dead Ringer' or 'Burning Up Time'. As Lemmy once said, 'You never forget your first love, woman or record.' *No More Heroes* remains my favourite Stranglers LP to this day.

In March 1979, I went to Germany on a three day school trip and was lucky to find a copy of *Black and White* with the extra seven-inch single. It had a traumatic effect on me as I was learning drums. 'Nice 'n' Sleazy' was easy to learn but I also learned 'Peasant in the Big Shitty' pretty quick! That whole record sounded amazing to these young ears, but I also felt like I had missed the whole thing, as both LPs had been released months before I heard the Stranglers for the first time.

But *The Raven* came out and I bought it as soon as it was released in France, making me feel more connected to the band. Needless to say, I was beyond excited to see the Stranglers in Lyon on that grey November day in 1979. The memories are blurry. I was a lonely and cautious 14-year-old kid and I didn't get too close to the action, to avoid bodily damage from furious punks. It was the first of many shows.

A week later, the Stranglers show in Paris was broadcast on French national TV, Live at l'Empire. Those live TV shows were like my Sunday morning church, with performances by Siouxsie and the Banshees, The Ruts, Devo, Ramones and more during 1979.

RAINBOW THEATRE

4 APRIL 1980, LONDON, UK

GRAEME MILNE

At the tender age of 12 in Aberdeen, Scotland, I discovered the Stranglers when my best pal's elder brother brought home a copy of 'Grip'. Their sound was amazing, and by far the best of any of the bands of the era. And they looked frankly terrifying,

Graeme Milne saw the Stranglers and Friends sans Hugh

scowling out from that classic single cover sleeve. Being too young to get into any of the venues they played in was a huge disappointment, but a couple of years later fate lent a hand...

One of my school pals, Richard, had recently moved to London and I was invited down for a few days. On the bus back to his mum's, we were flicking through a discarded paper and noticed an advert for a gig the following evening at the legendary Rainbow. The whole evening was then spent badgering this poor woman, who eventually crumpled and agreed to take us on the proviso that she could attend. Despite our perceived cool being in jeopardy, we agreed.

The next day we arrived to find the area was crawling with punks. We felt uncool and awkward in their presence so didn't linger. On entering we were handed a flyer. It read, 'Rats & Ravens Reject Reactionary Rock Radicals Rally Round' and next to it was a picture of Hugh Cornwell who, unbeknownst to us, had been given a two month sentence for possession. It was a bit of a blow but on closer inspection our eyes widened - the gig was going ahead. Tonight, it was Stranglers and friends, with various punk/new wave luminaries stepping into the breach. Man, what an experience.

Not only did they play the classics but also tracks from the recently-released *Raven*, including 'Sha Sha a Go Go', 'Ice', 'Dead Loss Angeles' and the title track. Sandwiched in between were 'Peaches', 'Toiler', 'Tank' and '5 Minutes'. I recall seeing Toyah Willcox, Nicky Tesco from The Members, Wilko Johnson, Richard Jobson of The Skids, Hazel O' Connor, Ian Dury and Jake Burns from Stiff Little Fingers and others tackling the aforementioned songs. The delivery was different and perhaps not always successful, but the energy, commitment and solidarity were there and to a 14-year-old from the sticks it was incredible to be part of it. I knew I was witnessing something special.

Myself and Richard periodically exchanged glances, nodding approvingly at certain points. His mum remained unconvinced and wore a sickly smile throughout which only added to our sense of rebellion. Part way through, and I think it was 'Nice 'n' Sleazy', a woman in a trench coat sauntered on and began to gyrate enthusiastically. Desperate to see we craned our necks, but the disapproving looks of Richard's mother had us drawing them back in like a tortoise retreating into its shell. Like Queen Victoria, she was not amused and her face wore an expression like curdled milk. We grinned like sharks.

At the end, the guests came on en masse for a rousing version of 'Down in the Sewer' which capped the night off beautifully. What a gig.

At this point, we were literally dragged out and onto the Tube to get home. I never found out what the encore was, if any, and felt annoyed to have missed it but I count myself lucky to been at that historic gig. Richard's mum, we discovered later, wasn't a fan, so I was grateful that she took us.

I still see the band when I can and have done so through various incarnations. They are still my favourites. Long live the Stranglers.

IAN (STUMP) MAGGS

Ian Maggs wrote to Hugh in Pentonville

When I was 15, I went to the first or second gig that the Stranglers ever played at the Marlowe Theatre in Canterbury. I was in about the seventh row back, and when the Stranglers came on, everyone surged back and all the chairs collapsed. My leg was trapped between the seat in front of me and my seat, and everyone was still falling back. I really thought my leg was going to be ripped off or badly broken, but two guys saw what was happening and managed to lift the front seat just enough for me to get my leg out. It was a lucky escape and could have been really bad for me.

Ian Maggs' bike Ratty

I was at the gigs at the Rainbow which featured many different artists taking Hugh's place for different songs when he was in prison on drugs charges. I sent the 'Nice 'n' Sleazy' record cover and two Rainbow concert tickets to Pentonville and asked if he could sign the tickets and, if they were about, the rest of the band to sign their names next to their pictures on the sleeve. Everything came back signed a few weeks later and I was well chuffed. I sold the items a few years later at a record fair and have always regretted it. I tried to track them down over the years but to no avail. I would love to get them back.

PETE NEWBURY

Jet made a marvellously rousing speech to open the concert. He had us all in the palm of his hand. 'We are all individuals, etc...' At one point, JJ dumped the bass guitar and wrestled Hazel O'Connor to the floor (in the nicest possible way). It was a fantastic concert. The support band was The Baldheads.

ANGUS JONES

I saw the Stranglers at the Rainbow when Hugh was absent at Her Majesty's Pleasure. I was 15 at the time and financed the trip by sleeping outside the Coventry Theatre overnight to buy Genesis tickets which I then sold on. The other musicians and bands that supported that night were amazing.

STEPHEN JOYES

I was there! Steel Pulse were amazing. So was Richard Jobson from the Skids. I bought Hazel O'Connor a drink, although I was skint. Afterwards, I went to the stage door only to see Toyah Willcox hanging out of an upstairs window screaming out and telling us all to fuck off and go back to our beds sits. I did as I was told!

MATTHEW ELVIS BROWN

Back at the Rainbow for the Stranglers and Friends while Hugh was down the 'Ville. By this time, I'd gotten enough nerve and familiarity with the bass to have formed a band with some like minds and we started putting our focus there for the next few years. The Stranglers were, and still are, a major part of the soundtrack to my life. JJ inspired me to become a musician.

I kept in touch with the news and releases over the next decade and a half but didn't see the boys again until Mark II played in my hometown at The Grand in Clapham Junction. My then girlfriend, Susana, and I took my dad and his girlfriend and I have lots of fond memories of that gig. From the opening notes of 'Genetix', I left my folks standing at the bar and went and joined the crowd. Susana later moved to Australia and saw the boys in 2020, Dave's last gig.

ROB MURRAY

I first heard the Stranglers back in 1977 on a waltzer ride at a fair on Clapham Common, and they have been the only constant in my life through the years since. I was a fledgling punk rocker, having a dodgy recording of the Pistols' first album, a pair of Dr Marten's and a leather jacket which I soon painted 'The Stranglers' on in white paint, which was the style at the time. I got the paint from an Airfix kit and kept having to repaint as it peeled off all the time.

Hearing that song was a life-changing moment. It was powerful, aggressive and loud and I soon got hold of the single and the albums. *Rattus* really cemented my love for the band. What an album! I still listen to it all the time and 'Down in the Sewer' is my favourite piece of music ever. I can't think of another song where four musicians, including two of the most outstanding players of their generation, complement each other as on that recording.

My first attempt at going to see the Stranglers was meant to be with some schoolmates who were going to see The Who at Wembley Stadium. We were not well off and I didn't have the money for a ticket or the travel, so I broke into a load of telephone pay boxes to get the two and ten pence pieces. I had amassed what seemed like a small fortune - enough for the ticket, travel and a hotdog. But when my mother found out that I had done this, she grounded me for a month and so no gig. Crime don't pay!

I had to wait for the 'Stranglers and Friends' gig at the Rainbow before I could get started. What a mind-blowing experience it was, and despite Hugh not being there. I went home from the gig, cut my headphone wires, plugged them straight into the speaker outputs and played *Live (X Cert)* at full volume until it was light the next morning.

A HIGH SCHOOL

1980, PARIS, FRANCE

ERIC THULLIER

My friends and I created a group which, in a very original way, we called The Meninblack. The day before our first concert, which we were going to do in our high school in Paris, I received a postcard that said, 'Hello Eric, we are in Paris to record a new album, I tried to call you but the number does not seem to be the right one... it would be nice to see you and you can reach me at the number... Hugh S.' I called and suggested that they come to our gig - our first gig! The next evening, we went on stage, starting with '5 Minutes', in front of JJ and Hugh.

NICE UNIVERSITY

20 JUNE 1980, NICE, FRANCE

MARTIN BLENCO

According to press reports, the Stranglers' PA broke down for a third time during their gig in Nice as a result of the university generators not being up to the job. Jet

Black told the audience that the university had refused to agree to the band using a more powerful generator because of the perceived fire risk it might create. Jean-Jacques translated the message into French for the audience and the band left. The audience, their gig left unfinished, rioted. Plate glass windows were smashed and trees within the campus grounds set alight.

COLSTON HALL

11 JULY 1980, BRISTOL, UK

MARTIN WALTERS

Martin Walters hasn't washed his shirt since JJ signed it

I was 15 and it was the first gig I'd ever been to. I went with my mate and his older brother. To say I was blown away is an understatement. We were made to sit in seats but when they came on stage all hell broke loose. Seats were damaged and there was pushing to the front. It was just brilliant for a 15-year-old. Inside the gig, I remember Dave's keyboards playing with my mind, JJ's bass hurting my chest and Hugh scowling at us all night. As well as the band, I really remember the back drop of a giant raven with a light beaming out of his eye.

We went around to the stage doors afterwards to see if we could meet the band. After a minute or two the doorman just disappeared, so what do 15 and 16 year old boys do? We ran inside and legged it around the back. There were no shouts of 'stop' or 'get out', just silence. So we ran around the corridors and up and down stairs and, all of a sudden, there was Jet walking down a corridor. 'Hello lads, what are you up to?' 'Looking for you,' was the genius statement we came up with. 'Wanna meet the rest of the band?' 'Yes please!' we all cried. And off we went, with Jet, back to the dressing room and there they all were. Jet introduced us and we had a great ten minutes in their company. Dave was quiet but nice, Jet just kept the conversation going, Hugh stood in the corner, still scowling, and JJ seemed really happy that we'd sneaked in. He signed my shirt for me.

After we'd said our goodbyes and were shown out, I nearly got arrested for not wearing a shirt whilst walking around Bristol by an over-zealous copper. Well, I didn't want to ruin that signature now, did I? And I still have that shirt all these years later, and it's still never been washed.

GAUMONT THEATRE

14 JULY 1980, IPSWICH, UK

PETE NEWBURY

Pete Newbury was at Ipswich Gaumont

I was hanging around near the back door when some clean-shaven guy with long hair and a haversack came out and walked straight past me. A few seconds later the penny dropped - it was Dave Greenfield, who had recently shaved off the moustache. I tried to catch up with him but to no avail. I remember Hugh's hypnotic guitar on 'Bear Cage' and how he used the volume knob on the Telecaster on the verses of 'Thrown Away'. JJ was wearing white braces, baggy trousers and black slip-ons. After the gig, again at the back door, I helped Hugh get to his getaway car (something sleek and black, with some very interesting female company inside). He said they would stop the car 100 yards up the road to sign autographs. In fact, he didn't stop for anything. I don't blame him.

I remember the *La Folie* tour at UEA in Norwich for one of the very first performances of 'Golden Brown'. It shocked the audience into momentary silence. Then there was huge applause. It was before the album's release date.

In December 2017, I saw them somewhere near Albi in France. I shook hands with JJ from the audience. But I was too drunk to say anything meaningful.

ODEON THEATRE

16 JULY 1980, BIRMINGHAM, UK

CLIVE ADAMS

Clive Adams was at Birmingham Odeon

In February of 1980, I tagged along with my older brother and his mate to the Birmingham Odeon to see the Ramones. Looking like the geeky schoolkid wearing the obligatory Snorkel jacket, I knew nothing about the band I was going to see. This gig changed my life forever and got me into music big time. I loved the uniform look, and the pop songs played at breakneck speed, but what really got me were the fans. I loved the leather jackets, the cool t-shirts, the spiky hair and the punk look.

I thought of the fans as a gang of nonconformists, outsiders and misfits, and I wanted to join. Not long after this, it was down to the Oasis market in Birmingham, where the tribes would assemble on a Saturday afternoon, to buy a leather biker's (Ramones) jacket.

In July, I took the opportunity to go and see the Stranglers with a couple of school friends. Unlike when I saw the Ramones, I knew who the Stranglers were – I'd heard 'Peaches' and 'Hanging Around' and was aware of their status in terms of English punk and new wave bands - but that was the extent of my knowledge. Little did I know at the time that this was to kick start my lifelong love for the Stranglers.

I vividly remember my brother coming home from the daily commute to his city centre office. He had seen some Stranglers fans gathering around the Odeon on Birmingham's New Street. He looked at me, worried. 'I've seen a load of punks in town', he declared, 'are you sure you're going to be ok at this gig tonight?' I could not answer his question truthfully. Although I had adopted a more appropriate look, at just 14 I lacked stature, toughness and confidence.

This was the *Who Wants the World* tour, and the single had been irritating the charts. The Stranglers began their set with 'Sha Sha a Go Go' and 'Ice' from *The Raven*. Then came 'Toiler on the Sea', 'Duchess' and 'Hanging Around'. Their sound was crisp and unique, complex and multi-layered but at the same time it was still accessible. I loved JJ's growling bass and Hugh's choppy guitar. With his dry wit, Hugh was a natural at playing the crowd. Dave Greenfield's keyboards set them apart from all the band's contemporaries and it was clear that these were being used in 1980 to drive the Stranglers into a new, more diverse direction where they would experiment with new recording techniques. Part of their appeal has been that they have never been afraid to experiment and push boundaries with their music.

It was clear that the Stranglers had their own unique fan base and I wanted to be a part of it. The uniform of mainly short hair, black jeans, Doc Marten's or monkey boots, leather jackets and Stranglers t-shirts, picturing the classic rat and raven logo, were the order of the day.

The throng of fans at the front of the stage pogoed at every opportunity and as we were standing in the centre stalls, I wondered what it would be like to be in there with them. There was an air of menace, tension and excitement in the Odeon, but this did not escalate into violence. I don't ever remember feeling afraid; if anything, I was more intrigued by the vibe of 'thinking man's thuggery' I was detecting. Shortly after, I went out and bought the *Raven* album, which to this day is probably my favourite Stranglers album.

I have since notched up over 100 Stranglers gigs, seeing them every time they have played in Birmingham and in venues all over the UK, though I understand my total is a meagre number compared to other die-hard fans. I have met fans at gigs and formed friendships with people that have survived for more than 30 years.

That hot July evening back in 1980 was a huge influence on me. I saw that the Stranglers were never a 'one trick pony'. They were and remain accomplished musicians, performers and songwriters. We have all got older over the years, and things have changed since 1980, but there is a talent, a stubbornness and gang mentality that still exists today.

The Stranglers are criminally underrated and should have achieved greater commercial success. Then again, being part of a band of outsiders who people love to hate has made me appreciate and want to follow the Stranglers even more.

GARETH NOON

The day after my younger brother Dave's 15th birthday, the Stranglers played Birmingham Odeon. I was taking him to the gig as it was the school holidays and I had taken a couple of days off work as my folks said I needed to look after him.

The band had recently been jailed for the fans

Gareth Noon's favourite Stranglers gig was at Birmingham Odeon

riot in Nice. Although the tour was called the *Who Wants the World* tour, I named it the *Jailbreak from Nice* tour. By now they were the band I wanted to see more than anybody else. They were almost becoming an obsession, and I was wearing all black, buying the records and boring my mates and my girlfriends, telling them that these were the best group that walked the earth.

Dave and I duly left Wigan mid-morning. Arriving early afternoon, we didn't have any idea where the Odeon was, but luckily it was more or less right next to New Street station. As we looked through the doors of the theatre, the door was unlocked so we had a look inside. In the background I could hear the band doing the soundcheck so we ventured further inside and into the seats. We managed to get halfway in and sat down as they played 'Toiler on the Sea'.

As they finished the soundcheck the band disappeared into the backstage area. We got up to leave when we heard somebody shout, 'It's not that way,' and we were taken over the stage to be met by Dave Greenfield. It was the first time I'd met the genius, and we chatted for a couple of minutes.

Although a hazy memory the set played consisted of 'Shah Shah A Go Go', 'Ice', 'Toiler', 'Waiting for the Meninblack', 'Baroque Bordello', 'Who Wants the World', 'Nuclear Device', 'Genetix', 'Princess of the Streets', 'Hanging Around' and 'Down in the Sewer'.

My favourite Stranglers gig.

PAUL CAREW

I was aware of the Stranglers and had collected any newspaper/music press clippings I could find. On holiday that summer, I heard a few of their songs on rare playings on the radio and decided I needed to hear more, but didn't have much money as a 12-year-old so waited until Christmas to get the *No More Heroes* album. It got played every day and at one point, when my friend came over one night, we played it at least eight times. I became obsessed but very annoyed at the band playing venues which were not on my doorstep or venues that were 18 plus.

Eventually, they announced a tour for the summer of 1980 but with a holiday abroad coming up, I didn't want to miss them. Dates were not announced immediately so I went around telling anybody who would listen that I would rather miss the holiday than miss the Stranglers. When the dates were finally announced, I breathed a huge sigh but now the thought of missing out if we didn't get tickets immediately crossed my mind. But my friend agreed to go into Birmingham and get them.

We broke up from school on the day of the gig. All my classmates knew how much I was looking forward to it. It was a scorching hot day and my friend and I caught the bus and discussed on the journey which songs we thought they would play. The anticipation was really getting to us and even though we'd been to other gigs, we hadn't seen 'our band' play before.

Paul Carew has collected a few Stranglers badges

After The Tea Set went down fairly well (for a support band), the chants of 'Stranglers, Stranglers...' got louder and louder until they came to a huge cheer and footstomping noise. The exact set is not something I remember but 'Shah Shah a Go Go', 'Ice', 'Toiler on the Sea', 'Duchess', 'Hanging Around', 'Four Horsemen', 'Down in the Sewer' and 'Baroque Bordello' were in the set and I often think it would be nice to hear a bootleg of the gig.

The volume really seemed to drive home the songs and it all seemed to be louder than any of the previous gigs I'd been too. You just lose yourself in the music and I could tell that my friend and I never wanted this experience to end, and the thought of having the next seven weeks off to talk about it was not lost on us either. The usual sarcastic comments from Hugh were always treated as banter and we all just laughed at it all as we were used to not taking it all too seriously, unlike the press.

The set list was varied and took in all the albums and I seem to recall two encores. I always hate that moment when the lights come on and it's a case of, 'You can all go home now as the band are finished and you only have your memories.' It was so unlike now, when you see all sorts of clips on *YouTube* from the if you went to the night before from people using mobile phones, and all very good quality.

Leaving the Odeon that night, we reflected on how much we had enjoyed it all and the thought of perhaps waiting another year to see the Stranglers seemed too far off. We did see them many more times after that, and they were always great with just a hint of menace in the air before they came on stage. I have tried to keep as many bits of memorabilia as I could over the years and have at least 95 per cent of it still, including the postergramme from that first gig. They were my first band and that feeling never leaves you, despite other bands coming along that you love.

My last date was the Stranglers at the O2 Academy in Birmingham in 2022, and looking around at the older faces amongst the crowd, I did wonder just how many had been at that gig in July 1980.

MAYFAIR

17 JULY 1980, SUNDERLAND, UK

PETER SMITH

The Stranglers were persona non grata in Newcastle after a riotous gig at the City Hall in 1977. It was almost three years before they appeared in the North East again, this time at Sunderland Mayfair (aka The Mecca or, previously, the Locarno).

A lot had changed in the intervening years. By 1980 the Stranglers had released four albums, the latest being *The Raven,* and had 10 singles in the UK singles charts.

Disaster also struck for the band in 1980 when Cornwell was arrested and convicted for drug use and sent to prison for three months in Pentonville.

I remember the Sunderland show as a good gig, but also being a little disappointed that many of the early songs had been dropped in favour of more recent tunes. A young Baz Warne was apparently in the audience that night. He would, of course, join the band some 20 years later.

APOLLO THEATRE

18 JULY 1980, GLASGOW, UK

CRAIG WOOD

Craig Wood's Stranglers jigsaw puzzle

I missed the early years of the Stranglers. When *Rattus* was released, I was still in primary school, but as I grew up, I became more interested in music and was led towards the punk bands my schoolmates listened to. I was told the Stranglers were the best, though the Old Stranglers were much better than the New Stranglers, with 'London Lady' being their best song. I did know a few Stranglers songs at this point: 'Peaches', 'No More Heroes', '5 Minutes', 'Go Buddy Go'. I live in Paisley, where we are known as Paisley Buddies, and this nickname has been passed onto the local football team, St Mirren. In 1977 the team were riding high under a young Alex Ferguson and the fans adopted the song as an anthem, singing, 'Go Buddies, go Buddies, go, go, go.' I also liked 'Freddie Laker' off *Euroman Cometh*. A local radio DJ took it up because he reckoned it sounded like farting into a vocoder.

I was 14 when I discovered the Stranglers for real. I borrowed *No More Heroes* from the local library and when I heard the way Dave's piano burst into 'English Towns' from the fading 'Burning Up Time' I was destined for a lifelong obsession. The first single I bought as a proper mature music fan was 'Bear Cage', followed by 'Who Wants the World', which was closely followed by the Nice incident.

I bought a ticket for their appearance at Glasgow Apollo, despite the fact that it was on Glasgow Fair Friday and my not having permission from my mum. I will always remember the way they started with 'Shah Shah a Go Go', in front of the spectacular *Raven* backdrop, and it's a song I now have a special connection with. I have always been disappointed that they have never attempted to reprise it post-Hugh. I think JJ is on record as saying he was embarrassed to think he could sum up the entire Iran situation in a five minute pop song. If this is the case then how does he feel about wearing a bowler hat on *Cheggers Plays Pop*? The song brilliantly portrays the atmosphere of the time, of the hot, dusty environment, the brooding malevolence of the crowd, the chaos on the streets, exactly as Huggin and Muninn would have relayed it to Odin. It's certainly one of the most evocative pieces of music I have ever heard. Burnel, you're a genius!

Throughout the summer and autumn, I acquired all the albums and as winter approached, I became aware that my favourite album was the (apparently maligned) *Raven*, and the title track my favourite song, along with 'Goodbye Toulouse', 'Dagenham Dave', 'Tank', 'Toiler' and 'Threatened'.

The Gospel According to the Meninblack was the first album I bought on release, and although there were solid moments – 'Four Horsemen', 'Hallo to Our Men' and 'Thrown Away' - a lot of it was quite weak. It was great to see the band on *Top of the Pops* doing 'Thrown Away', although I think they got the mix wrong, as every time they played it live the synthesizer sound was much bassier, instead of the beep-beep-beep-beep on the version released. (Not to mention Dave's slipped note.)

ELIZABETH MCCAFFARY-REID

I first heard the Stranglers blaring from my brother's bedrooms in 1977, day in, day out, for hours and hours on end. Previously I had been more of a Donny Osmond and Bay City Rollers fan but the Stranglers were just on another level.

My brothers, nephews, cousins and all their friends are all massive Stranglers fans. I've been to many Glasgow gigs since but my brothers have never missed a Glasgow gig and go to numerous UK gigs every tour.

I remember that first gig; I was only 14 and my brothers left me upstairs in 'The Royal Box' with their pals as they thought I'd be safer... back then, everyone used to pogo and the whole place shook.

I probably look the least likely Stranglers fan ever. I always wear pink and I love anything that glitters and sparkles. I recall being sent back upstairs by my brother, David, before leaving for my first gig and being told to get changed or they weren't taking me... I can't remember what I was wearing originally but I know that I changed into jeans and one of my brothers Stranglers t-shirts.

On the morning of a gig my brother, Brian, always texts me to arrange the time and meeting place for the gig and his texts always ends, 'No pink and I mean no pink!' When we have family get togethers, the generation above us - mums, dads and aunties all in their eighties - know the lyrics to every Stranglers song we play. It's crazy but brilliant to hear them all singing along.

Our 80-year-old mum still talks about knitting black jumpers with white sleeves to replicate the one worn by JJ on the *Black and White* album cover. Some of her friends helped out with the knitting as my brothers, cousins and their pals all wanted one and they had to be ready for an upcoming gig. They wore them for years!

Back in the '80s, before we had video recorders or *YouTube*, we would sit watching *Top of the Pops*, praying that they would be on and when they were, we didn't blink or even breath as we couldn't rewind and watch it again. We just had to capture every precious moment.

Seven years ago, I wrote to the Stranglers' manager, Sil Wilcox, and enclosed a card asking if it could be signed by the band for my brother's 50th birthday. He got it signed by The Wurzels by mistake (he manages both) so I phoned Sil and when he eventually stopped laughing, he promised to get it sorted for me, which he kindly did. My brother was delighted to receive the card but he also loved his Wurzels card and the story behind it!

I can't put into words what the Stranglers have meant to me and my family over the years. But as siblings, cousins and friends we are all very close, and that is because of our mutual love of the band. And for that, from The Lady in Pink to the Meninblack, from bottom of my heart, thank you.

Dave Greenfield's passing was like a death in our family. Before the 2022 Glasgow gig, I said to my brother and cousin, 'I wonder what it will be like when they come out on stage and 'Waltz in Black' starts? That song and the band's entrance always make the hairs on the back of my neck stand on end. The music started and Dave wasn't there and I turned to look at them and all three of us had tears in our eyes. My cousin managed to croak, 'Very emotional.' Only a true Stranglers fan would understand that.

DAVID REID

While eating at the dinner table, my brother and I said we liked JJ's black shirt that had one white sleeve, as on the *Black and White* album cover, and that it was a pity we couldn't buy it. My mum said, 'I can do that if you like, all you need is black wool and a wee bit of white for the arm.' She set off taking measurements and then got knitting. My cousin caught wind of the jumpers and asked for one too. Through gritted teeth, Mum said yes, and with the help of her friend Jenny she got them finished. She probably wished she had never opened her mouth. We all got the jumpers and showered our mum with love, and were instructed to all separately phone Jenny to say thank you. We thought they were so cool, and we took off to strutting around outside with them. Many people thought they were clever by saying, 'Did you run out of black wool?'

JAMES BECK

I met JJ Burnel in the foyer. I didn't have a ticket and asked him if he could put me on the guest list. He was very down to earth and said yes. We had a talk about some guys that were standing watching the sound check and he referred to them as a bunch of Durannies (Duran Duran were doing the rounds). It was a four thousand capacity hall and packed. I went up to the first balcony. The stage rapidly got engulfed by guys swinging from the balcony curtain onto the stage in a Tarzan fashion and I had to join in. There were 20 to 30 people on stage and after it was cleared we did the same again. But it was good humoured and only the Apollo bouncers took umbrage.

I had many conversations with JJ in the coming years and always found him to be interested in all kinds of subjects, from Japanese tuna fishermen to French World Cup footballers. We never spoke about music.

Back then, I was interested in a project called the Barlinnie Prison Special Unit. A guy I knew had invited me to visit it. It was a new concept, Scotland's ten most dangerous prisoners held in one mini jail in Glasgow. During my visit, I spoke to a guy who said he was a huge Stranglers fan and, knowing they were due in Scotland, I said I'd ask JJ if it was possible to carry out an impromptu visit to the unit.

It was a Saturday night show in Glasgow. I met up with the band in the old Kelvingrove Lorne Hotel in Glasgow's West End. I said, 'JJ, would you fancy visiting ten of Scotland's most dangerous prisoners in the special unit?' He said, 'Can you get me in and, moreover, can you get me out?' We met up on the Sunday morning and piled into a car that took us two stops along the M8 motorway.

On arrival, we signed in and a prisoner officer told JJ he was a huge fan. JJ said, 'Aw, that's a shame, can't you get a decent job?' but it was tongue-in-cheek. We were taken over to the small ten cell unit, with a hallway and huge gym and kitchens. As we went into the kitchens, a guy called Gary who was a huge bodybuilder and a life serving prisoner, was stirring a pot of chilli. JJ went up and said, 'How are you?' Gary said, 'I am well mate, I'm Gary.' I said, 'JJ's one of the Stranglers, Gary,' and they shook hands. JJ said, 'Yes, I'm a Strangler, as James pointed out,' and Gary said, 'Yeah, I've did a bit of strangling myself.' JJ laughed and said, 'Yes, but I do it with a smile on my face,' and Gary, our lifer, said, 'Yes, JJ, so did I.' It turned out this guy had strangled three people.

KING GEORGE'S HALL

22 JULY 1980, BLACKBURN, UK

RUSS LAMBERT

My first gig. I'm 14 and the band are due to play Blackburn King George's Hall on 22nd July. My dad has said he will take my two school friends, Ian and Mark, and myself to the concert and drop us off before waiting and picking us up afterwards.

Then, a problem. The band are arrested in Nice for inciting a riot at a local college and thrown in jail. Will the tour go ahead? The Stranglers - no strangers to controversy!

The band are released on bail and the tour will continue. That night sits in the memory now as fresh as the day it happened. The support acts were Headline and The Tea Set. I look around me taking in the atmosphere and the people. During the set for The Tea Set, an over enthusiastic band member knocks his mic stand off stage, hitting a member of the crowd. Slightly concussed, he manages to see the rest of the night out.

Russ Lambert's dad thought the Stranglers were 'bloody rubbish'

Around 9pm, the lights dim, 'Waltzinblack' plays over the PA and the band take to the stage. This is it. Three years of listening to their music and collecting the records, media cuttings and posters and now my heroes are on stage in front of me. They played 'Shah Shah a Go Go', 'Ice', 'Toiler on the Sea' and 'Four Horsemen'. And so it goes on, just over an hour of pure pleasure with Hugh and JJ prowling the stage, Dave playing rhythmic heaven on the keyboards and all kept in time by the wonderful Jet Black. Then it's all over, the lights come up and as we make our way out, there's my dad stood at the back. 'How long have you been there?' I ask him. 'I saw most of the act doorman let me in after I told him I was waiting for you three. Bloody rubbish, load of noise.'

42 years later, I still get the same buzz when the lights dim and that familiar rift fills the room.

CIVIC CENTRE

23 JULY 1980, CORBY, UK

TIM CORY

The first time that I saw the Stranglers was with my two brothers in our hometown of Corby. The steelworks were being closed down, it was a time of national industrial strife and the Meninblack came to play what was essentially one of their first charity gigs. As it was exclusively for us hard-done-to residents, tickets were only available from the Civic Centre on a Saturday morning and were strictly limited to two per person. The queue snaked for a mile.

At this time, our heroes were notorious tabloid fodder following Hugh's incarceration and the Nice affair. The gig itself was life-changing, as all of our first experiences of the boys were. For our 35 pence, we were all given the latest copy of *Strangled* mag, a classic green rat badge - and the Meninblack.

The Stranglers were at their ominous and threatening best to begin with. But the overexcited locals began throwing copies of *Strangled* at Hugh, and spitting at him too ('just like punks are supposed to be'). He was visibly upset by this and, as we were up at the front, my brothers Nick and Jon and my mate Andy were equally unenamoured of the flob! Hugh bitched back at the audience with typical elan. 'Haven't you learned to read?' and, 'I'm looking at my watch and it's 1980, why are you still spitting?' The gig was sadly curtailed after about an hour with no encore. In the car on the way home, Nick raged that JJ had only sung one song – 'Ice'.

● The Stranglers in action: The decibel level proved too much for some who left ashen faced — others showed their appreciation by jumping up and down.

Plenty of spit, not much polish

CORBY had its first taste of what a major punk rock concert is like last night.

The event passed off without any serious trouble — much to the relief of council officials and police.

An audience of 1,300 young people packed the Festival Hall to watch the controversial group The Stranglers.

And it was the group itself which had reason to feel annoyed with the behaviour of the audience.

The Stranglers returned earlier this month from a French tour in which they gained notoriety when a concert at Nice University ended in a riot with £10,000 of damage. They then generously fitted Corby into their British tour.

It was a special low price ticket concert — 35p instead of the normal £3 — and it was the band's gesture to cheer up youngsters in the unemployment hit town.

But despite this gesture some of the young audience crowded

● The police took the precaution of asking some of the boys to hand over the laces from their boots.

At one stage a microphone stand was pulled down and some of the stewards hired for the evening said they had to move in to separate and eject a few excited fans who were trading punches.

And if it was acceptable punk behaviour as far as the culprits were concerned, it certainly did not meet with the

he informed those spitting at him that it was affecting his guitar playing and if it didn't stop the group would cease playing.

Cornwell told the audience that the group were playing in Corby for nothing. In between songs he bemoaned the standards of education in the town and described the behaviour of some

first time in their current British tour didn't return for an encore.

Many of the concert goers wore the conventional punk outfit of black leather jacket and trousers, covered in various parts by chains, zips and pins.

Some wore leopard skin-style trousers, one boy sported a dog collar — the sort dogs, not vicars wear —

Tim Cory was at the gig the Stranglers played for steelworkers in Corby

Highlights? Spittle hanging from Hugh's Fender and the, 'This is the Lord's Prayer' intro for new song 'Hallow' - an epiphany for all that were there for Corby's first gig.

My brothers and I went to a gig together again in 2022 at the De Montfort Hall in Leicester – a sensational show. Thanks forever, boys. Long live the Stranglers.

LYCEUM THEATRE

27 JULY 1980, LONDON, UK

MARK LUFF

I wasn't a particular music fan until 1977 when at school one day, Gary Taylor, who was a friend of a friend, told me to listen to the radio that evening as the Stranglers were on. The first song I heard was 'Straighten Out' and the rest is history... My first gig had to wait for another three years when they played the Lyceum, supported by Hazel O'Connor, and my memory of that gig is not great as it's over 40 years ago. My gig total is around 85 to 90, which may sound a lot, but there are fans and friends I know who have seen the band hundreds of times. Getting married, the birth of my children and a few other family-related occasions are obviously the most important happenings in my life, but I still get 'that feeling' about a minute and a half before the band come on stage, when 'Waltzinblack' is played. You then know that it's nearly time and even though I have heard it so many times before, it still makes the hairs stand up on the back of my neck. I love that couple of minutes... people sing, hum, sway in anticipation and the excitement is palpable. And then the cheering when they walk on stage... just brilliant!

Mark Luff's singles collection

PAVILION

18 AUGUST 1980, BATH, UK

ALI BANKS

Ali Banks and photos she took of JJ

My then boyfriend and I had travelled from Newcastle with a tent to follow the Stranglers on the last couple of dates of a small summer tour called *Who Wants the World*. He'd already seen the band and met them once. It was my first Stranglers gig. This morning, we congregated outside Bath Pavilion from very early in the morning with other fans. It was a beautiful day and everyone was sat on the grass catching the sun. Suddenly, Hugh and this beautiful redhead came out and said they needed two people to help with the catering. My heart stopped as they pointed at me and this other girl.

I was only 15 and my life changed that day. I knew I'd need to work hard and this was a rare opportunity. (The other girl I remember doing very little.) I met the band and ended up sitting on Hugh's knee at dinner. I ended up firm friends through life with Simmy and Belinda, whose catering firm were called Out to Lunch and who were doing the last couple of dates of that tour.

The next date was Nottingham's Theatre Royal and we got in as guests and were guested and allowed in for the full televised show that was later broadcast on the TV programme, *Rockstage*. We met Hazel O'Connor, who has remained a lifelong friend.

During the gig, a bunch of skins were shouting and Sieg Heiling. One got up on stage and JJ barely flickered as he belted him, sending him flying over the audience. Amidst cheers, JJ carried on as if nothing had happened.

I worked for them again in Newcastle in 1981. JJ and my boyfriend had got on well at all the gigs; they were similar characters. I have seen the Stranglers often over the years, but never been backstage since. I have seen and spoken to Hugh a few times over the years, and he is just miserable and grumpy. The Stranglers changed my life and I will never be able to thank them enough, especially JJ and Dave who were always so kind and funny. I have made lifelong friendships and life decisions as a result of those few days. The Stranglers have been the soundtrack of my life.

PHIL COXON

My first gig was New Bingley Hall in May 1978 and then Loch Rock followed by three dates on the *Raven* tour, two gigs at the Rainbow when Hugh was in prison, 14 *Who Wants the World* gigs in the summer of 1980, 16 *Meninblack* gigs in 1981, 22 *La Folie* gigs in 1982 and seven dates on the *Feline* tour in '83. I particularly remember incidents involving JJ, and especially Bath Pavilion, where a small group of skinheads were being nuisances, creating a tense atmosphere. When one jumped onstage doing the 'Sieg Heil' salute, JJ promptly dispatched him to where he had come from with a crunching right hander. All the skins then legged it out of the hall to big cheers from the rest of the crowd and a great gig followed.

THEATRE ROYAL

19 AUGUST 1980, NOTTINGHAM, UK

DAVID LEIGHTON

My first encounter with the Stranglers would have been outside the public conveniences in Brinsley in Nottinghamshire in the summer of 1977. It may sound nice and sleazy but Brinsley bogs by the Rec was youth culture central for kids in that East Midlands pit village.

Standing in the entrance to the gents were my mate Drey's older brothers Arch and Pin and their mate Viv, chanting all aggressively at us young 'uns (we were 13 and them 16 or 17) something about 'beaches' and 'peaches' and 'sewers' and 'skewers'. 'What's up with them?' I asked Drey. 'It's a band called the Stranglers – haven't you heard of them? They're really good,' he replied.

I got someone to record *Rattus Norvegicus* and *No More Heroes* on a C90 cassette for me, and from then on we were full-blown fans and arguing the Stranglers cause against the other punk bands. They seemed to be a band you either liked or you didn't. There were no inbetweens. The hip people in London might have reckoned that punk was over by '78, but it wasn't if you lived in the sticks. We were soon being told, 'The Stranglers aren't punk' or, 'The first two albums were okay but the new stuff's shit.' Not for us it wasn't, and we were soon doing our singing in the bogs to *Black and White* and the *Raven*.

My older sister worked in Nottingham and punked me up a bit. She got me my first Stranglers t-shirt and one day told me the Stranglers were coming to Nottingham: 'Do you want me to get you tickets?' Too bloody right!

By now me and Drey were always in a trio with our mate Mick, who was a bit older and worldly wise and, strangely for that time and area, a big reggae fan. 'Will there be any birds there?' asked Mick (it was the Seventies). 'Bet there will be.' So, thanks to Jan, we were off to our first ever gig.

As we entered the theatre, I really didn't really know what to expect. We found our seats on the first balcony and spotted Sharon, a girl from our school, down in the stalls. She gave us a cheery wave. At some point Pete, one of the older lads from our village, appeared with a girlfriend in one of the boxes high to the side of the stage, spotted us and gave us a regal wave. They'd come down on spec and ticketless, and then got talking to some of the crew who'd got them in.

The atmosphere and anticipation was building. This was Nottingham pre-Rock City and the Royal Concert Hall, and it really felt like a big thing. I suppose it was Hazel O'Connor who broke our gig virginity. She was the support and plugging her *Breaking Glass* film, but there was no doubt as to the main event. From the moment the then unknown to us 'Waltzinblack' struck up and our heroes took the stage in front of a massive raven backdrop, the place went mad. We went mad!

Dave seemed to be surrounded by keyboards, reminding me of Herbert Lom in *The Phantom of the Opera*. Jet seemed to be in a world of his own, almost hunched over his kit and exuding power. Hugh looked like he had stepped straight off the cover of the 'White Room' single sleeve, telling us that the only time they'd played Nottingham before was the catering college to a bunch of blokes in chefs' hats. And JJ was just cool as fuck, from his skinny tie down to his whirling DMs. There was only one fella the ladies were interested in this night and – sorry, Mick, it wasn't you!

The gig was filmed for an ITV show called *Rockstage* and their edited footage doesn't show Hugh's girlfriend back on stage for 'Hanging Around' and '5 Minutes', interrupted by a stage invasion, and then in a flash it was over.

The local paper reported that the 'punk rock gig passed without incident other than a few broken chairs', but that gig sealed the deal for us. Mick was hooked (I like to think that he gave me Bob Marley and I gave him the Stranglers) and soon we were daveinblack, dreyinblack and mickinblack.

I've seen the band in all its forms many times over the years and been fortunate to have attended a few significant gigs in the Stranglers' story, including Hugh's last show at Ally Pally, Paul's last show at Rock City and one of Jet's last part sets in Liverpool. I also saw the two appearances at the Royal Albert Hall, a couple of conventions and a rather 'warm' night in York (which I think Baz would remember) and a bomb scare in Leicester!

One of my best nights was when I took Drey, who had emigrated many years earlier, to see the band at Warwick in 2015. He and his wife were buzzing for days after. I rate the Baz, Dave, JJ and Jet/Jim combo as my favourite live line up, and that Paul gets a raw deal from some. His enthusiasm kept the band going in a difficult time and the way the whole dynamic changed with him seemed a good bridge between the original four piece and the four piece now.

Album-wise, I don't think you can look much further than the first five albums, with *The Raven* just shading it for me, but after that I'd have the last four right up there and that *Suite XVI* is underrated.

I regularly go to the Theatre Royal with my wife to see all kind of shows, and whenever I enter the auditorium with the same green seats and stage curtain, I can't help but be taken back to 1980 and that raven backdrop. I'm sure the missus is sick of me telling her she missed the greatest act and show to ever grace that stage but, Susan, there really is no argument.

RIP Dave. Fly straight.

BRINSLEYBOGBOYSINBLACK

MICHAEL FISHER

Michael Fisher gets an autograph

The first time I came across the Stranglers I was a fresh-faced 14-year-old. It was 1977 and 'No More Heroes' came on the radio. 'Wow, this sounds fantastic,' I thought. It had the aggression of punk but sounded different, more melodic, and the keyboards gave it a different sound. I was straight down to my local Woolworths to buy the single, not realising that the album with the same title was also out. I bought them both, took them home and played them continuously on repeat until I realised the Stranglers debut album, *Rattus Norvegicus*, had been released a few months earlier, so I went off to my local record store to buy this album. First two albums acquired and played simultaneously, I was then hooked and eagerly awaiting every Stranglers single and album release.

The first time I got to see my heroes was in my hometown of Nottingham. It was an all-seater venue. You could feel the excitement in the air as the lights went down, 'Waltzinblack' came on over the speakers to a delirious crowd and on came the fab four and straight into 'Shah Shah a Go Go'. Everybody was up off their seats as the first song was coming an end and the band went straight into 'Ice'. Two songs in, I knew we were in for an unforgettable night.

BRADY'S CLUB

20 AUGUST 1980, LIVERPOOL, UK

MATTHEW SEAMARKS

I became aware of the Stranglers from hearing John Peel play them on his late night Radio 1 show in 1977 and 1978. But my real introduction to them was in a huge house in a town called Holywell in North Wales when I was 13. Somehow, I had been invited to a party thrown by seemingly wealthy parents for their newly teenage daughter. Now, after 45 years, I can't remember a single detail about how I got there or even the names of anyone who went. But what I do remember is that they had a dining room table full of alcohol and a front room with a sound system twice the size of our kitchen.

The DJ, with his open-necked shirt and cravat, played punk music accompanied by multi-coloured flashing lights and huge black speakers. At some point that night he played both sides of *Rattus Norvegicus*... and as the sound boomed out, and the older teenagers bounced, swayed and swaggered around the room, I fell in love with the greatest band in the history of the world!

From then on, I collected every record on the day of its release from the tiny record shop in the small town of Mold near where I was brought up. Sometimes we ventured further afield to pick up badges, imports or posters. I bought *La Folie* from Probe Records on Mathew Street in Liverpool. Pete Burns of Dead or Alive served me and said, 'What do you want to be buying that shite for?'

I saw my first Stranglers gig at Brady's (previously Eric's) at the other end of Mathew Street in August 1980. I was 15 and got a lift from the boyfriend of a girl in my class at Mold Alun Comprehensive. She couldn't go because she had a Girl Guides event so she offered me the spare ticket. Her boyfriend had a sky blue Ford Cortina with a beautifully painted Raven on the bonnet. If I'd asked my mum and dad if I could go, it would have been a straight 'no', so on the pretext of 'listening to records with friends' I was secretly off to see the Stranglers!

The venue was tiny and scruffy and really scary and I stood terrified at the back hoping I wouldn't be murdered. That was the first of many gigs that stretched through my teens and all the way through now to my 50s. I think it's 121 gigs as I write, and those gigs encompass the highs of the Royal Albert Hall and Stranglers conventions to the comparative lows of quarter full venues in Rhyl and Halifax. I've seen them in seven different venues in Sheffield alone!

At that Halifax gig on 5th November 1997, I waited for the band after they'd finished and said hello to Dave as he rushed past with his puffer jacket and shoulder bag. 'Trying to get to a bonfire night celebration, Dave?' I asked as he swept past. 'I *do* like a firework display,' he replied and, turning back to speak to me, he proceeded to tell me his top five firework displays in brilliant detail for well over 20 minutes. Apparently, a hilltop display on Sicily was his favourite... long before he was in the band.

Fast forward 20 years and I was with friends in Folkestone, waiting to go over to Ghent for the weekend. I had met Louie, the Stranglers' producer and sound engineer, at gigs over the years and we'd even done some recording with him as I'd been in a band with my schoolfriends since the very early '80s.

He wanted to know whether or not it was okay for the band to have a go at a song I'd written with a view to (maybe) possibly trying it out live. Previously I thought I'd reached the height of my devotion by getting a letter published in *Strangled* so this felt like a step up! I agreed (of course I agreed) and I think they've made it their own. Now I go to gigs and watch them play it. They've called it 'This Song', and now when I hear it, I think of how that Stranglers journey has come full circle. It feels like they set the template for me of the expectation of what a song could be... I just followed that and came up with something that probably sounds like something they would have written in the first place!

Only Stranglers fans really know the attachment and devotion they have to this band. They are part of our essential DNA. JJ, Jet, Dave, Hugh, Baz, Paul and John... and now Jim and Toby. Inspiring, imperious, melodic and dark. Soaring, thrilling, menacing and eloquent. One moment beautifully fragile and the next aggressively stark. God, I love their music so much and I literally cannot imagine a world without them. Ultimately, I can only thank whichever mysterious force has compelled them to make music with the integrity and beauty that they have. Thank you seems so totally inadequate.

EMERALD CITY

10 OCTOBER 1980, CHERRY HILL, NEW JERSEY

DAVE KELLY

I must be one of the first Stranglers fans in America, as I purchased my first Stranglers album in August 1977. What makes it special is the rat on the vinyl, as that was only sold in the UK. A&M records sold it in the USA, with the A&M logo on the vinyl. I was 16 years old in 1977 when I made a trip to Wales that August. I remember the day I landed in London, as it was my first flight, and when I landed, the big news was that Elvis Presley had died while I was in flight.

I was the guest of a family in Cardiff, Wales, who took me to a record store. I knew who the Sex Pistols were, but something attracted me to the *Stranglers IV* album. I purchased it, returned to Pennsylvania and have turned a lot of people onto the Stranglers over the past 44 years. I remain a proud fan, and follow them online, wishing they would announce one more tour in America.

I've seen them at Emerald City in Cherry Hill, New Jersey in 1980 and '81 and in 2013 at Union Transfer in Phildelphia on my 52nd birthday. A special memory is seeing them at Ripley's, a music hall on South Street in Philadelphia, in 1983. We stood next to the stage for that show and one of my friends was hollering 'Peaches' at JJ. He made a face and hollered back.

ALDO'S HIDEAWAY

16 OCTOBER 1980, LYNDHURST, NEW JERSEY

MARYANNE CHRISTIANO-MISTRETTA

I was just 16 years old and very excited to be going to see the Stranglers with a friend. But Aldo's was a nightclub and you had to be 18 to enter. My friend was of age and I borrowed his older sister's ID. The doorman looked at me and questioned, '26?' He looked directly at me and shook his head in disgust. I was shaking and terrified, but he let me in.

Back then shows started much later in nightclubs. I don't remember what time they were supposed to go on, but it was very late. So late that the fans were screaming nasty things like, 'C'mon you fucking limey bastards!' and throwing bottles at the stage. I didn't like that. I was a true fan and couldn't imagine doing something like that. I was also worried because I had a curfew. But I was right in front of 'the stage', which wasn't exactly a stage but right on the floor. I wasn't going to move.

Finally, around 12.30 am, they came out. It was outrageous seeing them so close up! I felt 'important', locking eyes with both Jet Black and Hugh Cornwell several times. Included in the set were 'Hanging Around' 'Who Wants the World', two of my favourites today. But back then I was thrilled to hear them do 'Tank'. It may have been the only song I knew back then, because with a $5 a week allowance, I couldn't buy that many records.

It was after 2am when I got home and my mother was furious. I was grounded for life. And the next day my ears hurt from the show.

POLYTECHNIC

10 FEBRUARY 1981, PLYMOUTH, UK

DEAN LEGGETT, DRUMS, BOB, ONE EYED WAYNE, JAMIE WEDNESDAY

Dean Leggett with his copy of Black and White

Although I was pretty up to speed on all the punk bands in 1977 and '78, I mainly bought singles. I made exceptions for the first Pistols album and first two Clash albums but otherwise albums were out of my price range. As my pocket money increased and I got a job working at the local Tesco, I was able to afford more albums. It was at Barry Gribble's house – he was one of my best friends, we were both 16 and lived in Redruth, Cornwall - where we listened to Stranglers albums, especially *Rattus*. He had it on constant play and was a member of the Stranglers Information Service, so always knew their news before the rest of us. He was a huge fan, much more than myself, and had every record.

Barry and I went to see the Stranglers at the Cornwall Coliseum in 1980 on the *Who Wants the World* tour and had tickets for the following February at Plymouth Poly on the *Men in Black* tour. But for some reason he couldn't come. I said to him, 'If I get to meet them by any chance, is there anything you want me to say?'

I travelled there by train and arrived four hours before the gig. Me and a few others were let into the soundcheck and afterwards we were invited into the dressing room, where we were given sandwiches and drinks. I spoke to Hugh, told him what Barry had asked and how he was gutted to be missing the gig. Hugh wrote his reply on the back of a paper plate, saying they'd be back. And true to his word, they returned to play the Cornwall Coliseum in January 1982.

I had all the early singles, but 'No More Heroes' was a particular favourite, as was 'Shut Up', the B-side of 'Nice 'n' Sleazy'. I can't say Jet was a massive influence on my playing, but there were some things I tried to copy, like the hi-hat patterns on 'Peaches'. He was much underrated as a drummer.

I didn't appreciate the Stranglers' albums as much as I should have, but these days *Rattus*, *Black and White*, and *The Raven* get played regularly at home. I bought everything up to around *La Folie*, but after Hugh left, I discovered new music and that was that. I've seen them in recent years, most notably in 2016 at Brixton Academy, when I shared a toilet cubicle with Stuart Pearce. The less we say about that, the better...

MOUNTFORD HALL

20 FEBRUARY 1981, LIVERPOOL, UK

TREVOR AINDOW

When I was 13, I wrote to Jean-Jacques Burnel and he wrote back to me. For a while, I was the talk of my school. I had forged a friendship with a guy who'd played on *Top of the Pops*. Even before hearing about JJ, I was dressing in black and wearing Doc Marten's; I had already picked up a bass guitar and was strongly into music. I was also into the martial arts scene (and Bruce Lee) and slightly later came the motorbikes.

I was introduced to the Stranglers in late 1976 on vinyl. A young Mick McGee, a founder member of Southport punk band Mayhem, said, 'We watched your face and body language change completely when playing *No More Heroes*.' *Rattus Norvegicus* I found out for myself.

Trevor Aindow's photo of JJ at the Brighton Centre on the Aural Sculpture tour

A chance came to see the Stranglers live at Liverpool's University, where I met JJ. The gig was beyond belief. From then on, I went to every single Stranglers gig possible, far and wide. They and their music often kept me sane in a mad crazy world. I did a little work for them, including newspaper write ups and running short articles about them, offering fans the chance to win concert tickets, and putting up hundreds of tour posters in the North West under instruction from Sil Willcox, the Stranglers' manager.

I completed the two *Dreamtime* tours, following the band from coast to coast. Many gigs on and much later, a gig at Warwick University in 1997 was another great show and I got to meet John Ellis before the show. The Royal Albert Hall was memorable for its sheer size and the awesome sound. Rock City in Nottingham through the Paul Roberts era (either with John or Baz on guitar) was always one to look forward to in a typical classy rock dive. The 2001 Stranglers Convention was truly remarkable, happening a couple of days after the USA's 9/11 attack. And a 2007 return to the

London Roundhouse was more than special, the video capturing Fansinblack at the front of the stage in the venue with the oddest history in the country. My friend Mick McGee (RIP) was working as floor manager and we attended the sound check. Seeing the band endlessly over the years has been a lifelong treat.

APOLLO THEATRE

21 FEBRUARY 1981, MANCHESTER, UK

DANIEL PRINCE

Daniel Prince was excited to be going into 'rough' Manchester

I was 14 years old and travelled from Oldham with my mate Gordy on the bus into Manchester. It was exciting, as we were only young and Manchester was rough in those days, and the Apollo wasn't in the best part of the city. We were also going to see one of the most intimidating bands around. We were already little Meninblack, having played their records to death, but this was taking it to another level.

The atmosphere was electric and the performance blew me away. Something changed in me that night. I became more confident, more independent. I got to meet JJ in New York in 2014, when he signed my ticket for the gig, and I told him that the gig in 1981 had given me a 'fuck you' attitude (in a positive way) for the rest of my life. He said, 'Oh dear!' I also got Hugh to sign the ticket at a local gig in Uppermill. He was charming and gregarious, contrary to the general perception.

DURHAM UNIVERSITY

23 FEBRUARY 1981, DURHAM, UK

PETRA JAGGARD

After the gig my female friend I were chatting to JJ outside the venue. That was until her older sister turned up on her motorbike, a devoted heavy rocker who wanted to see what all the fuss was about. JJ rode off into the night on the back of her bike. She didn't have a clue who he was but they did share a keen interest in Kawasakis.

The 'Fairground' intro is my favourite track. It leads us to the 'Meninblack', 'Nice in Nice' or 'Nice 'n' Sleazy'. After all this time, you make it look easy.

HAMMERSMITH ODEON

24 FEBRUARY 1981, LONDON, UK

ALDO CAPARCO

Aldo Caparco with Dave

I loved music from a very early age, and my favourite groups were ABBA and the Bee Gees. As a 12-year-old, I'd go and play pinball and bar football with my friends at a local café and it was on the café's jukebox that I heard 'Peaches'. I listened to the Top 20 on a Sunday evening and watched *Top of the Pops*. I remember hearing 'Something Better Change', 'No More Heroes', '5 Minutes' and 'Sleazy' and loving them all.

One of my best mates at the time had an older brother with a very impressive record collection. Everything was in pristine condition and chronologically ordered by band name and release date. When he was out, we would sneak into his record collection, dig out some LPs and tape them. One day my friend picked out *No More Heroes*. I'm not sure if I was there at the time, but I ended up with the cassette tape. I was 14.

As soon as I heard the opening of 'I Feel Like a Wog' I was hooked. It sounded so powerful and yet musical - and a little bit dangerous. I couldn't stop playing the album, and then my friend taped *Rattus* and *Black and White* for me. We had discovered something uniquely special. That keyboard and bass combination, those long instrumental sections, the guitar and keyboard interplay, the colossus that was Jet Black. The more I delved, the better it got and I was now a Stranglers fan above all else. I used my pocket money to buy *Rattus*, and played it every day after school on our family stereogram.

By the time of *La Folie* I was 16 and old enough to go to my first gig with three school mates. They opened up with 'Down in the Sewer' and I was in heaven.

APOLLO THEATRE

25 FEBRUARY 1981, GLASGOW, UK

ALLAN CRAWFORD

My journey began as a 13-year-old back in 1979. My mates were playing their older brothers' records – the Pistols, Ian Dury, SLF and the Stranglers. 'Duchess' was an early love. My memories of my first gig, on the *Meninblack* tour, are of the support act being chanted down by the 3,500 strong audience, the lights going out and stampeding fans running over me, in the stalls, to get to the mosh pit. Fans were climbing from the royal boxes over the PA onto the stage while vicious bouncers, dickied up like penguins, pulled back fans who were trying to get a 'bunky' onto the stage. JJ was dangling his leg over the 15-foot high stage above me, still belting it out on the bass, and I remember the spitting, the strippers, the audience as loud as the band, the heat and the sweat. What a gig. What a night!

Allan Crawford was at the Apollo in Glasgow in '81 and has met JJ and Hugh since

The baying crowd played up to the band and the band played up in response. The love affair was sealed for me that night. I've seen many bands at many venues over the years, but none had the energy, mischief and edginess of the Stranglers at the Glasgow Apollo.

MAYFAIR

26 FEBRUARY 1981, NEWCASTLE, UK

RUSS GOW

I have followed the Stranglers since 1977 and seen them over 40 times. Back then you used to have cameras confiscated by the bouncers but when I asked if I could take some photos at Newcastle Mayfair in 1981 for my student mag, they let me in... Although I wasn't a student I managed to catch a bit of history and although the photos aren't great quality, they are in my prized collection.

I also saw the band on *The Tube* in the '80s and Jet kindly gave me one of his drumsticks, which on the *Ruby* tour was featured with me holding it... It made my day. At *The Tube*, my mate asked Hugh to sign his trainer and Hugh took his shoe off and said to my mate, 'I will - if you sign mine first!'

I also saw the band at Sunderland Mayfair on the *Raven* tour. We were right at the front and my mate had a broken collar bone. When the band came on everyone pushed to the front. My mate was in agony so they crowdsurfed him to the back where the bouncers let us stand on some stairs and we had a great view. I also saw JJ use his karate to remove a fan jumping on stage.

BARRY LEWIS

I was a big fan of the Stranglers and seeing them play at the Mayfair Ballroom in Newcastle when I was 17 in 1981 was a memorable experience! I remember the crowd getting restless waiting for them to come on stage and when the support band (Modern Eon) came on there was a fair degree of hostility and I was hit on the head by a plastic beer glass that somebody threw at them. Their electronic music was deafening and the pitch was quite painful.

COVENTRY THEATRE

4 MARCH 1981, COVENTRY, UK

MIKE ABBOTT

My name is Mike Abbott and I'm a Maninblack. That may sound like the kind of introduction you might give at an Alcoholics Anonymous meeting, but the Stranglers are my 45 year addiction. It all started quite innocently, when I was 14 in 1977...

It was the height of the punk and new wave explosion. Like many other teenagers I was drawn to this revolutionary music. The Stranglers achieved three Top Ten hits that year. I saw them on *Top of the Pops*, playing 'Go Buddy Go'. I only had a cassette tape player so I had to rely on recording music off the radio (there was a skill to start and stop at just the right moment) and friends taping their records for me.

I had my own record player by the time of the release of *The Raven* and bought the last 3D picture cover version from Boots in Stratford-upon-Avon. The Stranglers

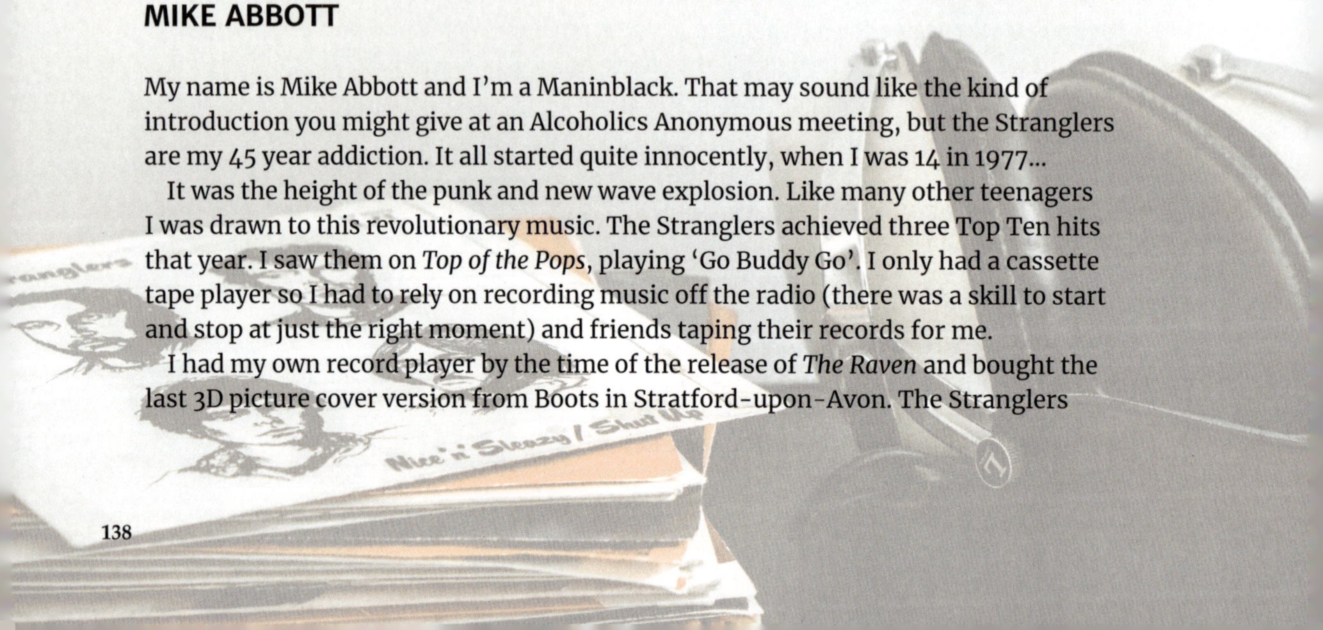

A. B. Cooper (Printers) Ltd. MANCHESTER

COVENTRY THEATRE, Coventry

Kennedy Street Enterprises presents—

The Stranglers

Wednesday, 4th March 1981

Evening 7-30

STALLS

£3.50

S 37

No Ticket exchanged nor money refunded
No Cameras or Recording Equipment.
Official Programmes sold only in the Theatre

Retain this portion.

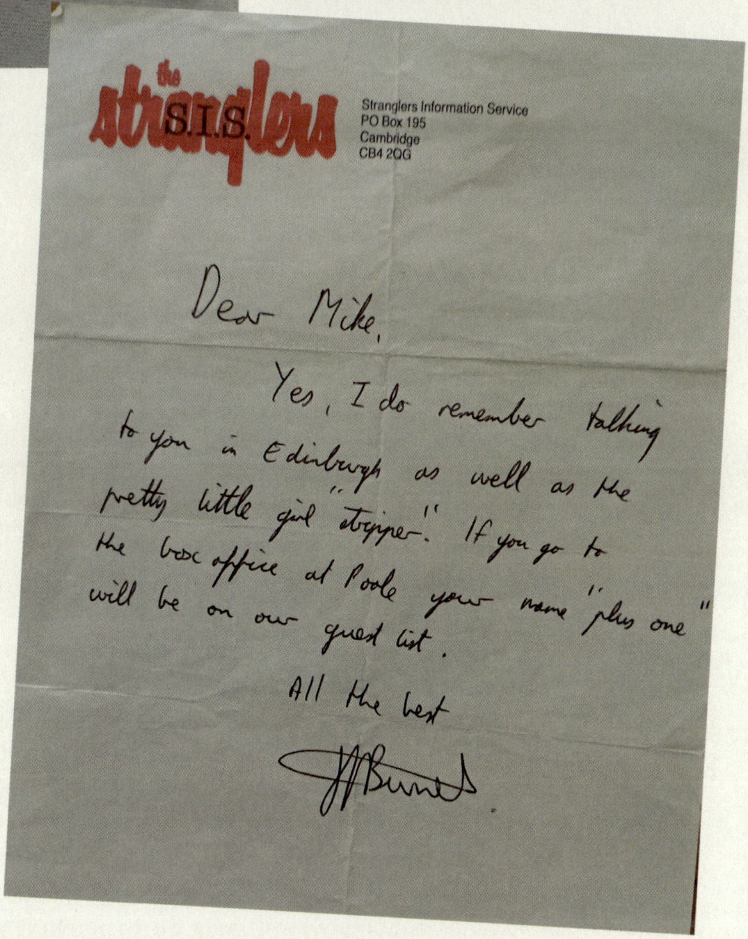

the stranglers S.I.S.

Stranglers Information Service
PO Box 195
Cambridge
CB4 2QG

Dear Mike,

Yes, I do remember talking to you in Edinburgh as well as the pretty little girl "stripper". If you go to the box office at Poole your name "plus one" will be on our guest list.

All the best

JJ Burnel

emerged as a band whose music I genuinely liked every track of. But it went beyond that; their sounds resonated inside me, generating an emotion like nothing else. Their music lured me in.

On holiday in the summer of 1980, I made friends with another fan and one night we decided to wear all black to emulate our heroes. It seemed to give me a sense of belonging, identity, empowerment and confidence. And so, outside of school and work, I would only wear black clothing for the next ten years. JJ has referred to the Stranglers as his 'gang' and I certainly felt part of that gang; the Stranglers were my band.

I collected anything connected with the Stranglers. My first car had a personalised windscreen sun visor strip, as was fashionable at the time, stating 'THEMENINBLACK', and I had a large translucent Stranglers sticker with ravens on it in the side window.

I had never seen any band live before March 1981 and nothing could have prepared me for this life-changing experience. Everyone was adorned in black and the tension grew in anticipation of the performance to unfold. The opening song, 'Threatened', was received like a volcano erupting – the seats nearest to the stage were dislodged due to the vast numbers of fans clambering to get to the front. Being in that mosh pit was absolute chaos, but exhilarating beyond description. I can liken the ecstasy of that gig to losing your virginity but it lasted 90 minutes rather than nine seconds!

I had been taken to another level and was truly hooked on this 'drug'. I would now see the Stranglers at every opportunity I could. I stopped counting how many gigs I've been to after reaching 100.

RICH MATHER

Rich Mather's first show was in 1981 (left, here with friend Denzil and son Jamie)

My first album was *Black and White*, bought from WH Smiths by my mum and endlessly played by me on my parents' old radiogram. It was amazing to see them play the full album all in one a few years ago in Oxford. I got backstage briefly that night and managed to shake Dave's hand.

My first ever gig was at Coventry in '81. I was 14. Me and four school mates were up in the circle looking down on the stage after having been dropped off by one of the dads. If my memory isn't playing tricks, the support act was, amazingly, Adam and the Ants, although I've never been able to find anyone else who can remember them. I can only assume this was a one-off pre tour gig for Adam himself just as he was getting big and about to embark on a major tour himself. The Ants had two drummers banging the hell out of their kits stage, left and right, and playing all the hits at a time when they were becoming a big thing.

The excitement waiting for the Stranglers was incredible. I'd never experienced anything like it. They came out and tore through a fantastic show. 'Toiler' was mesmerising. As a schoolboy, watching the mayhem down below from up in our circle also seemed a wise choice. I was a fan for life.

WEST RUNTON PAVILION

5 MARCH 1981, WEST RUNTON, UK

PETE NEWBURY

The West Runton Pavilion was a great venue on the north Norfolk coast, now sadly demolished. It was the *Meninblack* period. There was a lot of unnecessary spitting. Hugh stopped playing in the middle of a song and calmly wiped his guitar clean with a towel while the band carried on. Someone then annoyed JJ during the intro to 'Baroque Bordello' sufficiently for him to dive off the stage and show the offender the error of his ways. The story was hotly denied in the *Eastern Daily Press* the next day. I remember Hugh introducing 'Second Coming' by saying, 'This is a song about premature ejaculation.'

CORN EXCHANGE

6 MARCH 1981, CAMBRIDGE, UK

LAWRENCE FREEDMAN

I was down at the front and the worse for wear when I decided to get up on the stage. I fell over into Jet's drum kit. He ignored me and carried on playing. I don't think I can climb that high these days, so it's safe to say the drum kit remains in one piece. I've seen them every year over the past ten years and loved every gig. Thanks guys. Keep on strumming.

SAM MOLYNEUX-FARR

The Stranglers are probably the longest lasting relationship in my life apart from my mum. I'm born and bred Cambridge, UK but have resided in Oz for almost 20 years. How did the Stranglers come into my life? Well, as millions of us did, I was watching *Top of the Pops* on the BBC and it was there where I first saw the band, performing 'Go Buddy Go'. It was rocking, catchy, driving and aggressive. I may have only been 12 years old but JJ had me, all pouty and shouty, looking like he was ready to pick a fight. Dave was all dark hair and cheekbones in his famous green flying suit, playing the most aggressive and dominant keyboards I'd ever heard... ker-ching - sold!

My first ever gig (by anyone) was on the *Meninblack* tour. I was at secondary school and a lot of us wannabe punks and new wavers were going from my year. Most outstanding was a lad called Paul Meadows, who fancied himself as a bit of a hard man. His message to us all at school was that he was planning to 'get' JJ at the gig... blah, blah, blah!

The gig was great. One of my mates got called up on stage by Hugh so that she could give him the cane during 'School Mam'. And hard man Paul? We saw him try to scramble up the front of the stage near JJ at some point.

Monday morning, and back at school, we discussed the gig and agreed we had all had a great time. Paul Meadows had a black eye. It seems that JJ 'got' him and not the other way round, JJ having repelled him with his Doc Marten's to stop Paul climbing up on stage. How we laughed, and I loved JJ just a little bit more.

Many Corn Exchange gigs were to follow over the years. My favourite song is 'Go Buddy Go' as it was played at my Stranglers baptism, although '5 Minutes' runs it pretty close for the aggression and for JJ going off in French. And I love 'Midnight Summer Dream' for its whimsy and magic and un-Stranglers-ness.

My favourite album of all time is *Black and White*, which is a total epic from start to finish, and which has so much power and sound and is a keyboard masterpiece by Dave. When I heard Dave had died, I went straight to *Black and White* and had it on all the time when I was in the car, just driving around, crying.

RAINBOW THEATRE

7 MARCH 1981, LONDON, UK

DAS STEVENS

Me and my mate, both 16, took the short train journey from Stevenage to Finsbury Park. I was impressed by the support, Modern Eon, but the fans didn't agree, and I found out later that it was a tradition to boo the support off. The Stranglers themselves were awesome, with lots of *The Raven* and *MeninBlack* in the set. Me and my mate were both punk musicians at the time, and although we no longer play in bands and live 150 miles away from each other, we are still musicians. I dedicated my last solo album to Dave Greenfield.

KAREN ROGERS

We arrived early to try to meet the band as they arrived for the soundcheck and realised that the stage door was slightly open; when we looked in, we saw a small empty room just inside. As it was cold, we thought we would sit in there, expecting to get chucked out, but no one said anything so we stayed. After a while, someone kicked the

Karen Rogers was at the Rainbow in 1981

door. Saz opened it and in walked JJ. She asked him if he had kicked it and he followed her into the room and said, 'What's it got to do with you?', smiling all the time. Saz thought we were dead! Dave walked past and said, 'I'm with the band.'

STEPHEN PALMER

When I was 17, I happened to walk past the radio in the kitchen at home to hear a most amazing piece of music. I stopped, transfixed, listening to its swirling keyboards, hypnotic bass and snarled vocals. The track, I learned at the end, was 'Something Better Change' by a band called the Stranglers. I was hooked. The following year Peel played *Black and White* in its entirety on his radio show and I became a committed fan.

Four years later, I was at university near London. Following my usual intense scrutiny of the music papers, I discovered that the band were playing the Rainbow Theatre to support their *Meninblack* album. I knew I had to go... but there was a problem. I had black shoes and trousers, but no black jacket; you had to wear black to a Stranglers gig. I asked my mate, Dave Nye, if I could borrow his black leather jacket. Luckily, he agreed.

I took the train and Tube to the Rainbow, massively excited and rather nervous, wondering what it would be like. I stood on the right-hand side of the auditorium. It was amazing to see my heroes on stage. I remember JJ doing his karate kick thing best of all. The sound was incredibly loud, but the experience was fantastic, a dream come true. Unforgettable!

Stumbling out of the venue afterwards, I took the first bus I could find back to Waterloo station, realising that my right ear had gone almost deaf. I could just about hear the driver with my left ear. I sat back, tired, stunned and delighted...

IRVING PLAZA

4 APRIL 1981, NEW YORK, NEW YORK

PIERRE JOLICOEUR

The Stranglers first got my attention in the winter of '78 through CHOM-FM in Montreal hearing 'Grip', 'Peaches' and 'Hanging Around'. I was not 16 yet and had fallen deep into The Doors' psychedelic rabbit hole. The Stranglers were dubbed the 'English Doors' in North America and I was receptive to their vibe. I read about them in *Circus*, *Creem* or *Hit Parader* magazines. They had a mysterious and menacing aura and articles about them were hard to get hold of. I remember a quote from Hugh, 'This is a time of strife in England,' and a description of JJ's sound : 'The meatiest bass sound since John Entwisle.'

When CHOM chose to move to corporate rock and the new music scene went out of the window so no more Stranglers on the radio. But I had bought *Rattus Norvegicus* and I kept playing it to my friends and they liked it too. It mixed well with The Doors, The Who, CCR, Sixties psychedelic rock and the emerging new wave sounds that we consumed avidly.

In April 1981, I was a month away from turning 19 and part of a group of 35 students on a four day Easter college trip to New York City. Most of us were art or film students - and rock music fanatics! In a record store, I picked up the not even two months old *The Gospel According to the Meninblack* and saw the Stranglers logo. My curiosity was piqued by the design, the absence of a band picture and the unique calligraphy. I bought it.

The buzz spread that the Stranglers were to be playing at the Irving Plaza the following (Saturday) evening. This was pure synchronicity, a defining moment in life. And so we went, a bunch of wide-eyed and bushy-tailed youngsters. We got there at about 9.30pm, thinking the show would start within the hour. There were a few other people scattered about, but it was mostly us, naively waiting...

Two hours later, the crowd had grown considerably larger, and the New York punks were impressive, if not intimidating, we were starting to get nervous. At midnight, support act The Catholic Girls took to the stage and stormed through a furious 45 minutes set. And then there was what seemed like another endless wait.

At last, at 1.30am and four hours after our arrival, the Stranglers appeared to the sound of a strange ditty, which I would later discover was 'Waltzinblack'. The band launched into a slashing guitar rhythm on a mid-tempo beat full of tension. 'Threatened' had an agressive sound that reflected the current mood of the crowd. It was a pretty intense moment.

The band was so close to us! My friend Jack was sitting partly on the stage. Another friend, Michel Laplante, had the time to snap a couple of pics of JJ, before being told by security to drop it.

The band were on fire, delivering on all cylinders. They played most of *Gospel* plus some *Raven* tracks and a few from *Black and White*. I was... awestruck. At that moment, I got a solid fix. I had discovered, live and in 90 minutes, a corpus of three albums I had no idea existed, let alone how they sounded.

Hugh was in a great bantering mood, very talkative and telling the audience the correct time of day. 'This is 1981, not 1977 anymore!' He had the crowd in his hand.

Then we got to 'Nuclear Device' which faded into a very strange drum pattern, one that seemed to roll on itself, only to be stopped at the fourth beat by the hi-hat and immediately fall apart again. When Jet got into 'Genetix', I couldn't believe my ears. The beat morphed into another one you could dance to, and the instruments came together to deliver an astonishing, modern sci-fi climax.

The show finished at 3am and the crowd calmly dispersed onto the streets of NYC like a spent force. I was in total shock. My life changed at that moment. I was impressed beyond words. I was in a state of mind totally new to me, and no dope was involved! I had just witnessed the future of '80s rock, and it was the Stranglers.

The tour ended in Montreal in June with two dates. I went to the first. I have less vivid memories of that show. I came back for the *Feline* tour, where Hugh didn't utter a single word in Montreal and looked totally pissed off. The *Dreamtime* tour came through and I went. I built a nice collection of *Strangled* mags, and was into the band musically, intellectually and viscerally.

And it lasts, to this day.

ROCKSTAGE

JULY 1981

CRAIG WOOD

The Stranglers were going to be on a TV programme called *Rockstage*. I got my very own videotape for Christmas and I kept it waiting for the big event. Every Friday, I went to see my Gran so I could look at her *TV Times* to see if the next week would be the one. Motorhead, Girlscool, Madness, The Modettes, Joe Jackson, Orchestral Manoeuvres in the Dark all came and went before the Stranglers eventually came along, the last in the series, last week in June before the summer holidays. Eight tracks on a VHS cassette, and that became my most prized possession for years, perhaps even decades. I could easily have watched it a thousand times, especially to see Dave play 'Genetix'.

UNIVERSITY OF EAST ANGLIA

14 NOVEMBER 1981, NORWICH, UK

ANDREW HOOK

In January 1978, I was ten and a half years old and had been a punk for some time without really knowing what punk was. I was at the nebulous age where reality was only just starting to form around me and my world view was naïve and malformed. It wasn't even clear to me that punk was about music, but I knew it was political because a few of us at school had plans to sneak up behind Margaret Thatcher and pull down her underwear. Or was that '79?

One day my mate, Mark Dullea, said, 'If you're calling yourself a punk then you need to buy a punk record.' I went with my mum to Jarrold's department store in Norwich where she asked the sales girl if she had 'five minutes', whilst I saw the cover of the Stranglers' '5 Minutes' single beneath the glass counter. The lettering was LED red on a black background. I go giddy thinking about it even now. It was the first 'proper' record I would buy. Later in 1978, *Black and White* would be my first proper album. It stood to reason the Stranglers would be my first ever gig. I had a while to wait.

I was 14 in 1981. The Stranglers were on the first leg of the *La Folie* tour. I was told about the gig by a mate a school. Tickets were £3.50. I can picture that ticket now (the word 'Stranglers' in block capitals in yellow on a blue background) even though I haven't seen it in 41 years. I stored the ticket somewhere safe. It was a fetish, a talisman. I'd pick it up and look at it with reverence.

My dad worked security at the university that night and I walked down with him. I remember asking my dad if he could buy the tour t-shirt for me from the merch stall just inside the entrance and seeing surprised faces looking around. It wasn't very punk to have my dad there. I wore a black t-shirt, black corduroy trousers and black desert boots. My mate, Tim Caynes, had been to gigs before, and suggested we stand near a pillar, slightly above the mosh pit; sensible advice.

The band took the stage to the strains of 'Waltzinblack'. I remember menace, a cacophony, a melee. Opening with 'Non Stop', the band focussed on the previous four LPs, with nothing from *Rattus* which in hindsight feels odd. I loved it. With the Stranglers – with punk – I had found a home. I couldn't quite believe they were on stage. I never ventured into the mosh pit, but when the gig finished, and the song 'La Folie' played as an outro, I remember sitting on the steps near the now empty stage. Stunned and reeling. Strangled.

ODEON THEATRE

15 NOVEMBER 1981, BIRMINGHAM, UK

CLIVE ADAMS

Clive Adams has worn his jacket to over 100 Stranglers gigs

The Raven album gave us a taster of the new direction the Stranglers were to explore with their concept album, *The Meninblack*. It marked a turning point for the band, as every studio album from then on would see the band's music progress to a less aggressive and more commercial sound. With the release of the *La Folie* album, the Stranglers had lightened their mood and the new material had a distinctively more pop feel to it. Their date on the *La Folie* tour at the Birmingham Odeon is one that, after all these years, has stood out for me.

There were two support acts that night, a band called Taxi Girl and a barbershop quartet. If you were crammed in the front stalls waiting for the main band, you had little choice but to watch the supporting acts unless you wanted to lose your space at the front of the stage. It was customary practice at the tail end of punk for crowds to give support acts a rough ride. Verbal abuse and gobbing at the acts was rife that night. I remember a guy with a mop and bucket walking on stage before the Stranglers came on to wash away the gob!

The atmosphere that night reached fever pitch before the Stranglers even came on. The evening got underway with the now all-too-familiar 'Waltzinblack' intro and fans rushed the stage while the meathead security attempted to restore order. We were treated to five songs off the new album, with tracks from both *Black and White* and *The Raven*. I don't recall them playing any songs from *Rattus*.

For one of the encores, Hugh treated the crowd to the cocktail rendition of 'Bring on the Nubiles' before hammering into the full version. The fans wanted tempo and the band was obliged to play 'Duchess' and 'The Raven'. This culminated in a full-on-stage invasion and, with so many fans dancing on the stage, it was a struggle to see the Stranglers.

The gig finished with the title track from the new album and large figures walking out on stage to spell 'La Folie'. This was greeted with both bewilderment and some hostility from the crowd with chants of, 'What the fucking hell is that?'

Band and fans were in top form that night. The Stranglers were razor sharp, unpredictable, sophisticated, menacing, both moody and witty and, at times, borderline bizarre.

COLIN WEAVER

The final encore was 'Down in the Sewer'. In those days, you could stand right up against the stage and it was packed solid with a strong odour of leather and sweat. People knew that the gig was nearing the end so wanted to get on stage. Somehow, I found myself on the stage while waving to the audience and grinning like a Cheshire cat. I was then thinking, 'What the fuck do I do now?' By then, two further people had joined me on stage which I found comforting as a stage can be quite intimidating. I knew that what would be cool would be to do a JJ Burnel impression, when he goes on that walk. It would be super cool to see and completely original. By now, there were about ten people on stage and the roadies were telling people to sit down while the Stranglers played the last track. I have total respect for the roadies; instead of them throwing us off stage they could see we just wanted to express ourselves in a positive way. It was a great night out and the memories of that evening will stay with me forever. As I made it outside, I was still buzzing. On my way to the bus stop something felt different. I carried on walking and still felt a terrible draft. On checking the offending area, I realised I had a seven inch split in the backside of my jeans.

HAMMERSMITH PALAIS

17 NOVEMBER 1981, LONDON, UK

BILL ELLIOTT

Bill Elliott has followed the Stranglers for 42 years

I've followed them for 42 years. I remember finding *Live (X Cert)* in the local department store, hearing 'Grip' for the first time and thinking, 'What the hell is this' I first saw them at the Hammersmith Palais in November 1981 with Neil, Eddie, Steve and Michael (RIP Mike). Other highlights of the near 150 gigs I've seen down the years are:

- five nights at London's Dominion in February/March 1985
- meeting Phil on the ferry to Pink Pop in May 1985; 37 years later, we still go to gigs together
- the Cliffs Pavilion, Southend in March 1990, with Katina expecting our first
- the Cheese and Grain in Frome in 2010 and a bomb scare
- Looe Beach in 2012 with the rain lashing down and the waves crashing in
- an ill-fated trip to Moscow in 2015. RIP Swiss Chris
- buying Dave Greenfield a pint at the Centurion Club in September 2019. See you at the bar...
- Huxleys in Berlin in December 2019; my last gig with Mr David Paul Greenfield
- *Dark Matters*... welcome Toby, and back out on the road.

My favourite gig? Rattus at the Roundhouse in November2007 – two gigs in one after the restart. And 'Walk on By' is my favourite song. It perfectly captures the band's unique sound, and with typical Stranglers irony they didn't write the thing! Thanks to all band and crew members for the amazing nights you have given the Familyinblack down the decades.

GAUMONT THEATRE

19 NOVEMBER 1981, SOUTHAMPTON, UK

JEZ BOTTLEY

Jez Bottley (right) with fellow fans Andy Mills and Sarah Chapman

I got hooked on the Stranglers sound, sat in a car in Newport (Isle of Wight) in 1977, when 'Peaches' and 'Go Buddy Go' were played back-to-back on the radio on a hot summer's day. I was with my cousin, Greg, and we both thought it was so different. Greg influenced me a lot with music at that time but it was my mate, Steve Bull from school, who gave me full access to the Stranglers' albums in the early years by giving me recorded tapes of each album. Our record player wasn't great so I sadly had no desire to buy records back then. It was not until 1980 that I bought all the back catalogue on vinyl.

I lived on the Isle of Wight and growing up on an island was restrictive for access to live music, other than a local punk band or two. We had been due to go to the *Who Wants the World* tour earlier that year but didn't (perhaps my mum intervened?) so this was my first time off the Island with mates and no adult supervision! I was 16.

The gig left a lasting impression, not least with ringing ears for days afterwards, but the image stays with me of the end of 'Genetix' when the band's heads slumped as the lights went down, the synth faded and Dave sang 'Gene Regulation' ahead of the encores and close of the set. They were the first proper band I'd seen live, and I don't think there could be a better induction to decent live music - the energy and aggression was electric.

APOLLO THEATRE

23 NOVEMBER 1981, GLASGOW, UK

SCOTT KERR

Aged 12, I was visiting my cousin Gary and he let me hear *The Raven*. As soon as I heard it, I loved it. That weekend I took all the money I'd saved from my paper round and went to my local record shop, Europa Music in Alloa, and bought *Rattus Norvergicus*, *No More Heroes* and *Black and White* for £3.99 each.

Two years later, Gary came with me to my very concert... the Stranglers at the Glasgow Apollo. I was mesmerised, the concert was magic and it was being recorded by Radio Clyde, so I was able to tape the whole gig off the radio. Later the concert was released, on a CD called *Apollo Revisited*.

In 1984, I started work in the dockyard at Rosyth. I was a coppersmith and one of my mates was a plumber who also loved the Stranglers. Not long after we finished our apprenticeship, he left the dockyard to take up photography at college. That mate was David Boni... the jammy sod only became the official photographer and film maker for the Stranglers!

The Stranglers have been a constant throughout my life. I have taken my daughter to see them and am now waiting for my grandson to reach an age so that I can take him too. Throughout the highs and lows of my life, there are Stranglers songs that can instantly transport me back to those moments, good and bad. In many ways, these songs form an index of chapters of my life.

I've also stated that when I eventually peg out, I want my coffin brought in to the 'Waltzinblack' that was recorded at that very first concert because, in that crowd is a mesmerised yet delighted 14-year-old me, loving every minute and with my whole life in front of me.

I wouldn't change any of it, not even the really shit bits, as I wouldn't be who I am or where I find myself today, surrounded by a loving family and true friends.

Scottinblack, fading to grey!

Tim Bagnall's first of 92 Stranglers gigs (so far)

APOLLO THEATRE

25 NOVEMBER 1981, MANCHESTER, UK

TIM BAGNALL

The Stranglers have been one of the most important influences in my life. From the age of 15 to the age of 57, there's barely been a day they haven't been in my thoughts in one way or another. The first LP I bought was *Live (X-Cert)* and I was hooked from the first 'ow-ow-ow-ow' of 'Grip'. I liked plenty of other bands at the time, and many others since, but the Stranglers are a constant and more than just a band that makes music to stir the soul. They're an attitude, an education, a tribe, and that's all this young teenager needed onboard to charge into adulthood. My body may have deteriorated somewhat in the intervening years, but my head is still alive to those same feelings and the emotions that their music generates.

My fist gig was on the first *La Folie* tour. I went on the bus into town with two school mates who I still regularly bump into on tour. I've been to every tour since. There are many highlights but a few stand out; Wembley Arena in 1986 with the hilarious Keith Allen abusing the crowd, and all three nights at the Hammersmith Odeon residency in 1987. I have had some amazing times going to watch the band, 92 times up to now, and I never tire of listening to their recorded musical output. The fact there is so much of it means it is a hobby in itself collecting it. The digital world makes this so much more accessible which is great, but I miss a Saturday as a kid scouring Manchester's Underground Market, Clampdown Records in the Exchange or Affleck's Palace for bootleg tapes, imports and rare stuff. I have a Captain Pugwash chest with my collection in it. If there was a fire at home it would be the first thing out! Don't worry, the Mrs would be out too. She'd need to carry the other end of it, as it's a two-man job.

LYCEUM THEATRE

28 NOVEMBER 1981, SHEFFIELD, UK

GREG MCNALLY

Greg McNally was introduced to the Stranglers by a cousin

I was introduced to the Stranglers by my cousin in 1977 or '78 when I was 16 or 17. I was a bit studious, a bit of a nerd. Jane (not her real name) was three months younger than me and similarly scholastic but it came naturally to her; she didn't have to work as hard as me. Consequently, Jane rebelled a bit and was a bit of a punk; leather skirts, coloured hair, black finger nails and lippy. In my eyes she was the coolest. We got talking about music at a family do and she said the Stranglers were her favourite band. A few days later, I collected together all the money I had (which was not a lot) and bought *Rattus* at the local record shop; if it was good enough for our Jane, the coolest person I knew, then it was good enough for me. From the first three notes of 'Sometimes' to the water gurgling down the plug hole in 'Sewer', I was enthralled, surfacing only to turn the record over halfway through. It was mesmerising, every song a masterful blend of melodic keyboards and thumping bass like I'd never heard before.

The media portrayed the Stranglers as punks but this was far in excess of the standard three minute 'shout-a-long-a-three-chords' punk offering; it had musicality, melody and a dismissive attitude to the listener. The only thing I can compare it with is when my Dad took me to Anfield for the first time. I was six years old and hooked by the colours, the sounds, the smells and the excitement of what was going on in front of me. *Rattus* didn't have smells or colours, but it made up for it with depth and breadth and aggression and I was, again, totally hooked — I still am at 61 years of age. I have our Jane (not her real name) to thank, may she rest in peace.

My first Stranglers gig was in 1981. I was a student on industrial placement in Sheffield for six months so I had a bit of money. It was a stop on the *La Folie* tour and as well as the *La Folie* tracks they played some back catalogue stuff; 'Hanging Around', 'Heroes' and my favourite, 'Go Buddy Go', but, if truth be told, I can't remember a great deal about it other than Hugh's red socks, JJ's one-legged gyrating while playing and Dave's head just poking up over the massive bank of keyboards — oh, and a massive feeling of joy and satisfaction that I had seen the Stranglers perform, which could never be taken away from me. I've seen the boys many times since, in all their incarnations, including the last five or six gigs at the Hexagon in Reading (always on a Tuesday, for some unknown reason), and they just get better and better every time. The old songs are the best but Baz delivers them brilliantly even though he wasn't there when they were laid down.

My favourite track is 'Go Buddy Go', but that's this week. Next week it'll be 'Bitching', or 'Grip' or 'Heroes'. There are too many brilliant tracks to choose a favourite. However, the last two tracks of the *Live-X Cert* album are my favourite ten minutes of music anywhere (just ahead of 'Down in the Sewer' on *Rattus*). Like all live events, that particular performance is unique but these two versions of '5 Minutes' and 'Go Buddy Go' are the best I've ever heard in their construction and delivery. The intro to '5 Minutes' is a throbbing, cumulative addition of sounds from Hugh's guitar to JJ's bass with Jet's thump-thump-thump driving it forward. The live intro seems to be played in series rather than in tandem like in the studio, the live version taking 50 per cent longer than the studio one. 'Go Buddy Go' is again different from the studio (it is live, after all), with the two 'elbow rooming' bridges sandwiching Dave's magnificent solo. But the big difference for me is a small one; between the 'Go Buddy Go' chorus and the third verse there's an extra bar, as if JJ was taking a big breath for the final push. That small thing makes the song so much better for me. Both songs reflect and represent the Stranglers totally; powerful, expertly delivered, skilful, musical, and an attitude that says, 'I don't give a flying fuck about what people expect.' Utter perfection.

'GOLDEN BROWN'

RELEASED 11 JANUARY 1982

NIGEL PECKOVER

In early February 1982, 'Golden Brown' was riding high in the UK charts. I was 17 years old and the Stranglers were by far my favourite band. I had seen them live three times and had all of the albums and singles, but I had yet to buy 'Golden Brown'. I had asked a girlfriend out a couple of times, but she told me that one of her friends would really like to meet me. We met up and soon started to talk about music. Karen told me the singles that she had recently bought, which included 'Golden Brown' and 'The Model' by Kraftwerk. I invited her round to my house, expressly requesting that she bring these singles with her so that I could hear the B-side of the Stranglers single, 'Love 30'. I must admit I did not particularly like 'Love 30', but we have been together ever since, and are now married with three grown up children. At our wedding, we both chose a first dance. Mine was 'Golden Brown'.

Nigel Peckover met a girl who had just bought 'Golden Brown'

ABERYSTWYTH UNIVERSITY

22 JANUARY 1982, ABERYSTWYTH, UK

ANDREW BROWN

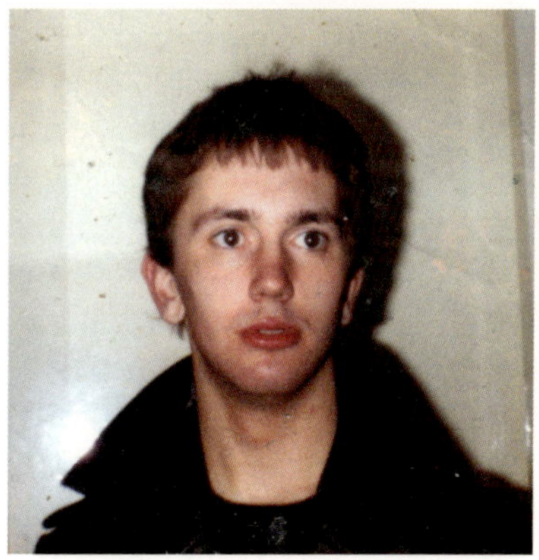

Andrew Brown was a fan from the age of 14

I was a fan from the age of 14. I discovered the band via a friend who lived in a village near Hereford and whose stepdad used to play *Rattus* on a cassette tape through a guitar amplifier so loud that the vicar used to come round from his house to complain. On holiday in sunny Tenby, my parents eventually surrendered to my plea to have my very own copy of *Rattus Norvegicus* from a local record shop and I remember handling that sacred piece of vinyl, barely able to wait to listen to it back home. A year or so later I used some of my meagre wages working in my Saturday job in a petrol station to buy *Black and White* from a record rack in the local newsagents. I was enraptured by the sounds. My apprenticeship as a fan was underway. I devoured the music, the attitude and the forthright intelligence of the material and the great interviews in the music press. But gigs were a thing of the future.

I saw them on the *La Folie* tour. I had a raging toothache but had paid for a ticket by working in the local vicar's garden (my friend and I used to joke that we were working for a maninblack in order to pay to go and see the meninblack). I turned up at Hereford train station on that bleak, bitter day and prepared myself with British Rail

Buffet tea and sandwiches and added painkillers. On arrival at Aberstwyth's epicentre of scholarliness, it was no warmer but there was a great pre-gig atmosphere and with some other fans I waited about to see any band members. Before long, JJ Burnel emerged and we gathered round while he sat on the floor in a light-coloured overcoat that he favoured at the time, adding names to a guest list for other gigs on the tour. Mine was included for Cardiff. In the hall was a table laid out for a pre-gig meal for the band members.

I got a position at the front almost within touching distance of the band and there began a blistering gig. Like all such Stranglers dates, it had the feeling of unity, of being a family. The music thundered along and was memorably embellished by Dave Greenfield's majestic and mystical flourishes.

My parents had agreed to collect me for the return journey as it was too late to travel back by train. My dad was waiting mesmerised at the entrance, having been able to enter and wait for me while the encore was underway. He said bluntly, 'I have never heard anything like it in all my life,' but looked like he might have been enjoying it!

On the way out, I saw an old schoolfriend who asked if he could have a lift home and my parents duly obliged, my mum well wrapped up in blankets in the passenger seat of our grey Vauxhall Chevette, recovering as she was from a heart attack.

There was snow on the way home and the drive was a little slower than would normally be the case through the winding Welsh landscape. It had been an amazing day and my friend and I rabbited all the way back despite our post-gig ringing ears. Around this time, I purchased some gig recordings on cassette from an enterprising Stranglers disciple in Bristol called Paul Whitrow. Some of my purchases led to visits to his parents' house in Long Ashton. He took me to Kinkade Brothers in Bristol, who made the guitars for Hugh and JJ which were used on *La Folie*. An accomplished keyboard player who could replicate the most demanding of Stranglers tracks, Paul was engaged in some capacity on the Stranglers-related single, 'My Young Dreams', a cover of a pre-fame Stranglers song on which Jet Black played. Paul's mum proudly told me about meeting Jet. Paul later went into music production but died a few years back and I gather Hugh Cornwell played at his wake. My brother lived nearby and so I contrived a reason to visit SIS (the Stranglers Information Service) at Shepperton Studios. I had purchased some things by mail order and asked if I could collect them when I was in the vicinity. It was just a sneaky way to have a chance of chatting about stuff and seeing stuff by getting inside the camp. The people in the SIS office were really nice. In 1983, the Stranglers appeared on *The Tube*. My parents' telly couldn't receive Channel 4. Undeterred, I called an aerial fitter in Hereford and asked if I could hire an appropriate aerial. 'No need', he said. 'Just come up to my place and watch it.' So off I went to the other side of town and watched it with a stranger and his children.

In 1993, I went to a Stranglers convention at New Cross and met Dave's wife, Pam. She showed my partner and myself the rats she and Dave kept as pets. I am proud to be a member of the Stranglers family. It has really enriched my life.

CIVIC HALL

26 JANUARY 1982, GUILDFORD, UK

MALCOLM WYATT

Malcolm Wyatt saw the Stranglers in their home town – photo Owen Carne

I reckon my Stranglers love started as much with my brother's copy of 1977 debut LP *Rattus Norvegicus* and 1979's *Live (X-Cert)* as those wondrous early singles, both heavily played cassettes bringing home the quality of a band that seemed far tighter than many of that era's fabulous but less accomplished three-chord punk outfits (he adds, with considerable hindsight).

It's difficult to recall my late Seventies thinking now, but while neither *No More Heroes* nor *Black and White* came my way for a while - even if a copy of the latter was feverishly borrowed from Surrey County Council's visiting mobile library - *The Raven*'s arrival around the time of my 12th birthday made another huge impression.

Again, several tracks take me right back, the singles 'Duchess', 'Nuclear Device' and 'Don't Bring Harry' never losing the'(Get a) Grip (on Yourself)', 'Peaches', 'Something Better Change', 'No More Heroes and 'Walk on By' first snared me. What's more, having quit my church choir earlier that summer, the image for 'Duchess' I saw advertised in *Smash Hits* - featuring those four 'angelic' choristers - truly resonated. I may not have looked the part, but I had punk spirit. And while I liked my choirmaster, accomplished organist Mr Bryant, I might have stayed longer if Mr Greenfield also featured.

What's more, the scout hall where the band practised in their formative days was at the end of my road, this reluctant Shalford 1st woggle-wearer having launched aptly named murder balls and bobbed for apples in wooden barrels one too many times in that iconic setting. Also, the first line-up of fellow Guildford luminaries The Vapors had practised at our village hall, while (whisper it) prog legends Genesis recorded across the railway tracks from my council house, Phil Collins and showbiz mate Eric Clapton having jammed on harmonica and spoons at the Queen Vic, opposite Lord Baden Powell's meeting place. Come to think of it, it's a wonder this rural Surrey setting doesn't appear on more rock'n'roll heritage tour itineraries.

In fact, word has it that in pre-deal days, Burnel, Cornwell and Greenfield were sporadically sent out around the area in one of Jet's ice cream vans to earn some cash for their keep, so maybe I once handed over coins for a 99 or Sunday lunch vanilla brick to Hugh. Either way, that surly rock 'n' roller with the greasy quiff would surely have riled my old man as we waited to be served.

In early January '82, I finally got to see the band at the Civic Hall in the neighbouring town where both the Guildford Stranglers and this fan were born. And, through the wonders of the internet, I can now revisit that night's show, that midwinter visit – the £4 ticket met by my labours at the village farm shop - coming at a time when 'Golden Brown' was four days off the start of a six-week stay in the UK Top Ten.

As it was, *La Folie* would be the first of seven LPs to not quite dent the Top 10 album chart, that and the previous year's *The Gospel According to the Meninblack* forming the core of the set that night, my fourth ever gig and second Civic visit. But listening back I'm there again, an Adrian Mole-esque 14 and the three quarters, the highlight for me being the song they launched into after walking on to a scene-setting 'Waltzinblack', the sublime 'Down in the Sewer'.

I still cite this show as the loudest I've attended in 42 years (close to 500 gigs), and listening back I found myself welling up re-hearing that early live outing of 'Golden Brown' recently, knowing all that followed for me and a band somewhat elevated in the public eye from there. As for their set, they hit top gear late on with 'The Raven' and 'Nuclear Device' before a 'Genetix' finale, but I was slightly disappointed at the time that so many of those songs I loved that formed the backbone of the first live LP and those initial four albums weren't there, my tender age meaning I'd effectively missed out on their first golden era.

Those who know *Live (X-Cert)* – a stunning stage record of a great band on their mettle from the moment those four grunts precede 'Grip' on track one - will not be surprised to learn there were dickheads continuing to think gobbing at visiting bands was acceptable, Hugh lashing out at the 'few idiots who still spit', segueing neatly from those 'unidentified flying objects' into 'Just Like Nothing on Earth'. And while overall there's comparatively little between-songs chat, there is an early spell where the lead singer does a little stand-up routine while Dave Greenfield and the roadies (queuing up like Rodneys, no doubt) dealt with electronica malfunctions ahead of 'Second Coming'.

'I tell you, if you're going to buy a synthesiser, don't buy it from Marks & Spencer's, 'cos they don't fucking work!'

He also tells a joke about Prince Charles and British Leyland, something of a historical timepiece itself now, and suggests if anyone sees locally-based legendary BBC producer Mike Appleton - the first producer of *The Old Grey Whistle Test* - they should sneak up behind and shout 'Stranglers!' to gauge his reaction, the quartet clearly still sore after the fiasco that saw them storm off stage at the town's University of Surrey during a televised late '78 *Rock Goes to College* performance, the organisers going against their wish to ensure at least half the tickets for the sell-out show went to locals.

Hugh added, 'We'd like to meet anyone who came to The Star in 1974 ... one of our first gigs.' And it seems somewhat prophetic considering 2019's PRS for Music Heritage award plaque unveiling outside that Quarry Street local, that he further suggests - regarding Jet's nearby Jackpot off-licence, 'They're thinking of putting a plaque on the wall outside, saying, 'Jet Black drank 3,000 gallons of gin on this spot between 1972 and 1974.''

What a night. What a band.

OASIS LEISURE CENTRE

30 JANUARY 1982, SWINDON, UK

FAL CARMICHAEL

The arse-spanking incident at the Oasis in Swindon on the *La Folie* tour? I have some grainy 110 photos of that somewhere!

NO NUKES FESTIVAL

9 APRIL 1982, UTRECHT, THE NETHERLANDS

ERIC VONK

I had already heard and read about the Stranglers, but my first encounter with them was in the winter of 1977 watching the Dutch equivalent of *Top of the Pops*, entitled *Top Pop*. It was the infamous miming session for 'No More Heroes' in which the band all mimed an instrument they did not play. JJ demolishing the drum kit was a sight to see. Apart from that spectacle, the song really hit me. I loved the snarly vocals and almost merry-go-round organ lines. Needless to say, I got the record soon after and the rest is history.

My first gig was the *No Nukes Festival* in Utrecht. I was very impressed by the whole day and atmosphere, and remember seeing members of Steel Pulse members helping Jet out with percussion on 'How to Find True Love and Happiness in the Present Day'.

I sort of lost track of the Stranglers in the late '80s, finding their sound too slick and commercial, I never really left the rat fold. Over the years I have seen them more than 50 times. I've travelled through half of Europe to see them, including Germany, France, Belgium and often to the UK. The Glasgow gigs I attended were amazing.

TOP OF THE POPS

5 AUGUST 1982, LONDON, UK

CRAIG WOOD

La Folie was a strange album, but what I liked most about it was 'Golden Brown' with the way it stuck out with its resonant bass sound. The layered harpsichord made for a real dreamy feel. (I believe the mix for the single is different, with some of the deeper harpsichord removed to emphasise the more metallic sound.) Imagine my surprise when I went out on a Friday night and all my friends were telling me about the Stranglers being on *Top of the Pops* the night before, playing their brilliant new single, 'Strange Little Girl'. I was raging. I had to go straight out the next day to buy it, then wait two weeks until the band's appearance was repeated on *Top of the Pops.*

OFF THE RECORD CENTRAL HALLS

18 OCTOBER 1982, GILLINGHAM, UK

DAVID JOHNSON

I have been a Stranglers fan ever since hearing 'Sometimes' and the lyric, 'Someday someone's gonna smack your face'. when I was just 13. It had quite an impact on a young teen. Back in the '80s, TVS (as it was then) had a weekly 30 minute *Rock Goes to College*-type show called *Off the Record*, with a different band performing live for half an hour each week. The Stranglers were invited to play.

The show's production team were quite shocked at the hordes of black leather jackets that turned up. There were loads of us, far more than they usually got for the show. The venue was full. A rather camp producer, checking his sound levels for the recording, asked us from the stage, and in a somewhat camp voice, to pretend we'd just heard our favourite Stranglers song, expecting a friendly cheery response. I don't think the reply from the masses is printable. The poor bloke didn't know what to do.

On the programme, whichever band was featured would fulfil their 30 minute slot and then stop. Not so the Stranglers. The fans had turned up en masse and so the band rewarded them with a full set. The producers looked around, very confused and annoyed, as the Stranglers did not stop playing after the scheduled 30 minutes. The producers didn't dare turn everything off for fear of death, and it was a good 90 minutes before they could dismantle their equipment.

GARETH SIMMONS

Gareth Simmons was at Gillingham's Central Halls with his mate Clive

My friend Clive and I went. We got a good position at the front, on the right of the stage as you looked at it. During the gig I persuaded the bouncer nearest to us to take a photo for me. After the last track of the encore, l jumped up on stage and got a photo of me with Dave Greenfield. When the house lights went on, we looked for the nearest stairs and found an elderly security guard blocking the way. I convinced him l was Hugh Cornwell's brother, although to be honest I don't think he knew any of the band members' names. We found the dressing room and the band welcomed us in. They kindly gave us some beers and we sat and chatted with them for a while.

Afterwards we walked down the grand staircase with them to the front doors, where other fans were waiting to greet them.

FELINE

RELEASED 22 JANUARY 1983

ERVIN SOON

I discovered the Stranglers' music in 1986 when my brother Allan brought a copy of *Feline* back from a visit to Finland. It looked so beautiful and sounded very good. He also bought the soundtrack to the film *Clash of the Titans*, thinking it must be the Clash... A little later I heard tape recordings of *No More Heroes*, *Black and White* and others albums and fell in love with them on first hearing.

HUGO HIGGINS

I enjoyed *La Folie* a lot (except for that one song; I really have a lot of problems with songs in my native language - I definitely heard too much French crap when I was a kid!), but then came *Feline*. I can't describe how disappointed I was when I heard songs from that album. I totally understand the need for bands to evolve or change their sound, but this was too far gone for me. I was heavily into harder sounding music like American hardcore and the switch to an acoustic and huge reverbed snare drum sound was definitely not for me.

CORNWALL COLISEUM

29 JANUARY 1983, ST AUSTELL, UK

TOBY HARRIS

Toby Harris caught the Feline tour

My first memory of the band was a couple of 1977 *Top of the* Pops appearances. But I got into them more seriously after stealing my older brother's '5 Minutes' single. My first gig wasn't until I was 15, on the *Feline* tour. I have a great memory of Hugh, mid-gig, saying, 'So this is the entertainment *Crapital* of the West?' I worked at this venue (in the Wimpy bar) as a teenager and so was able to get over to watch bands warm up. On the *Dreamtour*, and before the LP was released, I was the only person in the 'audience' as they rehearsed 'Always the Sun'. It was the first time I'd heard the track and I was blown away.

My favourite gig is Caerphilly Castle in 2019. Keep on rocking, guys – the 2022 gigs were awesome!

Toby Harris's garage is full of Stranglers memorabilia, including the full three-piece stage set from the 2010 tour

COLSTON HALL

31 JANUARY 1983, BRISTOL, UK

MIKE ABBOTT

In the spring of 1982, I went without a ticket to a sold-out gig at Warwick University on the second leg of the *La Folie* tour. I managed to buy one from a guy with a spare. As we chatted, it transpired that we lived near each other, so Jez Brannan and I became friends and toured together, seeing the Stranglers all over the UK.

Our first trip together was to Bristol on the *Feline* tour with my brother, Dave - now sadly departed. We slept overnight in my car in a multistorey carpark as we couldn't afford a B&B. In the morning, we went to the hotel where we believed the Stranglers were staying in the hope of meeting them.

We had waited some time in reception when Hugh appeared. Dave politely requested if we could take a photo to which Hugh very abruptly replied, 'No.' This took Jez and me by surprise, but Dave asked, 'Why not?' Equally short, Hugh retorted, 'Because I said so,' and walked off.

Shortly after, JJ emerged from the lift, looked at us looking nervous after our first encounter with Hugh. He said, 'What do you want?' I was thinking that this wasn't going to go well either. We explained what had just happened and JJ laughed, saying, 'Don't worry about 'Auntie' Hugh, he's often grumpy.' We got our photos and autographs, exchanged a few words and all was well. Dave and Jet followed and duly obliged with autographs and photos. We left the hotel happy.

STUDENTS' UNION

1 FEBRUARY 1983, CARDIFF, UK

STEVE BERMINGHAM

I had been going around with my punky girlfriend, Jenny, for about two years. This gig had sold out before me and my mates could buy tickets but Jenny had bought herself a ticket. So I 'borrowed' her ticket, made copies for me and my 20 mates and then replaced her ticket without her knowing I'd taken it. Except that I replaced her original ticket with one of the forgeries. On the day of the gig, I got in but all the rest – including Jenny – got caught! Thanks to the band they were all let in and we had a massive night out. I never saw Jenny again. It was worth it.

ROYAL CONCERT HALL

5 FEBRUARY 1983, NOTTINGHAM, UK

JOHN CHAMBERLAIN

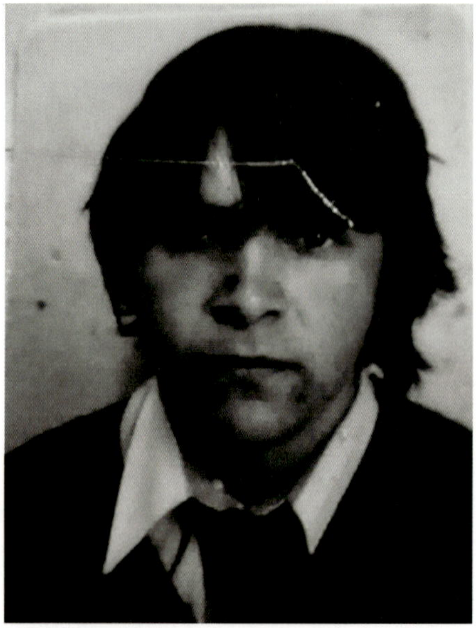

John Chamberlain got chucked out, but got back in

My dad drove me and my mates to Nottingham from Birmingham. I recall being surprised at the band playing such a venue and remember being in the bar and hearing a 'bing-bong' and the announcement that the Stranglers were on in ten minutes and that there was to be no standing up, which was met with much derision.

We had seats in the middle stalls and as the lights went down, we set off, hurdling seats to get closer to the front. I got from Row J to Row C and was pleased with my progress until I was pulled backwards by a bouncer and, joined by another bouncer, frogmarched out of a side door and into a corridor where another door was booted open before I was launched onto the pavement with the words, 'That's where scum like you deserve to be' ringing in my ears. I'm not sure what I thought. Probably, 'Shit!'

I made my way back towards the front of the venue. I could hear the muffled sound of the band in full flow. I saw an elderly doorman, a proper geezer in bow tie, dinner jacket, etc. and wandered to his door. I presented my ticket and he said, 'Hang on, the stub's missing.' I thought at this point to be honest and so told him the story, elaborating that I was from out of town, had no money, etc. He took pity on me and said, 'Don't do it again, in you come.' Bless him. I walked back in and at this point the bouncers had cleared the aisles so I walked straight back down to Row J, studying my ticket like I was lost and past the guy who threw me out. It was then that I realised why the bouncer was walking away from the front towards the rear, as Jet was stood at the edge of the stage, berating the gorillas in suits and threatening to pull the gig if they didn't clear off. I stood there proudly thinking, 'I wonder if he saw me getting chucked out?'

VERULAM ARMS

14 FEBRUARY 1983, WATFORD, UK

JOHN WOODCOCK, AGE 16

I got into the Stranglers at school about 1980 and first saw them in Hemel Hempstead in 1982. Aged 16, I started work in Watford as a trainee tyre fitter and travelled

Stranglers in pub gig

ROCK superstars The Stranglers have turned down a money-spinning concert at a top London venue — so they can play at a Watford pub tonight.

The band, who are on a sell-out tour, were offered an extra night at the 4,500-seat Hammersmith Odeon.

But they had already agreed to play a gig at the Verulam Arms in St Albans Road, North Watford — giving their services free for an old friend, the pub's landlord Joe S

The
Vale
costi

Joe Seabrook, left, with three of The Stranglers

cover expenses) sold out in just half an hour.

But among
guaranteed a

junction with Joe Seab

John Woodcock was at the St Valentine's Day Massacre and now goes to Stranglers gigs with his son Jack

the eight miles every day on my little 50cc Honda. One of my workmates drank in the Verulam Arms and, having seen me in my Stranglers t-shirt, he told me the Stranglers were playing there next month. I just laughed and said, 'You must be wrong.' He wasn't wrong, and I was even told when the tickets would go on sale. The band's friend and security guy, Joe Seabrook, owned the pub and they were doing the gig to help him promote it.

On the day the tickets went on sale I went to the pub along with some old school mates – Steve Davis, Chris Davis, George Walpole, Clive Bullock and Neil McBride – and we all managed to buy a ticket. We couldn't wait to see them play such a small venue, and all queued up outside on the night of the gig and were first in. Most of us went to Hugh's side and were right in front of his mic stand. The stage was about 12 inches high.

Dubbed the 'St Valentine's Day Massacre' on the tickets, we waited in anticipation for the boys to take to the twelve-inch-high stage! Before we knew it, they were there, starting with 'Nuclear Device'. My mate Neil was so close to Hugh that his over-hanging guitar strings were hitting him in the face, and after the second song, 'Toiler on the Sea', my friend asked Hugh to snip them off, which he duly did.

We were treated to close up views and brilliant songs such as 'No More Heroes', 'The Raven', 'Who Wants the World?', 'London Lady', 'Genetix' and more. It wasn't the best sounding gig I'd been to but it didn't matter. To see them so close up was a once in a lifetime opportunity. There was plenty of banter from Hugh as always, asking the locals why they didn't go to live music in pubs and generally having a go at them.

After the gig ended, I got on stage and went over to Jet's drums and nicked his empty beer can as a memento, which I still have today. The following night I went to London to see them at the Hammersmith Odeon, in a 4,500 capacity venue. I was 16 years old then and I'm still watching the Stranglers today, usually with my son, Jack.

HAMMERSMITH ODEON

15 FEBRUARY 1983, LONDON, UK

PAUL SMITH

I discovered the band when I was eleven and *Rattus Norvegicus* was released. An informed friend who knew what was what played and then lent me the album. 'How original and how brilliant,' I thought, with 'Rats Rally' going on to become my battle cry as I determined to better myself and my position. It still almost sends me into a trance as JJ plays the first few notes.

I bought *No More Heroes* belatedly as I had limited funds and I was playing it for the first time while three of my best friends and my girlfriend at the time were playing snooker on a six-foot table in my front room. 'Dagenham Dave' led into 'Nubiles' and, as 16-year-olds, we couldn't believe the lyrics and replayed the track in fits of

Paul Smith and his daughter Lex

laughter and astonishment.

I saw them live for the first time in the spring of 1981 on the *Meninblack* tour at Hammersmith Odeon with those same three best friends, and in early 1982 we were all there again for the *La Folie* tour. A guy playing spoons was one of the support acts. When the Stranglers were on, Hugh asked, 'What did people think of the guy with the spoons?' Despite being near the back, upstairs and only 15 years old, I yelled out, 'He should go and play with his fucking bollocks!' Hugh replied, 'I didn't ask for your opinion!'

And I remember the first of two nights at the Hammersmith Odeon on the *Feline* tour, where the band asked that the bouncers leave as they didn't want to see people's backs towards them. After a short delay, the Odeon management agreed but the following night's show was cancelled, as I found out when I went to the Odeon the day of the second show to be told by an officious man outside that this was due to the front seats being broken.

PALAIS D'HIVER

27 FEBRUARY 1983, LYON, FRANCE

HUGO HIGGINS

I was glad to see the band again in my home city, especially when they played the harder stuff, but I didn't really care so much when they used their acoustic instruments. Lyon was the centre of worldwide attention at the time because of the trial of Klaus Barbie, the so-called 'Butcher of Lyon', which brought journalists and TV reporters from all over the world to cover the event.

JJ talked about Barbie and added something to the effect of, 'Can you really blame someone who just obeyed orders? No! No!' which brought a lot of boos from the crowd. Some smart-arse threw a banana on stage. JJ picked it up and went, 'Hey, does the guy who threw this banana want to come onstage and have this banana stuck up his ass?' Incredibly, the guy went, 'Yep, it's me!' and got up on stage. Jet came out from behind his kit and grabbed the guy by the neck, while Hugh pulled down his pants, peeled the banana and gently stuck it into the guy's orifice... all this in front of a thousand people!

They released the guy, who then got the banana out of his hole, threw it into the crowd and left the stage with a big smile on his face. What a winner!

After my *Feline* disappointment, the following albums didn't do much for me either, especially that awful polished, uber-produced Eighties sound that was the thing in those days. By then I was totally hooked by hard-hitting and melodic bands such as Hüsker Dü and other crushing US bands. But still listening to the first four Stranglers LPs.

I saw the band one last time, in 1985 on the *Aural Sculpture* tour, in a huge place with a mainstream audience. That show didn't do much for me, unlike the Purple Helmets show I attended a few years later in Lyon, which was a very relaxed and fun show in front of a small but enthusiastic crowd.

I would have to wait until 2011 to see the Stranglers again, when they played my new home city of Montpellier. I wondered if I really wanted to pay 28€ to see an old favourite from my young days, thinking they would be tired, boring and playing the more mainstream songs... But how glad am I that I did when they started with 'The Raven' and played about 15 songs from their first four classic albums. I was super impressed by Baz's presence and his great playing and singing. He wasn't a poor copy of Hugh, but a great homage to the man and the songs. It just felt like riding a great time machine and I think a few tears flew!

Ten years later, and what a relief it was to attend another Stranglers show in Montpellier in December 2021 after a long and horrible concert abstinence because of Covid. *Dark Matters* is a great album, although it felt quite strange to buy a Stranglers album again, 30 years after *La Folie*. Standing up front near Baz and singing along brought back some cherished memories. Even if that proves to be the very last time I see the Stranglers, there's no sadness to be had. The Stranglers have been a huge part of my humble life and their songs will always remain the perfect soundtrack to it!

READING FESTIVAL

26 AUGUST 1983, READING, UK

JONATHAN STUBLEY

After a terrific support set by Big Country, the Meninblack took the stage as headliners on the Friday night of the festival - much to the bemusement of the assembled heavy metal fans. Hugh expressed his surprise that they had been booked for this event but the band played a superb set including 'Toiler', 'Heroes', 'The Raven', 'Duchess' and 'Sewer'. The bit that sticks in my mind was the band sporting long black 'metal' wigs as they emerged to play an encore of 'Nubiles' and 'Genetix'. 'Well, this *is* Reading!' quipped Hugh.

STEVE HULME

At Preston Guild Hall, a guy got on stage to show off his Sid Vicious tattoo on his back. Me and a couple of mates got on to drag him off but Hugh said, 'Hang on,' and disappeared off stage. He came back with a banana, asking us to pin the lad down and de-bag him. Hugh then stuck the 'nana where the sun don't shine before the lad was booted off stage. Tough gig!

Steve Hulme and his mate Bish danced onstage at Reading Rock

At the *Reading Festival* 1983 on a Friday night, we had been on the lash all day. In an atmosphere of expectation and adrenalin, the Meninblack came on at night to a mighty cheer. A couple of songs in, the crowd surged forward through the over-zealous bouncers and me and my mate Bish took our chance, jumped off a couple of blokes' backs and managed to get on to the stage, which was bloody high up. We were immediately met by more bouncers, but JJ told them to do one and we were live on stage with JJ, dancing with our heroes in front of tens of thousands! We were up there for two or three songs and left feeling elated. I will never forget the thrill and experience... happy days... amazing band.

I still see them every time they play the Tivoli in Brisbane. Please give it one more go, lads!

ROB MURRAY

A huge bottle fight had broken out and one bottle hit the girl I was with in the face. I marched into the clearing between the two sides and shouted, 'Come on, then, I'll have the lot of ya!' I ended up black and blue from the pounding I took from the bottles that hit me from both sides. A mistake.

ICP RECORDING STUDIOS

JUNE 1984, BRUSSELS, BELGIUM

ERIC THULLIER

My old friend, Olivier, and I had been invited into the studio by JJ. At one point we were asked to do the backing vocals for Spain. We gathered all our strength to shout, 'Spain, Spain, Spain,'. We probably could have asked for a fortune for our performance...

ROYAL COURT THEATRE

20 FEBRUARY 1985, LIVERPOOL, UK

TONY MELIA

Tony with the cat

JJ and Tony Melia with the cat

In late '77 you had a choice of the Bee Gees or the Stranglers and I chose the Stranglers. I borrowed *Rattus Norvegicus* and *No More Heroes* off a friend, and then in 1978 came the single '5 Minutes' and I just fell in love with them. There was no looking back. I was 16. I wasn't really into punk and I thought the Stranglers were a bit more creative than punk, although punk was in their locker.

I first saw them in 1980 at Brady's in Liverpool, which used to be Eric's. Altogether, I saw them five times with the original line up – at the Royal Court in Liverpool in 1981 and again in 1985, on the *Aural Sculpture* tour, at Preston Guildhall and at Birmingham Hummingbird. I've lost count of how many times I've seen them since Hugh left in 1990. They started to tour quite heavily and I went to see them at any opportunity.

Hugh left after the 1990 tour. It was a very strange atmosphere on that tour. I couldn't quite put my finger on what it was. The album, *10*, didn't make much of an impression on me. I heard there were tensions in the band but I didn't think he was going to leave. I saw the headline in the *Daily Mirror:* 'Stranglers front man has left', and I thought, 'What a load of rubbish.' And then I saw it in one of the music papers, *Sounds* or the *NME*, and that's when I thought, 'There's some truth in it then. He's gone, he's left.' I was devastated.

Alexandra Palace was his last gig. He was the only person who knew he was going to leave. The story I heard is that he was watching the cricket and Devon Malcolm was batting and Hugh said to himself, 'If Devon Malcolm hits a six, I'm going to leave the Stranglers.' And Devon Malcolm hit a six, and Hugh thought, 'If he can do that I can leave the Stranglers.'

He rang Dave Greenfield first to tell him. And then he rang Jet Black and he rang JJ last. Burnel said, 'I'll tell the others,' and Hugh said, 'No, I've already done it.' He said he did it over the telephone rather than to their faces because he didn't want to be persuaded to stay. He had threatened to leave before, in the early Eighties, when he fell out with them and they'd persuaded him to stay. In 1990, it was the end. He and JJ weren't getting on and were going in different musical directions. Hugh didn't mind being in a pop group whereas JJ wanted to be in a cool cult band with their own following. And that's what I wanted when I was younger. I wanted them to be 'my' group, my special band. But Hugh was a bit more ambitious and a bit more commercial and wanted to get into the charts.

The inner sleeve photograph of *Rattus Norvegicus* includes a photo of the band taken in a house built in 1798 called the Old Knoll in Blackheath in London. The band are standing between two pillars in the photo, apart from Dave, who's sat with a cat on his knee. I always wondered if it was a real cat. Many years later, I had a video called *Screentime* which had six Stranglers songs on it including a song called 'Midnight Summer Dream', in which they went back to the house six years later to shoot the video. At the end of the video, the camera was outside the house and it showed a sign saying 'Old Knoll for Sale'.

My partner Fran said she was working in Blackheath and so we went to Blackheath to look for the house but we couldn't find it. Fran said, 'I'll just go into an estate agent and ask where it is,' and one of the guys in the estate agent said, 'I can tell you exactly where that house is' and gave us the address. So we went to the house, pressed the intercom and chatted to the people inside, but they wouldn't let us in.

The owner of the house was Mr David Redlick. He told us the house used to be owned by an antiques dealer called Warner Daly. I found his phone number on the internet and spoke to him on the phone. Warner remembered the original photograph session for the album cover, but not the video. I asked him for his address and sent him a copy of the video.

Warner sent me a postcard thanking me for the video and he invited me to his house just off the North Circular, where he went through the artefacts that feature on the cover of the album. He pointed to the cat on Dave Greenfield's knee and said, 'I've still got that cat.' He reached up to a cupboard and pulled the cat out. It was a painting of a cat on a piece of cat-shaped plywood. It had been part of an art exhibition in 1973, but wound up on the street when the IRA exploded a bomb there. One of Warner's friends found it in the street and gave it to him.

If I had a time machine and could go back to any one gig, it would be the Royal Court gig with the brass section in early '85. I remember Hugh and JJ wearing leather jackets right the way through that gig and many years later, when I met Hugh Cornwell, I said, 'I really enjoyed the Stranglers at Liverpool Royal Court.' And he said, 'It was freezing that night.' And that's why he kept his leather jacket on.

I always thought Hugh would go back. But not now. It's not going to happen, is it?

ODEON THEATRE

22 FEBRUARY 1985, BIRMINGHAM, UK

ANDY KENDALL

Andy Kendall saw the Stranglers at Birmingham Odeon

When I was six years old my elder brother, Nick, bought a cassette home, which contained two songs, 'Pretty Vacant' by the Sex Pistols and 'Peaches' by the Stranglers. I remember thinking that 'Peaches' was the weirdest thing I had ever heard. Up until then, I only owned records by The Wurzels and Laurel and Hardy, so this was something of an awakening at such a tender age. We all thought 'Peaches' was very daring with its explicit language. It was around this time that kids at the local park were putting safety pins in their mouths to make it look like they were pierced, which I naturally tried to do myself.

Little did I know at this point that the group performing the song would have a profound influence on me as I struggled through my teens to navigate life. It was the summer of 1977 and punk had hit the provinces. There was no shortage of young people in my home town of Nuneaton donning safety pins, spiking their hair and wearing odd socks in an expression of defiance.

Later that year, I heard a song on a cassette that had been used to record the charts from the radio. We had a cheap cassette player that we used to hook up with a microphone to record the chart rundown from a separate radio on a Sunday evening. You had to try to get people not to talk as it would pick up the slightest noise, not to mention having a propensity to feedback. It must have been autumn half term, as I remember listening to the song over and over in the morning and again over the next few days. I had to keep rewinding the cassette back to Ram Jam's 'Black Betty', which I patiently had to wait for the ending of before the infamous rattling bass and drum intro kicked into the magic that was 'No More Heroes'.

That was the start of my love affair with the Stranglers. Soon after, they appeared on the children's TV show *Tiswas*. Hugh and Jet were being interviewed by Sally James and Hugh kept lobbing sweets (or nuts) out of a paper bag up in the air for the kids sat in the audience behind them to catch. We thought this was very punky and funny. And I remember my middle brother and I visiting our cousin in Huddersfield and miming repeatedly to the *No More Heroes* album with improvised instruments.

1982 was the year I became an obsessive fan. I got a copy of *Live X (Cert)* from my eldest brother. The album reawakened my fascination with the Stranglers' sound. I would spend hours trying to draw photos of the band from the tiny images on the inner sleeve. Around this time, I paid another visit to my cousin's house where he introduced me to the bass guitar. I realised how much I loved the sound of JJ Burnel's bass and decided I wanted to be him. He looked incredibly cool and his bass sound was like no other. That was the start of my life as a musician, and many years later I would play bass in the group Kolony. We never made it to the big time, but our single was played on XFM radio and for a while a certain Ian Grant (yes, the same Ian Grant!) was trying to get us publicity and support on a tour. The highlight of this period was getting a support slot with Big Country at Shepherd's Bush Empire.

The first time I saw the Stranglers was at Birmingham Odeon in February 1985 with my brother, Phil, and a couple of his friends. It was my first proper gig and I remember being astonished at how many Stranglers fans existed as I made my way through the foyer of the venue. It was rare that you ever saw anyone in the street wearing a Stranglers t-shirt at this point in their career. I was mesmerised by the multitude of hundreds of painted jackets and paraphernalia.

I had waited what seemed like an eternity to see the band, so I was very excited. The music playing through the PA before the band came on was a succession of Vladimir-themed songs the band had recorded as B-sides and solo projects, so I was quite certain this was the beginning of the build up to their taking to the stage. The tension was building.

I knew the band must be about to hit the stage, though I was confused as to where the mic stands were (it turned out the band were using radio mics). My mate, Gary, asked me to turn around and look up at the circle. From where we were standing in the front stalls, it was an impressive sight; a sea of a thousand heads or more spanning the auditorium. As the last Vladimir song ended, the house lights dipped and the audience roared.

The unequivocal tone of Hugh's voice delivered the 'Aural Sculpture Manifesto' through the PA and there were just a tantalising few moments left before I would finally see the band that I adored and who were my world. 'Behold, the Stranglers bring you *Aural Sculpture*' and, with that wait over, a strobe light dominated the scene and I saw the back of JJ running across the stage. Then a flashing image of Hugh appeared from nowhere and he began to play the first notes of 'Something Better Change'. It was the loudest thing I had ever heard in my life!

Jet's snare kicked the song into action and there was an explosion of coloured lights as I was propelled forward and found myself clinging onto a spider web punky jumper not unlike the sort JJ wore late '77 and '78. I was quite small for a 14-year-old and battled to stay standing with the crowd surging forward. Simultaneously, the music was incredibly loud and distorted, because we were very near the PA. It was the most terrifying and wonderful thing I had ever experienced! Fortunately, one of our party managed to drag me out to safety and I was able to pogo to the gig with joy thereafter. It sounds like a cliche, but it really does still make the back of my hairs rise when I think of that moment in time.

DOMINION THEATRE

27/28 FEBRUARY 1985, LONDON, UK

LEE WILLIAMS

In 1978 I started secondary school. Punk had evolved (or dissolved) into new wave and the Stranglers had put out *Black and White* and pretty much ruled the singles chart. Making new friends who had older brothers, I was introduced to the Stranglers and haven't looked back since.

Lee Williams first saw the Meninblack in 1985

Seeing the Meninblack for the first time should've been at Hammersmith Odeon in 1983, but alas that was cancelled due to issues with the security (bouncers). 1985 was the year of my live baptism, by which time they were already eight albums strong. My anticipation for the shows in London at the Dominion was through the roof. I had saved up my money from my first job to buy loads of merchandise, along with going two nights in a row.

The opening notes of 'Something Better Change' had me jumping up and down like a fucking frog on steroids, which didn't stop until the last encore. By the end of two nights of this, my knees were black and blue from the seats in front but I didn't care. I had at last witnessed the full force of the Stranglers. Their brooding music giving way to more melodic tunes was an aural delight.

As much I have developed a love of different genres of music over the years, and fads have come and gone, my undying love and admiration for the Stranglers have only grown. I always felt a natural affinity for them being the outsiders. For fuck's

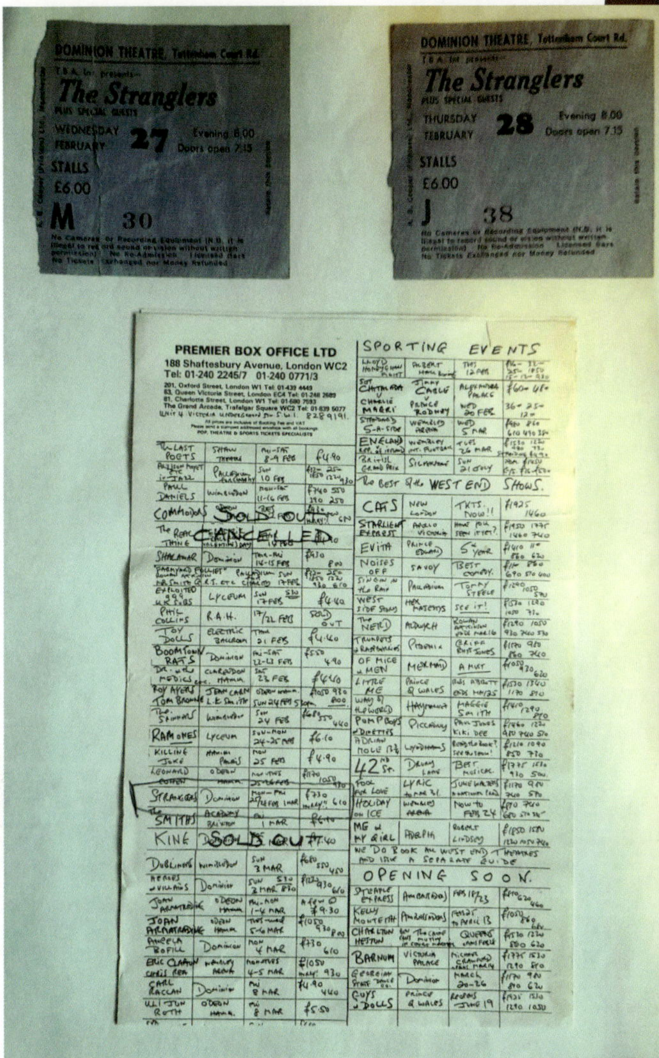

sake, they released a punk single with saxophone! They have carved their own niche in music history. Walking their own path has enabled them to stay true to who they are, even through line up changes, and even with the sad death of Dave, they managed to put out a chart-topping album.

I have met many of the fantastic Familyinblack along the way, and

Lee has met Dave (above) and Hugh (opposite)

love being forever associated with the Stranglers. Having clocked in at over 100 times of seeing the band live, it's never enough. For me there will never be another band like 'em. I even named my second son Jet. Fly straight.

BOURNEMOUTH INTERNATIONAL CENTRE

3 MARCH 1985, BOURNEMOUTH, UK

JAMES MCCARRAHER

I first saw the band on their *Aural Sculpture* tour. A group of us travelled from Romsey and it was a massively exciting occasion. We were surprised to find the support act was a ventriloquist with a monkey. When he realised he had lost the audience (he was persistently coined), he proceeded to shove the monkey's head up its arse, which was rather funny at the time. The Stranglers were magnificent and we shouted to each other excitedly over the music as each song was played, chattering animatedly and dancing to the older songs.

A few months later, I was at a record fayre in Southampton and saw a bootleg tape of the very same gig. Without hesitation I was parted from my cash and my mate Pete Rickman and I huddled around a tape player to relive that wonderful night. And what did we hear?

Pete and I chatting throughout the gig with the music in the background. We must have been standing next to the bootlegger!

HORDERN PAVILION

10 MAY 1985, SYDNEY, AUSTRALIA

DAVID PETERSON

I was living in Sydney at the time of the *Aural Sculpture* tour and went to the Hordern Pavilion show. I didn't know much of the Stranglers music in those days apart from hearing a few songs on the radio but I was curious about them. I mainly went because Hunters and Collectors were the support act. Before the boys came on stage, they played the 'Aural Sculpture Manifesto' with an

David Peterson was at the Hordern Pavilion

accompanying slide show which whipped the crowd into a frenzy. It was a fantastic performance and before the show was finished, I knew I was going to their second Sydney show at Selina's at the Coogee Bay Hotel a few days later. By the second date I'd begun a love affair with the band that endures to this day. This was the tour when the whole stage including the drum riser was covered in white sheeting. The boys (of course) were in black, which made for some nice stage lighting effects. It was the first time I'd seen a band wearing headset microphones that didn't require a cable and so JJ and Hugh were strutting all over the stage.

I didn't get to see them again until 2016 when I saw them at Thebarton Theatre in Adelaide. They were still as great as I remembered them from 30 years before, and I've subsequently seen them in 2018 at the Thebarton Theatre and in 2020 at the smaller and more intimate Governor Hindmarsh Hotel in Adelaide. I have special memories of seeing Dave play that night.

PINK POP FESTIVAL, BURGEMEESTER DAMEN SPORTPARK

27 MAY 1985, GELEEN, BELGIUM

MARK CONNOLLY

Mark Connolly was at the Pink Pop Festival in 1985

I went to the *Pink Pop Festival* with SIS (Stranglers Information Service). I was at the front by the fencing and a journalist starting to talk to us. He then tried inciting us to cause trouble and tear the fence down. Being the law-abiding citizens that we were, we respectfully declined. However, the Stranglers came on and after a few songs stormed off the stage, never to return. Unfortunately, this resulted in us trying to tear the fence down! The journalist was very happy and took a few photos and gave us the thumbs up.

On the coach returning home, we approached the Belgian border and were informed that border control may search us. This caused one of the passengers near to me to panic. He had bought a stash of weed. Someone had a loaf of bread and so several of us ate weed sandwiches. I didn't, because I am a law-abiding citizen.

The coach stopped at border control and a couple of officers walked down the coach and picked two to be searched. Guess who was one of the two? Yes, yours truly. Luckily it was not a full body and cavity search! Not that they would have found anything as I am a law-abiding citizen (as previously stated).

ROB MURRAY

After seeing the 'And Friends' Rainbow gig, I went to every London and the South East gig for years as well as festivals home and abroad. At the Pink Pop Festival, we had a 'Brits versus Locals' footie match on the field and one of the Belgian guys ran into a wasp's nest and got very badly stung.

Dave, who had travelled with us on the coach, had fallen asleep drunk on the field and the medic guys came and put him on a stretcher and wouldn't let him off despite his protests that he was fine! He didn't make the coach back and I didn't see him again for a few months.

And I remember driving back from a gig in Eastbourne. I was dying for a pee and pulled over on a sleety black night to go by the side of the road. I couldn't see a thing and, as I tried to find a hedgerow, I fell straight into a ditch that was full of something like slurry. It stank so much that I ended up taking my clothes off and binning them. I drove home naked, hoping I wouldn't get pulled over.

The band have really influenced my life in a lot ways, and may even have kept me alive. Throughout school, I only had one idea of what I wanted to be when I left, and that was to join the army and become a paratrooper I applied as soon as I could, and had to wait quite a long time before I could go through selection and then training. I had started to learn the guitar and the first song I learnt was the bass line to 'Peaches', followed by 'Hanging Around'.

I spent hours sitting there trying to learn the songs. There was no internet or *YouTube* then so you had to do it by ear. By the time I got to basic training, I was in a band and wanted to be just like JJ Burnel. I had also taken up karate which later turned to boxing. So by the time I got to basic training for the army, my whole attitude had changed. I loved the physical side but hated the discipline and the sergeant going on about dying for the Queen. I called him a dick or something and got a right good hiding from him in return. Not long after, the major called me in to discuss my attitude and it was decided there was no future for me in HM Forces. The following year, so many of those guys were killed in the Falklands. I can't help thinking that if I hadn't started playing guitar and wanting to be in a band so much, I could well have gone to the Falklands and been killed myself.

Years later, I told this story to Hugh, who my band supported, and he was great to us. It was the first time I had met any of the band, as I'd avoided it in case they turned out to be dicks. However, I have met them all a few times now and they have been great every time. My band still plays and we try to put in little Stranglers references

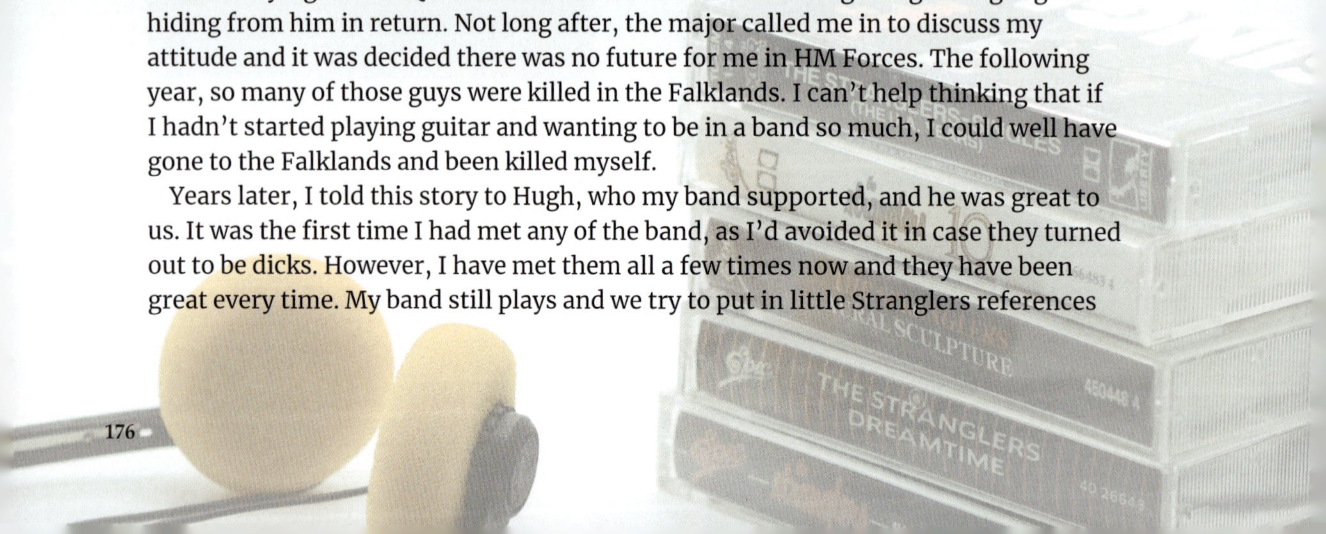

to songs here and there. My biggest ambition is to support the guys one day. Time's running out but we'll keep trying.

I still go see them whenever I can. I have taken two of my three kids to see them and I have pictures of them with JJ and Baz. There's just my little boy to go. He loves the music. His favourite song is 'Nice 'n' Sleazy', or 'squeeze it', as he calls it.

I don't cry often, but I did when Dave died. It made me realise that a huge part of my life will probably come to an end soon. It amazes me that the band can still touch me all these years later, as they have with the latest album. Thanks for being there for so long and for the memories. Like the song says, these are from the smiles when I look upon your face.

ROCK IN ATHENS, PANATHINAIKOS STADIUM

26 JULY 1985, ATHENS, GREECE

JONATHAN STUBLEY

This was the first time that I had seen the band abroad, having driven all the way from England, via Belgium, Germany, Italy and what was then Yugoslavia to see them. The stand out memory is the opening number, 'Nice 'n' Sleazy'. This was the only time that I have ever seen the band take the stage one at a time. Jet ambled out first, at about 0.3 miles per hour, before taking his seat and starting up that familiar drum pattern. Hugh was out next, joining in with a staccato B minor on his guitar before Dave appeared behind the keys. JJ was out last, ripping in to the famous bassline, and we were away. As you would expect, it was rather hot in the mosh pit and the crew took to soaking us with a hose pipe.

My other highlights and lowlights include: seeing Hugh play as a Strangler for the last time on the *10* tour in Brixton in 1990; walking out in tears during 'Toiler' at a Mark II gig in London in the '90s, thinking it was all over; the 'resurrection' of the band as a four piece in 2006 at the Shepherd's Bush Empire, with the added pleasure of meeting Baz and Dave at their hotel after the gig; going to the Albert Hall for the Proms; *Rattus at the Roundhouse*; the 2011 Convention in London; seeing Jet perform with the band for the last time in Bristol; the premiere (and last ever showing?) of the film *Death and Night and Blood* in Brixton; and the 2019 tour, the last time that I saw Dave play with the band. And 2021 saw a triumphant return in Valenciennes with Toby, followed by two fantastic gigs - at Brighton and Cambridge - in memory of Dave.

SOMETIME IN 1986

SOMERSHAM, UK

JEZ BOTTLEY

I had taken up Karate around 1982. In 1986 and I found myself posted to RAF Wyton in Cambridgeshire and in a dojo in Somersham with none other than Sensei Burnel. I recall being very apprehensive on the day he first showed up but he's a very humble guy, especially in the dojo, and I really enjoyed my time training with him and being a founder member of Shidokan UK.

At the Stranglers Convention in 1992, JJ led a karate workshop and as part of that I had to punch him. This was a test of strength and conditioning as JJ took punches from various karateka but it was my punch that made him rebound, wince and say, 'Now that's my student!' In 2022, he stabbed me in the chest with his powerful finger and said, 'You should never have stopped training.' He was right.

During the time that I knew JJ, whilst he lived in Somersham, I felt very blessed to share time with him and occasionally other Stranglers at the Windmill pub or in his studio, where I heard previews of various Stranglers albums before they were released. I got to see the band rehearse in his studio on one occasion, and it was interesting to see the inner workings of this band – warts and all!

I also spent a couple of hours in Paul Roberts' company one sunny afternoon at JJ's house. JJ was away and Paul was house sitting with his girlfriend. It was around the time of *About Time* being rehearsed. He's a really lovely bloke and it saddens me when people malign him. I went to see him perform at the Brewery Tap in Peterborough some years after he had left the Stranglers and he remembered my name. I was impressed!

On my 40th birthday in 2005, Hugh Cornwell played the Wood Green Animal Shelter in Godmanchester. Imagine that - my hero playing the sleepy town where I live. I snuck round to the Portakabin that was Hugh's dressing room, with my mate Andy as back up, to ask Hugh if he'd dedicate a song for my birthday. He was rehearsing with his band. The door was wide open but I tentatively knocked on the door between songs and made my request. His response… 'Fuck off!'

I've been fortunate to see Baz and Dave perform in Somersham a number of times over the years, and two lovelier chaps you'll never meet. It's so sad that Dave is no longer with us. I'd often asked Baz if I could play drums for him and Dave when they play but never got the gig and never will now. They say you should never meet your heroes but I'm glad to have met all of these heroes over the years. What a band.

12TH ANNUAL WORLD BATHTUB RACING COMPETITION

6 JULY 1986, CAGNES-SUR-MER, FRANCE

PAUL JENNER

In July 1986, JJ and a group of fans participated in the 12th Annual World Bathtub Racing Competition down in his early stomping grounds in the French Riviera. The crew created a Viking long ship of sorts, christened the Ravenlunatic, from bath tubs and buoyancy aids and carted it all the way from the UK to Cagnes-sur-Mer by coach to take part in a 500 metre race for human powered craft.

JJ had seen this event the previous summer with his family, who lived in the area, and thought it might be worth a crack to enter a British team of Stranglers fans, so the *Stranglers Information Service* set about orchestrating a motley gang of folks to take on 'The Challenge'.

Through word-of-mouth, the initial meetings in North London brought a slew of ideas and participants eager to knock together a three-bath prototype, strap it to a van and test it in a local pond. JJ participated in these early sessions, hauling the tubs onto the van and testing their sturdiness in and out of the water. Despite many spills and dunkings, avoiding sewage outlets and rethinking the float formation, our newly painted jet-black vessel was ready for sturdier testing in Cambridgeshire. But our shenanigans attracted the ire of the locals and then the boys in blue, who came down to investigate but left us to it following a water safety lecture.

Onwards in a bath-carrying convoy to a quarry lake near JJ's place in Cambridgeshire, watched this time by Dave and Pam Greenfield who delivered, the Challengers reassembled the craft - now including a dragon figurehead, *Raven* shields and mast with a red *Raven* logo sail - to put it through its paces once more prior to the French trip.

Allons en France! After a seemingly never-ending coach journey to the Côte d'Azur, bedecked in our Challenge t-shirts, we arrived in Nice with a day to spare to chill out in the sun prior to the big event. Come race day, the weather had turned and blue skies had made way for the overcast tones of a storm somewhere out in the Med.

Spirits remained high as we agreed who would sail with JJ in the Ravenlunatic. I was one of the lucky six. JJ registered our craft with the committee and set about adding to our fierce-looking boat with the crew all in black by spraying our hair red with matching red beards!

We marched our vessel down to the packed harbour, ably supported by our cheerleaders the Stranglerettes, waving our hammers, growling and making general Viking noises, and ready to launch our beast against the massed amazing-looking creations of the French, Swiss and Germans which included a football pitch, a banana boat and a tank! Once we had launched into the marina, the banter and baiting started with our raucous crew boarding other vessels and pelting them with eggs and fruit following JJ's cry of 'attaaaaack!'

CAGNES-SUR-MER
OFFICE MUNICIPAL DES ANIMATIONS ET DES FETES
★★★
12e CHAMPIONNAT DU MONDE DE COURSES EN BAIGNOIRES

★ Diplôme d'Honneur ★
décerné à

M. Paul Jenner

Le Délégué Culturel pour la Baignoire Jeune :

Le Concierge du Complexe Portuaire :

1986

La Présidente du Home-Club Nautique :

Le Plombier Chef :

Paul Jenner and JJ took part in the World Bathtub Racing Competition

All photos Paul Jenner

The race got underway just as a squall arrived, and negotiating the choppy open Mediterranean outside of the marina proved a challenge for all of the racers. Charging headlong into three-foot breakers, we went for broke, narrowly missing other boats in an effort to distance ourselves from the narrowly encroaching shoreline. We persevered, powering forward past the early leaders and through the waves. Then – disaster! A wave crashed into our bows, turning us clean over. We tried in vain to right her as the bath tubs did as they should – hold water – but no amount of Viking helmet bailing would get us back on track and we ended up beached as part of the day's jetsam.

We were cover stars of the following day's *Le Nice Matin* - which said of our efforts that we didn't even have time to 'invoke Nelson' to save us from our predicament – but the Union Jack was to be seen as I emerged from the surf with our flag, salvaged from the mast.

Despite no one winning or even finishing the race – out of 18 teams, six didn't even start and five didn't reach 200 metres - the Ravenlunatic team were surprise winners at the evening reception recognising our efforts and us being British! JJ's acceptance speech stated that God had smiled on us with English weather for the day… to no avail. Each of the crew received a medal and JJ took home the trophy.

The following day the challengers took a trip to Grasse, perfume capital of the South, for an afternoon picnic at an idyllic hilltop lake, messing about on the water prior to the journey back north to the UK. A great fan event but we've yet to take up 'the challenge' again!

SCOTT NEIL

'Build a boat from old bathtubs, make it look like a Viking longship and then race it in the sea.' As madcap enterprises go, on a scale of one to ten, it was right up there at twelve point six.

It all started when Jean-Jacques Burnel watched the annual international bathtub race at Cagnes-Sur-Mer, near Nice, in the south of France in 1985. He wanted to assemble a team for the following year, and early in 1986 put an invitation out through the Stranglers Information Service seeking fans willing to come together to build a bathtub boat.

For me and best pal Rob, both aged 19, being 'up for a lark' was a quintessential part of life. We trundled 100 miles for the first meeting of The Challenge group in a semi-detached house in North London. A mixed group of about 20 gathered. JJ came too. We drew up a plan of action, indicating which components we could source for the bathtub boat and bring along to the next gathering, when work would begin. Before departing, we tested the structural integrity of the roof of a London black cab by sitting on it for a team picture.

I secured a dozen large plastic containers that could be used as buoyancy for the boat. These were fitted in place at the first working weekend, where the bathtub boat started to take shape. The design was a Viking longship, after the instrumental track 'Longships' on *The Raven*. The main sail and team t-shirts would feature the raven logo from the album. The boat would be known as the Ravenlunatic.

Scott Neil was one of those who took part in the bathtub challenge

The boat was soon in transit, or rather strapped to the top of a transit van. We took it to a nearby public pond in Barnet, North London to test its seaworthiness. Who knows what the locals thought of this motley bunch paddling the lake in three bathtubs? However, one of them not only thought, 'Call the police.' They actually did.

Two police officers arrived, having been told that some kids were messing about on the lake. The officers were surprised to find the 'kids' were clearly not wet behind the ears (well, not yet as we hadn't capsized). JJ was a virtual elder statesman kid at 34. The lead officer gave an obligatory spiel about the importance of observing the rules of water safety, then beat a retreat. Meanwhile, we were delighted the boat floated, albeit in a slightly bouncy Loch Ness Monster fashion. A bit of lateral strengthening was needed.

The boat building and testing then moved to rural Cambridgeshire. A quarry lake near JJ's home became the venue for further sea trials. The bathtubs were painted black and a dragon masthead was added, along with a central mast and black sail with the depiction of a red raven.

With the boat now starting to resemble a Viking longship, a call was made to a freelance music press photographer encouraging him to hasten to the lake near St Ives for a few snaps. A group of us, including the Stranglers' keyboardist Dave Greenfield, hopped into Nik's black cab - the one with the now slightly dented roof - for a short ride to a disused quarry lake.

It was a tight squeeze in the taxi. Greenfield had his shoulder travel bag - an ever-present accessory, the contents of which followers of the band have forever guessed at. He rested his enigmatic bag on his lap. I gazed at it and wondered if perhaps it contained one of his many pet rats, the rodent synonymous with the band since their debut album *Rattus Norvegicus* nine years earlier. But no question was asked. What else was I, a teenager awed by the presence and aura of mystique of the musical maestro, to do? Besides, there was work at hand to test the bathtub boat.

We assembled at the quarry lake to take the boat out for a few laps. The afternoon was ticking away - where was the freelance photographer? There was a call. He had reached St Ives, but it was St Ives in Cornwall, some 300 miles away. Fortunately, a second photographer was despatched and reached the lake before the sun went down to capture the Ravenlunatic in all her glory. The snaps appeared in the *Record Mirror* and *Melody Maker* music papers.

Everything was ready. At the beginning of July, a 52-seater coach took the team and the boat almost 800 miles to the south of France. The bathtubs were stowed in the luggage compartments. A further 20 supporters joined the trip, helping reduce the cost-per-head of the journey. With everyone decked out in black Challenge t-shirts, featuring *The Raven*, we turned heads on the promenade at Nice. Viking headgear, fake red beards and our posse of pom-pom cheerleaders completed the scene. We were ready to rumble.

The Ravenlunatic was reassembled on a stony beach at Cagnes-sur-Mer, a few miles from Nice. A race team was picked from the original core group. The rest of us helped and added vocal support from the beach and quay.

Then something freaky happened to the weather. A storm squall suddenly blew in from nowhere, which meant the race itself did not really take place. The boats played around in the safety of the walled harbour, until a few tried their luck against sea god Neptune, including Ravenlunatic. None survived intact.

But really the escapade was less about the actual race and more about putting together a team, and over the course of four months building a faux Viking longship from a few bathtubs, having fun and forging friendships along the way. The next day the coach was driven into the wooded hills surrounding Nice where there was a freshwater lake that JJ knew of. There we spent an afternoon swimming and floating around in salvaged pieces of the Ravenlunatic. Among those at the picnic was graphic artist Jean-Luke Epstein, who had helped construct the boat, and who designed the majority of the Stranglers' record covers during the 1980s.

Before leaving this idyllic location, we posed in front of our trusty Wallace Arnold coach for a mass picture of crew, boat-building team and supporters. And then it was over. The spring and summer of 1986 was all about having a spirit of adventure, going into the unknown, doing something a little crazy and different and having fun. It was a madcap enterprise worthy of celebration.

PLAYHOUSE THEATRE

25 OCTOBER 1986, EDINBURGH, UK

MIKE ABBOTT

On the *Dreamtime* tour, Jez and I had found out which hotel the Stranglers were staying at and ventured there after the gig. There were quite a few other fans in the hotel lounge bar and we got chatting to a girl who was on her own. Before the band entered the room everyone was asked to leave. However, the girl declared that she was there to collect a signed *Dreamtime* LP. At the gig, Hugh had invited girls to dance on stage to 'Nice 'n' Sleazy' with the best dancer getting a signed copy of the as yet unreleased new LP. She got to stay and, as we were with her, so did Jez and I.

We had a few words with Dave and Jet before we went over to Hugh at the bar. I told Hugh of my Stranglers addiction, to which he remarked that perhaps their records should come with a health warning. I commented on the hot girl from Xmal Deutschland, the support band, who were also there. Hugh proceeded to introduce me to her, probably to get rid of me.

We got to sit down with JJ who talked about motorbikes, holidays and winding Hugh up amongst many other things. I remember the girl who had won the LP inviting JJ to afternoon tea, which I thought was a bit odd and probably not on JJ's agenda but he did reply in a gentlemanly way. I mentioned that tickets for gigs were sometimes hard to get – this was before the internet and when you couldn't even phone to book, as application had to be by post unless you visited the box office in person. JJ kindly offered to help out if ever there was a problem.

Afterwards, I drove us to Carlisle where we were stopping at another fan's house before travelling on to the Newcastle gig the next day. Jez promptly fell asleep in the car. Becomingly increasingly tired myself, I stopped in a layby to get 40 winks. Jez woke up in a panic, thinking we had crashed!

ODEON THEATRE

29 OCTOBER 1986, BIRMINGHAM, UK

STEVE BIZLEY

During the mid to late '80s, the music wasn't as good as it once was. There were very good tracks on each LP, but the albums didn't quite have the full punch of the first releases. But I remained loyal and continued to attend as many gigs as possible. On the *Dreamtime* tour, I waited outside Birmingham Odeon for the band to arrive. It seemed like an age. It was the first time that I realised that Hugh didn't have full respect for loyal fans. Having waited to get the *Dreamtime* LP signed – all the other band members signed the cover, and JJ in particular was very kind, signing it 'to patient Steve' - Hugh was confrontational and simply scribbled a few meaningless lines. It was a real disappointment.

Despite this I continued to follow the band in different cities – London, Wolverhampton, Oxford, Leicester, Birmingham and a turning point for me was Newport. I went to the gig and took my place at the front as usual and, as always, I was pushed against the barrier. The day after my ribs were really painful and I realised that, at the age of 30, it was time to step back a little from the front!

READING UNIVERSITY

17 MARCH 1987, READING, UK

ADAM BROADWAY

Adam Broadway was at Reading in 1987, and Cambridge in 2022

I had already seen the Stranglers four times. My first gig was *Reading Rock* in 1983 with mud and hippies. The university gig was full of local punks and post-punks plus a few students. The locals seemed to be the dominant crowd. A few punks and skinheads were down the front next to the stage and seemed a bit lost in time. They

started to gob onto the stage, and at Hugh, who stopped the gig and shouted at the 'gobbers' to stop saying something like, 'Oi, you lot! Fucking grow up, punk died years ago and so did spitting. Carry on and we'll stop the gig!' Those responsible were truly humiliated. They stopped and the show continued.

BARROWLAND BALLROOM

22 MARCH 1987, GLASGOW, UK

STEVE GLADWIN

Steve Gladwin with JJ

I was born in 1968 in Glasgow, so I was too young for the Stranglers' early days. But I was a fan from the age of ten when me and my older brother shared our pocket money to purchase *Black and White*. I never managed to see them until two consecutive nights at the Barowlands for the *Dreamtime* tour. I have seen them well over a hundred times since. The *In the Night* tour stands out. When Paul Roberts took the helm after Hugh's departure, he put a spark back in the band and didn't get the credit he deserved for keeping the band going. My most memorable gig was 1991 in Milton Keynes. It was a great, sunny day that was broadcast on Radio 1 and I'm still listening to it today.

HAMMERSMITH ODEON

30 MARCH 1987, LONDON, UK

ANDY KENDALL

Andy Kendall saw three nights on the Dreamtime tour and got the band's autographs

The years rolled on and I started to increase the number of gigs I was attending per tour. Standout memories include climbing up on stage and dancing next to JJ at Bradford St George's Hall, getting autographs at various events and sound checks, two coach trips to Europe, and meeting some great people along the way. At Hammersmith Odeon in 1987, the band played a three-night run on the second leg of the *Dreamtour*. We stayed in a less than salubrious hostel near Gloucester Road Underground station for these gigs and got autographs on the last afternoon. At the soundcheck on the last day, we were complaining about the bouncers not letting people who had stalls tickets move to the front, and I naively thought it would be a good idea to ask Hugh if he could do something about the situation. His eyes flashed at me and he said, 'Oh the bouncers! Well, you talk to this man over here...' which was embarrassing, but funny too.

As it happened, we had a chat with the head of the venue security and he got us down to the very front, which was a great way to end the tour before heading back to the comparatively sleepy Midlands. I do believe it was at this event that I met über fan, Owen Carne, in the upstairs bar, a man well known to all fans and a diehard supporter. Our paths crossed many times over the next few years and occasionally I have been able to sell him the odd poster that he doesn't have, but it's rare, as he has just about anything that's worth getting your hands on.

During these years there were some eventful moments, which unsurprisingly involved JJ. I remember at Warwick University on the *Dreamtour* when an annoying character got on stage (he had been annoying people in the audience) and wrestled the band's minder to the floor of the stage. JJ promptly walked over and put his foot on the guy and looked like he was pointing at him and doing something with his arms. The guy got up with his nose bleeding and arms in the air, as if in victory, and jumped back into the audience.

On another occasion, at Wolverhampton Civic Hall, someone in the audience threw water and it went over JJ's bass. Incandescent at the irresponsible behaviour of this individual, he stopped playing, pulled his bass above his head and smashed it to the ground. He then made an announcement that if the perpetrator had any balls, they should make themselves known. He jumped down off the stage and I could not see clearly what happened but was told afterwards that he head butted somebody!

The Stranglers provided the perfect escape from the struggles of life at school and the boredom of living in a parochial town in the Midlands. For years I would hop on the train on Saturdays over to Birmingham, often on my own, to seek out rare records and posters. I think the independence I craved and enjoyed gave me the confidence and desire to break out from my humble home town life and head off to the smoke for life at university. So, thank you Stranglers, for my degree!

Whilst I'm not quite the obsessive fan I once was, they will always be my favourite band and I am eternally grateful for their helping shape my life.

UNIVERSITY OF WARWICK

16 APRIL 1987, COVENTRY, UK

MIKE ABBOTT

Perhaps the most bizarre Stranglers gig I've ever attended. For some reason the gig was switched from the Butterworth Hall to the Student Union building. It was rammed with people trying to see the small put-up stage from any vantage point they could. It really wasn't appropriate for a gig this size. Coventry City were due to play Leeds United in the FA Cup semi-final in a few days and in the mayhem before the Stranglers came on, some Coventry fans started their football chants. Myself and other Leeds fans present reciprocated with our songs and the atmosphere was becoming increasingly tense – until the Stranglers emerged and all football differences were forgotten.

HOLLYWOOD PALLADIUM

8 MAY 1987, LOS ANGELES, CALIFORNIA

PAUL NEYRINCK

Paul Neyrinck was part of a ruse to fool Hugh and the others into believing there was press interest in LA

My friend Dean Peterson and I travelled to Los Angeles in 1987 to see the Stranglers around the period after *Dreamtime* was released. We got in the queue at the venue very early, around noon - just us and a few other people. Shortly thereafter, a woman approached us and explained that a local college newspaper had failed to show up for an interview with the band and asked if we would like to meet the Stranglers. The only caveat was that we would have to pretend we were reporters scheduled to interview them. After assurances that we would not lose our place in line, we agreed to the charade.

She took us to the rooftop pool of a nearby hotel. Jet and JJ were there. JJ was extremely surly and when Dean asked him a question, he replied rudely and then abruptly left. Jet, on the other hand, was incredibly friendly and walked with Dean and I down a dark hallway and into a room, where Hugh was relaxing. I asked Hugh about 'Mayan Skies' and he talked about how he was inspired by a trip he made to Mexico. Dean, sitting on one of the twin beds, noticed a sizeable stack of pound notes within easy grasp, but resisted the temptation.

Afterward, they took us back to the venue and our place at the front of the queue. I have long since felt guilt for being part of a ruse to fool the band into believing there was interest from the local media.

ASTORIA

29 APRIL 1988, LONDON, UK

ADRIAN ANDREWS

It was almost a case of blink and you missed them. If you lived too far from London it is all

the more likely that you would have missed them. The pulse of The Purple Helmets throbbed with vigour for a couple of short years, in which time they only played a glanful(sic!) of gigs in the London environs, plus some brief appearances in France.

The Stranglers had toured heavily throughout 1985, 1986 and into 1987 playing dates all over Europe and in the US and Australia. The Stranglers were overdue for a break.

To a fan like myself, 18 in 1987 and only recently for the first time in possession of some disposable income (thanks to my weekends spent mopping up blood as a domestic hand in my local A&E department), this band hiatus, whilst deserved, was quite frankly a major disappointment for me. I had some money, independence and was raring to go, but The Stranglers had gone to ground.

I did what I could in 1988. Tickets were bought for a planned AIDS benefit at Wembley Arena in where the band were to play alongside The Communards, amongst others. As a result of bad promotion, this gig was pulled and although JJ responded to my written moan by putting myself and Steve Tyas on the guest list for the band's gig in Berlin the following month, the logistics of getting to a gig in the Middle of East Germany ruled the offer out. Dusseldorf and Milton Keynes followed, but two dates were a poor substitute for a tour.

So how exactly was this Stranglers shaped hole in my life to be filled, enter the form of The Purple Helmets (on reading that line back it sounds wrong in every way!).

The Purple Helmets brought together JJ, Dave, well known Stranglers associates, Alex Gifford and John Ellis with Tears For Fears drummer Manny Elias completing the line-up. If the SIS press release for their album 'Ride Again' is to be believed, The Purple Helmets were true rock survivors having completed the traditional Beat group apprenticeship of amphetamine fuelled nights in the clubs of Northern Germany before burning out on the West Coast of America on a breaker of alcohol and Class A substances. But old rockers never die and the lure of the boards brought these five men back together in 1988 to do it all over again. As promotion it read well, but as to its authenticity, well I had my doubts!

In truth The Helmets first stepped out in Rennes in late 1986, but then went to ground again until 1988 when starved Stranglers fans had the first opportunity to see them play dates in London.

It was the first opportunity to see the band in what for me was to be something of a pivotal gig. Three of us made the journey up from my hometown of Burgess Hill (incidentally scene of a very damp, low key date on the 2000 'Alone and Acoustic' tour, a gig I am sure JJ would rather forget, if he has not done so already!). My travelling companions on the day were Adam McCready (an old school friend and a Damned fanatic to boot) and Steve Tyas (with whom I was reunited through the back pages of *Strangled* after meeting at the Reading Festival appearance the previous August).

Taking the tube from Victoria into the centre of town, a search for a cash point took us round the back of the Centre Point building at the junction of Tottenham Court Road and Charing Cross Road. It was here that our paths crossed with another group of people who, judging by their attire, were in the area for the very same reasons as us. Amongst this group were Owen Carne and Paul Cooklin, who became friends then and remain friends to this day.

As fans started to congregate, we took ourselves off to 'The Tottenham', a pub whose facia boasted that it was in fact 'The Only Pub In Oxford Street'. Of 'The Tottenham' even though logic says this must be the case, I would say that it is also the worst pub in Oxford Street and yet in the years to come, it became a regular gathering point for Stranglers related events (I suspect that the pub's proximity to the Dominion Theatre where the band played five consecutive dates on the Aural Sculpture tour is the likely reason it was used as a meeting place).

This was going to be a late one as the doors to The Astoria were not due to open until 11pm. And so it was that we had the chance to make the most of the available licencing hours. This of course meant that the majority of the audience that night were perhaps less 'clear thinking' than perhaps they would be for a normal gig. Either way it seemingly gave the venue security (let's call them 'Bouncers' here) all the excuses they needed in order to apply their heavy discipline with impunity. The violence at the hands of the bouncers is my enduring memory of this gig, both before and during the Helmet's set. A succession of punters were manhandled down the steps to the right of the stage to be delivered into the hands of more bouncers who delivered further blows before ejecting the bruised 'miscreant' through a rear door and onto the street. A similar fate almost befell Steve Tyas. In the gent's toilet (also down those same stairs) Steve has emptied a soap dispenser to respike his hair (those were the days!) and on leaving the loo, a wobble must have caught one of the bouncers eyes. Apparently reading this to be a sign of imminent trouble, a wide-eyed, soapy Steve was picked up (we were all young and skinny then) and hurled through the back door. I am not brave so I can only assume that it was dutch courage, I started to argue with the bouncer to get Steve back into the venue... and somehow it worked.

Nerves were a bit frayed by the time the band eventually came on at about one in the morning. However, tiredness and the early onset of a hangover were swepy away with the opening bars of Sam The Sham's 'Wooly Bully'. 'We are The Purple Helmets... coming from our hearts into your heads' announced Alex Gifford. The set was great, it being, with one exception, a track by track run through of the recently released 'Ride Again' album, with an additional 'I Saw Her Standing There' thrown in for good measure.

It is worth pointing out here that whilst I was familiar

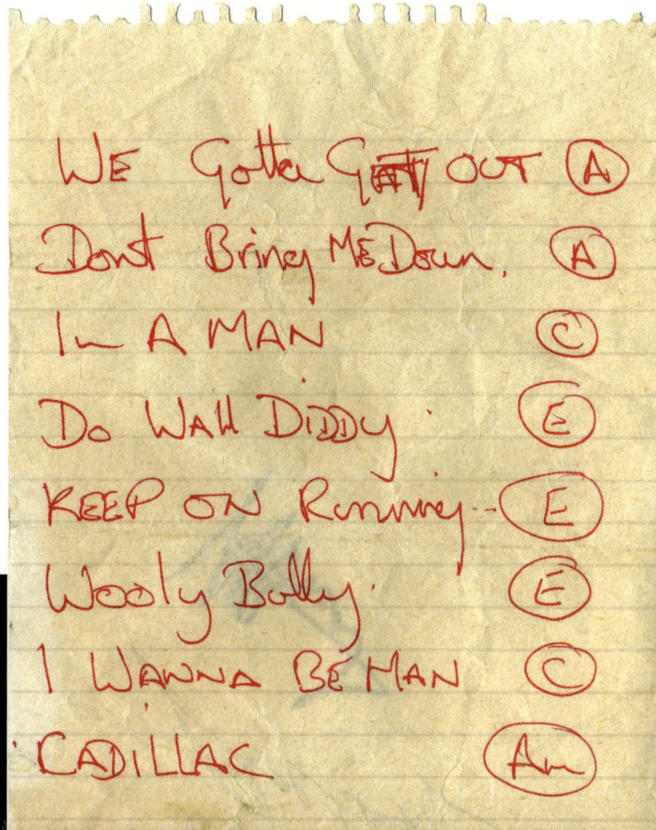

Adrian Andrews on stage with JJ

with some of the songs, many of them were completely new to me (after all I was just 19 and most of the bands of the sixties were as obscure to me as the Stranglers should have been to my own children, were it not for an intensive programme of indoctrination applied from an early age!) The Who and The Kinks? Yes, yes. But The Nashville Teens and Them?

After about an hour the evening's (or rather morning's) entertainment came to an end and with no possibility of getting back to Sussex we headed around to the stage door in the hope of having a word or two. Sometime later, JJ and Dave emerged and duly signed autographs for the gaggle of ardent or stranded fans (both in my case) still loitering by the exit. This was the first time that I had met any of the Stranglers and at the time it was an immense thing. I recall at the time I was struggling with the bass line to a song, 'Strange Little Girl' it was (how so you say, but I was never any good!). JJ gave it some thought, then fingered out the notes on his forearm. This was really something for me, a personalised, albeit brief, bass lesson from Jean Jacques Burnel no less!

As JJ and Dave drove away from the venue, this was our cue to head south. We walked through to Victoria from where we were able to a milk train as far as Gatwick Airport where a couple of uncomfortable hours sleep were attempted in the lounge (these were less security conscious days) before taking the first available Brighton train to complete the homeward journey. Once home, it thankfully being a Saturday, some sleep was possible before regrouping in my local to recount our encounters of the previous night.

HESSENHALLE 1 BERLIN

12 JUNE 1988, BERLIN, GERMANY

COLIN WEAVER

The very first time I heard of the Stranglers was when trying to do some homework (very badly) whilst listening to Top of the Pops in the background. I looked up at

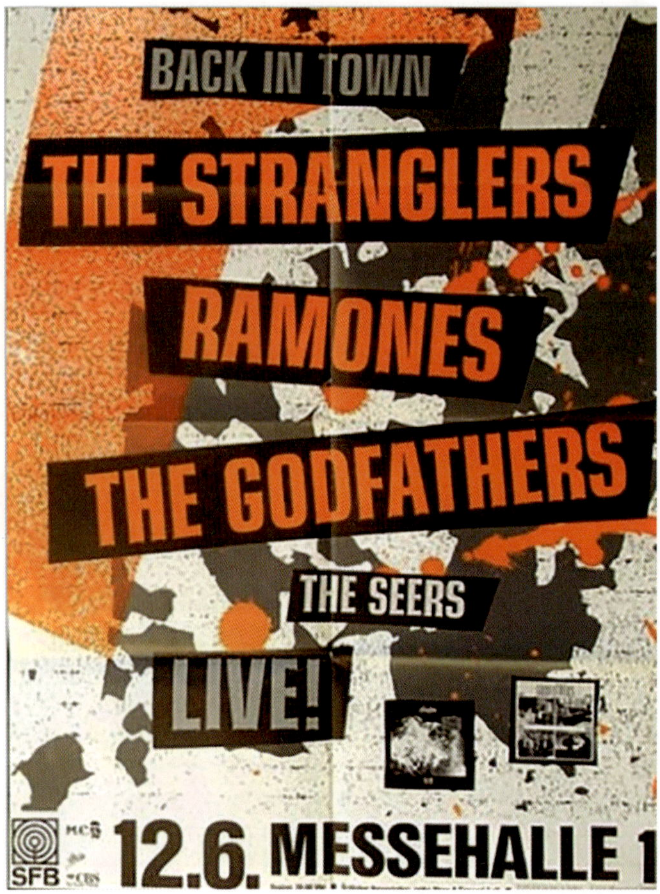

Colin Weaver caught the Stranglers live whilst on holiday in Berlin

the screen and there were the Meninblack playing a really catchy tune called 'Go Buddy Go'. It was love at first sight. It was 1977 and I was 13.

Although I would see the band whenever they came to Birmingham or the Midlands, I really wanted to see the band on foreign soil while I was on holiday. I knew a German guy by the name of Hans Wehr who I was going to see in Berlin in June 1988. Hans and Klaus met me at Berlin Tegel Airport. As we were heading off to the car Hans said, 'Because it is your birthday on the 9th, I have got you a present - a ticket to see the Stranglers.' My reaction was, 'You gotta be fucking joking!'

The arena hosting the gig was massive. I was standing pretty close to some Scottish soldiers who were having the crack amongst themselves. We got talking and they said how they loved being stationed in Berlin because of the nightlife. Then one said, 'Hey, watch this mate.' One guy was lying flat on his back while his pal proceeded to jump up and down on his stomach. The one on his back seemed to really enjoy himself. I thought, 'I hope we don't have to take it in turns.' Just at the right time I found a distraction as who should walk in but Joey Ramone. 'Hey lads, look over there!'

The Stranglers were the headline act. The guys walked on stage to rapturous applause. JJ was wearing a kilt, to the delight of the Scottish contingent. It was a fabulous concert.

PHILIPPSHALLE

13 JUNE 1988, DUSSELDORF, GERMANY

ALAN BATY

Alan Baty was in Dusseldorf in 1988

This was an official SIS trip. Trevor (aka Podga) and myself were two North East lads in our early twenties and we made our way down to London to board a fans German gig bus via Harwich, to see the band play with the Ramones in Dusseldorf. At the same time, the European football championships were on. England had not qualified. It was around this time that English football teams were banned from European competition for well documented reasons. I was expecting the worst.

Podga and I somehow managed to get into the venue as the soundcheck was starting. There was a back door open and with trepidation we crept in and found ourselves at the side of the stage. We saw a little door at the side of the stage, so we opened it and went in. We shut the door and found somewhere to sit right underneath where the Stranglers were sound checking. After about five minutes that door opened and we were discovered by a cleaner. Next thing we knew, we were being dragged from under the stage with not too many questions asked and we were unceremoniously thrown out from whence we came. I can't remember that much about the gig but I do know there seemed to be a lot more German Ramones fans than Stranglers fans, and they weren't happy they weren't the headline act. They also didn't like it when we pushed forward to get them out of the way for the main event of the evening.

STU WEST

I undertook a 24-hour coach journey conveying dedicated Stranglers fans from London Victoria to Dusseldorf, Germany in 1988. The line up was fantastic - the Stranglers, the Ramones and the Godfathers along with the Seers. The journey started late afternoon on the Saturday, two days before the gig, and I was truly not prepared for the endurance of pain and boredom of such travel. The adrenalin soon subsided when the first numb bum was experienced! The thought of having to do this again for the return journey was soul destroying. The carrot of the bargain price for such a trip had tempted me to apply for my first ever passport. The lack of air conditioning on the coach, the sweatiness, my lunchbox empty, all my water consumed, the cramps in my legs, the back pain from the uncomfortable seats - and we hadn't got to the ferry yet! Sleep was attempted but it was quite useless. This journey did not seem like a good idea now.

On arrival into what was probably the parking area of the Philippshalle (I was delirious at this point so details are vague) on Sunday afternoon, there were quite a lot of Stranglers fans waving at our coach and shouting and waving albums excitedly in the air. What a welcome.

As our party descended onto terra firma, it dawned on us that these fans thought we were the band and that our coach was the band's bus! Pens were thrust in our direction to sign their albums and singles. We laughed this off and walked away, but these people were very insistent and demanded signatures. As I was nearest, I agreed to be JJ Burnel and three others decided to be Hugh, Jet and Dave. Weirdly, it worked and off they scuttled, very happy with their bogus signatures. I had to pinch myself to see if I was actually still on the bus and hallucinating all this while and whether maybe in reality I was somewhere in the English Channel. But no - it was real enough.

Backed up by plenty of great German beer and newly formed friendships, the gig on the Monday was quite superb. It's always a treat to hear the song 'Who Wants The World?' in the set.

So I guess this is my confession to posing as JJ. I actually am a bass player, but not that bass player. I joined The Damned in 2004 for a journey of another kind of insanity.

MARQUEE CLUB

24 JUNE 1988, LONDON, UK

ADRIAN ANDREWS

Arranged as a private party for subscribers to *Strangled* magazine this was my one and only gig at one of the most famous rock venues in the world. Shortly after this gig, The Marquee Club (which in it's present location had played host to The Who, Hendrix and Bowie etcetc) upped sticks and moved to a larger premises in nearby Charing Cross Road.

Supporting The Helmets on this occasion were JJ's Belgian mates Polyphonic Size. At some point prior to their set, I met a girl, Gunta, who would in time become my wife.

Adrian Andrews at the front of the Marquee stage

BLACKHEATH CONCERT HALL

24 OCTOBER 1988, LONDON, UK

ADAM SALEM

I discovered the Stranglers and their music at the age of four, in 1986, when my uncle decided he'd had enough of my play list of *Thomas the Tank Engine and Friends* on repeat. I had just been given my first Fisher Price cassette player and he gave me a cassette which just said 'The Stranglers' on it. Out went Thomas and in went the Stranglers!

The first song I ever heard was 'Something Better Change', and I remember being blown away by the intro. I used to rewind the tape just to hear it over and over again. From that moment on, and much to my mum's horror, I was a Stranglers fan. I already had *Rattus Norvegicus* and *No More Heroes* and over the course of the year, my uncle gave me copies of *Black and White* and, at the age of five, what became my favourite album of all time, *The Raven*. It's like a soundtrack and a story to which all of the songs fit. 'Longships' going into the title track, 'The Raven', is sheer musical perfection. 'Dead Loss Angeles' goes into the brilliant 'Ice' and so forth, and can you get as perfect a song as 'Baroque Bordello'?

I used to write into SIS a lot when I was younger, and one day when I got home from primary school at ten years old, I found out my letter had been printed in Volume 2 Number 35. That made my day!

I first got to see the band on the *Coup de Grace* tour at Blackheath. I was amazed at how good they were and it was great to see them live in person. Since then, I have seen them 168 times – and counting. I use all my holiday at work to follow the band. My manager always asks me, 'Don't tell me you're going to see the Stranglers again, Adam. Aren't you getting bored of it?' to which I reply, 'No!'

The most memorable times of seeing the band are on Owen Carnes' seven 'Wonky Bus' coach trips to see the band in Europe, starting in 2009 at the Paris Olympia. *La Folie* and *Feline* are particularly big in France so we are often treated to deep cuts that aren't as popular in England. We got the brilliant 'Midnight Summer Dream' with its segue into 'European Female', and at 2014's Lille gig we even got 'La Folie'. There's something for the die-hard fans every time we go to a gig. We think, 'Maybe they will play such-and-such a song,' and it's always a rare treat when they do.

LIVINGSTON FORUM

10 JUNE 1989, LIVINGSTON, UK

DEREK LOWE

I bought tickets for myself and three friends - Paul, Jim and Donald. I hadn't seen the Stranglers with Paul before so we were looking forward to it. I went up to Paul's house on the outskirts of Glasgow city centre for a few drinks to get us in the mood for the gig… as you do! I then began wondering when we were going to get the train in, so I asked Paul to call Glasgow Central to find out the train time. He came back in a bit of a panic. The next train was at seven o'clock and it was already just past six. I called Jim and Donald and told them to get moving. We all got to the station with seconds to spare only to see the train already leaving. The ticket office informed us the next train wasn't until nine o'clock. We were in danger of missing some or all of the gig. Thankfully, Donald's sister let him borrow her car. We got there in time to hear them play new tracks from the forthcoming album, *10*, including 'Let's Celebrate' and 'Someone Like You'. It was a bit of a stressful evening but ended up being a brilliant one.

DAVID GLADWIN

David Gladwin with Jet

My first gig was actually JJ Burnel in the Glasgow Pavilion in 1979 but one of my favourite ones was June 1989 at Livingston Forum. It was a scorching day in Scotland and the gig was packed to capacity.

BRIXTON ACADEMY

12 JUNE 1989, LONDON, UK

JON HOLLAND, AGE 19

Jon Holland dragged himself out of bed to see the Stranglers

I had spent most of the week in bed with glandular fever, feeling close to death. But the ticket on my bedside table was haunting me. With all my remaining energy, I dragged myself out of bed and walked the mile and a half to the venue. As I turned the corner and the Academy came into view, I was surprised by the emptiness of the street. I continued walking but my brain was telling me something was wrong. I arrived and found the doors to locked. I stood there in a daze and finally asked someone what was going on. 'The Stranglers?' he said, 'they were here last night.'

I looked at the ticket... I was a day late. I couldn't believe it. I remember the despair I felt. I could have stayed in bed. I felt like shit.

If there's a moral to this story, it is, 'Don't go to a fucking gig if you've got glandular fever!'

MARQUEE

9 OCTOBER 1989, LONDON, UK

ADRIAN ANDREWS

As mentioned earlier, in the 16 months since their previous engagement at the Marquee, the club had moved a few hundred meters to a new location. Details of this gig are very sketchy in my mind, although looking back on photos of friends at the event it can be guaranteed that at least an hour or two had been endured pre-gig in The Tottenham.

Two things have stayed in my mind from this gig. Gunta and I (now an item since shortly after the first Marquee gig) were in the foyer, close to the doors onto the street, when Dave sauntered in clutching his bag of mysteries. Greetings were exchanged before a rather inebriated Gunta suggested that The Helmets could play in her Ealing bedsit. Dave, then spent the next five minutes explaining in Greenfield-esque detail, the logistical and technical reasons why this wouldn't be possible!

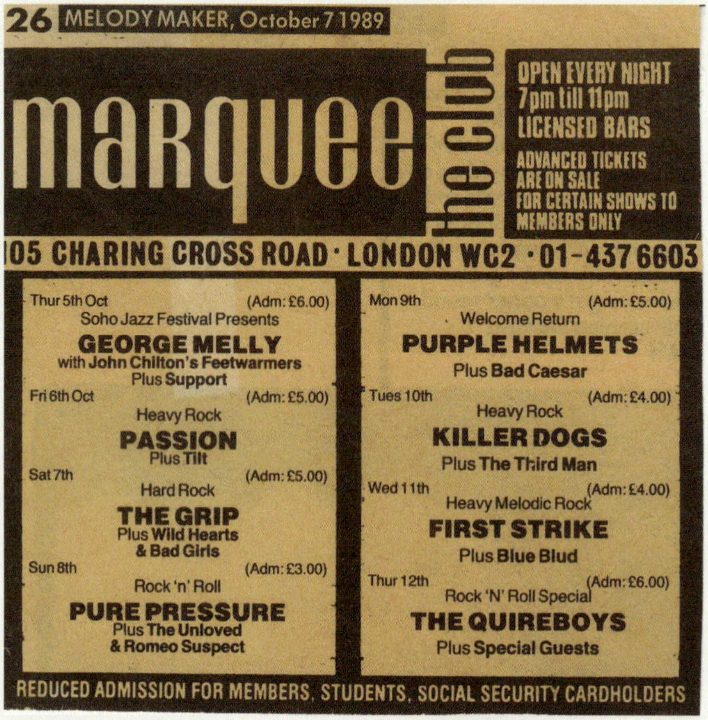

This was one of the last, if not the last full gig played by The Purple Helmets.

The only other recollection I have if of my introducing Gunta to JJ. They shook hands as JJ waited expecting her to say something, but alas no words were forthcoming! Such was the extent of his gallic charm over her at the time!

And that was it for me. The Purple Helmets were a brief musical deviation for band and fans alike. The intimacy of those few gigs offered many of us a chance to interact with the band in a way that had not been possible for a long time, which was great. Perhaps more importantly for me, at this time enduring friendships (not to mention a marriage!) were formed which are reinforced periodically in the pubs of London (happily not The Tottenham)!

ARTS CENTRE

20 FEBRUARY 1990, POOLE, UK

WARREN MEADOWS

I have so many memories of past Stranglers gigs over the years, and I was lucky enough to get close to the band in the years before I had kids. Mind you, some of those memories might get me into trouble. Like the first time I took my girlfriend, Cheryl, now my wife, to see them in 1990 on the *10* tour. I saw their bowler hats in the back of this car. That's how I spotted them on the M5 initially. Yeah, I know they used them on the *Dreamtime* tour, but they were there. I also knew they used white Ford Scorpios 2.9s. So I thought, 'Ideal - they will take me straight to the venue!', the venue being Poole Arts Centre and me having no idea where it was.

Anyhow, they realised they had a tail, so being in a fast car their driver put his foot down. However, I was in a blacked-out Ford Capri 2.8i, and we ended up hammering along at... well, let's not mention the speed... until we got to Poole, where they indicated right and then went left. I hung on in there though and we arrived together at the venue, their driver shooting straight over to my car, followed by JJ. I got out and JJ said, 'Hey, it's you! What's occurring?'

He was very intrigued by Cheryl and signed her stuff - not bad for a first meet. He then asked her if she wanted to get up on stage in the gig. I declined his kind offer on her behalf, fearful that she would be stripped off on stage. I hadn't seen any shows on that tour. My fear for Cheryl came from flashbacks to the *Aural Sculpture* tour in '85 when a bloke got up on stage at Preston Guild Hall and JJ and Hugh downed guitars, stripped him off and shoved a banana up his arse.

It turns out Cheryl would just have got a spanking off Hugh for 'School Mam', and some freebies. She's not forgiven me.

MIKE ABBOTT

My mate, Andrew Law, and myself had tickets for a gig on the *10* tour. A couple of weeks before the gig his wife, Jane, decided she wanted to go as she had never seen the Stranglers. The gig was now sold out but Andrew, having probably been bored by my countless tales of Edinburgh, scoffed saying it was alright as I knew JJ and would get her a ticket. With the pressure on, I decided to write to JJ via SIS, referring to the evening with the girl at Edinburgh on the premise he was more likely to remember her than me. Thanks JJ – you didn't let me down and we were added to the guest list much to Andrew and Jane's amazement. If I ever had one cool moment, that was it.

ASKER'S ROADHOUSE HOTEL

20 FEBRUARY 1990, ASKERSWELL, UK

LILY URIKO

I was cashing up at Asker's Garage when in walked several hungry guys. I had no idea who they were and could only offer them crisps, chocolate, etc. I told them we could walk to the Roadhouse which was part of Asker's as I had to cash up there and, although it might be closed, they did have a bar and food. We walked in and Paul, the cook, was in the kitchen closing and cleaning it down. I told the guys I could do them drinks but would have to see about food. I went into the kitchen and asked Paul if he could feed a few hungry people. He gave me this look to say, 'I have just finished.' I said, 'Okay, it's cool. Help me serve them drinks,' which he was happy to do. Paul came out to help and what came out of his mouth next was, 'Fucking hell, I was at your gig! What would you like to eat?'

Lily Uriko first met the Stranglers when she was working

I served them drinks, took their food order and helped cook. I asked Paul, 'What gig?' He said, 'The Stranglers are on tour and played at Poole Arts Centre.' It turned out to be an unforgettable night. We fed them and they had the freedom to drink, play snooker and relax as we were closed. I was lucky enough to have conversations with them and I even had the cheek to ask JJ if they would gig at Asker's! (I put gigs on at weekends).

JJ was very polite and said they also went out as The Purple Helmets... interesting. He also spoke my language - Japanese. Another interesting fact. So I was learning about the Stranglers. I remember Dave's happy smiling face, with a drink in one hand and a snooker cue in the other. A good night was had by all and I have been a fan ever since. They put us on the guest list and away we went, to as many gigs as possible, the first being Torbay Leisure Centre the very next night.

CIVIC HALL

1 MARCH 1990, WOLVERHAMPTON, UK

IAN EMERY

When I saw them again in 1990, they were now an eight-piece band with three in a brass section and John Ellis on additional guitar. This was another great gig but someone threw a pint at JJ and he stopped playing and the band followed suit. JJ shouted, 'Who threw that?', the seas of the audience parted and a blond-haired punk stood there trying to look hard. JJ threw his bass down, jumped off the stage and the punk tried to throw a punch at him! JJ leaned back, dropped a head butt on the punk's nose and down he went. Security led him away and, with much applause and cheering, JJ returned to the stage and continued with the set.

HUMMINGBIRD

11 MARCH 1990, BIRMINGHAM, UK

PHIL CHARMAN

Phil Charman and son Alfie are both Stranglers fans

I had just turned 15 when I first saw the Stranglers at the Hummingbird so was just about old enough to get into the venue. This was the start of my Stranglers journey, and it was terrifying and brilliant. I have followed them on every tour since. In 2007 I had twin boys and have brought them up in the Stranglers. Alfie in particular started to get into the music and so I took him to his first gig in Guildford in 2017, aged ten. He spent the night on the rail at the front and got Jim's sticks at the end of the gig. He was hooked! He's been to many more gigs since then and he's following in Jim's footsteps, being a drummer in his own band.

This year the circle was completed as I took my now 15-year-old son to the last full tour, 32 years after I went to my first gig at 15 years old. Alfie has collected many of

Alfie (between Jim and JJ) was on the rail at this gig

Jim's sticks over the years and, being a fellow drummer, we were lucky enough to go to soundcheck in Cambridge before the gig, meet the band, have some photos and a guided tour by Jim and, to top the day off, Alfie got to play on Jim's kit. It doesn't get any better than that!

Thanks to JJ, Baz, Jim and Toby for an amazing time, and thanks to the Stranglers for so many good times over the years - memories that will last forever!

PHILIPSHALLE

28 MAY 1990, DÜSSELDORF, GERMANY

MARCEL VAN OOSTERHOUT

Marcel tracked the band down in Düsseldorf

In January 1988, something on the radio got my attention. Sweet harpsichord sounds filled the room. I knew the song, I heard it before, but I had never had a look at the band behind it. The music enchanted me and I had to find it on vinyl. I took a train to Amsterdam and there it was, on the *Collection 1977-1982* album. A new world opened to me, a world I finally felt connected with. I wanted more. My vinyl collection started to grow, and all my money went on black vinyl from the bandinblack.

Searching for news of the band was pretty difficult in a country where the band was not that popular. At the local newsagent, I discovered the *NME* and *Melody Maker* and kept looking through them for articles about the Stranglers. I subscribed to *Strangled* and bought merchandise from SIS. But what I really wanted was see the band in real life.

The band not playing in the Netherlands but I heard that the band was playing in Düsseldorf in Germany on the European leg of the *10* tour. My only chance to see them was to go with my dad to Germany. I was so nervous that day. Outside the Philipshalle, we met Owen Carne and Steve Tyas, the start of a long-time connection with both. The gig was great, although the hall was really empty. But my dream of seeing them live had come true. Sadly, it was the first and last time with Hugh as he left a couple of months later.

FRANCK HÉNOT

I was chatting to JJ in French when Hugh left the band and I still remember like it was yesterday. He asked me to speak English and said, 'You've got a Yorkie Frenchie twang!'

ANDY HODSON

I saw the Stranglers at Swindon's Oasis Centre. JJ slapped a naughty boy who annoyed him. It was good-humoured fun, but the press made it into something nasty and violent. Bloody idiots.

FORT REGENT

1 JUNE 1990, ST HELIER, JERSEY

JUSTIN CAMPBELL

This was my first proper big band gig. The Stranglers amazed me in so many ways – the incredible wall of sound, the musicianship. I was in awe watching the band. About 30 minutes in, a really stupid skinhead jumped up on the stage, no doubt showing off. JJ, whilst continuing to play bass on 'Go Buddy Go', removed the skinhead from the stage with one small kick. The dopey skinhead flew backwards into the crowd, who had seen what happened and who all moved quickly to the sides, leaving the skinhead to inevitably lose against gravity and hit the floor, to then be carried out of the hall and ejected from the premises.

The gig was incredible and one of the best I've ever seen. We were Mods at that time, and seeing the Stranglers opened our minds to the more punk/rock/alternative music that was around then and, of course, the earlier '76 to '79 punk stuff. Thank you, JJ and the boys.

ALEXANDRA PALACE

11 AUGUST 1990, LONDON, UK

MICHAEL FISHER

My black Astra filled with petrol, Stranglers sticker firmly in place, off down the M1 to the Alexandra Palace I went. I was excited about seeing my heroes again after seeing them three times previously on the *10* tour in Nottingham, Sheffield and

Birmingham. Once in the venue, the excitement was building and it wasn't long before the lights were dimmed and 'Waltzinblack' came on over the speakers. A foghorn sounded and spotlights simultaneously shone upwards and it was one of my all-time favourite Stranglers songs, 'Toiler on the Sea'. Great opener. Then it was onto the opening bars of 'Something Better Change'. Wow! Two great songs to start the show with. This was going to be a great evening with the Meninblack with a varied set list played over the night, although I thought 'Punch and Judy' was a strange one to finish with. Overall, it was another great concert and I was one happy Stranglers fan as I got back in the Astra for the drive back up to Nottingham, not realising the devastating news that was to follow with Hugh leaving the band.

SCOTT HOWIESON

I had driven from Leeds to the Alexandra Palace and slept in my battered old Talbot Sunbeam, waking nice and early on the morning of the gig. I spent the morning walking around the grounds of the palace. There was a significant amount of Stranglers fans around the grounds. I met a bunch of lads who had travelled down from Scotland who introduced me to a delightful drink called Buckfast - it was the first and last time time I ever drank it! The gig itself was enjoyable, and proved to be a significant gig in the history of the Stranglers.

RICH MATHER

I've seen them many times over the years since Coventry in 1981, mainly with my best mate, Denz. Other gig memories are Sheffield City Hall on the *Aural Sculpture* tour and Jet having to re-start 'Punch and Judy', and Hugh's last gig at the Ally Pally. It was a huge crowd and a great night out, but somehow it was all a bit muted, and we found out why the next day. There was lots of brass with the horn section, which wasn't so much to my taste. It felt like they were losing their way a bit and the performance seemed subdued.

MIKE ABBOTT

I had just started dating a beautiful girl and informed her that I would next see her after I had seen the Stranglers. 'Where are you seeing them?' she naively enquired. I then rattled off about ten places. I was very keen on her and so kept in touch by sending a postcard from every gig – there were no mobiles then. The strategy worked as I have been married to Becky for almost 30 years now!

Becky did come with me to a few gigs after I returned, the most famous one being Hugh's last at Alexandra Palace. As always, I went to the action at the front leaving Becky by herself towards the back - she was okay about it, especially when a guy tried to chat her up. With the departure of Hugh, I didn't expect the band to continue so I stopped wearing black all the time, thinking perhaps I should move on too.

OLD TROUT

25 FEBRUARY 1991, WINDSOR, UK

RICH MATHER

There was then a gap to Paul's first ever gig. He was so excited and couldn't believe he was singing for a band he had adored from afar for many years. He gave it his all and put on a show, and although it was a very different experience, we warmed to him and accepted that the Stranglers were still there, but just a bit different. He was like a kid in a sweet shop – it seemed like every song he sang was him living the dream.

WOUGHTON CENTRE

27 FEBRUARY 1991, MILTON KEYNES, UK

TONY ARMITAGE

Tony Armitage and his mate Gary were mistaken for the band

After the Hugh years of largish venues, cancelled last minute gigs and long journeys, the intimate Woughton Centre in Milton Keynes was my second gig of the Paul and John years. Myself and long-time Stranglers bud Gary made the 25 mile drive from Luton at around midday. I can remember an overcast day as we found the venue. We were the only people in sight. The smiling manager of the venue came out to welcome us before taking us around the venue, pointing out various areas. It dawned on us that he thought we were the band or the road crew. We smiled and said our goodbyes until later.

When we returned to the venue, a side double door was open so we stood inside. We found ourselves feet away from the road crew, who were in high spirits. One guy was setting up Dave's organ. He called over to the others, 'Has anyone got any spray?'

They responded, 'Do you mean the spray that removes stuff?' 'Yes.' 'The stuff that comes in a can?' 'Yes!' 'The stuff we used last night?' 'Yes, that's the stuff.' 'No, we don't have any!'

We were then spotted by management and security asked us to leave. We returned later to a packed hall. I had ticket number one, which I treasure to this day. The band were in top form as we stood at the back, although I saw many fans just walking to and from the bar. I still wonder how much of the gig they saw?

GOLDWYN'S

28 FEBRUARY 1991, BIRMINGHAM, UK

MICHAEL FISHER

This was the Stranglers Mark II and a small venue with a capacity of about 500. You could actually believe that you were transported back to 1977 in a small sweaty venue packed to the rafters. On came the band with the new lead singer, Paul Roberts. They played the old songs with the same menace and vigour as the early days. There was no need to worry – the Stranglers were back and here to stay. Paul was the perfect match for the band, with his vocal range suiting the band perfectly.

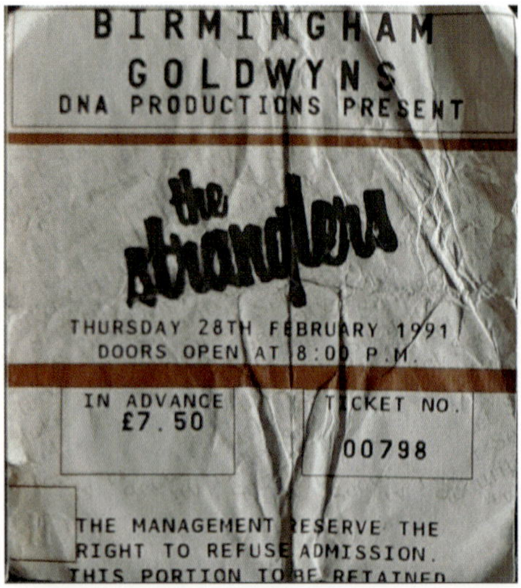

STEVE BIZLEY

That first line up with Hugh, JJ, Jet and Dave will always be special. Yes, Hugh was grumpy and it's clear that, by 1990, the band were no longer the force they once had been. I was gutted when Hugh left and thought that was the end. How wrong I was. I have fond memories of seeing the new version of

Steve Bizley and his Stranglers birthday cakes

the band in a small club called Goldwyn's, in Birmingham. It was one of the very early Mark II gigs. The band had a new found energy. Of course, it wasn't the same. It was a different band.

I also saw Hugh in the same venue doing his solo work. He sadly once again proved to dismiss his fans, not even coming on for an encore. Perhaps because it was a very small crowd?

I'm not anti-Hugh, but nor have I gone out my way to see him again. He left and the band moved on, simple as that. The 1990s were in many ways the wilderness years, but Paul and John were still very much part of the journey. Again, some of the new material worked – much didn't. But there is something about being a Stranglers fan that results in loyalty. I continued to follow them wherever they went.

DAVID THOMPSON

Hugh Cornwell had quit the band on August 11th following their gig at Alexander Palace. It felt like the end of an era, the breakup of a family, or a death of a friend, or perhaps all of these rolled into one. It marked a changing of the guard as Paul Roberts was introduced to the band. There was much debate around Roberts' style and whether this was a good move for the band, but for me it ushered in a new era and a refreshing change, especially as John Ellis had cemented his place with his silky guitar skills.

For five Stranglers fans (for the moment we'll call them the Stranglers V) from the Black Country, the new line up heralded a new chapter in their story of following the band through thick and thin. The band

David Thompson was part of the Stranglers V

was greater than any one person and the V were willing to cut Roberts some slack. What transpired was a whirlwind period of following them around the country, culminating with a sojourn to France to see them promote their new and first album under Roberts, *In the Night*. This new and exciting period started at Goldwyn's in Birmingham. It was quite a shock to see this new singer, sporting foppish hair and a very different singing style; the jury was definitely still out.

1992 finally saw the release of *In the Night* and there followed an extensive tour of the UK and the rest of Europe. The Stranglers V were galvanised into action. The album contained some very interesting tracks underpinned by, as ever, excellent base lines and spiralling keyboards. In time, tracks like 'Time to Die', 'Heaven or Hell', 'Sugar Bullets' and 'Brainbox' became standards in the band's live repertoire and seemed well-liked by the fans, who were still turning up in droves. The Stranglers V were there in force at Nottingham, Wolverhampton, and for a particularly memorable and storming gig at Coventry's Tic Toc club in the autumn of '92.

KING TUT'S WAH-WAH HUT

3 MARCH 1991, GLASGOW, UK

DEREK LOWE

King Tut's is a very small venue and I was shocked when I heard the Stranglers were playing a gig there. Tickets were going to be like gold dust, going on sale at nine o'clock one Friday morning. Thankfully, I worked nightshift so getting the chance to buy tickets wasn't a problem.

But the ticket vendor was the Virgin Store in Union Street, Glasgow and when I arrived there was a big queue. A friend of my ex-wife joined me in the queue. I finally got my turn to buy two tickets, which was the limit each purchaser was permitted, and once I had handed over my money and got my tickets, the sales assistant announced that the gig was sold out. I had bought the last two tickets. My ex-wife's friend's face was a picture.

THE BOARDWALK

6 MARCH 1991, MANCHESTER, UK

TIM BAGNALL

Tim Bagnall was at the Boardwalk to see the new 'post Hugh' line up

I saw Hugh's last appearance at Alexandra Palace. The band had clearly run its course. The energy levels had dropped and the concert seemed laboured. I was then at the Boardwalk in Manchester - a small sweaty club and a million miles away from the pomp and majesty of Alexandra Palace - to see the new line up. The performance was also different. I was close up to the band and remember 'Hanging Around' being played. As the guitar strummed intro began, JJ was not happy with the tempo and started to pump his fist to accelerate the pace. By the time the bass thudded in the band were at 100 miles per hour. The crowd were going mental and I remember thinking, 'This is fucking brilliant!' Not everyone is a Paul Roberts fan but in many ways he saved the band. He gave them a shot of adrenalin exactly when it was needed. This was one of the most notable gigs for me, and I've never seen them play a pedestrian gig since.

Julie Ballantyne (in the Elton John shirt) met JJ and Dave after an Elton John gig

A SNACK BAR

JUNE 1992, NEAR BALDOCK, UK

JULIE BALLANTYNE

My pal and I had travelled down from Fife in Scotland to see Elton John on tour and were staying with my aunt and uncle in Suffolk. Post-gig, we stopped off for some food at my favourite snack bar near Baldock in Hertfordshire. As we sat munching our rolls, an off-white Discovery Jeep parked up behind me. I started shaking like a leaf, realising who had got out of the vehicle - JJ Burnel and Dave Greenfield. I nervously approached them and asked for an autograph on the only bit of paper I could find in my car, and to have a photo with them, which the snack bar person kindly took for us. Meanwhile, JJ ripped the piss out of me for wearing an Elton John t-shirt. I was mortified!

BARROWLAND BALLROOM

4 OCTOBER 1992, GLASGOW, UK

CRAIG WOOD

At Christmas 1990 I met my old pal up from London who told me the band had been on the TV earlier that week with their new guitarist. When I asked what was wrong with the old one, he told me Hugh had left. It had happened four months earlier and I hadn't even heard. I did, though, become aware via the press that the Stranglers had recruited Paul and were going to continue. In 1991 I was working and had some income to dispose of. I recorded the Maine Road or possibly the Milton Keynes gig off the radio and listened to Paul's efforts. The bloody brass section was gone but Hugh's singularly refined vocal had been replaced with a bland estuary-English one. The jury was well and truly out.

Then I discovered a tape of the stolen demos for sale (sorry, lads). Hearing 'Time to Die' was a serious OMG moment for me. It was fantastic, from the atmosphere of the sample to the dirty guitar and Dave's big, phat, meaty chords. I made a half-hearted attempt to get a ticket for the gig at King Tut's, but I was still unconvinced.

I bought *In the Night*, which was all right I suppose, but I was very disappointed on listening to 'Time to Die'. Obviously, the *Blade Runner* sample had to go, but the dirty guitar was gone, replaced by John Ellis's Hollywood effort (which a friend said sounded like The Shadows) and Dave's big chords were lost as well, replaced by a paper-thin vocal sample whilst the guitar was much more prominent.

When the band played Barrowlands in 1992, I thought twice about it. It wouldn't be the same without Hugh, but with Dave and JJ they were still worth a look. They kicked off with 'Time to Die' before segueing into 'Toiler', then 'Sometimes' and 'I Feel Like a Wog'. I had seen the Stranglers ten times previously and always stayed on the periphery, carefully taking it all in. But this time I found myself subject to a strange urge to get up and dance. I made my way straight into the crowd and pogoed away to my heart's content.

What a gig, what a performance! Wouldn't be the same without Hugh? Too right - this was better! But trying to convince anyone else was an impossible task, with most of my friends dismissive about any mention of the band Mark II. (Their stance changed when they saw the painful cabaret act that was the DVD of the Ally Pally gig).

I had accepted Paul, but coming back on stage for the encore, he said what a great gig it had been and it was true that Glasgow was 'the best venue in England'. Well, the roof nearly fell in as an enraged, jeering crowd started to chant that most Scottish of

Scottish expressions, 'Ya dirty English bastard!' Paul was very apologetic as he tried to worm his way out of it with his Scottish credentials. 'I was born in Scotland', he began. 'I have relatives near here in a place called Paisley.' I couldn't believe it. One of the Stranglers had relatives living in my home town. I have kept an eye out for them over the years, but to no avail.

ELYSEE MONTMARTRE

16 NOVEMBER 1992, PARIS, FRANCE

PAUL SHEPHERD

Paul Shepherd got to go backstage at Rock City

In September 1992, the Stranglers released their first post-Hugh album, *In the Night*. As a fan since '79 (where I was exposed to side-A of *Rattus* on a summer holiday – a family friend forgot to tape side-B), I went along to Selectadisc in Nottingham to buy the album. Inside was a piece of red card which said 'Win a Trip to Paris to see the Stranglers'. Details entered, into the post it went. A few weeks later, the phone went and I was the lucky winner. This pleased my new girlfriend (and future wife) no end, as well as the Seletadisc manager who also got to go.

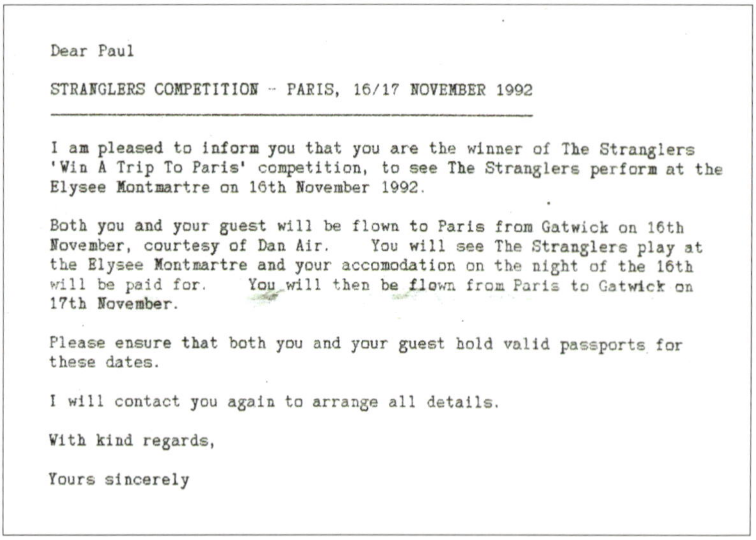

Dear Paul

STRANGLERS COMPETITION - PARIS, 16/17 NOVEMBER 1992

I am pleased to inform you that you are the winner of The Stranglers 'Win A Trip To Paris' competition, to see The Stranglers perform at the Elysee Montmartre on 16th November 1992.

Both you and your guest will be flown to Paris from Gatwick on 16th November, courtesy of Dan Air. You will see The Stranglers play at the Elysee Montmartre and your accomodation on the night of the 16th will be paid for. You will then be flown from Paris to Gatwick on 17th November.

Please ensure that both you and your guest hold valid passports for these dates.

I will contact you again to arrange all details.

With kind regards,

Yours sincerely

Paul Shepherd won a trip to Paris

The confirmation letter arrived outlining the arrangements. The Paris gig was in November with flight and hotel arranged. However, I had just started to work as a teacher and the flight was on a Friday. Thankfully, I had a very understanding head who allowed me to swap my non-contact time.

The letter also had an invite to meet the band before they played Rock City in October. I turned up on the day in best black threads and leather jacket and was taken backstage where I got to chat with the band prior to having a photo taken with them, plus I got to meet Nottingham Forest and England legend, Stuart Pearce.

A month later, we arrived at Charles de Gaulle Airport where we were supposed to meet members of the tour crew who would take us to the hotel and then the gig. Unfortunately, we somehow missed them and ended up getting a taxi into Paris and having to convince the door staff at the gig that we should be allowed entry. We got to see the Stranglers play another great gig. The night was finished off with a walk down the steps in Montmartre where part of the 'La Folie' video was shot.

30 years later, I was back at Rock City for the tribute to Dave tour, this time with my daughter.

L'UBU

11/12 MARCH 1993, RENNES, FRANCE

DANIEL HYDEN

The first time I saw the Stranglers abroad was in Rennes in 1993. I spoke to Paul after the second gig and asked if I could have a drink with them because we were off home the following day. He told us to come back about an hour after the gig had finished. We did, and had a fantastic time – free beer, free champagne, even free cigarettes. It was a brilliant night.

Daniel Hyden saw the Stranglers in France

Years later I also had a beer with them in Wolverhampton

with my seven-year-old son. JJ picked him up and paraded him around to the other fans. I was so proud.

DAVID THOMPSON

In 1993 we saw them at the Aston Villa Leisure Centre and Oxford Apollo and met some of the band for the first time. Jean-Jacques was a real gent and thanked us for the birthday wishes and good luck messages for the forthcoming French tour. Having discovered the dates of this (and I don't know how we did, in those pre-internet days) we decided to hop over to France to see some of them. We decided not to go to Paris - we wanted something more personable, more approachable and engaging, and somewhere that offered up more than one gig. The two gigs on consecutive nights at L'Ubu stood out, and Rennes was just a ferry crossing and a few hours' drive away.

It seemed a small venue and we didn't want to risk travelling all the way there only to miss out if all the tickets were sold. However, with the help of a fluent French relative we managed to send a fax (remember those?) to the venue.

Five of us – me plus Phil, Jan, Dan and Lynne - plus baggage crammed into a VW Polo. It was the end of the working day and we needed to catch the overnight ferry from Portsmouth to Le Havre and through Brittany. But we had barely made it to the Stourbridge ring road before the exhaust on the car started making a right old racket, putting the trip in danger. But our driver, Phil, managed to find a salt-of-the-earth Black Country fitter to patch it up and we were on our way.

On arrival in Rennes, we found accommodation at the Hotel d'Angleterre. Once we were checked in, we couldn't wait to get to the gig but there were hours to kill. Some of us decided to see if we could get in on the sound check. I still remember hearing Jean-Jacques singing a song I'd never heard of, to this day, but unmistakably it was them. After a bit of hanging around (by us, not a rendition of the song) the band members drifted away and were good enough to say hello. I think Jet thought that, because I'd got skinny legs, I was French! They seemed genuinely surprised and appreciative we'd travelled all that way to see them, although the conversation quickly turned to news of the previous night's Arsenal result (they beat Crystal Palace two-nil in the League Cup semi-final second leg).

Some of the band were worried about the acoustics but we were told that the design of the venue, small as it was, replicated that of the shell-like shape of the ear, all to aid the sound quality. The locals seemed friendly and accommodating and on the first night we hooked up with a few students and ended up at a local nightclub.

After the first night, we saw Jet Black walking to a pre-gig meal the following afternoon but left him in peace. Paul and John popped up throughout the day and posed for pictures and autographs. At one point I had to drag Dan out of a bar (he was trying to calculate how many more glasses of wine his remaining francs would buy; we'd only been there two days and it seemed to have become his local) to say hello.

At the end of the second gig, an impromptu post-gig party took place at the venue. We found Paul, John, JJ and Dave G having a shindig with a few French fans, as well as Lynne and Jan. Dave Greenfield was his usual gracious self, approachable and quietly spoken. They chatted to us about what we did back home and some of the gigs we went to, and I vaguely remember chatting to DG about life after death and various esoteric things. By this time the beer was kicking in I think, and so my ability to splutter bollocks was greatly enhanced. JJ cracked open a bottle of champagne, although the jury is out as to whether he shared any of it.

Some band members tried to wind up the male contingent of the V, saying that the girls were being chatted up by some French fans, but we weren't having any of it. In the end, the L'Ubu staff got fed up with all of us hanging around and called time on us and the band. We said a fond adieu to each other and drifted off into the night. After the Rennes encounter Jean-Jacques referred to us as 'the famous five'. That could be interpreted both positively or negatively, but I'll take that.

ROYAL ALBERT HALL

13 JUNE 1993, LONDON, UK

TINA HAGEN-HURLEY

I wasn't there at the beginning but, boy, how I wish I had been. I was a 13-year-old girl growing up in West Germany when I first saw 'No Mercy' on Sky channel, the only UK channel we could receive at the time. I was instantly taken by these cool guys, and I ripped every single Wham! and Frankie Goes to Hollywood poster off my bedroom wall the same day. Replacing them with posters of the Meninblack, though, turned out to be a lot more difficult than expected. Since I couldn't get hold of them in the boring small town we lived in, and with the invention of the World Wide Web being almost another decade away, I started looking for pen friends in England as a way of getting hold of posters or magazine cuttings of the

Tina Hagen-Hurley wanted to marry Hugh

Stranglers. Some obliged but some saw through my cunning plan pretty quickly and the letters dried up soon.

When I finally managed to get my hands on a poster, my mum came into my room exclaiming, 'Mein Gott sind die hässlich!' (My god aren't they ugly!). I didn't speak to Mum for a week before I announced that, one day, I was going to marry Hugh (sorry JJ).

I soon discovered the early stuff, which no one else around me seemed to have ever heard about. Songs like 'Straighten Out' and '5 Minutes' were perfect catalysts for my teenage aggression, but when I played them to friends I was met with bewilderment, which was kind of what I wanted, because it made me 'the only Stranglers fan in the village'.

What can I say? Time wasn't on my side and the first live gig I managed to attend wasn't until 1993 after moving to Chorleywood to work as an au-pair girl. It was at the Royal Albert Hall and by then the boys were fronted by Paul Roberts.

Hugh leaving the band didn't stop me in my pursuit of him. In the year 2000, at one of his solo gigs, I got invited backstage at the Borderline where I finally had the chance to tell him about my teenage fantasies of becoming Mrs Cornwell one day. When he told me with a wry smile to come back in a leap year, I was finally cured.

After a period of not following the band, I was reminded of how powerful the Stranglers were on stage and how much their songs meant to me when Baz joined. My British husband and I have rarely missed a gig at the Brixton Academy since, and we continue to travel over from Germany to see them.

CROSS CHANNEL FERRY

AUGUST 1993, THE ENGLISH CHANNEL

ANDY MCKENNA

A new boy had transferred over to Bury High School from Ireland. He was a bit of a rum bugger to say the least. However, we got on and became friends. He introduced me to the Stranglers by selling me a secondhand *Raven* and *Black and White* - I didn't ask who was the first hand! *Black and White* was first on the turntable and it blew my mind. Then came *The Raven* and that was it - my heart and creative musical soul

Andy McKenna met Dave on a train

were sold to the Stranglers. If I ever had thoughts of a musical career they were gone - how the hell could I compete with this? This was musical perfection.

Over the years I've been to many gigs, met the guys and generally loved every aspect of my life involving the band. My wife now loves them and my mum and dad loved 'Golden Brown', so the Stranglers got everywhere (apart from to my brother, who's not a music fan).

I was in the British Army and serving at an AFCENT unit in The Netherlands. Going on leave, I would drive from camp to Calais and catch the ferry to Dover and then drive to Manchester for some R&R (mostly involving boozing and/or a Stranglers gig). On this occasion I was walking through the cabin trying to find a place to sit when I spied a remarkably familiar figure - could it be Dave Greenfield? Yes, it most certainly was.

I asked if he minded if I sat with him and, him being an absolute gent, he didn't mind at all. The hour or so crossing passed in a blur. We talked about where I was stationed and it turned out the Stranglers had just played Maastricht, we talked about cars and we talked about what he was doing in mainland Europe (working on a project in Paris with JJ and John Ellis). This was before mobile phones and compact digital cameras, so I went and bought a paper from the shop and asked Dave to sign it as my best mate (another Andy) would never believe I'd met him otherwise.

Eventually, the ferry docked and it was time to go our separate ways. As is the general way of things on a ferry journey, a quick visit to the ablutions is necessary before the drive home. We went to the same place (but weren't co-located) and this, I think, is the measure of the man. He waited outside for me to exit, shook my hand and we wished each other well for our respective onward journeys.

He was a true gent and gave his time freely. It was great seeing other people trying to guess who he was. What a loss not only to the world of the Stranglers but to the world in general. Dave was not only a musical genius but someone who had time for everyone and was one of the most down-to-earth people I've ever had the pleasure to spend time with. RIP Dave Greenfield - you will always be missed.

OLYMPIA THEATRE

12 AUGUST 1994, DUBLIN, IRELAND

CIARÁN PEPPARD

I came to the Stranglers at what may have seemed like a low point in their long and illustrious history. As a child of '76, perhaps I was imbued with some of the spirit of that year when I bought the *Greatest Hits* album on its release in 1990. At the time, my awareness of the band was based on 'Golden Brown' and 'Peaches', and I'd liked what I'd heard. The talk in the music press was that the band was finished, having suffered the loss of Hugh Cornwell, and the decision to continue with a new singer was treated with more than a little mirth by the music papers. However, the band continued on their journey, and I started to delve back into the back catalogue, buying *Rattus* and *No More Heroes* on cassette and moving on to buy up all the albums available to me.

October 1994 brought my first opportunity to see the band in concert, at Dublin's Midnight at the Olympia, and the excitement for me was seriously off the scale. I think it was the band's first Irish gig since the *Dreamtime* tour, so a lot had changed. The intro of 'Waltzinblack', the stage antics of JJ (described by one review as *Corrie's* Des Barnes' more unhinged brother), Jet's menacing presence and Paul Roberts' best Iggy Pop, was all topped off by Dave. What to say about Dave? All the things I took for granted subsequently were brand new to me that night. The rats attached to the keyboard rig, the downing of the pint during the 'No More Heroes' solo, the whole mesmeric keyboard/organ/piano sounds he produced – unforgettable. I left the Olympia at 1.30am an even more rabid convert to the band.

And that's where I've stayed for the last 30 odd years. I've seen the band countless times on their visits to Ireland, and the gigs have become even better as the years have gone by, as Baz's contribution has enhanced their sound and reshaped it for the 21st century. But I'll still remember the house lights dimming and the opening bars of 'Waltzinblack' booming out of the PA on that chilly autumnal night in Dublin. It stays with me as a landmark in my live music adventures over the last four decades.

Long live the Meninblack.

HMV STORE

16 MAY 1995, BIRMINGHAM, UK

IAN EMERY

1995 saw the Paul Roberts/John Ellis era and the *About Time* album and tour. When Paul Roberts joined the Stranglers, the hostility towards him was terrible. I saw him when the Stranglers played Goldwyns in Birmingham and he had abuse and missiles and everything hurled at him. But he stuck at it, bless him.

Ian Emery with his signed copy of Girl from the Snow Country (Dutch sleeve)

They did a record signing for *About Time* in HMV in Birmingham. I had had two heart attacks and was recovering from having died for 15 minutes. All five members of the Stranglers were sitting scribbling away. I had met Jet Black when he did his launch party for a single called 'My Young

Dreams', an old Stranglers demo he had re-recorded, so I had some banter with him.

He was first in line. He looked at me, grinned and said, 'I know who ate all the custard creams.' I said, 'You can talk, you fat bastard!' At which there was silence as JJ looked at me. Then Jet laughed, 'How are you?' and we had a quick chat.

I'd brought my copy of JJ's single, 'Girl from the Snow Country', for him to sign. I put the single in front of him and he picked it up and said, 'Where did you get this from?' I told him I'd bought it from a proper record shop on its release and said, 'Is it genuine?' He said, 'Yes,' and signed it. Paul Roberts picked it up and said, 'I'll give you £200 for it.' I said, 'Not after JJ's signed it, you won't.' Jet pointed at me laughing and shouted, 'He's trouble.'

I got into a conversation with Paul about my illness and I said that I was seeing them at Wolverhampton Civic on the following Monday and that I would be at the front on the left balcony. He said, 'Okay, see you then.' On the Monday, Paul stopped the show mid-gig and said, 'One of our oldest fans has been ill – can we give him some applause?' and before I knew it, the lights were on me. I thought, 'Bloody hell, they remembered.' I liked Paul Roberts, but what went on in the band was a different matter.

In 2019, I met the band at Rock City in Nottingham and spoke to Dave for the last time. Baz took the mickey out of Walsall FC, as he always does when he sees me. I saw them in February 2022 at the De Montfort Hall in Leicester, a great venue. I was in the balcony and JJ acknowledged me when they were playing 'Peaches'.

They are still part of my life. Ladies and gentlemen, the Stranglers!

BARROWLAND BALLROOM

9 JUNE 1995, GLASGOW, UK

CRAIG WOOD

There were more gigs at the Barrowlands, each similarly impressive, until *About Time* came on the scene in the summer of '95. This was special. I remember standing in the crowd, filled with expectation as the lights went out and a clock like the label of the album was projected onto a screen counting down. As it hit zero, it exploded into the Stranglers' logos and the familiar opening bars of 'Waltzinblack' filled the air. Excitement rose within the crowd as Jet appeared, in full hairy monster mode, followed by Dave - proper Dave, without a ponytail or a skinhead, exactly as he looked on the *Meninblack* tour. Both waved in acknowledgement of the reception they received, then Dave put one hand on his top sampler, the other on his MiniMoog, nodded to Jet and...

It was '(Get a) Grip (on Yourself)' and I couldn't believe the way Dave's keyboards blared out the opening notes like a howitzer as, simultaneously, psychedelic oil film images were projected onto the stage as the other three band members came on stage. It was absolutely breathtaking. When the band has played this track recently it has never been the same, with Dave's sampled version of the intro being merely a grunt-grunt-groan-groan-grunt, lacking the spectacular sharpness witnessed that evening.

This was a memorable gig, and I loved hearing 'Goodbye Toulouse' and 'Straighten Out' live for the first time ever.

OLYMPIA THEATRE

25 NOVEMBER 1995, DUBLIN, IRELAND

PETER KELLY

On a Sunday morning in 1995, after a great midnight in the Olympia gig, I spotted the band in a corner of Dublin airport waiting for their flight. I excitedly grabbed a pen and paper from my girlfriend and made a beeline for JJ to get an autograph. He was very polite and courteous and answered the one question that my over-excited brain managed to blurt out. He then directed me to where the rest of the band were before I could form a second one. With me safely dispatched, he quietly sidled up to my girlfriend, who was watching the proceedings with amusement, to have a chat. Did she enjoy the gig, he noticed her in the front row, where was she from, etc. By the time I finished collecting autographs from the rest of the band, who were all very gracious, my girlfriend was looking very smug and JJ was nowhere to be seen.

EFFENAAR

6 APRIL 1996, EINDHOVEN, THE NETHERLANDS

ROB BURG

Rob Burg got to review a Stranglers gig for his newspaper

Ever since the Stranglers started, I've been a fan. I bought my first records in 1976. The first concert I saw was in 1983, in Den Bosch, Netherlands. Later I saw the band three times more. One of them was in 1996. I am a reporter, working for *ED* (*Eindhovens Dagblad*), a regional newspaper in the south of Holland. That night I attended the concert and wrote a review for our paper.

This is the translation:

It is no fun for any rock, punk, metal or any other group to be haunted again and again by the image from a greying past. The London group the Stranglers understand this. For many years, new albums by the Stranglers were invariably set against the first two albums, *Rattus Norvegicus* and *No More Heroes*. Well, those discs were well worth listening to, especially compared to the work of other bands from that punk era. It's not so strange that the Stranglers actually preferred not to be labelled as 'punk'.

On the other hand, the 'Meninblack' were lucky because they happened to play the right music at the right time: hard, short and powerful songs with lyrics that razed the muzak of the post-hippy generation to the ground.

However, the fact that the group of Hugh Cornwell, Jean Jaques Burnel, Jet Black and Dave Greenfield also managed to produce many nice records in the following years (*La Folie*) was noticed by few. People wanted to hear the gory lyrics and raw sounds of 'Peaches' ('Walking on the beaches, looking at the peaches'), 'Feel Like a Wog' and 'Something Better Change', on which it was so nice to pogo.

The young crowd that had flocked to the Effenaar last night in hope of getting some of that old stuff poured over them were lucky. This was no less true for the people in their thirties, who were clearly less strongly represented. About half of the set consisted of old work. From the 'Waltzinblack', the quirky instrumental in 3/4 time with the nervous giggles of a bunch of mean sewer rats, to the encores with 'Hanging Around' and 'No More Heroes'. 'Golden Brown' was also performed, as was 'Let Me Introduce You to the Family', which can be found on the same album, *La Folie*.

Last night the Stranglers proved that musically they still stand their ground, despite the advancing age of, especially, drummer Black and keyboardist Greenfield. A minus however were the vocal qualities of singer Paul Roberts, who replaced Hugh Cornwell a few years ago. The man's voice is too polished, too smooth and perhaps too beautiful for the rawness that is typical of the Stranglers' best work. He does his best, comes into his own in the most recent Stranglers work, but really can't stand in Cornwell's shadow when doing the old romps.

And the fact that Dave Greenfield can play the incomparably beautiful keyboard solo of 'No More Heroes' with only one hand, and clearly wants to prove this to the audience by drinking a cup of water with the other hand, is a circus act that the band is unworthy of.

KAMMGARTEN

20 APRIL 1996, KAISERSLAUTERN, GERMANY

MICHAEL MCCLUGHIN

A stand-out gig, and definitely my proudest, was in April 1996. A friend had married, moved to Germany and had her first child. That was my excuse to pay them a visit and, miraculously, I timed it so that we could all get to the gig in the Kammgarten. However, our timing on the day was off and the three of us arrived a few hours before the gig, but just after the lads, by then including Paul Roberts, were finishing off their hot and sweaty (it appeared) soundcheck. We ended up sharing a few drinks outside in the sun with JJ and Paul, who were both showing off their physiques, which in JJ's case certainly didn't put me off my man crush.

Both were very patient, posing for a variety of photos (there were no selfies back in '96) and they seemed genuinely interested in our different stories as to how we happened to be there. They then invited us to join them after the gig for some drinks. Needless to say, I couldn't believe it, and duly celebrated some more before the gig.

When we finally got inside, we were amazed to find we could walk right up to the stage, which was about the height of a chair, where we took up my now customary left-hand-side viewpoint, in front of you-know-who. As the gig progressed, the locals behaved like Germans, and were literally very standoffish, affording us plenty of space to show them how to pogo, old school style. We were having a ball, but then it came to the encore, and someone nodded at a few of the crew standing to JJ's right, to 'ask' if it was okay for me to join him on stage, and got the thumbs up. I can only conclude that they had seen us earlier with JJ and Paul and thought why not!

I didn't need a written invitation, so within seconds I'm 'dancing' JJ-style (though not as nimbly) behind the man himself, and of course, he's aiming for me with those DMs, which I just about managed to avoid. Next thing I know, Paul is mimicking me from centre stage, and we end up having a limbo dancing competition, mid-song.

To this day, I don't know (to my eternal shame) how many songs I was up there for, nor which songs they were. I just jumped back off the stage again when I knew I should and re-joined my friends. And, as good as their word, we joined all of the band after, chatting away with Dave, Jet and John as well, but again, my memory is fuzzy on what we chatted about. Though I know my 'dancing' came in for some stick!

STAMFORD BRIDGE

7 DECEMBER 1996, LONDON, UK

ANDY MILLER

Andy Miller met JJ at the Bridge

I went to watch my football team, Chelsea, play Everton. I took my seat in the Old West Stand and, halfway through the first half, I noticed a chap in a jacket with Triumph emblazoned across the back. It was JJ. At half time, I made my way down to where he was sitting and cautiously approached him to ask, 'Are you who I think you are?' He looked at me and said, 'Whom am I, then?' I responded, 'Jean-Jacques Burnel.' He replied, 'Correct, and you are?' I blurted out, 'I am a *Strangled* subscriber.' He pushed his hand forward and shook mine and said, 'One of the family, then.' We chatted for a few minutes, and he told me that the Stranglers would be playing the Royal Albert Hall the following year with an orchestra, and he might wear a suit.

After the match had finished, I made my way up the stairs in the stand and who should be standing there waiting for me? Yes, JJ and his son Jeremy. I walked with them to the train station after getting him to sign my match programme. It really was a special moment. A few months later, I went to see JJ perform an acoustic gig in Swindon and he saw me outside the venue and shouted out, 'Hi Big Fella – been to any football matches recently?'

And when I saw the band at the Royal Albert Hall the following year, he did indeed wear a suit.

Ross Stothard thought his unit was winding him up when they said the Stranglers were going to entertain the troops

---

DISUSED FACTORY

MAY 1997, GORNI VAKUF, KUPRES, BOSNIA

ROSS STOTHARD

Whilst serving in the British Army, and having just recovered from a badly broken leg, I re-joined my unit who were serving out in Kupres, Bosnia in 1997 in support of peace operations. I arrived out there to be greeted by my troops with an enthusiastic, 'Hey Sarge! Guess who's out here playing on the CSE (Combined Services Entertainments) show?' 'Only the fucking Stranglers!' was the answer. Now, my troops knew I was a lifelong fan – I'd seen the boys play a few times before I joined up in '84 – and I was a prime target for a good wind up, seeing as I'd just arrived in the country.

But it turned out to be true and that the boys had been scheduled to play about ten gigs, headlining the shows for the all of service personnel stationed out there. Unfortunately, tragedy had struck back in UK with John Ellis's dad and the band had returned. By the time I'd arrived out in Bosnia, the boys had come back to play out the final three remaining dates of the shows. The first one was that very night in a little enclave called Gorni Vakuf in a disused, former tomato processing factory. The place was inhabited by a Fusiliers battalion, and they hosted the show.

It also just happened that some of our radio operators, who were having a quiet tour, volunteered to crew for the boys for the remaining shows. Dave very generously shared his obligatory pint of Bacardi and Coke with me and, God bless him, it's still my weapon of choice to this day.

I was given a straight choice of going to that show or the next one at Tomislavgrad. I opted for the next day as I had to sort my shit out. That show was the absolute dog's bollocks. We were treated to all the new stuff from *Written in Red* and the best of the best from every album prior. The stage was about three feet high and there was no crowd security. We were all just stage diving and crowd surfing the whole show. We even joined Paul at the mic a couple of times. I was lucky enough to get backstage for a few beers with the boys, where I chatted with Jet, JJ and Dave and explained I'd first seen them at Bridlington Spa in 1978.

The next day my boss, on hearing how big a fan I was, gave me 'leave pass' to go down into Split, Croatia to see the final show that night. Watch my fucking tracer (as the expression went) and so I did, at record pace in the Land Rover. Arriving at the show at the end of the opening number, I got a greeting from the mic from JJ. The show was rocking from the word go.

It was held in a big rubber hangar in the Mediterranean heat, and Paul and JJ were stripped to waist only three numbers in. Everyone in the mosh pit was stripped to the waist too, while the boys were really playing at full pelt. Paul came to the mic a bit pissed, because the troops in the mosh were breaking open their dayglo Cyalume light sticks and striping everybody. I think he was worried that the fluid might be poisonous and he got splashed in the face. Oops.

I also remember the opening to 'Nice 'n' Sleazy' being prolonged and turning into an ad-hoc jump around and then the band going back to 'Sleazy' and the vocals kicking in. That was a gig to remember.

At the end of the show, I was allowed backstage again as I was wearing a black long-sleeved crew shirt with 'Nice 'n' Sleazy' in white script on the chest and the rat logos in blue running down the arm. Security parted like the Red Sea and let me in to sit in the press conference and have a few beers with the boys. I got a knowing wink from Jet.

I've lost count of how many times I've seen them play. And guess who got Covid and couldn't go to the final tour? Stranglers 'til I die. MIB.

ROYAL ALBERT HALL

13 JUNE 1997, LONDON, UK

STEPHEN CARR

Stephen Carr stayed in his seat at the Albert Hall

I've followed the band for over 40 years, travelled to venues all over the country, and seen them live probably 70 times or more. It would be impossible to pick a favourite gig, but one that particularly stands out was the so-called 21st anniversary gig at the Royal Albert Hall in June 1997, when the band was accompanied by the Electra Strings Orchestra. The layout of the venue meant I had to remain seated throughout, one of only two occasions I've seen the band live and not joined in the ruck in front of the stage, which gave me a totally different perspective of a gig.

I attended the Stranglers' convention weekend at Brean back in 2001, which provided a relaxed way to chat with some of the band members. However, my favourite Stranglers memory came a few weeks earlier when I spent a couple of hours in the company of my hero Dave Greenfield at his pub, The Windmill, in Somersham, Cambridgeshire. A quiet Tuesday evening with hardly anyone else in the bar meant I had Dave to myself for much of the time. There was no superstar about him, a more down-to-earth chap I couldn't have wished to meet as he shared band news with me. Pity I didn't have a camera with me that evening. Those memories quickly came flooding back when the shock news of his death was announced in 2020.

The three main passions in my life have been West Bromwich Albion FC, Worcestershire County Cricket Club and the Stranglers. Of the three, I would have to say that the Stranglers have given me most pleasure – certainly there have been far fewer ups-and-downs following a band than there have been following a football or cricket team. 'Waltzinblack' is a classic piece of quirky Stranglers music. I tried to persuade my fiancée, Sandra, to walk down the aisle to it on our wedding day but her being a conventional lady, it was quickly vetoed. However, it is on the playlist for my own funeral, and will be played at the start of my last 'gig', just as it has been played at the start of thousands of Stranglers gigs over the years.

UNKNOWN VENUE

NOVEMBER 1997, FALKLAND ISLANDS

JAMES MCNAIR, THE INDEPENDENT

In 20 years of gig-going, I have never witnessed a concert quite like the one that took place that evening. Whatever one thought of new members John Ellis and Paul Roberts, they brought an energy to the band that Hugh Cornwell simply didn't have. There were no bouncers, the bar didn't close, and when the Stranglers encored with 'No More Heroes', they triggered a king of hyper-catharsis amongst the squaddies which remained gloriously unchecked.

'I went to see the Stranglers play in Port Rush in Northern Ireland when I was 13 years old,' Flight Lieutenant Gareth Scott told me afterwards. 'I can't believe that they came all the way up here to play to 35 people. It was absolutely fantastic.'

JJ: 20 YEARS AGO, I WOULD HAPPILY HAVE POSED FOR A PICTURE WITH ONE OF THOSE SHEEP. I'D EVEN HAVE GOT ITS BACK LEGS INSIDE MY WELLIES

TALKING TO THE INDEPENDENT

MORECAMBE DOME

18 NOVEMBER 1997, MORECAMBE, UK

JILL SANDERSON

I was 24 years old and had given birth to my first son, James John, eight days earlier. I'd been following the Stranglers since I was eleven, and the chance to see them so close to home was not to be missed. Off I went to the gig alone, leaving James with his dad and great grandma and a bottle of expressed milk. The gig was amazing – no surprise there.

After any gig there is always an element of sweat, but that night there was the added bonus of breast milk flowing – I hope the guy in front of me in the mosh pit didn't realise. I got back home to find James crying for milk. He'd finished the bottle I'd left a while back and was hungry. I must admit, I felt a little guilty but no harm done.

24 years later and I finally managed to convince James to attend a gig at the Manchester Apollo in February 2022. We were in the mosh pit, and it was another fantastic gig, no surprise there. When we left the venue James turned to me and said, 'I get it now Mum'. On our walk back to the car a rat ran across our path, a message from Dave if ever there was one, and an emotional end to our evening.

So many gigs, so many memories but those two mentioned are very special to me. The two loves of my life - my kids and the Stranglers.

FRAN CHAMBERS

I probably completely ignored the Stranglers in the late Seventies. I started seeing them in about 1998. I wasn't originally a Stranglers fan. I found them rather misogynist so I avoided going to see them. But when I did go and see them, I just saw them in a completely different light. And Hugh's just a very intelligent lyricist. I've seen Hugh many, many times and if he was playing, I'd always seek him out.

Fran Chambers with Hugh

GLORIA O'CONNELL

I remember seeing Jean Jacques Burnel take a full pint of beer straight in the face whilst playing in Wales, dismount the stage and smack the culprit in the mouth for his stupidity. Good on you, Mr Burnel.

CIVIC HALL

20 OCTOBER 1999, WOLVERHAMPTON, UK

GLEN JONES

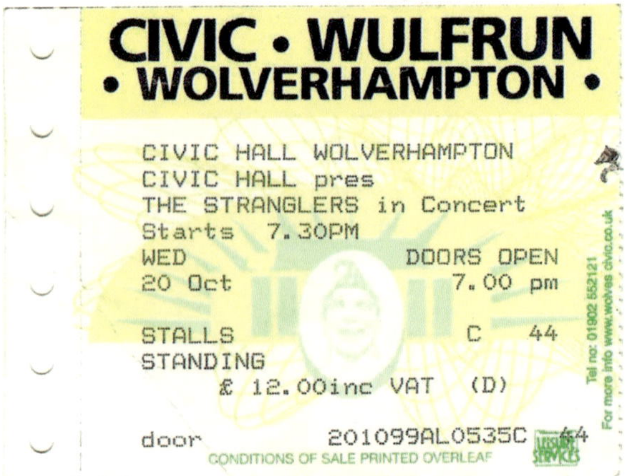

CIVIC • WULFRUN
• WOLVERHAMPTON •
CIVIC HALL WOLVERHAMPTON
CIVIC HALL pres
THE STRANGLERS in Concert
Starts 7.30PM
WED DOORS OPEN
20 Oct 7.00 pm
STALLS C 44
STANDING
£ 12.00inc VAT (D)
door 201099AL0535C
CONDITIONS OF SALE PRINTED OVERLEAF
Tel no: 01902 552121
For more info www.wolves civic.co.uk

I was late to the party, as it were. As I got into music around 1990, I heard a few Stranglers tunes, so saved up pocket money to buy the *Greatest Hits* and then the entire back catalogue. Hugh had gone by then. My first Stranglers gig was in Wolverhampton in October 1999 on the *Hits and Heroes* tour. It was also the first gig I took my now-wife to. She was one of probably only five ladies in the crowd. It was her first gig full stop, and we were right at the front, so she was impressed with Paul getting his top off, especially when he leant over her. The gig was stopped because someone stole Paul's gold necklace. The place went mental for 'No More Heroes' at the end.

CSE TOUR OF CYPRUS

JULY 2000, CYPRUS

KEVIN TERRY

I saw the band in Cyprus when I was in the army in 2000. What a great night. I was thrown on stage as I was doing the photos.

JJ BURNEL ALONE AND ACOUSTIC TOUR UNIVERSITY OF SALFORD

4 DECEMBER 2000, MANCHESTER, UK

CHARLIE BRADDOCK

Charlie Braddock misheard JJ

Some years ago, JJ Burnel did a solo acoustic tour, mainly of small venues and universities. The tour was entitled, *Alone and Acoustic*. I was sat right at the front during the Salford University gig, as JJ discussed his love of all things Japanese. He then posed the question, 'Does anyone here know what Manga is?' Quick as a flash, my hand shot up. 'Yes. It's a large tropical fruit with a big stone in the middle.' JJ stared at me with a bewildered expression for a few seconds, before saying, 'That's a fucking mango!'

PONTINS HOLIDAY CENTRE

14 - 16 SEPTEMBER 2001, BREAN SANDS HOLIDAY PARK, BURNHAM-ON-SEA, UK

TIM BAGNALL

Tim Bagnall was at Pontins

I saw the Mark II line-up loads of times after that first time at the Boardwalk. I had some great times: the conventions, the legendary Royal Albert Hall concert and a mad night in Halifax when the sprung floor broke at the front and became like a trampoline for the first few rows. I remember Paul laughing as we all bounced ever higher in unison, terrifying. The *Atlantic Rock* festivals in 1999 and 2000 were excellent too, the second one with Baz having joined the band.

I remember the *Pontins Weekender* – another legendary one. My mate arrived late on the second day. He was driving a flash Mercedes S500 at the time and as he pulled up at the entrance, he noticed that, strangely, the staff had formed into a line for him. After lowering the window down the most senior guy there looked in and said, 'Oh thank fuck for that, we thought you were Mr Pontin.' Brilliant.

YUKA TAKAHASHI

After I came back to Japan from the UK in the early Eighties, I started work and wasn't really listening to any particular band for quite some time. In 2001, I saw a guy at work one day in a black t-shirt with the Stranglers logo on it. We started talking about the band and he told me they were holding a weekend convention in September at Weston-super-Mare in the UK. I really wanted to see the band again and so had my friend in London arrange everything. At the convention, I realised what I was missing. Their live performance was amazing. Their old songs didn't sound old at all and the new ones sounded good too. That made me want to see and listen to them more.

I then found out that SIS Japan still existed so provided Rieko (who was running it, although it wasn't active at all then) with photos and a review from the convention. I was so impressed by the band and excited, but there was almost no one talking about or promoting the Stranglers in Japan. So I thought, 'If no one else does it, I'll do it.'

With the help of friends, I posted a review in a music magazine, carried out an interview with JJ for a different music magazine, provided information about *Gankutsuou*, a Japanese TV animation series from 2004 which JJ did the soundtrack for, to Adrian of The Rat's Lair (the Stranglers' official online merchandise shop), who shortly after suggested that Rieko and I start the official website, which we did.

I translated the lyrics of JJ's tracks on *Gankutsuou* and started helping him as his interpreter which led me to also help his karate organization with interpretation, arranging their trip in Japan, etc. I also flew to the UK for the annual UK tour and began writing reviews on our website.

The Stranglers came to play at the *Summer Sonic* festival in 2007 and Punkspring in 2010 but in 2019, the band finally returned to Japan for their three gigs in Tokyo after an absence of 27 years. These were some of the best gigs I've been to. It was personally very emotional but the band was on top form and the atmosphere superb. We were talking about having them play again in 2021, if possible, but due to Covid it has not happened. It's never going to be the same without Dave, even if they come again.

NIGEL PECKOVER

I played against the Stranglers team in the 5-a-side football competition held at the Pontins Convention in 2001. It was great to speak to Baz for the first time, and I also had some nice conversations with Paul and Jeremy Burnel. My team included three members of a Stranglers tribute band called No More Heroes (I was not one of them) who were pretty good at the time, so it was great to play against our heroes at football. The game was very exciting, but our team was not very popular with 100 per cent of the crowd as we beat the Stranglers team 3-2. I was certainly The Man They Loved to Hate as I scored all three of our goals.

I discussed the game with JJ sometime later at a record signing event and he asked if I was the player who injured Jeremy in the game. I genuinely don't remember doing so, but if I did I am sorry!

BAR CUBA

5 DECEMBER 2001, MACCLESFIELD, UK

LIONEL J MAJOR

When JJ was touring with *The 3 Men and Black* in 2001, I ventured from my digs in Manchester to nearby Macclesfield. Arriving at the venue early for the sound check, the roadies were setting up and there was no security so I just walked in. I could hear someone speaking in French, presumably on a mobile in a room. It was JJ. Eventually, he emerged from the room and, as he was about to walk past me, I politely asked him if he could spare a few moments of his time. We spent a good few minutes chatting while he signed items of memorabilia. It was JJ himself who asked most of the questions. He was very affable.

MAGIC BUS

7 NOVEMBER 2002, MARCON, VENEZIA, ITALY

MICHELE SAVOLDI

Michele Savoldi with the Stranglers and The Mugshots

I fell in love with the Stranglers in 2000. The following year I gave life to The Mugshots, my own band very much inspired by the Stranglers and by Alice Cooper:

many years later (2019) I even managed to see them both playing in London at the O2 Arena.

It was 2002 when I first saw the Stranglers live at the Magic Bus in Marcon, Venice. It was an incredibly energetic show despite the lack of audience: every other concert I've attended to in Italy was actually much more packed with people. After the show I managed to record a brief interview with Paul Roberts and gave JJ a demo of my band. After a few weeks, I sent JJ an email and to my surprise he replied with a few pieces of advice for our music. A friendship developed...

In 2004, I attended the London after show party at the *Norfolk Coast*'s presentation gig. I met JJ, Dave Ruffy from The Ruts (who produced the Stranglers' album) and a weird but lovely friend of his who looked like Miles Davis and gave me some hash! Over the following years, I kept JJ updated with the releases from my band and eventually, in 2007, we supported the Stranglers at the Transilvania Club in Milano.

2011 marked the 10th anniversary of The Mugshots so we organized a concert/party sponsored by Triumph Brescia (our hometown): JJ was meant to be a special guest but he couldn't come for personal reasons, so Baz Warne together with TV Smith from The Adverts – joined the party and we experienced an unbelievable weekend. Three years later we supported the Stranglers at Vox Club in Nonantola, Modena and at the New Age Club in Roncade, Treviso. I have a very fond memory of myself, Dave Greenfield and JJ Burnel on the Stranglers' tour bus smoking weed while talking about the italian political situation.

In 2019 I attended two gigs, one in Bologna – with an aftershow experience on a beautiful terrace of a hotel together with JJ and Baz... and some joints as well – and one in Torino, where I managed to introduce renowned Italian singer Enrico Ruggeri to his youth hero - JJ Burnel!

During the pandemic, The Mugshots released a single, recorded by each musician separately, to raise funds for a local hospital since Italy was suffering some hard times. Baz Warne provided a beautiful guitar solo and the *Sunderland Echo* penned a beautiful article about the collaboration. I loved the fact that Baz told the journalist that, 'The Mugshots are buddies of the Stranglers.'

QUEEN MARGARET UNION

16 NOVEMBER 2002, GLASGOW, UK

YVONNE MORRISON

I've been going to Stranglers gigs since the '90s. I was working for the promoter at this gig

Yvonne Morrison had a ciggie with Dave

and sitting in the production office myself. Dave came in and asked if he could have a ciggie in there, as he wouldn't smoke in the dressing room. I said no problem and we chatted for about 20 minutes, him regaling me with some old gig tales, whilst all the time transferring cigarettes from a packet into a gold cigarette case. He talked about his love of ale, his pub and how, back in the day, he would have quite a few pints on stage, but would then have to wait for Hugh to play a long guitar solo so he could nip off stage to the loo and get back before the end of the guitar solo. He then said that lately he had switched to Bacardi and Coke, as the guitar solos weren't now quite long enough to cope with pints of ale. Great man, great band. Don't stop touring please.

RECORDING STUDIOS

7 NOVEMBER 2003, BATH, UK

STEPHEN HOWARD

I have been a Stranglers fan since buying the 'No More Heroes' single in 1977. They are a band who have soundtracked my life and provided great moments of enjoyment and excitement, whether that be from new releases or gigs. The band, well JJ, also provided me with a once in a lifetime experience. In the early Noughties, as the internet gathered pace and influence, I decided to set up a website about the band. It was one of those basic Freeserve-type websites. I used the site, which I called 'Written in Red', to collate news from various sources with regards to releases, tours, etc., and it covered the band, Hugh Cornwell and the solo work of Paul Roberts. This was all taking place in the time between *Coup de Grace* and the release of *Norfolk Coast*.

I was also an active member of the 'Burning Up Time' fan forum. One day a forum member put out into the open an e-mail address for JJ relating to his activities with UK Shidokan. There was a general lack of information at this time about the band's activities and the forum member suggested whether it would be worth e-mailing JJ. So I took the plunge and e-mailed JJ. I introduced myself and explained what I was doing, asking if he could provide any information.

A few days later, I got an e-mail back from JJ in which he gave some information about the band working on a new album, which was to become *Norfolk Coast*. In thanking JJ, I asked if I could contact him again in the future and he agreed. This set in motion a regular exchange of information about the album for me to publish, some of which was exclusive.

One day, in late summer 2003, I received an e-mail from JJ that I could never have expected: an invite to join him at their studios near Bath for a pre-release listening party for the new album. As I was travelling from Manchester, JJ also arranged overnight accommodation in a nearby hostelry. So, in November, off I set to Bath with my mate, a fellow Stranglers fan who JJ had agreed could come along.

JJ met me in the Tuckers Grave pub where we had, in those parts, the obligatory cider, and where he explained it would be just us and music journalist, John Robb, and that we would be going for meal later. I had expected it to be a mass attendance event, so I was suddenly even more awestruck; this was basically a personal event with JJ. We were then whisked off to the band's base where we met Baz and Paul too and were given a guided tour.

We then went into the studio and, straight off the mixing desk, the brilliant opening to 'Norfolk Coast' echoed around the room. As it kicked in, JJ did one of his karate kicks. As the album progressed there were looks between all present which said 'wow'. After the listening, it was off for something to eat and more talk about the album and tales from the band's past. Some of the band's entourage were also present and I was introduced to Dorothy Howe, who would be handling the promotion and publicity for the album.

JJ then took us back to our accommodation and arranged to pick us up the following morning to take us back to the station. On the way he passed me a press pack and we stopped off for coffee and more Stranglers conversation. In the months that followed, I was able to continue to provide regular updates from JJ and Dorothy about the release of *Norfolk Coast.* The album is widely agreed to have been a turning point in resurrecting the band's profile, and to be a part of that was a great personal experience and privilege. I continued with the website up to and just after the release of *Suite XVI* and received a similar invite which I couldn't accept due to family reasons.

It's often said you should never meet your heroes. I did, and it was one of the greatest experiences I have had. For a five or six-year period I was able to be a cog, albeit a little one, in the history of the Stranglers. The fact that I was allowed to be shows the unique nature of this band, who have always been close and appreciative of their fan base. I lost touch with JJ afterwards, but I will forever be able to remember his friendliness, kindness, and the unique experience of my 'fifteen minutes of fame'.

SEC ARMADILLO

19 DECEMBER 2003, GLASGOW, UK

CRAIG WOOD

By the time the millennium came around the band had a website that kept us up to date with all the latest news. One evening I surfed in and discovered one Baz Warne was a new Strangler, following the departure of John Ellis. I was not sorry to see John and his thin strings go, and in fact looked forward to seeing, and hearing, the new boy after Dave was quoted as saying the Small Town Heroes wrote some good tunes.

The new boy did well at his first proper gig in October 2002 at the QMU in Glasgow, where the sound was unfortunately shit. A few new songs were aired and 'Peaches' and 'Death and Night and Blood' emerged from the closet. I then travelled to see them play at the Falkirk Festival in May 2003, where they were really good, playing 'Curfew' for the first time (to my ears anyway).

All this was leading up to *Norfolk Coast*. I remember a post on the website saying that the title track would be played in advance of the album release on an online radio station. I would guess there were thousands just like me tuning in to hear it, and it didn't disappoint.

This proved to be an album I really liked, especially 'Big Thing Coming', which I had heard when they supported UB40 at the Glasgow Armadillo. At this gig, as the band played 'No More Heroes', I looked around me. There was no sign of the girl with the cleavage like a folded mattress who always gets JJ's plectrum, so I carefully calculated where he would be, got into position and held my hand out in hope of a handshake with the legend, if not an actual plectrum. Instead, I felt a cold clammy presence in my hand and discovered JJ had given me his bottle of Holsten Pils. As I stood transfixed, and a little disappointed, I realised I had an actual JJ souvenir in my hand, just as the steward came over and snatched it out of my hand saying, 'No alcohol allowed in the auditorium!'

THE JUNCTION

5 OCTOBER 2006, CAMBRIDGE, UK

ADAM BROADWAY

I moved to Cambridge around 1988 and was present when, on Valentine's Day 1990, the Cambridge Junction opened. This was a much-needed venue for a city that was missing out on many new and well-established bands, especially indie and post punk groups. The Stranglers played there a few times.

Cambridge Junction in October 2006 was my 500th gig, according to my rough records. And Cambridge Stranglers gigs, being the home town of some of the band, always had a bit of special feel to them. The crowd were warmer and there was good camaraderie. The band also seemed just that bit more engaged.

The crowd were loud and boisterous. A few younger members of the crowd thought it was a good idea to climb on stage. Fair enough, we used to do this a lot back in the 1980s. However, this time JJ seemed to have had enough. One fan jumped up onto the stage and started dancing around. JJ went alongside him and lifted his foot and placed it nearly under this guy's chin. The fan fell to the floor... it looked like he was out cold. However, he soon got off and jumped back into the crowd. The gig continued.

I have seen the Stranglers 15 times. They remain one of the UK's best ever bands, consistently getting better and better. The last gig I saw them play was the last gig of the sadly postponed last tour... February 2022 at the Cambridge Corn Exchange. I am not sure if I was ever as tense and emotional before a gig. Dave Greenfield's death in 2021 hit me very hard. I have no idea why. I only met him very briefly once, and never knew him, but as a now local Cambridge inhabitant I could feel the love for and bond with him. Friends tell me how he had gone to their wedding, or how he'd say hello while sipping a pint in the Red Lion in Histon.

To this day, I do not know how Baz and JJ performed the solo in 'And If You Should See Dave'. It makes me emotional now, just thinking about it. So, thank you, the Stranglers. You mean a lot to me.

THE MAJESTIC

10 MARCH 2004, CANNES, FRANCE

TIM BAGNALL

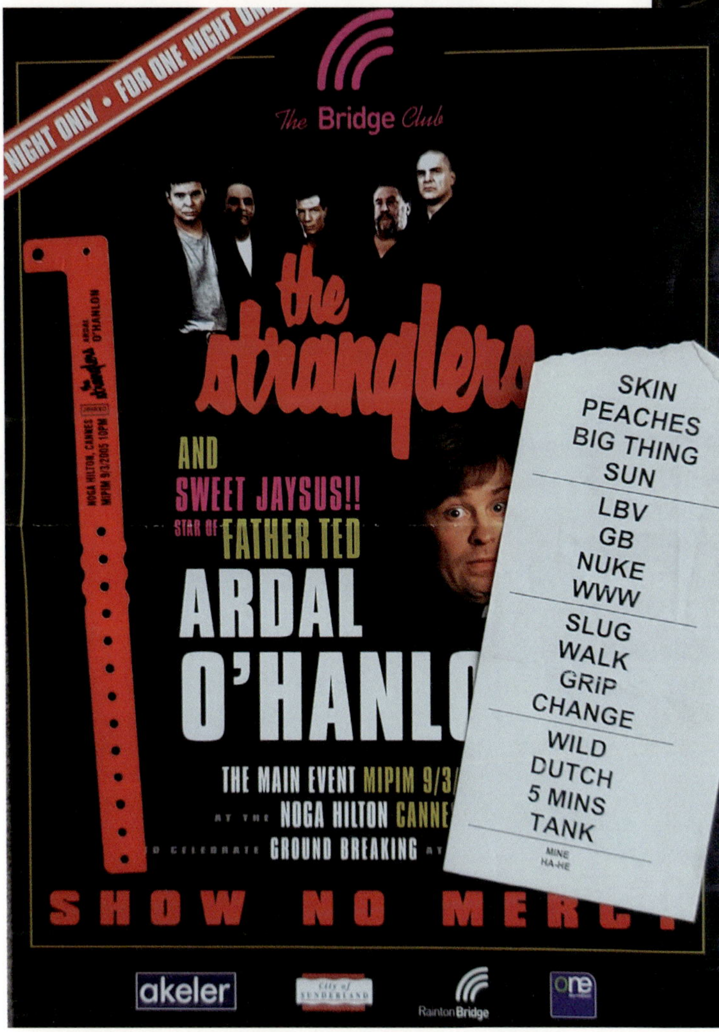

Tim Bagnall's work's piss-up in 2004 included the Stranglers as the corporate entertainment - and they were back in 2005

I worked in the property sector for a few years. The annual trade event is called MIPIM and is usually held in Cannes. Lots of industry people launching projects, selling their services, and generally getting pissed for a few days. In 2004 some genius managed to book the Stranglers.

Crammed onto a tiny stage, it was great to be up close and personal with the band. There was still a handful of real fans amongst the property fraternity, so when Paul struck the wood block during 'Always the Sun' the familiar response echoed back at him – 'whayy' – and there was a collective 'for fuck's sake!' from the band. There's no escape. They were so good they got booked again the following year. It was another storming gig, just as claustrophobic as the previous year. It was fascinating to watch them interact at such close quarters.

BARRYMORE'S

19 OCTOBER 2004, OTTOWA, CANADA

MARTIN ALLAN

Martin Allan caught the band on their way to the Ottawa gig in 2004

I live in Canada. The band don't come through here very often, so I always try to make the most of my chances to see them. Back in 2004, the *Norfolk Coast* tour was announced with two dates within a few hours of my town (St Catharine's, which was the first gig of the 1993 North American tour) and I made plans to attend both. My wife and I found extremely cheap flights to the first show in Ottawa, and we booked that and the Toronto date. We arrived at the airport for our flight and were going through security when my wife was instructed to remove her boots for further inspection. As she was removing them, I heard a man with an English accent behind me shout, 'Woo-hoo, strip search!' I turned around to find myself face to face with the entire band and a couple of the crew.

I had a great time chatting with JJ and Jet in the deserted departure lounge and with Paul, Dave and Baz (who was playing his first North American show with the band) while waiting for the bags to come out at the Ottawa end of the flight. I've had a few meetings over the years with various members of the band but none as random as this.

A friend went to interview the band at their hotel once and called me to say he had some pictures that I'd probably never seen before. He was made to conduct the interview with his trousers around his ankles and in return got some pretty funny pictures of the band in the same setup.

LE KRAKATOA

18 NOVEMBER 2004, BORDEAUX, FRANCE

EWAN MURRAY

I remember going to Le Krakatoa, Bordeaux in 2004 on the *Norfolk Coast* Euro tour and meeting so many great people. Also, there were some great trips to Prague, Milan and Lyon. I also had a great laugh on my birthday in Eindhoven in 2015, meeting up with so many of the Familyinblack.

WESTLANDS LEISURE COMPLEX

22 OCTOBER 2005, YEOVIL, UK

BRIAN ASTLEY

Although I had seen them in 1986, I didn't see them again until 2004 in Newport, some 18 years later. They then advertised a gig in Plymouth, which I had booked a hotel for, etc. but it got cancelled and I'd lost out on some money. The merch girl, Annie, put me on the guest list for Yeovil. I got a train to Bristol and then it was a two hour or so bus journey from there. It was a few months after my dad died and I was still very emotional at the time, but it was probably the gig and the trip that started me on my Stranglers gig adventure, which has taken me to many places.

PAUL DIXON

It was the *Norfolk Coast* tour. I walked back stage and ended up chatting to the band and being handed a plate by JJ and invited to help myself to the buffet.

SUITE XVI

RELEASED 18 SEPTEMBER 2006

CRAIG WOOD

I started to travel to see the band whenever the opportunity arose. In Perth, we arrived early and scouted out the venue. We became aware of a small flurry of activity outside the concert hall. It was Baz going in for the sound check. I shook hands with him and he told me JJ was in the cafe opposite. There were a few people around him as he was trying to sidle off. One was a peroxide-blond '77 style punk who kept distracting him as I tried to attract his attention. JJ happily posed for photographs with him as I meekly tried to attract the legend's attention. ('Ehmm, excuse me, ehh, Mr JJ'...) Eventually I got my 15 seconds and I shook the hand that had played 'Tank' so many times. 'I've waited 25 years for this moment', I said. 'You could say we grew up together', he replied. And then he was gone.

Then the website announced that the band had played their first gig as a four piece after Paul had left. I had accepted Paul, though others had never taken to him, but I didn't feel this was a particularly bad thing, or sad either for that matter. *Suite XVI* was in the offing, and the gig on the tour was really good, being heavy on the JJ vocal side, and Baz seemed to undergo a bit of a personality change, as he went from the quiet boy with his head down concentrating on playing his guitar to quite a brash character as a frontman.

The album was brilliant. The band had produced the absolutely wonderful, the sublime, what is still the best track of the twenty-first century in 'Barbara'. The initial burst of bass, the guitar, the piano, the way Dave bubbles and sparkles through the chorus, the growing, squealing organ growing through the second verse, the e-theremin and the wonderful melody of the chorus, not to mention the solid wall of bass throughout. What a song. And there was also 'A Soldier's Diary', 'She's Slipping Away', 'Summat Outta Nowt', 'Relentless' and 'Bless You'. It was a brilliant album full of big hitters.

JJ was quoted as saying the band were always meant to be a four piece, and that having a frontman singer was a mistake. I couldn't agree more with him. The original four Stranglers were all instrumentalists, and this was what made their sound so special, peaking with the Raven. I recall JJ on *The One Show* explaining the intro to 'No More Heroes' as the band members wanting to show off to each other. The Stranglers were always at their best using their instruments to do their talking for them. The guitar in 'Toiler' and the apocalyptic ending to 'Genetix' were only two examples of what the band did best, and here they were 27 years later back on track.

EMPIRE

6 OCTOBER 2006, SHEPHERD'S BUSH, LONDON, UK

STEVE WORRALL

Although the Stranglers were one of the most important and much-loved bands of my youth - it was JJ who inspired me to pick up the bass, and I'd love to say I was loyal and stuck with the band after Hugh's departure; I didn't stop supporting my team when they sold my favourite striker - the fact is that I'd kind of started losing interest even before Hugh left.

I wasn't a huge fan of *Dreamtime*, and *10* was even worse. Despite a couple of decent tracks, I felt it was ruined by poor production, and the fact that the biggest hit off the album was a rather pedestrian run-through of '96 Tears' probably summed it up. So I can't just blame Paul Roberts. Like a lot of Team Hugh fans, I'd already given up a bit. I was there at Hugh's last show at the Alexandra Palace, but it was tired and lethargic, as the live video evidences pretty conclusively. It definitely felt like it was the right time for the band to call it a day (or night).

I was interested when JJ, Dave and Jet got a new line-up together with singer Paul Roberts and guitarist John Ellis, and I checked out a couple of their new songs, but I didn't like Roberts' voice and just felt the quality of their songwriting was lacking something.

It took the release of *Norfolk Coast* in 2004 to pique my interest again. The reviews were good and other Stranglers-fan friends were making positive noises. I got the album and was impressed - John Ellis had been replaced by Baz Warne on guitars, who also contributed some songs, Roberts' singing seemed much better - but most importantly, the crunching bass riff on the opening (title) track was immense. This was more like it! Dave Greenfield's trademark organ was back too. It was a really fresh, invigorating return to form.

Things really took a massive upturn for the band with the release of the superb *Suite XVI* album in September 2006. Roberts had left, the band reverting to their traditional four-piece line-up, with JJ and Baz Warne sharing lead vocal duties. Baz was a revelation, not only on the album but live too, and the gigs were fantastic.

I took the plunge and went to see them at Shepherd's Bush Empire and was totally blown away. The sound and energy harked back to *The Raven* era, and I felt like a teenage fan again. Baz was so good that you forgot about Hugh. There's no point trying to compare the two. He takes the role perfectly - the old songs are handled in a respectful manner, but he injects his own considerable personality and style into proceedings. He's a great singer and guitarist and there is an undoubted chemistry and bond between him, the audience and his bandmates.

Most importantly, the new songs finally stood up to the best of their impressive back catalogue; 'Unbroken', 'Spectre of Love' and 'Barbara' in particular were to me at least to be ranked among all their classics. I almost felt vindicated, like maybe I wasn't the only one who'd had this journey with the Stranglers, and not the only one to see the light again since, after many years in a Stranglers-less wilderness.

CORPORATION

7 OCTOBER 2006, SHEFFIELD, UK

MICHAEL FISHER

In 2006, my favourite band were playing just up the road in Sheffield at the Corporation. I hadn't got a ticket, and it was a last-minute thing, but I decided I must go and see them because it was just a short drive from Nottingham. I managed to pay on the door. Once in the venue, I was pleased to have made the journey. It began with the usual formula – the lights dimmed and 'Waltzinblack' blasted out of the speakers. On came the band with no Paul. I hadn't realised he'd left the band. So back to the original number of a four piece. It seemed to look so natural and right, with Baz taking on Paul's singing duties and JJ back on lead vocals too. After a great show and a new line up, I took the short journey back up to Nottingham, looking forward to a new era of the Meninblack.

EXETER LEISURE CENTRE

23 JUNE 2007, EXETER, UK

GEORGE WALKER

I was 11 years old and it was a rainy day in Exeter. Being so young I didn't know what to expect. Arriving at the venue to see everyone head to toe in black, sporting Dr Marten's and jet black hair, was very intimidating for a young boy. But as soon as the lights went down and 'Waltzinblack' started playing, my heart raced with excitement. JJ had just started playing his Shuler bass. I remember hearing his bass sound thump through my ears and chest and thinking, 'This guy is the fucking man.' JJ is a fierce-looking man, but he could see I was with my father. It was our way of sharing a bond, going to see the Meninblack growl through a set. It was that very moment which inspired me to play bass.

MARKTROCK

25 AUGUST 2007, POPERINGE, BELGIUM

ESKA GEBRUERS

The first time I saw the Stranglers I was just six years old but I still remember it vividly. My dad is a big fan – he first saw the Stranglers in Viane, Belgium in September 1992. We live in Belgium and we've been going to London for seven years now, just to see the Stranglers! We've seen the *Decades Apart* tour at Hammersmith Apollo in 2010, the Black and Blue tour at the Apollo in 2011, the *Giants* and *Feel It Live* tours at the Roundhouse in 2012 and 2013, the *Ruby* tour at Hammersmith in 2014

Eska Gebruers first saw the Stranglers when she was six and now she's a huge fan

and in 2018 we were at Brixton Academy. We've seen the Stranglers at Fiesta City in Verviers (Belgium) in 2015, and in Bierfeesten in Oudenaarde (Belgium) and Nirwana in Tilburg (The Netherlands), both in 2016.

And in February 2022, we went to both concerts in London. This was very emotional for us - the first time seeing the Stranglers perform without Dave. Tears were shed both nights. Two things I'll never forget: on the first night, a man came up to me and said that he recognised me from seeing me on concerts when I was little; and on the second night, a man told my dad, 'Your daughter knows every word to every song... She's perfect!'

Fun fact: I always want to stand on Baz's side (sorry, JJ!) For me, he is a real Strangler. I don't know the Stranglers without him.

ABC

1 NOVEMBER 2007, GLASGOW, UK

CRAIG WOOD

The band's next appearance came as quite a surprise. There was no mention of anything unusual as we made our way to the ABC in 2007, expecting the normal setlist of well-established favourites along with one or two surprises. When they started with 'No More Heroes' quickly followed by 'Ugly', there was no sign of anything out of the ordinary. But then JJ addressed the troops and told them that this was the thirtieth anniversary of the *No More Heroes* tour coming to town and him being chucked down the stairs by Strathclyde Police, and they were going to play the same set. What can I say? The crowd went mad, and there then followed a very special and memorable gig. Spare a thought for my mate; he couldn't get to empty his bladder as there was no 'Golden Brown' or 'Always the Sun'.

TIM BAGNALL

On my list of memorable gigs is the trio of performances that made up the mini *Rattus at the Roundhouse* tour in 2007. It was a repeat of the exact set they played 30 years earlier at the Roundhouse. I said memorable, although I'm surprised that I can remember any of it. Me and my mate Fraser flew up to Glasgow for the first gig. Needless to say, beer was drunk on the way, and we were on top form by the time we arrived at the ABC. Unfortunately, they had run out of draught beer and we had to make do with two bottles of Pils in a pint pot each time we went to the bar. Bad decision – we got absolutely battered. Glasgow is traditionally acknowledged as one of the best gigs on tour and the city did not disappoint. The band were on fire and the ABC went mad.

After an extra night in Glasgow, we got the train down to Manchester where once again the beer was flowing freely. Meeting up with a few old faces in traditional pre-gig pub the Jabez Clegg, we then went on to a rammed Manchester Academy for a repeat performance.

JAMES BECK

In 2007, I was so addicted to stage-sharing with the band that I got myself in a bit of a pickle. I had been given a pass by the Stranglers' tour manager Gary Knighton to take residence in one of the upper circle boxes. After one vodka too many, I climbed down the trellising of the stage and discovered that I was too far away from the stage - and too far down to return to base. In essence, I was rather goosed. All I could do was await Big Allan Robinson to come to my rescue, and after a debate over who was getting to keep me, ie. was I the property of the Stranglers or Strathclyde Police, Gaz Knighton informed me that at one time Carling Academies had considered bringing a charge of incitement against me. Some smart arse recorded my exploits and it went viral, the clip becoming known as 'Spiderman joins the show.' To this day, Baz comments on that fateful night.

ROUNDHOUSE

4 NOVEMBER 2007, LONDON, UK

MICHAEL MCCLUGHIN

We were treated to one and a third concerts, thanks to a few issues with Dave's kit, and a great line from JJB: 'Fuck the curfew... We do what we fucking want.'

TIM BAGNALL

We caught the train again the next day to London for the final date. The gig was heaving, and the bar was rows deep. Gear failure meant the concert was restarted and we got to hear half the set again. This was the best gig of the three, probably because of the historical context, and it rounded off an amazing few days of following the band, meeting old friends and new.

O2 ACADEMY

3 NOVEMBER 2008, NEWCASTLE, UK

IAN CUNNINGHAM

I went with a bunch of mates to the O2 Academy. It was a cold night and, thinking this homeless guy looked rather cold, l took off my coat and gave it to him. He was very grateful and after a brief chat l caught up with everyone and we went to the pub for a few pre-gig drinks. We joined the queue outside the O2. It was when l got to the front that l realised that my ticket was in the inside pocket of the coat I'd given away. l legged it down towards the railway station to where the homeless guy had been sat but there was no sign of him.

l wasn't going to miss the gig, so l decided I'd try and buy a ticket from somebody outside the O2 and headed back. Guess who l found trying to sell my ticket? He even tried selling me it until l told him it was my coat he was wearing. Many grovelling apologies later l was in the O2, and had a great night. I've seen the Stranglers many, many times since, most recently at Newcastle's City Hall. l keep a tight hold of my ticket.

Ian Cunningham gave his coat to a homeless guy, and his gig ticket too!

SHEPHERD'S BUSH EMPIRE

14 NOVEMBER 2008, LONDON, UK

STEVE ANSELL

On my 50th birthday, my good friend Adrian said that for my birthday he would take myself and my wife Joanne to see a show in London with dinner and a hotel as a present. Checking my diary, I saw that the Stranglers were playing at Shepherd's Bush empire so I said, 'I really want to go and see the Stranglers that night.' He replied, along with Joanne, 'You can see them anytime, but

Steve Ansell with JJ

you're only 50 once.' Reluctantly, I agreed but I was very disappointed.

Come the day, Adrian and Eileen picked myself and Joanne up to take us both to London. On arrival at the hotel, in Shepherd's Bush, we checked in and went for a drink in the bar. Shortly after this, Paul Roberts, Baz Warne, JJ Burnel and Dave Greenfield walked through the bar on the way to a sound check. Unbeknownst to me, one of Adrian's friends was something to do with the tour. Adrian said, 'I think the game is up.' It was a set up; we had guest list tickets for the show, which was awesome. After this, we all went back to the hotel and all the Stranglers came to the bar for some drinks, allowing me to get some photos with the band. I was one happy person that night.

ALHAMBRA THEATRE

27 FEBRUARY 2010, DUNFERMLINE, UK

STUART SIMPSON

Stuart Simpson has amassed a lot of Stranglers memorabilia

I remember going to see the Stranglers with my dad who got me into their music when I was 16. The first time I saw them was in the Alhambra, Dunfermline, and they quickly became one of my favourite bands. Over time, I have collected various memorabilia, including newspaper cuttings: some of which date back to the 1970s.

I remember going to see the Stranglers movie, *Death and Night and Blood*, in 2019. I was one of the few people to see the film as, sadly, it didn't get released. This is a particular stand out memory for me as the original drummer, Jet Black, turned up and was welcomed by a standing ovation – I had goose bumps. The film itself was fantastic and a bonus was my name being in the credits.

The standout Stranglers gig for me was at Caerphilly Castle in 2019 when they were supported by Ruts DC. Everything was excellent: the weather, the sound, and the performance.

My favourite song is 'Something Better Change' because I feel it's still relevant today. Things do need to change; people can be nasty especially just because someone looks different. The song stands against that. Not to mention the raw vocals from JJ Burnel.

I was born too late to see them in their heyday, but I've followed them through the years I have been around and have loved every minute of it.

PUNKSPRING FESTIVAL, MAKUHARI MESSE CONVENTION CENTRE

4 APRIL 2010, CHIBA, JAPAN

CHRIS DIXON

When I was a young whippersnapper, I bought a cheap tape recorder and began taping random songs off the radio. One of those songs was 'Something Better Change', and I wore the tape out listening to it. It was 1977 and my dad sneered at me, 'You don't like punk, do you?'

'What's punk?' I replied, never having heard the word. And I'd never heard of the Stranglers either, for that matter – I was only eleven – but as I got older and grew more aware of the important things in life, I came to love this quirky, aggressive, tender, menacing, intelligent, sophisticated band. And, several decades later, I still do!

So it was with huge excitement that, in early 2010, I heard the Stranglers were coming to Japan – where I had been resident since 1988 – to play at the Punkspring Festival. I was finally going see my heroes in action for the first time. I was not disappointed. It was without doubt one of the best gigs I have ever seen – and I have seen a *lot* of bands. And then – I couldn't believe my luck – in November 2019, the Stranglers played their first full live shows in Japan for 27 years. Three whole nights in Tokyo, bringing my Stranglers total to four.

Baz... What a great voice this man has, at once sexy, threatening, lascivious - and serial killer! JJ, grinding away with that bass sound that makes the Stranglers so recognisable. Dave, a firm favourite of the crowd, whose every little synthesised ping drew a squeal of admiration. And Jim, whose awesome drumming deservedly earned him JJ's moniker, 'Son of Jet'!

One night, I attended a meet-and-greet and sound check. 'Never meet your heroes, Chris,' cautioned my friend John, 'they'll only disappoint.' But they did not disappoint. They were gracious and pleasant. JJ was engaging, and most interested in me and my life in Japan. There was no sign of an ego that demanded to be the centre of attention. I was impressed by their curiosity – which I guess is one of the reasons the Stranglers' music is so creative and original.

It was just six months after these shows, six months after I shook the hand of the great Dave Greenfield, that he passed away. I was shocked. But what a legacy he leaves...

WYESIDE MUSIC FESTIVAL

21 AUGUST 2010, HEREFORD, UK

POPPY SAVAGE

Although I wasn't alive when the band first formed, they have been a vital part of my life, something that I share with my dad. He introduced me to the Stranglers when we travelled to and from his house every weekend, starting with the *Black and White* album. We would mime Dave's amazing keyboard solos and shout the lyrics together in the car. These journeys hold some of the best memories of my childhood. Since then, we have attended gigs at Birmingham countless times and have heard all of our favourites. My fondest memory is sneaking backstage at *Wyeside Music Festival* in 2010 and meeting JJ, Jet and Dave. My dad and I saw people going to 'meet the band' and he ushered my sister and I to get past the side of the stage, knowing this would be the only chance to meet them.

18-year-old me ran into up to JJ with a smile plastered on my face, 'Hi, I'm Poppy'. JJ smiled and replied, 'I am sure you are.' They were kind enough to have their photos taken with me before we were escorted back to the festival. The Stranglers have continued to inspire me, even helping me to achieve my music degree, using their story and musical style within my analysis. Without the passion they have shared with me I wouldn't have been inspired to learn keyboard, perform in a band, and become a music teacher. But, most importantly, I wouldn't have shared so many wonderful moments with my dad.

JOHNNY NORGROVE

We travelled to this gig only wanting to watch the Stranglers, so made the unwise decision to head into Hereford and drink the under-the-counter scrumpy at each pub. Some of it looked like it had frogspawn in - but it was tasty! We headed back to the venue and met up with some top Welsh lads who I have met up with at gigs over the years. The festival had been rearranged and there weren't many folks there, so the atmosphere was flat. And to make things worse, the heavens opened. The rain wasn't as bad as at the *Looe Festival* but the downpour made it very muddy.

The band seemed subdued, but I was having a great time jumping around on my own and my cider-addled brain thought it would be a good idea to get on the stage. This was despite me being in the process of having a tooth implant and having a temporary plate which was like having a beer mat in my mouth. I went head first over the first barrier and just about scrambled up on to the stage in front of JJ, who luckily smiled rather than sending me back with a boot.

Delighted I had cheered JJ up, I did a little jig which was brought to an abrupt end by a security chap yanking me away while I was trying to say 'cheers' to JJ.

Unfortunately, it caused my false tooth to shoot out and land at JJ's feet! I struggled with the security chap and called JJ to get me my smile back. Whilst continuing to play on, JJ used all his karate skills to flick my tooth back to me which I popped back in my gob! I was then ejected but ran back round to watch the rest of the gig.

The incident was caught on *YouTube* and what I missed (because I had departed the stage) was JJ in bits and then going over to Baz to tell him what had happened and him bursting out laughing. So my mission to cheer them up succeeded!

I was a custody sergeant in the Old Bill and my colleagues would show the *YouTube* video to someone brought into the cells in handcuffs. It was a great way of calming them down and breaking the ice by showing them that police are humans too.

RADISSON BLU HOTEL

21 OCTOBER 2010, SLIGO, IRELAND

JIM O'MAHONY

I have been a fan since the late Seventies and have seen them live seven times. The first time was at the Arcadia Ballroom in Cork when they were promoting *The Raven* and since then I've seen them in Sligo, Belfast, Dublin, Limerick and Dublin again.

The Sligo gig in 2010 took place at the Radisson Blu Hotel in Rosses Point. I didn't manage to book a room there but was able to book a B&B very close to the venue. My wife and I travelled up from Cork on the day of the gig by car, an arduous five-hour journey due to roadworks in the West of Ireland. By the time we got to our accommodation, it was very close to gig time.

The Stranglers were brilliant on the night with Baz playing a hilarious version of 'My Lovely Horse' from the TV show *Father Ted* which went down a treat. Towards the end of the gig, Baz kept saying, 'See you in the bar after the gig.' I said to myself that I had to get to the bar at all costs and asked the bouncer afterwards if the Stranglers were going to be in the hotel bar. He declined to answer and blocked our passage, telling us that only hotel guests were allowed in. Out the door we went, fairly disappointed.

Mother Nature called on leaving, so I went back into the hotel and asked the same bouncer if I could use the toilet so he let me in. On coming out, I somehow managed to exit another door and, lo and behold, I was in the hotel bar. I rushed back out and called my wife and we went back and into the hotel bar this new way, avoiding the bouncer.

I could see Jet and Baz holding court at the back of the bar. I was starstruck when I saw Jet. What a legend. I had a wonderful conversation with both, but particularly Jet. I told him I had first seen them in the Arcadia in Cork all those years ago, when they were promoting *The Raven*, and asked him for an autograph. I only had on me a receipt from a fast-food outlet we had stopped at on the way up from Cork. Jet was just about to sign it when I saw a lady to his right, who was observing in an over protective way, advise him not to sign it. But Jet was having nothing of this and signed it no problem. Having Dutch courage due to the drink I had taken, I asked him, 'Who is she?' His answer was classic. 'She's the Strange Little Girl,' he said, with a twinkle in his eye.

JOE COLEMAN

Joe Coleman and his wife Olivia were staying at the same hotel as the Strangers

I have been a fan for 40 years and have seen the Stranglers many times. I picked fruit and vegetables in the fields of Ireland to get money to buy *No More Heroes*. I was up on stage at the Olympia in Dublin in the Nineties and about to shake hands with Paul Roberts near the end of the gig when security grabbed me and threw me out. I was left outside in the street minus my Stranglers t-shirt and heard the band playing another three songs from outside.

In 2010, my wife Olivia and I were lucky to be staying in the same hotel as the band and had a drink with the lads. JJ spoke about the bass guitar and his pal Lemmy from Motörhead, who was sick at the time. We also spoke of his karate and his love for motor bikes. And we spoke about Hugh leaving the band, which he didn't want to talk about too much, which is understandable. Baz spoke about Sunderland - even though I am a Leeds United supporter! Jet Black spoke about his Irish connection to County Roscommon, and Dave was just a pure gentleman.

MICHAEL MCCLUGHIN

2010 brought a random appearance at a music festival in Sligo, Ireland and a gig that was like a school dance, in the ballroom of a hotel. Making sure I got there in plenty of time, it was only right to bounce into the bar, next to the ballroom, and listen to the soundcheck over a few amber nectars. To my surprise, it wasn't long before JJB, Baz, Jet and Dave had the same idea. I had come prepared... with my picture of me on stage in Germany.

Now, over the preceding (and receding) years, I'd made a point of tapping the top of my chrome dome, and pointing at JJB during gigs, accusing him falsely of going bald, which still remains completely untrue. I'm not sure if he came over to my table to give me the kicking I deserved, or if he'd remembered my 'dancing' on stage in Germany or maybe it was just that I pointed at my pic, and made the international sign for, 'Can I have your autograph please?' (which confusingly is the same as the, 'Can I get the bill please?' one), but I was soon joined by JJ and Baz, happy to chat and sign my photo.

JJ asked me what I was doing 'over here' and when I said I'd only had to drive down from Belfast, he brought my man crush crashing to the ground with the gut-wrenching line, 'I thought you were Welsh!' But my crush was instantly back on when he called over Jet and Dave to sign my photo, which now takes pride of place - on canvas - in my man cave. It was a great close-knit gig, drinking in the bar with all the band and most of the audience until 2am!

MANCHESTER ACADEMY

26 MARCH 2011, MANCHESTER, UK

CAITLIN TENCH

I first saw the Stranglers at the wee age of 11. Since then, I have seen them every year with my dad. Throughout my teenage years, the Stranglers were to me what One Direction were to my friends. I obsessed over and loved the band like a teenage girl does: they were ingrained into my personality. I made a Stranglers cushion in Year 8 Textiles. I mentioned them in my German speaking and writing GCSEs wherever possible. I spoke about them nonstop and paraded around every day in the *Feel It Live* 2013 tour hoodie.

Caitlin Tench was just 11 when she first saw the Stranglers

I matured out of this fangirl stage, and then developed an even greater appreciation of them. The music saw me through lows and brought me many highs by taking me away in their sound and, at times, making me feel like the dog's bollocks. I've completed my GCSEs, A Levels and a degree with the Stranglers providing much needed light through all the hours of study.

The music brings back amazing memories of me and my dad that I will cherish forever. My favourite memory is of listening to 'Never to Look Back' on every single journey from my swimming lessons and my dad doing the keyboard motion like John Candy in *Planes, Trains and Automobiles*. I will always go to gigs with my dad but probably none will be as special as going with him to see the Stranglers.

I have only been there for a small period of the Stranglers' lifespan, but they have been there for the majority of mine, and for that I am endlessly grateful.

THE CAMDEN CENTRE

19/20 NOVEMBER 2011, LONDON, UK

At the 2011 Stranglers Convention in London JJ did a cooking session, creating pad thai. Whilst he was preparing and cooking the food, Baz was providing a running commentary and it was fucking hilarious. He said that he needed to wear his glasses to read the prompts but that his son had told him that, when he wears them, he looks like a U-boat commander.

Another highlight was when JJ presented the winner of a competition to win a Stranglers custom Triumph motorbike at Jack Lilley Motorcycles in Ashford. There weren't many members of the Familyinblack there that day. JJ was in fine form and chatted with us about the forthcoming *March On* tour and what songs they should play.

Andy Miller saw JJ auditioning for Masterchef

ALAN BATY

I had bought tickets for my wife Kate and myself for the Stranglers Convention. Unfortunately, for family reasons she couldn't go so I had a spare ticket. With it being a sell out, Owen Carne had made a list of people who were waiting for any spares to come up and he put me in touch with Billy Green from Glasgow. I gave Billy a call, and once we had softened our accents a little so we could both understand each other (me being a Geordie), we got on very well on the phone. The only problem was the double bed at the B&B at Kings Cross. Sharing with a friend is one thing but sharing with someone you'd never met was another. After all he could have been an axe murderer! I contacted the B&B and thankfully they changed it to two singles.

Eleven years later, Billy and I have remained great friends and been all over Europe on Wonky's and countless UK gigs. We have become very close friends and have got to know each other's families. He takes me to Celtic games and I take him to Newcastle ones. He even came down for my mother's funeral a few months back, which I will never forget. It's a privilege to know him and it would not have happened if it wasn't for the best band in the world.

CORN EXCHANGE

8 MARCH 2012, CAMBRIDGE, UK

TOM WILLIAMS

Tom Williams has a favourite sweatshirt

Back in 2011 I discovered the Stranglers and was introduced by the song 'No More Heroes', which I loved lots. It was my all-time favourite, and at the time I was in Year 8 at school it made me think, 'Wow, what a band'. I was happy the tour then was *Black and Blue* with the support of one of my favourites, Wilko Johnson. I saw the Stranglers for first time at Cambridge Corn Exchange on the *Giants* tour, which was amazing. As the years have gone by, I have become a bigger fan and made everything count in every way I could. As well as the t-shirts I bought at gigs, I also love my vinyl, and especially cherish when I met the band members in 2019 at the Brixton O2 Academy.

O2 ACADEMY

12 MARCH 2012, OXFORD, UK

GUY WESTOBY

As a teacher I took a minibus full of students to see the band at the tiny sweatbox that is the Oxford O2 Academy. As a lifelong fan myself (40 plus gigs and counting), I often shared the love with my students but in 2012 the BTEC Music Technology students had to study the 'punk and new wave' genre as part of their course. Although I'm an RE teacher, because of my well-known love of the band, the Head of Music asked if I could teach that part of the course. Naturally I jumped at the chance and I greatly enjoyed teaching the one lesson a week I had to talk about and play punk and new wave music. Of course, it was biased towards the Stranglers...

Once the tour was announced I asked the class if they fancied a trip to Oxford to see the band and they were all keen, so I put in a request. Thankfully the headteacher agreed, as long as I put together a detailed risk assessment - a pre-requisite of all school trips these days whether to Alton Towers, an art gallery or wherever. I had to identify possible risks and the measures I had to put in place to manage them - I wrote about the 'dangers' of the moshpit but suggested it was unlikely as most Stranglers fans were middle-aged men who'd be nodding their heads and tapping their feet rather than bouncing around in a moshpit. I promised that I would discourage our students from joining in if a moshpit developed (yeah, right...). After the risk assessment went through the checking process, we were granted permission, and on the day set off in the minibus after school, getting to Oxford in plenty of time to park up and get to the gig.

After seeing the band many times myself, I knew it wasn't the best they've played, but it was unfortunately the gig just before which the mighty Jet Black was taken ill to hospital and replaced at the last moment, so understandably the others were a bit tense. However, my students absolutely loved it and indeed made up the majority of those in a small moshpit at the front. I bet there's not many RE teachers who have taken a school trip to see the Stranglers! Although I'm now close to retirement from teaching I still push the Stranglers on my RE students, some of whom have become fans themselves and even bought t-shirts. After all, a quality education isn't just about what you learn about in your subjects, is it?

OLYMPIA

13 APRIL 2012, PARIS, FRANCE

JOHN GRIFFITHS

I've been a fan since '77 when my next-door neighbours played *Rattus* to me and I was hooked (that bass and keyboard combo). I remember the excitement with school

John Griffiths and wife Pauline met the band backstage in Paris in 2012 and Guildford in 2013

mates of that summer with 'Peaches' and seeing the 'punk bad boys' on *Top of the Pops* for the 'Something Better Change' video. Apart from when Paul Roberts was in the band, I've seen the band almost every year live from 1978, including Toby's first gig in Valenciennes in 2021.

John Griffiths' dog is named after a certain bass player

There are a couple of very memorable gigs. Firstly, the Rainbow in 1980 whilst Hugh was in jail, the one which had all the guests, including my co-hero Ian Dury, doing 'Bear Cage'. I was also at the infamous Hammersmith Odeon gig of 1982, where Jet again made a speech slagging off the bouncers for having their backs to the band (not unreasonably, to keep an eye on the fans), but the great man took umbrage to that 'insult'. Once they were removed the seats got trashed in a semi-riot. Unfortunately, the next night, which I also had tickets for, was cancelled.

Perhaps the best gig I went to was at Glasgow Apollo in 1985 whilst I was at St Andrews University. This was a real eye-opener for a soft London lad with the tough old city back then and the crazy crowd. It was an absolutely amazing atmosphere with Hugh on good form, baiting the Jocks as only he could – and getting away with it. I also remember ladies coming on stage naked to 'Sleazy' and then getting dressed during the song, with a GLC ban on stripping imposed on the band. Like every fan, the band has been the soundtrack to my own life. The highs and lows are perfectly reflected in Baz's masterpiece, 'Relentless', my favourite song.

My wife and I were lucky enough to meet the band in 2012 and 2013, and after the Paris Olympia gig we had a really nice chat with Dave, who despite being tired after the show was a true gent in giving us his time.

We recently got a new rescue dog from Rottweiler Welfare Association who was named Jax. We didn't particularly like the name, but it was best to keep the 'ax' in the name for easier recall. So, after a run through of rhymes, what could be better than Jean-Jacques? But I would never have expected my wife Pauline to ever have shouted in our home, 'Jean-Jacques, stop licking your balls!'

DAVID TELFER

I've been extremely fortunate to drive the band on a couple of occasions. I had just finished driving a tour with Therapy? and was due to fly out to Milan to join the Stranglers tour. On the way to the airport, I got an emergency call from the tour manager. 'We have run out of Warburton's crumpets. Can you pick some up on the way to join us?' I went through customs at Glasgow Airport with my suitcase loaded with said crumpets. I arrived at the tour bus at around nine in the morning when the band were sleeping and put said crumpets next to the toaster. One of the crew was awake and toasted a couple. All of a sudden, I was surrounded by band and crew delighting at the smell of toasted crumpets. Proper old school rock and roll.

LOOE MUSIC FESTIVAL

23 SEPTEMBER 2012, LOOE, UK

NICK EASTERBROOK

I bought *Rattus Norvegicus* in a small record shop run by the father of a friend of mine in the town of Looe in Cornwall. It was 16 August 1977, the day Elvis died. And from that moment I became a fan of the band. I have followed them through the ups and downs over the years. I moved away from Cornwall to London and have made some of my greatest friendships through a shared love of the Stranglers. I saw the band a few times with my sister and so it was inevitable that when it was announced that the Stranglers would play the *Looe Music Festival* in September 2012 we would go. My band were playing in my town, where the journey had all started, and I went with friends and family to accompany me. It was a magical conjunction of the stars. A few years earlier, the band had played at the *Daphne Du Maurier Festival of Arts* just down the road in Fowey. That was the most bizarre time I saw them but Looe was the most magical.

The day arrived and the rain was falling so hard that you couldn't see from one side of the valley to the other. People often imagine Cornwall as this sunny holiday spot. But this was the reality for me and again it brought back those childhood memories. It couldn't be any other way. We made our way to the beach, not believing the gig would go ahead. And for some time, we thought it would be cancelled. And then over the golden sands the opening bars of 'Waltzinblack' played out. And there they were, my heroes playing my town, on my beach in the horizontal rain. In the houses high on the hill behind the town, people were leaning out of the windows. People poured out of the pubs and onto the beach. Soon there were 5,000 of us witnessing this event. The revolting conditions only served to bring the audience and the band closer together.

As always it was us against the world. And we won.

TOWNSVILLE ENTERTAINMENT CENTRE

10 DECEMBER 2012, TOWNSVILLE, AUSTRALIA

CHRIS WHITWORTH

I first got into the band after listening to *Rattus Norvegicus*, which also delivered my favourite tune of theirs, '(Get a) Grip (on Yourself)'. I remember my dad saying Dave was just copying Bach and he was nothing new, and my mother being disgusted at the lyrics of, 'Some day I'm gonna smash your face'. They never seemed to play where I was posted in the British Army, so it wasn't until I emigrated that I finally got the chance. I first saw the band when they played in Townsville, Australia.

They appeared on breakfast TV that morning, which was the first time I saw Jim as the new drummer. Later that day I went with my wife to the hotel where they were staying and whilst grabbing a beer, I was stood next to Jim, although at the time I wasn't too sure it was him as I'd only seen him for a few minutes earlier that day.

As we were leaving the hotel, Dave Greenfield was walking in. I'm unable to describe how I felt, but to say I was in awe of him is an understatement. I shook his hand and explained the band were my favourite and how great it was to meet him. He then asked me, 'Where's the boys then'? I said, 'I think Jim is by the pool, maybe they were with him.' It was also like I'd known him for years, so laid back and friendly.

To this day, I truly regret not going with Dave to meet the rest of the band. I even wrote a letter to them, which I handed to reception inviting them round my house for a barbecue – but to no avail.

The consolation was that Baz handed me his guitar pick at the end of the concert that night, which is now framed and a family heirloom.

O2 ACADEMY

16 MARCH 2013, BIRMINGHAM, UK

SIMON ATKINS

I regret never seeing the band play live during the Paul Roberts era. Despite remaining a fan, the level of excitement I first got as a teenager from listening to the band's music wasn't rekindled to the same extent until I heard *Norfolk Coast*.

The next time I saw the band play live was on my birthday in March 2013 at the O2 Academy in Birmingham, and I have been present at every gig they have played at that venue since. There has always been a fantastic atmosphere at the Birmingham gigs, and some particularly memorable moments. One that sticks in my mind is in 2016 when a fan interrupted proceedings by coming up on stage to propose to his girlfriend... Luckily, she said yes!

BRIGHTON MUSIC HALL

4 JUNE 2013, BOSTON, MASSACHUSETTS

JOEL GAUSTEN

Joel Gausten met the band at Brighton Music Hall

In 1988, an 11-year-old boy went left of the dial and heard the Stranglers for the first time. 25 years later, he finally saw the band perform live – VIP pass in tow.

In 2013, the Stranglers toured the United States for the first time in two decades. When word got out that the Meninblack would be playing at the Brighton Music Hall, I knew that I not only had to go but also had to make a point to shake the hands of the musicians behind some of my all-time favorite songs.

Meeting up with the band as their crew wrapped up the soundcheck, I was immediately taken by how friendly they were. Dave Greenfield greeted me with an ear-to-ear smile and an enthusiastic handshake, while frontman Baz Warne and co-founder and bassist JJ Burnel could not have been nicer. All three seemed genuinely pleased to be playing the States and meeting people on the road, despite the fact that the great Jet Black was too ill to drum on this Stateside jaunt.

Soon after leaving the fellows to their pre-show business and hopping out of the bar to get some fresh air, I received a message on my phone from Massachusetts resident, original Gang of Four drummer and all-around great guy, Hugo Burnham. He wrote that he was in town for the gig and having a bite down the street. Warm, good-natured and armed with a sharp sense of humour, Hugo is always fantastic company. It was great to catch up with him.

The crowd inside the club boasted some of the friendliest people I've ever met at a show. This included an incredibly nice and talkative husband-and-wife team who first met at a Stranglers gig in the late Seventies – and who brought their adult daughter along for this most recent ride. Very cool.

The Stranglers were absolutely amazing. Newer material like 'Freedom is Insane' mixed flawlessly with classics like 'Peaches' and 'Golden Brown' and proved that a band could be at the top of their game nearly 40 years after their first show.

I was blown away by the band's spirited rendition of 'Always the Sun' (a brilliant tune from 1986 that proves that the Stranglers were one of the very few bands that made the leap from punk to pop in the Eighties with great aplomb), while my jaw continually hit the ground thanks to Dave Greenfield's (often one-handed) keyboard mastery. And seeing Hugo happily sing along and bang his fist in the air next to me as his fellow old-school UK punks blazed the stage was a thrill in itself.

Some nights are just perfect, you know?

APOLLO THEATRE

8 MARCH 2014, LONDON, UK

MICHAEL MCCLUGHIN

The *Ruby* tour was time for me to pass on my love of the band and their music to my 15-year-old nephew, Rowan - not that he much choice. We had travelled over to watch Chelsea beat Spurs 4-0 at the Bridge (sorry Baz, I know you ain't a fan of the 'Landan' clubs) and he was given two choices; stay in the hotel room all night on his own, or join me at the gig and run the risk of me buying him a pint or two. He didn't really know the music at this point, so was a bit reluctant to go, but eventually made the right decision. Half way through the gig, I looked at him beside me and I could see that he too was hooked, just like me at my first gig. Boom!

We both got the bonus of Jet and young Jim, the newbie, rolling on the skins together... relentless! Rowan is now well and truly in the Familyinblack and got his girlfriend, Amy, to join us in Newcastle in 2022.

2020 brought the heart-breaking news about Dave 'Fly Straight' Greenfield; for me, it really did feel like a loss in the family, as I felt I knew him having grown up with him for over 40 years. The news came at a particularly difficult time for me, as I was about twelve months into a very bad period of depression and anxiety which knocked me for six. His passing made me reconnect with the music of my youth, and the Stranglers in particular, which went a long way to helping me recovering my mojo.

Thank you also to Jim and Toby, for helping my heroes to evolve and to keep going. Gents, never under estimate the part you have played in treating thousands of fans to a great night out over the decades.

Long live the Stranglers.

BUT

3 April 2014, Madrid, Spain

EDUARDO ALCOLEA MARTÍNEZ

Those were other times; we only had a radio cassette. I had heard a piece of 'No More Heroes' on the radio and I liked the chorus. One day I finally managed to record it, but the song had already started. I had an instrumental part in the middle of the song, and the end. I played it many times and was in awe at how well the keyboard notes were chosen, their elegance, and how quickly they evolved. There was a running tune with the individual notes and another with the whole. The keyboard evolved to bass beats and drumbeats, and with a beautiful bass beat the melody was resumed to start the final part of the song. The drums were incredible, it underpinned the rhythm of the song perfectly in tune with the bass and the singer's voice resembled that of my childhood best friend... I didn't know the name of the group nor that of the song. There was no internet, and I was studying only French (not English) in high school. It took me almost a year to find out what group it was.

Finally, my sister told me the name of the group, the Stranglers, and that they had released an album. I loved the name. I went to the Corte Inglés department store and there was *Rattus Norvegicus*. I have never enjoyed a record (on cassette tape) so much. I had one hour a day assigned by my mother in which I was allowed to listen to it on our old orange Köening radio-cassette with black buttons. I played it over and over again and I loved it.

I began to follow the instruments individually; I saw how they mixed with each other. The rapport was sublime. It was without a doubt the best band I had ever heard. I already knew at that very moment that they were going to last for many years, that it was not a one-song group and 'goodbye'. The solidity of their music was amazing. I especially loved the bass. I also knew that it was not going to be a very famous group, because detecting the strange beauty of their music was not within everyone's reach. It wasn't a bunch of easy choruses that you get tired of the fourth time you hear them. It was a rare beauty, that you could listen to in many different ways without getting tired. I loved the bass, hearing that forcefulness was practically a vital necessity. I was happy: hearing the music of the Stranglers made me happy.

I set out to make a poster. I found a photo of the Stranglers in a newspaper. On the photo I painted the contours in a transparent plastic, I projected it with a projector that fable with plywood, nails, a bulb, and a battery, and drew the four silhouettes on the cards placed on the wall. Then I painted everything in black and white tempera. I nailed it well into the wall with plugs and I had it about eight years. It was huge.

I have seen the Stranglers seven times in Madrid and once in Cambridge. The first Stranglers concert I (almost) attended was in 1980 in my neighbourhood. I almost faint when I saw the posters. It was at the Rayo Vallecano Soccer Stadium, and a crowd of almost 5,000 people turned up, but the concert was rained off. I waited until everyone left and the stadium was empty. A few days later I returned my ticket to get a refund, but later regretted having returned it.

In April 2014, I went to a concert on the *Ruby* anniversary tour with my brother and two sisters. I saw JJ Burnel throw his plectrum towards the audience, landing in an area between the fence and stage. I was bewildered that no one had noticed and quickly jumped over the fence and grabbed it. At the end of the concert, Baz Warne looked at me and threw his plectrum in the direction of my head. It hit my sister in the face and the plectrum fell at her feet. Again, I quickly reached down and picked it up. Everyone was looking around for the plectrum and for a while they kept looking. A girl said to me, 'You haven't taken the two, have you? Because you must share.' Of course, I denied it, so they kept looking...

In 2017, I travelled 1,800 kilometres to see the Stranglers in concert at the Corn Exchange in Cambridge. I was at the concert with my daughter Diana, who was 11 at the time.

53 DEGREES

6 JULY 2014, PRESTON, UK

KATIE ANDREW

Katie Andrew has seen the Stranglers 38 times since 2013

I first got into the Stranglers in late 2012 on a holiday to Perth in Scotland. My father gave me a few CDs to put on my iPod, including *The Raven* and *Gospel According to the Meninblack*. After that week in Perth, I was totally hooked and later saw them on their *Feel It Live* tour in 2013 in Glasgow. Since then, I have been lucky enough to have seen them another 38 times. My two stand out moments are meeting JJ in Preston in 2014 outside 53 Degrees and him jumping down off the stage to give me his plectrum, which I have framed next to the single I got signed that day, and then getting into the soundcheck in Birmingham 2018 when it was snowing. I was with a friend and we were the only two people waiting to meet them.

My favourite song is 'The Raven'. I have very fond memories of listening to it with my dad as he explained his theories about the album. And 'Strange Little Girl' reminds my family of when, as a little girl, I'd dance and sing along to a VHS tape of the Stranglers live until 'Strange Little Girl' came on. Then I'd sit on the floor and fall asleep.

I have to thank the Stranglers for so many great things in my life but most importantly they saved me, as a teenager I suffered with my mental health and without their music and the wonderful friends I've made from the Facebook groups and meeting them at concerts I really don't know where I'd be.

MALCOLM WYATT

While I'd caught and enjoyed the Stranglers back in my hometown and theirs, Guildford, in early July 2003, playing the Guilfest event with Paul Roberts on lead vocals, that show was more about headliners Madness and support act The Undertones for me. But the Stranglers were on top form at a University of Central Lancashire headline show at Preston's 53 Degrees eleven years later.

I'd caught Hugh Cornwell's three-piece band delivering a blistering set at the same venue a year earlier, each song from his solo catalogue followed by a Stranglers classic.

Baz Warne was out front and already long since proven, Jet Black having by now vacated the drummer's stool, 'consigned to the bench amid health concerns' as I put it at the time, Jim Macaulay, promoted from within, putting in a commanding shift between the sticks. On something of creative and inspirational high following acclaim for 2012 LP *Giants*, in an add-on to the *Ruby* anniversary tour, it felt so good to be back listening to Jean-Jacques' trademark growling bass and Dave's distinctive keyboard flourishes.

Again, Team Stranglers came on to 'Waltzinblack', back from its loan spell with the late Keith Floyd. Baz quickly proved his worth – as if he needed to – on 1978's 'Toiler on the Sea', before heading back a further year for landmark '(Get a) Grip (on Yourself)', the number I so wanted to hear on my first live sighting in 1982.

We were also reminded of the band's pop craft on 1984 hit 'Skin Deep', and then got a taste of *Giants* as JJ offered a pensive 'Time Was Once on My Side'. The less 'PC' Stranglers then got a look in on 'Nice 'n' Sleazy' and 'Peaches'. JJ was thrown a pair of briefs and Baz complained that the price tag was still on.

Their more recent output was again showcased by 2006's reflective 'Relentless', before a further trip down memory lane with my personal highlight, 'Duchess', and then that album's evocative title track, 'The Raven', JJ taking over. And there were plenty of smiles from Dave along the way, happy behind his towering bank of synths, contributing vocal harmonies and expertly multi-tasking, not least supping his ale mid-song.

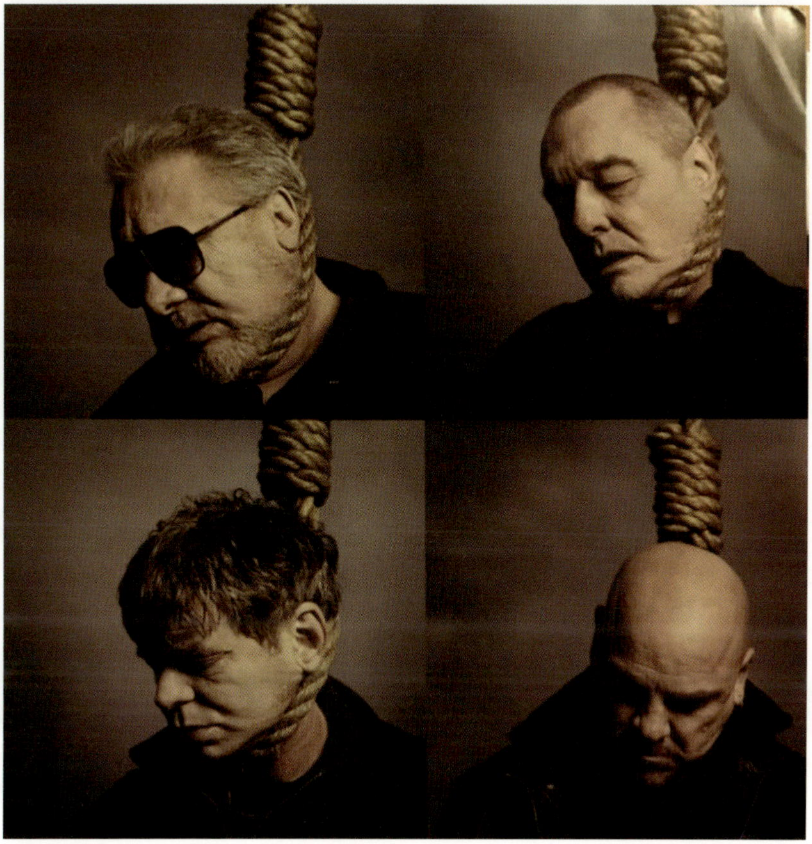

'Golden Brown' got a warm reception but the choruses were louder on 1986's poignant 'Always the Sun', perhaps the closest thing there is to a Stranglers anthem. Yet there's no polishing the rough edges, 'Death and Night and Blood' from *Black and White* keeping us on our toes and the ageing punks happy, 'Nuclear Device' having a similar effect before a majestic cover of 'Walk on By', that patented Stranglers sound beautifully complementing Bacharach and David's classic.

The supreme 'Hanging Around' and 'Curfew' kept the stage divers and old faithful down the front happy, with appreciation too for the now decade-old 'Norfolk Coast', before the set reached its climax with '5 Minutes', 'Something Better Change' and 'Tank', heralding an explosive finish.

Baz did much of the between song talking and added a personable North-East twist to a few crowd-pleasers as well as some neat guitar touches. Similarly, Jim played his part, adding the mettle to ensure that spine remains in shape – flying straight with perfection, you could say.

There was plenty of chanting for Jet before the encore. Baz reported that the 76-year-old was on the mend and determined to rejoin the squad soon – his Makem impression of the man himself was well worthy of the cheer it received.

With that, JJ teased us with a bit of bass-kidology, hammering on his trusty four-string, setting the venue throbbing before that magical intro riff led us into 'No More Heroes', still as potent all those years down the line, on a big night of nostalgia and much more.

ALBAN ARENA

7 JULY 2014, ST ALBANS, UK

DAVE TOMLINSON

Dave Tomlinson with JJ and artwork

My mum took me, along with three of my school mates, to see the Stranglers for the first time in the UK just over 40 years ago. I immediately became a fan and have followed the band loyally ever since. I have lived in New Zealand for the last 30 years and when they visit the southern hemisphere, I take my wife along to the gigs in New Zealand and Australia. The last two trips back to the UK have 'happened' to coincide with British tours.

In 2014, my mum noticed that the Stranglers were playing in her hometown of St Albans, so she bought tickets for her and Dad. Both of them were now in their late seventies and Mum walked with crutches. She wrote a letter to the band explaining how her son in New Zealand was a big fan and that she would like to get a photo of her with the band to send to me to 'show off' and handed it in to the merch stall. Somebody there was good enough to pass the letter onto the tour manager, who said that he would see what he could do.

Mum and Dad took their seats upstairs. Halfway through the show, Baz asked for the house lights to come up and then said, 'Where is Angie sitting? You wrote us a letter about your son in New Zealand. Where are you, Angie?' After a few minutes he was able to pick her out and he said, 'Angie, make your way down to the foyer during the next song and our tour manager will meet you out there. And don't forget your camera!'

Mum made her way down to meet the tour manager, who took her through to the side of stage. After they had finished the song they were playing, the band brought her out onto the front of the stage and had the tour manager take a photo of her with them and in front of the crowd. Amazing!

I know that the band have always ripped through their set at shows and seldom waste much time with crazy antics, and indeed Ava Rave confirmed to me after seeing my post on Facebook that Jet can't recall the band ever stopping mid-gig for a photo with a fan, let alone a 70-something-year-old lady on crutches. But there you go.

Now, whenever I see the band on tour at the airport or pre-show, etc., JJ and Baz always ask, 'How's your mum?' Just like the nice boys that they are.

On the last tour to New Zealand, I had mentioned to JJ that I had painted a couple of pictures of him and asked if he would sign them if I brought them to the Auckland sound check. He signed one of them, 'To Dave, for all the years, and Mum too.'

SUB89

8 JULY 2014, READING, UK

MARIA MELIOUMI

Maria Melioumi got a mid-concert kiss from JJ

I was introduced to the Stranglers by a groundbreaking radio station in Toronto, Canada which played music other stations did not. I first met them in 2013 when they played the Danforth Music Hall. I then travelled to the UK several times to see them live.

In July 2014, the band played two memorable concerts. The first was in St Alban's on July 7. They were in good form and all pistons were pumping. At one point, someone threw a beer at JJ during 'Hanging Around'. JJ was not pleased, but

Rob Ockford has a large Stranglers collection

Stranglers fans at a Manchester gig in 2014 – photo Matthew Elvis Brown

he finished the song and then went hunting in the audience for the offender, who quickly disappeared. JJ came back onstage and cleaned up the mess as liquids can present problems for their equipment. While he was on his hands and knees mopping up the beer, Baz joked that JJ cleans his whole house for ten quid.

The next night in Reading was intimate – a 600 capacity venue. Baz commented that it was like being in someone's living room and there was not a lot of ventilation. At one point, JJ said to the audience that Baz thought people would want to hear 'Golden Brown' which they had played the night before, but he thought the audience would prefer to hear 'La Folie', and he put it to a vote. 'La Folie' won. At some point, JJ got down into the press pit and kissed the hands of several women at the barrier in his slow, seductive way. I was one of the lucky ones!

During the final song, 'Tank', JJ got into the press pit again and interacted with the audience, while Baz altered the lyrics in fine Stranglers tradition. It was definitely one of the steamier concerts they played. The intimacy and the audience participation was great.

ROB OCKFORD

As part of the stage set for the *Ruby* tour in 2014, the band had four huge gold frames behind them with screens in them playing videos, and once the tour was over, they were put up for sale on eBay. Whilst the auction was live, I was on holiday with my family in Cornwall but I managed to win the auction and purchase one of the frames. I had to make plans to collect it from Bath. I was contacted by Louie Necastro, and I said I would collect it when I was on my way home from my holiday. However, I was towing my twin wheel caravan which could make things problematic. I managed to find the farm where I was collecting the frame from and, after a quick chat with Louie, we decided to load up, but it was not going to be easy.

The frame was in two halves and they were massive so there was no way they were going in the back of my pick up. I finally decided to see if they would fit in the caravan, and Louie looked at me as if I had lost the plot. It looked impossible to get them in, but after an hour of impersonating the Chuckle Brothers – 'me to you to you to me' - we finally manged to get them inside the van, but it was really tight and no thought was given to how I was going to get them out. This was a brand new caravan, and we must have been mad to even attempt to load them, but there was no way I was going to leave them.

Whilst we were at the farm, Louie showed us the studio and it was great to see where some of my favourite albums had been recorded, and we also took pictures of JJ's famous green bass and the keyboard that Dave played on 'Golden Brown'.

When we got home, it was a nightmare getting the frames out of our caravan and into the house, and I wish I had thought about this before I purchased them. The frame is about three metres tall and two metres wide, and it was just too big to display as a complete item, so I have put the top half on my lounge wall and the other half around the window in our music room. Even though I say it myself, the frame looks superb and it is a great talking point. My friends think I'm mad.

I have collected music memorabilia for years, and I have loads of Stranglers-related items, with various items on display in two rooms and all over the staircase walls. I would keep hanging stuff up, and I have a very understanding wife but I am under orders that enough is enough, so a lot of it is packed away.

MARCH ON TOUR

FEBRUARY 2015

SIMON SMITH/DELIC

Interview with JJ Burnel, February 2015, talking about *March On* tour.

I started by asking him how Jet (Black) was, and whether he was going to be able to play on the tour?

We don't know is the simple answer. He wants to be part of it but even when he came along last year, he was less and less of a presence live-wise. But he's still lurking in the shadows, and he still has an influence in the band.

It's just difficult. He was Mr Rock and Roll, and several decades down the line there's a price to pay. Last year he did 20 minutes in the first show, which was down to ten minutes by the second show, and he was having to have oxygen as soon as he came off stage. His body's just giving up and has been for a few years really. It's not a sudden thing. We'll have to see.

I have been coming to see you live for many years now, and it strikes me that the live shows have been building up: the venues fuller and the crowds more diverse. Last year's 40th Anniversary Ruby tour was a particular high point. Do you feel that there is extra pressure on you now?

Not at all, you can put as much pressure on yourself as you want. We're not promoting anything. We're going out because we enjoy playing together so much. It's amazing the feedback we've been getting for the last ten years. It has been getting better and better and more and more fun. There has been more of a communion with our audience in recent years. It's a symbiotic relationship with the fans and I'd die if I couldn't play anymore.

The audience is more mixed than ever before. There are people who gave up on us during the Paul Roberts and Jon Ellis years; then there are people who stuck with us; and a whole new young audience too. Those who look at the world in a slightly different way and think, 'I like this bunch of old bastards, I know some of their music, I want to familiarise myself with their stuff because they're not like *Pop Idol* or *The X*

Factor.' People see us as being 'the real thing' and I think we have integrity. So people are coming to see us for all different reasons.

O2 ACADEMY LIVERPOOL

9 MARCH 2015, LIVERPOOL, UK

EDWARD MCCORMACK

I was a bit of a late starter in discovering the Meninblack, with 1979 being the year of my real introduction via the *Live (X-Cert)* and *Raven* albums, two of several that have shaped my life. I've seen the band live in Liverpool during their numerous tours, and I've been lucky enough to meet the lads in person several times thanks to Jet's wife Ava Rave and Liverpool music hero, all round good guy and friend of the band, Ian Prowse.

Many years of aural pleasure followed my introduction to the Stranglers as I collected all I could, while the internet and social media pages eventually brought many fans together. Several years ago, a fellow Maninblack posted a fun survey on one of the band's Facebook forums. He was asking for fans thoughts on what our beloved band should open the shows with on their upcoming tour. There was even a fun prize up for grabs, a copy of *Written in Red* on CD in its original blood cover packaging.

The tracks that immediately came to my mind were my long-time personal favourites, 'Longships' and 'The Raven', which continue to inspire me to this very day. There were many replies and suggestions, but the likes for my choice were creeping up and, lo and behold, I eventually and unexpectedly won the disc.

There was, however, more to the tale. I was informed that all the suggestions would make their way to the band, for them to consider. A few months down the line, there I was at the O2 Liverpool, and I think you know what two tracks the band opened their set with. My mind was blown.

Oh, and sitting backstage post-gig in Liverpool a few years earlier, chatting to JJ about his favourite French vineyards and my vast *Jaws* (*Le Dents De La Mer*) memorabilia collection while sharing one of his favourite bottles of red is another story...

O2 ACADEMY

28 MARCH 2015, GLASGOW, UK

JAMES BECK

In 2015, I entered a competition to win a pair of limited edition Stranglers Dr Marten's and a night in a hotel to end the Stranglers tour in Glasgow. I also entered a competition to do a meet and greet with Status Quo. I forgot I'd entered them both. I was in Glasgow when I got a call from a woman called Billie Baier at Dr Marten's. She said, 'James, I have great news for you. You've won a competition.' I said, 'Oh fantastic, I've always wanted to meet the Quo,' and she said, 'Sorry?' I said, 'Status Quo. I'll be meeting the Quo, won't I?' And she said, 'No, but I'm happy to tell you you'll be meeting the Stranglers.' I said, 'Oh, fantastic. I know Baz and JJ and young Jim, and thanks very much.' She gave me Gaz Knighton's number and I went along to the Carling (O2) and JJ said to me, 'How's you, James?' and I said, 'I'm well,' and Baz said, 'James won the Doc Marten competition,' and I blurted out, 'I do apologise, but I thought I'd won the meet and greet with Francis Rossi.' I didn't realise how ungrateful I sounded, but I got my Doc Marten boots.

CATHEDRAL QUARTER ARTS FESTIVAL

1 MAY 2015, BELFAST, UK

GRAEME (MULLY) MULLAN

The rumours had been rife throughout the last legs of the *March On* tour that the Stranglers were going to be returning (after too long) to my hometown to play Belfast in May. Back in my hotel in Kilmarnock after the gig that night, I received a text from our Ulsterman in Madrid that the gig was confirmed, the contract signed - talk of Sil flying up to Aberdeen the night before now seemed to make sense. However, nothing could be posted on the website until the *Cathedral Quarter Arts Festival's* official launch, but who needs to see it in print? The gig was on and that's all I needed to know.

As the big day approached the social media pages and text messages were red hot with who was going, where we were meeting, what time people were getting in to the various airports, ferry terminals, bus stations - where they were staying and, most importantly, what time was the pre-gig social.

The morning of the concert, and after a plethora of texts and mobile calls, I was off to meet up with the already incumbent Familyinblack in The Crown Bar Liquor Emporium. Entering through the stained glass windowed doors and setting foot into the dark interior, I was immediately transported back in time to the late Seventies. This was the bar we all used to meet up in before Thursday night gigs in the Ulster

Hall. Me and my Strangler buddy were drinking our pints of Harp on 4th October 1979 when we were here for the Stranglers *Raven* tour, watching *Top of the Pops* on the old TV above the doors as The Police walked on the moon.

I came across the Family and after greetings, hightailed it to the bar for a round of drinks. Liquid downed, food ordered and consumed, the craic was flowing - as was the alcohol - and more comradesinblack were arriving in dribs and drabs. Soon it was time to make a move, as some were getting concerned about queuing to get into the venue - no amount of me explaining that Belfast doesn't do queues so there was no need to worry would suffice – and we progressed to the next drinking establishment, which was opposite Custom House Square, the venue for tonight's gig. McHugh's Bar already had a few Strangler t-shirted people thronging around and supplied the perfect view of the tent and surrounding area to spot the best time to head in - as if that was going to be an issue.

Eventually we made our move. The support act, a local ska band called The Aggressors BC, who were halfway through their set. The steady flow of people entering the event was building but there was still no queue. Entering through the festival security, we progressed into the main marquee - bar to the left, merch to the right. It was a long way to the stage, but with the roof and walls bedecked in white fairy lights it looked quite impressive. We made our way right up to the front barrier where The Aggressors BC were skanking their way through the remainder of their set.

After a long break between bands, the Stranglers entered around 9.20pm to a rapturous cheer from the welcoming Belfast audience. Belfast crowds might not be in a hurry to see a band, but they sure as hell know how to make one feel at home. With a nod of appreciation, and after acknowledging the presence of the girls in their regular spot on the barrier, JJ immediately kicked into 'Toiler on the Sea'. The powerful bass and driving drums were joined by Dave's keys picking out the melody and Baz's descending guitar signature. The crowd went wild, jumping up and down and singing along. Is there a better track to start a gig? It also meant I had another different song played at each concert I had attended this year. We were then treated to very much the same sort of set list as played on the recent tour.

The fifth song in gave us a stupendous version of 'Four Horsemen' - a favourite of mine form the *March On* gigs – and the band were obviously well rehearsed and tight as a gnat's chuff. A guy in a *Rattus* t-shirt a couple of people over shouted, 'Play something we know,' and was given immediate short shift as he was informed, 'Fuck off. If you were a fan, you'd know them.' 'Golden Brown' appeared early in the set and I left my second row position to depart for a smoke, missing Baz's guitar solo fuck up, which amused JJ and which Baz went on to play in reprise post-song.

Back in again just in time for '5 Minutes', I stayed back to see if the sound quality was any different. For a marquee gig, the sound was really good - far better than the Roundhouse, for example. And from anywhere you stood, you got a decent view of the band onstage. Making my way forward again, I bumped into a few people I knew and stopped for a quick greet. Not quite making it back to my original starting position, I stood to the side as the band were motoring through the set, 'Time to Die', 'Norfolk

Coast' into 'Wog'. There was little mid-song banter from the band tonight. Baz did ask if the crowd were enjoying themselves at one point and questioned someone who was shouting up at him, but even on repeated asking what he was saying, he couldn't make out the thick Belfast accent and gave up.

The songs were coming thick and fast - one classic after another – and there was very little to complain about in the performance. 'Peaches' was given a rapturous acknowledgement. The car crash keys of 'Lost Control' sounded superb. 'Duchess' saw the crowd once more raise the roof and no doubt pleased our *Rattus* t-shirt guy, and a stunning 'Curfew' saw the end of the set. A short break then saw the band return for the extended jazzy prog-punk improvisation of 'Walk on By'. As I made my way back towards the front, JJ began the bass crunching, ball-rattling intro to 'No More Heroes'. The crowd were stunned as many were 'feeling it' for the first time and, as the iconic G-string riffage crashed towards the opening chords, the audience erupted en masse. It just doesn't get any better than this - to witness your band, in your city, seeing the crowd react in this way - justifies why I love this band. Baz said that if someone invited them back they would certainly be over again, and I think the crowd would definitely turn out again to see them.

As the strains of 'Meninblack' began to echo round and the lights went up, I struggled against the exiting crowd, making my way to meet up with those I had left at the barrier earlier. Set lists purloined, plectrums gathered in and drum sticks begged from Jim McCauley, the customary photo shoot was commencing. More catching up with friends and chat about the gig was in progress, as we made our way outside. We were ready to move on for some post gig refreshments.

I directed our black bedecked group round to The John Hewitt pub and after getting served we found ourselves in a tight wee corner table for the debriefing. Another couple were sitting there - both had also been at the gig - and they couldn't believe the various accents - all friends, all over for the gig - and were completely gob-smacked when we all regaled how many gigs we had attended this year already.

Eventually, it was last orders and time to depart. As I knew it would be difficult to find their way back, I walked a few people to their hotel before making my own way home. Strolling along (minding my own business) with a contented smile on my face, it had been a fucking excellent day and night. Everyone seemed to have had a good time. Belfast, you did me proud.

HORSESHOE TAVERN

28 JUNE 2015, TORONTO, CANADA

MARIA MELIOUMI

This Hugh Cornwell solo concert was his second visit to Toronto in 18 months, this time performing at the Horseshoe Tavern, where he also played when he was in the Stranglers. On both solo tours, he started with a song from his 2012 CD *Totem and*

Taboo and moved to a Stranglers song, then alternating between the two.

In keeping with his buoyant mood, he delighted the audience with several upbeat Stranglers' earworms, such as 'Skin Deep', 'Grip' and 'Straighten Out'. He may have been nostalgic, since he included songs about his ex-girlfriends – 'Duchess', 'Strange Little Girl', and, debatably, 'Golden Brown', on which he handled the guitar solo quite well. He did have requests fired at him, and at one point, he asked calmly, 'Do you mind?'

Maria Melioumi saw Hugh Cornwell perform solo in Toronto

Cornwell was in a playful mood. Early on, before beginning a Stranglers song, he teased the crowd by telling them the next song was 'No More Heroes' and then he and the band launched into 'Dagenham Dave' instead. He bantered with audience members. Four songs in, he asked people seated at the back of the club if they were comfortable and whether he should order any food for them. He shared the titbit that people in Scotland call him Shug (a diminutive for Hugh). A couple of songs later, he commented on the cold and rain the city was experiencing and how lately, it always seems to rain in Toronto during the Pride celebrations. Kayvon, a British ex-patriot, called out that he had brought the bad weather. Cornwell replied, 'I brought it? I just came from Califor-nae-ay. It's 100 degrees there and sunny.'

Further evidence that the Cornwell of yore has resurged was his trademark lyric altering, which he did with 'Peaches'. He asked, 'Is she trying to get out of Toronto?' and he could think of worse places to be, like Mississauga, a boring city on the western edge of Toronto.

The set lasted an hour. The crowd wasn't having that and cheered and clapped for more. Cornwell & Co retook the stage, and as Hugh adjusted the strap for his guitar, various requests were volleyed at him such as 'Nice 'n' Sleazy'. Ever the deadpan artist, he scoffed, but first up was indeed 'Nice 'n' Sleazy'. From there, they moved to 'No More Heroes'. However, without JJ's familiar bass pounding and digit-dextrous intro, it seemed a little lacking.

After an enjoyable performance Cornwell came out and interacted with the fans. He easily chatted with people, signed CDs and graciously posed for pictures with them. Just two weeks before, a tour bus pulled up in the middle of the road in front of the venue where Paul Weller had played, 15 minutes after the concert, and Weller made a dash for it from a locked side entrance before fans realised what had happened. Some contrast.

THE VENUE

14 JULY 2015, MIDDLESBROUGH, UK

LES TAYLOR

Les Taylor was at the Teesside gig

I have been a Stranglers fan since first hearing 'Peaches' on the radio in 1977. The thing that roused my interest was the bass line intro to the song, as it sounded different to everything else that was being played at that time. The song sounds just as fresh as it did all those years ago. On Bastille Day 2015 in sunny Middlesbrough, my mate Greener and I, having purchased tickets a few weeks before, ventured down to Teesside for the gig. After finding our digs and then venturing round a couple of bars, we eventually ended up at the Venue.

As usual, we missed the support act and waited for 'Waltzinblack' to start. We ventured to the front. The band were as tight as ever, everyone was on their game. On the way to the bar to get another round, I decided to ask for a pen and piece of paper, constructed a note and promptly marched back down to where we were standing. When there was a brief break in the set list, I threw the note on the stage, next to Baz's mic. After the next song, he noticed the paper with my scrawl on it. I basically asked when the band were going to play his home town, Sunderland. I think he had difficulty deciphering my note as he peered at it and then said, 'Soon', threw it back on the ground, and promptly started another song.

Four years later, at *Rubix Festival* in 2019, underneath Penshaw Monument, we were there again with some of the lads. It was Baz's homecoming, and again, a brilliant gig. They headlined the Saturday night and rounded off a perfect day. Baz commented that he was happy to be playing his hometown, and had caught up with family and friends, but he did note one or two were caught up in fights at the front of the crowd, and the band had only played for ten minutes. This was the last gig we saw which featured Dave, so looking back, a rather poignant moment.

Moving on, Greener and I travelled to Glasgow and Manchester and saw the band at home in Newcastle for the Final Full tour. Three brilliant gigs again, with the first two really enjoyable for not being at home. Toby, having filled the void left by the great man, was given a worthy reception from the fans at all three gigs. It's amazing how JJ just keeps going. The bass lines during the three gigs just roared, Baz was brilliant as ever and Jim was excellent. He just seems to go for it every time, especially when they play 'Tank'.

Long may they continue.

FIRST DIRECT ARENA

27 NOVEMBER 2015, LEEDS, UK

HOLLY-LISA MELLOR

I was 14. My dad was going to see the Stranglers supporting Simple Minds and his friend was meant to go with him, but in the end his friend wasn't able to attend. I was handed a stack of Stranglers CDs and told, 'See what you think.' I enjoyed their music and said I wouldn't mind going to see them. With that, I was! After that, I wanted to see them again, so we saw them on the *Black and White* tour in 2016 at Bristol O2 Academy. I'm now 21 and have seen them over 20 times. While waiting in the queue, I have met some lovely people and we often pass the time waiting to go in discussing various things, which always helps take your mind off things if it's a particularly cold night!

Holly-Lisa Mellor captured the Stranglers in action in 2022 - photo Holly-Lisa Mellor

Holly-Lisa Mellor met Baz in 2017

One of the stand-out shows for me was Birmingham O2 Academy on the *Definitive* tour in 2018, where Baz handed me a set list, towel and pick. The set list I managed to get signed by the band and has pride of place on my wall. Another stand out show was when my dad took me to Bologna in Italy to go and see them a couple of days before my 19th birthday. At the end of the show there, Baz again handed me his pick.

My all time favourite song has to be 'Toiler on the Sea' as it was first song I ever heard them play live, but other favourites include 'Tank', 'Walk on By' and 'Last Men on the Moon'. And *Suite XVI* is a very underrated album.

I often think about my dad's friend who couldn't attend the Simple Minds. I probably would never have heard of the Stranglers if it wasn't for him!

O2 ACADEMY

12 MARCH 2016, BIRMINGHAM, UK

SIMON SMITH/DELIC

I've been seeing the Stranglers live for nearly 40 years. There is no band that I have seen more. I've seen the Stranglers be brilliant, and I have seen them when they appear to have lost their collective way and fall short of expectations. I've seen them play to packed houses and I've seen them play to less than half-filled halls. Yet I have never, never, seen the Stranglers play like I did at the Birmingham O2 Academy. It was a brave move to tour the *Black and White* album in its entirety. It is a magnificent album but one that is challenging to play and challenging to listen to. It is serious music with serious themes; this is not a move a band looking for an easy life would make.

The Stranglers' *March On* tour is a phenomenon that has been growing year by year; the halls have been getting fuller and the dates more numerous. The easy thing to do would be to sit back and play the hits. Here though, for the first time in my memory, was a set devoid of 'Golden Brown' but replete with classic and new tracks that did more than blow me away. It made me wonder where the band could possibly go next.

Coming on to the traditional 'Waltzinblack' I felt excited yet unusually apprehensive about how this would play out. Yet from the first chords of 'Tank' the band were immediately on it with this huge battering ram of a fans' favourite. 'Nice 'n' Sleazy' duly followed and so far, it could have been any year's gig. Then 'Outside Tokyo' powerfully kicked in, JJ Burnel's bass runs really hit the ears, and the band smashed what is quite an empty and spacious song, turning it into something even more substantial. As the 'white side' progressed it became clear to me that the Stranglers were nailing the album, culminating with a pulsating 'Toiler on the Sea'. So far so good, but now the tricky bit of communicating the darkness and experimentalism of the 'black side'.

If anything, this sounded even more fierce, but it was not just about power. The subtlety and the profound nature of the album really came through, you could feel them letting themselves go on the choruses of 'Curfew' and sensed the menace in the verses. Burnel's vocal and bass duet on 'Threatened' was immense, and 'In the Shadows' really stood out, sounding utterly contemporary and exciting: further compelling evidence that here was an album that managed to be experimental at the time, and yet still sounds fresh nearly 40 years later.

'Do You Wanna?' and 'Death and Night and Blood' retained their bleakness but were somehow revitalised here. For me, though, it was 'Enough Time' which really stood out as the track which exemplified this performance. Transformed brilliantly for the stage, I noticed how hard the band were working to communicate the track to the crowd. As on the album, Burnel's bass was front and centre, but Baz Warne worked tirelessly and always looked in control of tracks that were so personal to the authors. Dave Greenfield seemed in his element with the abstract keyboard work on the album, and in Jim Macaulay, the band have a drummer who can more than hold his own. Indeed, this was moment for me when he completed the move from stand-in to permanent member of the band. Jet Black not forgotten but succeeded by someone who seems to understand the importance of curating the Stranglers' legacy in its own particular way.

With the album completed, many bands would be content and take its collective foot of the pedal with a safe remaining set. Not the Stranglers, who, without pausing for breath, burst into a tight and visceral version of 'Grip' and followed it up with a *Black and White*-era cover version 'Walk on By', delivered with such verve and nuance that it achieved the seemingly impossible task of wringing even more out of this Bacharach-David classic.

What really struck me about the rest of the set was that there was no let up, the tempo remained high throughout and there was a good mixture of newer and older material, none of which sounded out of place. This for me was a band that had had to rehearse harder than usual to get to grips with the difficult *Black and White* material, the pay-off being that it was tighter and more coherent than ever.

Beyond that, however, this performance also confirmed that this was not just a 'black and white' band, but all shades in between. They were smooth and untouchable during 'Always the Sun', rocked out like a lo-fi garage band on 'A Soldier's Diary', and were the cheeky seaside-postcard chappies on 'Peaches' (although even this track seemed more powerful than usual). On 'Go Buddy Go' they were the house band working hard so we could party, an impression aided by a fan proposing to his partner of 32 years on stage. 'Norfolk Coast' was punchy and controlled, 'Princess of the Streets' as sleazy and grubby as ever, and 'Nuclear Device' epitomised the almost communion-like relationship between band and fans. Add to that a searing finale of 'No More Heroes', the twenty-ninth track of the set, and you get a performance that was nothing short of triumphant.

Johnny Norgrove's daughter Lydia got to meet the band at soundcheck

O2 ACADEMY

13 MARCH 2016, BIRMINGHAM, UK

JOHNNY NORGROVE

I was at home with my nine-year-old daughter Lydia when I got a call from Jim Mac to say the band were having a sound check in half an hour if I wanted to pop down. Lydia and I shot down and enjoyed a behind-the-scenes look. After the sound check, we took some pictures and were invited to take some on the stage. Baz appeared from nowhere and put a guitar on Lydia for a brilliant photo before JJ appeared and complimented her on her bright pink Dr Marten's. I sheepishly admitted to JJ about being the bloke who lost his tooth at the Wyeside Festival in 2010 and we had a quick chat about the upcoming Australian tour (which I was lucky enough to go to).

JJ then asked Lydia if she was coming to the gig and she said, 'No, I'm too young.' JJ replied, 'Rubbish, you will be my special guest' and he arranged for her to sit upstairs on the front row. He waved to her when he came out and blew a kiss to her at the end. What a fantastic gesture.

O2 ACADEMY

17 MARCH 2016, SHEFFIELD, UK

JOANNE CLIFFE

Joanne Cliffe in Sheffield with JJ and Baz

My first Stranglers gig was in 1980 and I'm still going strong. They have been the soundtrack to my life and, with my birthday in March, I was able to celebrate on tour.

I've kept all my tickets and set lists plus a drum stick and a plectrum or two. I was star struck a few times, enough to talk utter nonsense to Dave who was kind enough to say 'yeah' on repeat...

the stranglers
1979 - 2015
STRANGLERS
ACCES BACKSTAGE
13 NOVEMBRE 20H - ZENITH
EXONÉRÉ
DIVAN DU MONDE
PLACEMENT LIBRE
ROUNDHOUSE
ECHO arena liverpool
LISBON CALLING
Meat Loaf
the B-52s
LONDON SHEPHERDS BUSH EMPIRE
ESPACE JULIEN MARSEILLE
THE STRANGLERS
ACCES LIBRE
the stranglers 10
THE STRANGLERS DREAMTIME
THE STRANGLERS-SINGLES

L'OLYMPIA
THE STRANGLERS
JEUDI 5 FEVRIER 2009 20:00
ACCES LIBRE
ENCEINTE GENERALE
A2
WEEK END
La Sarthe
24 HEURES DU MANS
The Stranglers
Thu, 18 Mar 2010 19:30
Standing
CAMBRIDGE CITY COUNCIL
SJM CONCERTS PRESENT
THE STRANGLERS
FRIDAY 19TH MARCH 2010
DOORS 19:00
the stranglers
13 juin 2009 - 24 Heures du Mans
Happy birthday Michel
LE BATACLAN
THE STRANGLERS
JEUDI 25 MARS 2010 19:30
ASSIS - DEBOUT
PLACEMENT LIBRE
GRAND AUDITORIUM
PALAIS DES FESTIVALS
CANNES
THE STRANGLERS / KILLTRONIK
SJM Concerts present
The Stranglers
Plus Special Guests The Popes
Cambridge Corn Exchange
Thu, 8 Mar 2012 19:30
Standing
962
o2 academy
THE STRANGLERS
O2 ACADEMY BIRMINGHAM
SAT 10 MAR 2012 6:30 PM
ROUNDHOUSE
The Stranglers
Plus Special Guests The Popes
Friday Evening
09 March 2012
Fête du Cognac
Entrée 5€
Samedi 28 juillet 12
WOODSTOWER 2012
DF CONCERTS PRESENT
THE STRANGLERS
FRI 01-MAR-13
DOWNSTAIRS STAND
O2 ACADEMY GLASGOW
ticketweb
o2 academy
O2 Academy Birmingham, Birmingham
Brighton Dome Concert Hall
The Stranglers
40th Anniversary Tour
Thursday 6 March 2014
Stalls General Admission - 688
GIANTS AND GEMS: AN ALBUM COLLECTION
ATG TICKETS
Leas Cliff Hall, Folkestone
THE STRANGLERS 40TH ANNIVERSARY TOUR
SJM Concerts Present
The Stranglers
Eventim Apollo
Saturday 08 March 2014
Stalls Standing
L'OLYMPIA
THE STRANGLERS
LUNDI 7 AVRIL 2014 20:00
LI 0205
GRATUIT
TRANSBORDEUR
VILLEURBANNE
THE STRANGLERS
Brighton Dome Concert Hall
SJM Concerts present
The Stranglers
Plus Special Guests
Tuesday 03 March 2015
Stalls General Admission - 92
MARCH ON
AAA
SJM CONCERTS PRESENTS
THE STRANGLERS 2015 + SPECIAL GUESTS
THURSDAY 5 MARCH 2015
G Live
ROUNDHOUSE
SJM Concerts present
The Stranglers
plus Special Guests
Friday 06 March 2015
Level 2 Standing
HARLEY-DAVIDSON EURO FESTIVAL
REO rock
REO VEILING ROESELARE
the stranglers

APOLLO THEATRE

26 MARCH 2016, MANCHESTER, UK

ANA MARIA NAZARIO

Ana Maria Nazario was at the Apollo in 2016

Just as I feared, getting a standing area ticket for the Stranglers at the Apollo was really not a good idea at all. I got squashed at the front and the tall man behind kept hitting my head when he was clapping. I didn't even have enough room to clap, and couldn't breathe at one point from too much pushing from behind. Oh dear. But The Alarm were brilliant, with Mike Peters absolutely amazing.

After The Alarm's set I had to go out and get some fresh air. Also, I wanted to ask security if I could switch from standing downstairs to the seating area upstairs. Fortunately (or I should say unfortunately for the Stranglers) it wasn't sold out and there were lots of empty seats upstairs, so I had the whole of the last row to myself.

I did buy a t-shirt from the vendor outside. I know it's bad - I should really only get official merchandise - but I couldn't resist the £5 tag.

When I was a teenager in Manila, there was this new wave station, WXB102, where they played a lot of alternative music - stuff you wouldn't normally hear on regular commercial stations. You had to have a good radio antenna though. That's where I used to get my unusual music from. And the 'jeepney' public transport ride from home to uni and back - that was like a mobile club. I left the Philippines in 1989, though from friends' Facebook posts I know new wave is still alive and well back home. The Stranglers were popular in the Philippines in my youth, and we regarded them as new wave. I think it was 'Golden Brown' that first made me sit up and listen. Then 'Always the Sun' - so awesome. And then I heard the cover version of 'Walk on By'. That was awesome too.

ACADEMY

27 MARCH 2016, BRIXTON, LONDON

STEVE WORRALL

There is something slightly unsettling about the *Black and White* album and the atmosphere that pervades it. It's like watching a particularly effective psychological thriller or horror movie. You know? That feeling when, even after leaving the cinema,

Steve Worrall saw Black and White revisited at Brixton Academy – photo Steve Worrall

you're left with a lingering sense of dread and have that irrational urge to check under the bed before you go to sleep.

It's totally unique, a genuinely innovative, ground-breaking album with twisted time structures, weird angular guitar riffs and snarling vocals. There's that immensely powerful production and the iconic but weirdly compelling cover art... and that's before we get to the bass! *Black and White* must be the ultimate bass album, JJ Burnel in inspired form throughout. Instead of following the commercially successful *No More Heroes* with more of the same, the Stranglers really went for the jugular, miles ahead of most of their contemporaries, who were either imploding or churning out punk-by-numbers, and produced this timeless album.

It's almost like it was beamed down from another planet. There was nothing to prepare you for *Black and White*, probably only Wire and Public Image Ltd making similarly challenging music. Of course, the Stranglers never get paid their dues. Yet the band have always thrived on being outsiders, surviving the departure of not just one but two lead vocalists and the semi-retirement of legendary drummer Jet Black, to play packed out venues across the globe. And the decision to embark on an ambitious tour to play the *Black and White* album start to finish in 2016 proved I wasn't the only one who always believed it should be lauded up there with some of the greatest albums to have come out of the punk and post-punk scenes.

As the familiar strains of the 'Waltzinblack' intro music filled a packed-out Brixton Academy, the Stranglers took the stage and launched straight into explosive album opener 'Tank'. We knew what was coming but it still took the breath away. They always had a gift for writing evocative songs and 'Tank' could not have been better named. Unfortunately, health issues prevented Jet from touring, his place behind the drum kit taken by Jim Macauley, who at first glance bore a youthful resemblance to the fast approaching 80-year-old. And just as the addition of Baz to the line-up seemed to reinvigorate the band, Jim upped the energy levels even further - I don't think the band had sounded so fresh and exciting for many a year.

Next up was 'Nice 'n' Sleazy', the LP's only single, and with its skewed take on a reggae rhythm and JJ's iconic leering bassline it's another perfectly-titled track. 'Outside Tokyo' is a twisted baroque-style waltz that slows the pace momentarily before 'Hey! (Rise of the Robots)' crashes in. This is probably the closest the band get to sounding like a punk rock band. In fact, it sounds like something you might have heard in the Roxy in 1976, with its quick-fire Clash-like '1977' guitar riff intro. It canters along at a fair pace and is all over in two glorious minutes. It's a shame they didn't get a saxophonist on stage to try and replicate Lora Logic's inspired playing from the album.

Next came 'Sweden (All Quiet on the Eastern Front)', inspired by Hugh's time studying at Lund University, in the 'only country where the clouds are interesting'. Although the band filmed a humorous video for the song, it was somewhat surprisingly only released in Sweden (and in Swedish), so remains in my mind the greatest single that never was, Baz wisely opting to stick with the English language album version on this occasion.

'Toiler on the Sea' is again one of those wonderfully evocative songs, an epic seafaring tale made up of different sections, similar to 'Down in the Sewer' from *Rattus Norvegicus*. You can really picture the grey skies bearing down on the rain-lashed boat being tossed on dark waves as the metaphorical crew battle against the elements. It's this almost Viking-inspired imagery I see carried over to *The Raven* a year later. 'Curfew' is a blistering, paranoid track seething with unsettling riffs, stabs of keyboards and the fear of unwelcome invaders with the power to 'turn the day into night', while 'Threatened' is in a similar vein with its pumping and pulsing heartbeat drumming and afforded the bizarre sight of people around me joining in, singing such choice lines as, 'Man killed by luxury, man killed by falling tree.'

'In the Shadows', with its fuzzed beyond recognition bassline, was always the weak link for me and hearing it played live didn't really change my opinion. Dave Greenfield took over lead vocals for the sinister 'Do You Wanna?', which segued into the superb 'Death and Night and Blood (Yukio)', the hairs on the back of my neck standing up as the two songs collided.

I wasn't sure if they would include 'Enough Time', as it's a difficult enough track to get your head around as a listener let alone as a musician, but they managed the very weird time signatures and off-kilter riffs expertly. As the song slowly wound down, the stage lights came on, the stage suddenly awash in a blaze of colour, and the band starting the second half of the set with a stomping '(Get a) Grip (on Yourself)'. What followed was an excellent pick of singles, classic tracks and a few surprises, including 'Walk on By', initially given away as a free seven-inch single with the album. There were also a few tracks from *No More Heroes*, including 'Dead Ringer', 'Something Better Change' and a blistering 'I Feel Like a Wog', and 'Nuclear Device' from *The Raven*.

The sublime 'Always the Sun' was played under a beautiful orange sunset light show and sounded superb, followed by a surprise 'Princess of the Streets' from *Rattus*, JJ's voice on top form. The older, more familiar numbers were punctuated by songs from the last three Baz-era albums, 'Mercury Rising' from *Giants*, 'I've Been Wild' from *Norfolk Coast* and then - one of the highlights - a superb 'Relentless' and

‘A Soldier's Diary’ from *Suite XVI*, the latter a bit of a throwaway thrash.

It wasn’t the most inspiring selection of newish tracks when you think of the quality of some of the others they could have chosen, but they seemed to go down well. Anyway, with a back catalogue of such diversity and quality, they could have played for four hours and still people would complain they didn’t hear their favourite song. Besides, for the well-deserved encores we were treated to ‘Peaches’, ‘Hanging Around’, ‘Go Buddy Go’ and, of course, ‘No More Heroes’. And as I made my way out of the venue, I made my mind up to go along to see them in Reading a few days later. I had to get another fix of *Black and White*.

PIRAEUS 117 ACADEMY

16 NOVEMBER 2016, ATHENS, GREECE

PROFESSOR CSABA ANDRÁS DÉZSI

Behind the Iron Curtain in Hungary in 1978, it was not easy to get the records of western bands. The father of one of my friends (Károly Palotai) was a famous international FIFA and UEFA football referee, and I used to write out for him the lists of the records he should bring me back from his trips abroad. That’s how I received the Stranglers’ *Rattus Norvegicus* and the Sex Pistols’ *Never Mind the Bollocks* albums. I was at grammar school and punk music wasn’t known about in Hungary, so hearing it for the first time had a very big impact on me. Since then, I have bought all the Stranglers albums, but I could never get to any of their concerts. In the meantime, I became a medical doctor, a cardiologist and a university professor.

In 2016, my wife Veronika surprised me on my birthday by taking me see the Stranglers in Athens. I said that I wanted to meet one of my favourite bands in person so we went to the Piraeus 117 Academy Club in the early afternoon. We could hear the band doing their soundcheck but the local organisers of the concert threw us out and would not let us go to the stage. I told my wife that it wasn’t a problem. Wewere going to stand at the door and wait for it to open for the concert starting six hours later.

A lady came out. She was drinking coffee and smoking a cigarette. She spoke English well, which is not typical of the Greeks, and I told my wife that I thought she was with the band. I explained to the lady that I had got the concert ticket as a birthday present and that we had travelled to Athens from Hungary just to see the Stranglers. I asked her if she could get us in to meet them and take a photo. She said she would go in and ask. She came back after some minutes and took us to the stage, where the whole Stranglers team was. As we were approaching the stage, JJ greeted us in Hungarian, ‘Jó napot kívánok!’ It was a fantastic feeling. He said that he learned this greeting – ‘Good day’ - from a Hungarian friend.

On the stage, we got their autographs and took the long-awaited photos. It was a fantastic experience to meet the members of my childhood favourite band - JJ Burnel,

Dave Greenfield and Baz Warne - and they were very kind. As the door closed behind us, I said to my wife, 'Damn it, I forgot to ask for a guitar pick!'

Needless to say, we were the first ones to enter the hall at the start of the concert and stood in the middle of the first row, at the age of 57. It was a fantastic concert. All I had to do was to get a guitar pick!

During the concert, JJ recognised me in the front row, and I indicated to him to throw his guitar pick to me. He did, but the pick bounced off my chest and fell to the ground. I threw myself on the ground, but the pick fell through some iron railings and I couldn't see it. A stranger patted my shoulder. I thought there was going to be a fistfight, but he just gave me his phone to use as a torch and make it easier to find the guitar pick. I was completely astonished. Greek people are so polite! I found it, and I have kept it as a souvenir ever since. It was a fantastic experience.

At one point, Baz stopped the music and asked the audience to stop smoking because, although smoking was allowed, there was an awful lot of smoke on the stage and it interfered with their singing. As a professor of cardiology, I completely agreed with him that people should not be smoking!

O2 ACADEMY

15 MARCH 2017, LEEDS, UK

SIMON SMITH/DELIC

In all my 35-ish years of seeing the Stranglers I have never seen them so happy on stage as at this gig. They were clearly having a ball up there and that came through in the music which was a brilliant combination of professionalism and swagger as they ripped through 26 tracks from one of the best and most eclectic back catalogues in rock.

There are far too many highlights to go through them all but the opening salvo of 'Longships', 'The Raven', 'Straighten Out' and 'Grip' were a fantastic mixture of power and melody and were viscerally exciting. Hearing 'Four Horsemen', 'Nice in Nice' and 'Curfew' for the first time in years was great and I was so happy that they played the amazing 'Baroque Bordello'. Elsewhere, there were some storming post-Cornwell tracks, especially 'I've Been Wild', 'Norfolk Coast' and 'Lost Control', all of which sit well with the older stuff. But the highlights for me were an absolutely storming 'I Feel Like a Wog', the ever amazing 'Walk on By' and, finishing the main set, an overdue 'Down in the Sewer', which was as good as anything I've seen the band do over the years. Any words I use to describe it here aren't going to do it justice. You know those moments at gigs when everything just absolutely clicks? It was just phenomenal.

The Stranglers seem to go from strength to strength. They have somehow come through 40 years of gigging and releasing records with an integrity that few can match. While they are inevitably playing the game a bit more these days, they are still ploughing a fairly unique furrow away from many of their peers.

O2 GUILDHALL

20 MARCH 2017, SOUTHAMPTON, UK

LINDA TUTTON

I remember the first time I saw Jim on drums, at Portsmouth Guildhall. It was then that I realised that Jet was really unwell and might not be playing with the band for much longer. Thankfully Jet is still with us, and Jim has become an integral member of the band. I remember Southampton Guildhall in 2017. It was the very last time the guys ever played there. The sound was truly awful, to the extent that Baz actually commented on it and said they would never play there again. And they never have.

And my last memory is a very recent one, at *Rebellion Festival* in 2019. Why did it take them so long to realise this was an awesome festival? I'm glad they decided to return in 2022.

LE TETRIS

27 NOVEMBER 2017, LE HAVRE, FRANCE

SCOTT PHILP

Scott Philp wound up on stage in Le Havre

I have lost count of the number of times I've seen the band live, often denying I've been at a certain gig only for someone to produce a photo of me there. Apparently, it must be over 200 gigs from the 1970s to 2020s but who knows and who cares? I saw them sober for the first time in Glasgow in 2022 and remarked, 'Have they always been this good?'

The photo of me on stage at Le Tetris, taken by Audrey Grant, is a great memory. It was a great gig with us hoisting up different familyinblack members for each song; the locals started queuing up for their turn. Obviously, I baggsied 'No More Heroes' (my all-time favourite) and ended up on stage thinking, 'I can do JJ better than him!'

After 45 years following the Stranglers, gigs are now almost as much about meeting up with the familyinblack as they are about the band and the music – almost! I have made some real friendships over the years. It was a great touch by the band to use a photo of the Albert Hall familyinblack crowd for the cover of *Friday the Thirteenth*, even if I say so myself. That's a younger me on the cover with my arms in the air, along with many familiar faces, all waiting for the Meninblack to play an encore.

KRAKATOA

2 DECEMBER 2017, MÉRIGNAC, FRANCE

MARK TUTTON

This gig was booked way in advance as a mini break, but just a few days before, my father Tony Tutton passed away, throwing everything into chaos. After a long chat with the family and my wife, Linda, it was decided that we would go. The gig was mainly French fans with a few English people in the crowd. As the band took to the stage, my arms were raised and I sang along with every song, getting some strange looks in the process. Then came to the song which reminds me of my dad, 'Always the Sun'. I clenched my hands, kissed them and raised them to the sky, seeing in my mind's eye my dad with a big smile on his face looking down on me. Now whenever I hear the song at a gig, I stop and do the same thing. I was a bit of a wreck at the end, but the wife looked after me. I can't thank the band enough for the gig, it was something I needed.

IRONWORKS

9 MARCH 2018, INVERNESS, UK

BARRY GUNN

The last time the Stranglers played the Ironworks I attended with my daughter and son. My daughter had arranged for me to meet the band, but it fell through. We had, however, arrived early and the young bloke on the front desk suggested we wait at the back, as the Stranglers were in doing a sound check and we might catch them coming out. Three of us approached them when they came out, after listening to some of the sound check. I was starstruck but we

Barry Gunn saw the Stranglers at the Ironworks in Inverness

Barry Gunn was up on the balcony – photographer unknown

managed to ask JJ if I could have my picture taken with him and he obliged.

I said, 'Hi, I'm Barry or Baz – like him (gesturing towards Baz Warne who continued to walk past): bald and I sing, but better than him.' 'It wouldn't be hard', joked JJ. He took an interest in my daughter who was dressed up nicely for the occasion but was taking the pictures. My son was looking on and Dave Greenfield went over and watched the unfolding picture-taking while sparking up a conversation and smiling as only Dave could. They then went off in a car.

We went for a few drinks and a meal and went to the gig. My daughter knew somebody at the door who gave us a VIP pass, so we got seats up in the balcony with access to the bar upstairs. In the pictures published from the back of the stage, behind the Meninblack, we can be seen up in the balcony saluting them at the end.

What a night. I had only seen the Stranglers in Scotland on a limited number of occasions. My son and daughter grew up listening to Stranglers tracks in the house and car and were blown away by the gig. My daughter is a music teacher and teaches keyboard, so knows exactly just how good Dave was.

I have been an ardent fan since 1977 and love all the different line ups and styles and directions the band have taken. My favourite albums are *Rattus* and *Raven* from the older times but *Suite XVI* and now *Dark Matters* bring fresh direction and power. How on earth do you choose favourite songs? 'Genetix', 'Bless You', 'Laughing', and 'Stallion' are outstanding. 'Ugly', 'Sewer', 'Summer Dream' are classic and 'Grip', 'Tank' and 'Toiler' are all incredible live. Listening to these songs shaped the person I was and made me reflective – wondering about things I had never thought about. The Stranglers are interesting, talented people with so much to say. It's been some journey through life with them all. To have your family share it is a privilege and to meet these guys in person was unreal.

STRUAN J

I had listened to the Stranglers music for many years before I was old enough to attend a gig. Finally, I was, and I was blown away by how well the band played. The feeling of the bass vibrating through the floor was exhilarating. After attending the Inverness gig, I went to see the Stranglers again in Dunfermline in 2019. I was meant to see them in Glasgow in 2020 but... After the rescheduling of dates I finally managed to see the band in Glasgow in 2022. Finally being back in the room with my favourite music blasting out and everyone enjoying it was the best feeling in years. I even got a photo with the band (minus Jim, who was too fast getting into the venue!)

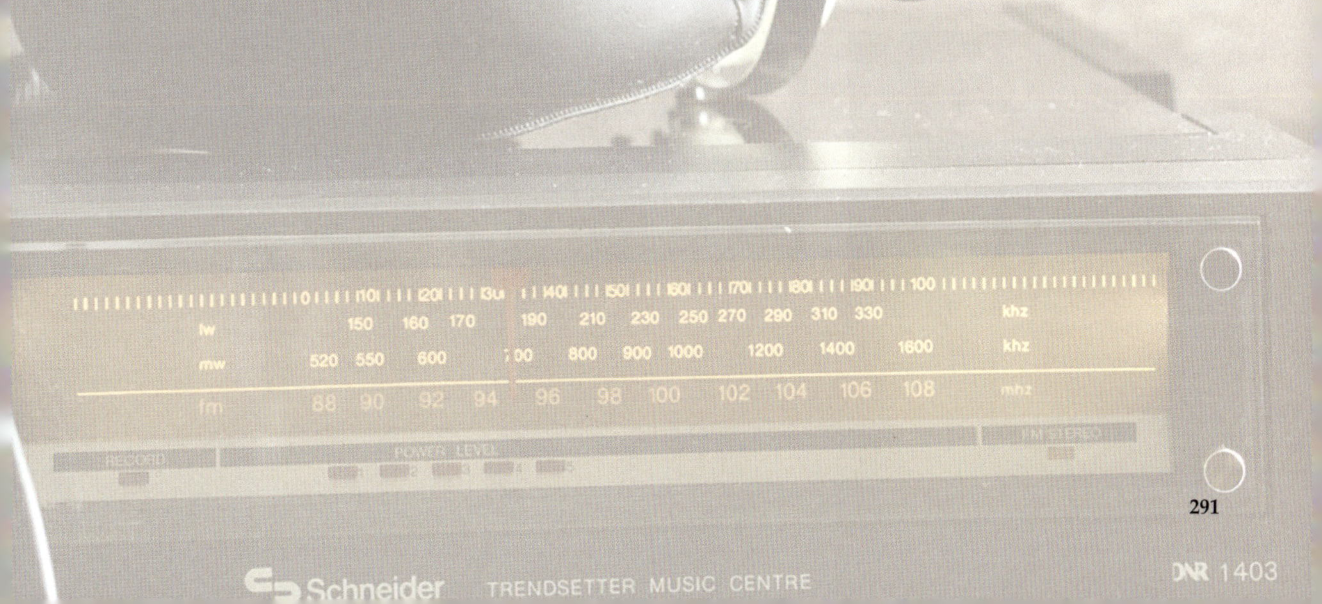

GUILDHALL

13 MARCH 2018, PORTSMOUTH, UK

ANDY MILLER

At the tail-end of 2016 my health changed considerably, and I went from being an active person with a really active job, an avid gig-goer, busy social life etc, to a mere shell of the person I was. So began a long, long journey

JJ signs a guitar, Andy Miller with Dave. Jet and Baz and JJ on stage

Andy Miller didn't think he'd make it to the 2018 tour.

of hospitals, doctors, tests etc, which has just gone on and on until the present day. Subsequently, my attendance at gigs began to fall away. I managed to get to six gigs on the 2017 British tour but the final night I attended at Brixton Academy really drove home to me that I was not in a good place at all, and really struggled. For the first time ever, I just wanted the gig to end. I never thought I would ever have said that about a Stranglers gig. I made up my mind that I had probably seen my last Stranglers gig.

When the 2018 tour was announced, I resigned myself to the fact that I would not be up to going to any of the gigs. However, Owen Carne, who runs the Stranglers website, contacted me. He said that by hook or by crook I would be attending at least one gig on the tour, that he would get me to and from the gig, and that I would be on the guest list and looked after for the whole evening. The gig was to be at Portsmouth Guildhall, though I was still filled with trepidation about how I would feel. On the day of the gig, I was picked up by Owen and his wife Jacquie and driven to the venue. We had a drink in the pub opposite and then went into the venue, where I took up a seat at the back by the mixing desk. It seemed really strange to me to be watching the greatest band on the planet sitting down, but I resigned myself to the fact that this would be the way if I was to attend gigs going forward. The Stranglers played a blinding set that night and I really enjoyed the gig even sitting down.

After the gig Owen and Jacquie took me backstage. As we walked into the backstage area, I saw JJ in conversation with somebody. He saw us, promptly came over, asked how I was doing, and was really concerned about my health situation. He said if I wanted to go to any more gigs on the tour, or future gigs, to get in touch and I would be put on guest list. He even suggested I could sit at the back of the mixing desk with Louie. JJ's words were, 'You are one of the family and we look after members of our family.' This meant so much to me. To think I first saw this guy on *Top of the Pops* in 1977, snarling with menace, now talking to me like this – it really brought home to me what this band are about. Baz then came over and again, like JJ, was concerned about what had happened to me. Though he did say, 'I have missed your ugly mug at the front.' Typical Mackem cheeky bastard that Mr Warne is, but all said in jest, and he loves the banter, does Baz. We did laugh.

To spend those ten to 15 minutes with these two guys in light of my circumstances meant so much to me and spoke volumes of them both as men and how much they value the fans of the band. Over the years I have met the band members on several occasions but that quarter of an hour in Pompey in 2018 will always sit there as a really special moment.

The Stranglers are the greatest band ever. End of.

O2 ACADEMY

29 MARCH 2018, NEWCASTLE, UK

JIMMY TURNER

Jimmy Turner got to meet Baz and JJ

I work with a lad called Kev Stores, who's an old pal of Baz Warne. Kev knew I was a big fan of Baz, starting from his days in the Toy Dolls, and Kev promised me and my pals, Paul Trotter and Tony Hunter, that he would sort it for us to meet the band after the show in Newcastle 2018 in their hotel. I didn't think it would happen but it did! We had a great couple of hours, mainly with Baz. What fans didn't know was that JJ had a chronic bad back and probably should have cancelled a couple of shows but didn't. I got to meet Baz and JJ again the following year.

APOLLO THEATRE

31 MARCH 2018, MANCHESTER, UK

BAZZA CRIDLAND

When Alfie, the older of my two boys, had received multiple sessions of conditioning by listening to their music, I decided to take him to a gig. He said he enjoyed it but wouldn't bother going again; no issues there and the 'take the boys to a Stranglers gig' box was half ticked. The younger one, Archie, was a different proposition. Exposed to the same level of musical input from the band on an almost daily basis, he was not bothered about going to see them live. What the actual fuck.

Bazza Cridland and son Archie were at the Bull's Head

It took a few years of consistent questioning, err, I mean asking, if he fancied joining me at a gig before he gave in – I mean said 'yes'. I think this was more to do with his mum asking him to go so she wouldn't have to keep hearing about it from me every tour.

We went to the Manchester gig, the last of the tour. With our hotel booked, we set off on the drive up north. I was trying to contain my excitement whilst Archie was just sitting quietly on his phone for the entire journey. We booked into the hotel and headed to the Bull's Head where I introduced him to fellow fans. With the gig done and after one hell of a night in which the 'take the boys to a Stranglers gig' box was well and truly ticked in style, we headed back to the hotel.

Next day on the drive home Archie said, 'I wasn't that bothered about going but only said yes to shut you up.' Fair point, I admired his honesty. 'But I loved it'. I grinned, thinking, 'I knew you would'. However, when he uttered those immortal words – 'when can we go again?' – I nearly exploded. The 'next gig' was in Belfast which was booked within 24 hours of getting home. That, and quite a few more gigs since then, and Archie is the greatest gig buddy I could ask for.

The experience of seeing the band live, along with the brilliant fans who accepted him as if he had been going forever, played a big part in his journey. The Stranglers, I fucking love them.

OLYMPIA THEATRE

1 MARCH 2019, DUBLIN, IRELAND

COLUM O'BYRNE

Colum O'Byrne rediscovered the Meninblack

In 1977, our household in Dublin City would all sit around to watch the weekly rendition of *Top of the Pops* on BBC on Thursday evening. My older sister and brother were starting to get into music and I watched and listened with complete disinterest. Then this band called the Stranglers appeared, looking moody and menacing with music to match. I was hooked immediately and now I needed a record player.

My dad, under pressure from the three of us, came home one evening with a High Fidelity record player. Now we needed some vinyls. My sister bought a Steely Dan album, my brother the *Greatest Hits* of the Stylistics and I came home with the sublime and brilliant masterpiece, *Rattus Norvegicus*. The flame was now well and truly lit and every album, single and 12-inch was obtained. A fully-fledged membership of SIS ensued (I still have all my copies of the magazine) and there was a wardrobe change to black. What a band, with superb musicianship and a brilliant live act. I bought records by other acts but my favourite band was - and is - the Stranglers. The solo albums were all purchased to boot.

Disaster struck - Hugh Cornwell decided to leave the band. I was devastated. I continued to buy the new releases but my flame was not burning as bright. I still went to gigs of both the Stranglers and Hugh Cornwell and supported both out of loyalty. I just never felt the chemistry of the band suited being five in number and always felt something was missing. My listening of the music was firmly belonging to all the albums up to and including *10* and, in fairness, *Time to Die*.

Five or six years ago I opened a Christmas present from my son and, lo and behold, there were two tickets for the Stranglers playing in Dublin at the Olympia Theatre. I was pleasantly surprised and what a live act still. They were back to a four-piece, the chemistry was superb and the musicianship just the best. Baz was superb on lead guitar and vocals, Jim excelling on drums and there were the two masters, Greenfield and Burnel. My mind was blown and the love affair was re-ignited. I couldn't get enough. I bought *Coupe De Grace*, *Suite XVI*, *Norfolk Coast*, *Acoustic in Brugge* and *Giants* all in quick succession. More live concerts followed and I was hooked again. Gems like 'Relentless' and so many others would have remained unheard if not for my son. Then the sad news of keyboard maestro Davie Greenfield passing away was offset a little by the aptly named *Dark Matters* and another vinyl masterpiece was born. 2022 saw a trip to the *Rebellion* Festival with my son in August, the Olympia Theatre in Dublin in September and Copenhagen in October.

If a wish could be granted, I would love to meet my heroes. What a memory that would be. But then - No More Heroes anymore! Long live the Meninblack.

THE HEXAGON

12 MARCH 2019, READING, UK

RUTH RAE

Back in May 2018, I decided it was high time I took my (then seven-year-old) son Iain to see my favourite band. Fortunately, the Stranglers were playing the 6pm slot at the charity festival *Concert at the Kings – Rock Against Cancer* in Wiltshire, and we were ready, in our Stranglers t-shirts, down at the front. My son is autistic, and music has always been a large part of the bond between us. He had great fun, singing along to the songs with his own favourite words, a big smile on his face. The band noticed him and were smiling too. At the end of the show, drummer Jim Macaulay wanted my son to have his sticks but didn't quite make the throw and they landed on the wrong side of the barrier

Ruth Rae with her son Iain and JJ

for us. I eventually managed to get one for him after a heated debate with the two middle-aged people next to us who decided they had a claim on the sticks, despite Jim clearly indicating who they were meant for.

The following year I made a special request of the band, asking if I could bring my son along to the sound check at our local venue to make up for the lost drumstick. To my huge surprise I received a phone call from JJ Burnel himself, inviting us down. The Stranglers crew were absolutely brilliant with my son, putting on the full lighting display and even allowing us onto the stage. I had a lovely long chat with JJ, and got to have a few words with Baz and Jim too, while my son made some pigeon noises into Baz's microphone and skipped around happily taking everything in. We thoroughly enjoyed the sound check, having the whole hall to ourselves to dance around to 'Baroque Bordello'. Afterwards Jim kindly presented my son with a set of two drumsticks and we had a quick photo with JJ and left floating on the clouds.

I returned alone later for the full show, which was excellent, and kept looking at the stage, thinking how my son and I had been on it just a few hours earlier. The Stranglers really do appreciate and care about their fans, from the oldest to the youngest.

O2 ACADEMY

14 MARCH 2019, NEWCASTLE, UK

JAY NELSON

I first got into the Stranglers through my dad as they are one of his favourite bands. However, he is only a fan of the Hugh era of the band; personally, I enjoy every iteration. My first Stranglers gig was in Newcastle back in 2019 and all I think about now was how lucky I was to be able to see Dave play live. I have great memories from that gig - the set list was outstanding with many of my favourites being played such as 'Uptown', 'Princess of the Streets' and 'Last Men on the Moon'. Jake Burns from Stiff Little Fingers was in the audience too as SLF were playing the same venue the next day.

O2 ACADEMY

15 MARCH 2019, LEEDS, UK

LESLEY STEAD

I asked Dave for a photo with him and my husband John and his brother. My husband first saw the Stranglers in the late 1970s when he was 15 years old, at Sheffield Top

Rank on the Black and White tour. They were supported by a then unknown band, which turned out to be the Human League.

APOLLO

30 MARCH 2019, MANCHESTER, UK

JACK HARKINS, BASS/GUITAR/ VOCALS, UHR, BLANKETMAN, THE COMMON COLD

Jack Harkins with JJ Burnel, and his signed Gospel LP

I was 14 when I first saw the Stranglers, at Bearded Theory in Derbyshire. I knew the hits but was hooked as soon as the bass intro to 'Toiler on the Sea' set things off. I'd never heard the bass guitar sound like that and immediately because completely infatuated with playing bass. Fundamentally, I learnt how to play by locking myself in the attic and learning their first six albums.

What I found particularly role model-esque about JJ was how in the context of punk and the wider context of being a person, he seemed to create his own style and make his own rules in life. This was something I mimicked, as you do as an impressionable kid. I imagine that's what's been lasting for me, and I hope I'm doing so now.

Album-wise, the one for me has to be *The Gospel According to the Meninblack*, because although *Black and White* really feels like a complete masterpiece, *Gospel* is just completely off the wall and is total creativity, without the shackles of genre or style. That period after *The Raven*, where you could hear anything from beat jazz poetry to Europop whilst maintaining their own isolated aura, made them so much cooler and is a testament to that total creativity that set them apart. An honourable mention to JJ's *Euroman Cometh* too.

I've lots of great memories of my time watching the Stranglers, with the standout for me always the lack of barrier between audience and band. Seeing the Stranglers was an immersive experience for me, and an inspiring one at that. They had a superb sense of humour too. As an aspiring young bassist, I recall JJ looking down from the crowd, asking me if he was playing the bassline to 'Baroque Bordello' correctly. That was really funny, and a really amazing thing to do for an impressionable young chap like myself.

Then there was my last pre-pandemic memory of the band - and my favourite – when I was drinking at the pub next to Manchester Apollo's stage door and JJ came out, shouting me and giving me a big hug. A band with true respect for their fans, and it's reciprocated.

THE REGENT

29 MAY 2019, LOS ANGELES, CALIFORNIA

JANELLE FRESE

Janelle Frese and her daughters are the California Peaches

I was 12 when I first heard the Stranglers on KROQ radio in 1979. Rodney on the 'ROQ played an import. My first Stranglers album purchase was *Aural Sculpture* and I played it over and over again in my room while staring at the pictures of the band and learning every word to every song. When I joined my first band (as a 16-year-old novelty girl drummer) I made my bandmates learn 'No Mercy'. We called ourselves The No Names and my drumming was fully inspired by Jet Black (of course!).

In the early 2000s, my daughters were ten and eight when they really started listening to the Stranglers around our house and singing along to the many Stranglers CDs I'd acquired over the years. They loved all the singles and more. They grew so enamoured of music, and the Stranglers in particular, that they started picking up instruments and teaching themselves to play.

In 2013, they formed their own band, the Nesting Dolls, and began playing live shows around town. They became friends with Keith 'Monkey' Warren of The Adicts, and in 2017, the Nesting Dolls opened for the Adicts at the House of Blues in Anaheim, California.

Monkey realised the girls had grown up to be big fans of the Stranglers, so when the Meninblack were on tour in the States in 2019, he invited them to take a road trip to Las Vegas to see the Stranglers headline the Punk Rock Bowling Festival. Mikayla and Marlena enjoyed meeting Baz and snapping a few photos and videos from their backstage view of the show.

A few days later, I took my daughters to see the Stranglers at the Regent in Los Angeles. This would be my first and only time to see the band. Marlena dressed up in a peach dress, Mikayla wore jet black and we were among the few female fans in the mostly male crowd. I can't tell you how many times we heard somebody mutter, 'Nice peaches' to us.

I loved the Regent show so much. I swear it seemed like JJ was playing and singing directly to us during a few fun moments. The band were on fire and performed an amazing set that we will never ever forget. As a drummer, I was always hoping I'd get to see Jet Black play, but when I saw Jim, I understood the power of Jet's legacy. We never thought this would be the last time we would stand in the presence of the genius wonder of Dave Greenfield. We are forever touched by his awesome magic and keep him in our hearts forever. These special Strangler moments, these shows of May 2019, left beautiful memories forever engraved on our hearts and in our musical minds and will last a lifetime and beyond.

Dear Fabulous Stranglers, we love you and thank you for the 45 years of music and magical punk-foolery! Love and gratitude always from the California Peaches - Janelle, Mikayla and Marlena.

KUBIX FESTIVAL, HERRINGTON COUNTRY PARK

6 JULY 2019, SUNDERLAND, UK

MICK ASTON

Mick Aston proposed to wife Keren at the Kubix Festival with a little help from friend Sarah and from Baz

I met my wife Keren after we both followed the band on Facebook groups. Keren had met the band when she was only 15 over 40 years ago. I first saw the band at the Theatre Royal in Nottingham in 1980 and have followed them ever since. At the *Kubix Festival* in 2019 we got a message to the band, with help from our dear friend Sarah 'Saz' Chapman. Baz announced my proposal to Keren in front of a few thousand Stranglers fans. There's a clip on *YouTube*. It was such a fabulous day.

BUTLIN'S RESORT SKEGNESS

6 OCTOBER 2019, SKEGNESS, UK

AL TIFFEN

Al Tiffen saw the lads at Butlins in 2019

I was 15 when my big brother bought home the *Rattus Norvegicus* album. He had to order it in from the record shop and it took two weeks to arrive. We played that album until it nearly wore out. My favourite track was 'Sometimes' and I'd get goosebumps grooving to the monster punchy basslines. Listening through headphones I really heard those swirling keyboards, the jagged guitar and the great vocals and lyrics.

I bought *No More Heroes* with my first pay cheque. That was the start of my life with the best band ever. I bought everything. I saw them in Portsmouth sometime in the Eighties, and then at Butlin's in 2019 with Baz. He's a great singer and guitarist with a fantastic sense of humour; a real man of the people. I have played bass myself in bands all over the place, always trying to emulate the power and feel of JJ. It's no particular sound – it's the attitude. I saw the guys on the *Dark Matters* tour in Norwich. They opened with my all-time favourite Stranglers track, 'Toiler on the Sea'. Brilliant. All I can say is thanks for being part of my life.

ESTRAGON

30 NOVEMBER 2019, BOLOGNA, ITALY

STEFANO PEPPINI

I attended the Bologna gig in 2019, the last in Italy with the beloved Dave. My (love) story with the Stranglers begins quite late, with *Aural Sculpture* and *Dreamtime*. I was a teen and I liked what I heard. I decided to discover more and went backwards to *Feline*, then *La Folie* and eventually found the great box set, *The Old Testament*.

Slowly but steadily, brick by brick, as the Romans built their roads (and consequently their empire), I fell in love with this wonderful and multiversal band. Now I give the entire discography a go on my FLAC reader every month or two. I just can't live without them. They are my all-time favourite band. It would be The Beatles, but The Beatles are kind of out-of-competition.

MELKWEG MAX

5 DECEMBER 2019, AMSTRERDAM, THE NETHERLANDS

WANDA STRUBBE

It took Wanda Strabbe over 40 years to get to a Stranglers gig

I'd been listening to their music since 1977 and had tickets for concerts before, but something always came up that stopped me seeing them. I lived in southern Italy for 30 years and never went to a gig. December 2019 changed my life. From the first note of 'Waltzinblack' until the last, I was totally amazed and enchanted. 'What am I looking at? What is this? Who are these people? This is more than just music.' Everything was perfect and I now understood the important role the bass guitar could play in music. After this gig, I took the bass I had bought back in 1981 out of the cupboard again.

When the *Final Full* tour was announced, I was really angry at myself that I had considered some things in the past more important than going to gigs and that I had wasted the tickets.

During lockdown, the Stranglers themselves suffered with the death of Dave, but tried to stay in touch with the fans via the 'Rat Chat'. It was really great to hear something now and then. Fans from all over the world began having a Zoom meeting every Saturday which I started attending called The Raven Inn. At the start of each meeting, we would raise our glasses to Dave Greenfield.

Four great fans organised it all and a Stranglers-related subject was chosen beforehand. Topics included the records, comparisons between records, time periods and individual band members. There was a quiz (which I understood very little of due to my poor English and because some information was missing). The questions were very detailed and there were quite a few Stranglers 'walking encyclopaedias' amongst the fans. I had a lot to learn and I did, thanks to The Raven Inn. Since the end of lockdown, The Raven Inn meetings have switched to monthly and topics include upcoming gigs.

Having only seen the Stranglers live once before, I am now at 19 times. My first post lockdown was in France. We all had to sit down and I wore a Stranglers motif facemask. Friends and family sometimes say, 'You have seen them already, haven't you?' The only answer I know is, 'Yes, and when are you coming too?'

FUZZ CLUB

13 DECEMBER 2019, ATHENS, GREECE

FOTINIJJ GIANNOPOULOU

In May 2019 I saw a poster on the side of a bus saying the Stranglers were coming to Greece. I was nine years old and it would be my first ever gig. On the day of the gig I woke up at seven o'clock in the morning. I skipped Friday lessons to get to the gig, going with my parents from the city of Patras to Athens, me in my *Black and White* t-shirt. We arrived at 5pm and I waited outside to see JJ but I was too shy to shout out to him or tell him how much I love him.

When I saw JJ on stage, he looked at me. I shouted loudly, 'JJ, I love you so much!' I wanted to hug him. He answered, 'Okay,' with his big wide smile. I gave him two sketches, a white flower and a letter. He gave me his plectrum, Jim gave me his drumsticks, Baz talked to me and I smiled at Dave and he smiled back. What a night!

My favourite song is 'Peaches'; I have it as the alarm that I wake up to in the morning. JJ has taught me to love the bass and he's the reason I love French and Japanese culture. For me the Stranglers are JJ. He has changed my life.

Fifiejjinblack, Greece.

TOWN HALL

13 FEBRUARY 2020, CHRISTCHURCH, NEW ZEALAND

PAUL WESTWOOD

When I left Blighty for New Zealand ten years ago, I thought I had seen my last Stranglers gig. Since then, I have been lucky to see the boys on four occasions. New band member Jim has filled Jet's considerable boots well and has inspired me to start playing drums in my late fifties. (I'm also proud that he's a fellow Brummie.) JJ still kicks ass. Baz has kept the on-stage banter going and he's an awesome guitarist to boot. They have even developed an awesome football set piece where Dave flicks the glass onto Baz's head who nods over for the volleyed finish from JJ. One from the training ground.

I last saw the Stranglers, with Dave, in Christchurch in 2020. It was only a couple of months prior to his passing, and although he played brilliantly he didn't look well and I had a feeling I may not see him play again. My youngest son Harry and his wife, Yuxin, were there and I have promised them my entire Stranglers collection when I pop off this mortal coil. I hope I get to see the band again before that happens.

Despite the distance apart that we now live, I'm still in touch with my old mate Jones and we still chat about our love for the Stranglers. He says that we are really lucky that we were smitten so young and we that got to follow the best band in the world. He's totally right.

DAVE GREENFIELD

3 MAY 2020

CRAIG WOOD

I discovered Dave had died when I looked at my phone and saw that 'Dave Greenfield' was trending as a search term. To say I was numb would be an understatement. This was my hero gone, the one person who I admired more than anyone else in the world, and who had such a profound effect on me for 40 years. That evening I wept, more than I had done for the passing of members of my own family. This after all, was the death of the Stranglers. The closest I ever got to Dave was when the *Aural Sculpture* tour came to Glasgow. A friend had told me he had just walked into the Apollo unchallenged whilst The Jam were doing their soundcheck, so I resolved to try the same. With a small group of friends, we waited at the stage door whilst Hugh and JJ arrived in a car, with JJ disappearing inside like a streak of lightning and Hugh stopping to sign one single autograph.

Only a couple of minutes later, Dave and Jet walked along, both of them pausing to chat. I recall one guy quizzing Dave about the set list.

'You playing Ice Queen tonight, Dave?' 'No.' ''Genetix'?' 'No, we haven't rehearsed it.' ''Hanging'?' 'Yes, yes, we are playing 'Hanging Around'.' At this point I rather awkwardly put my hand out and patted Dave on the shoulder, saying the immortal words, 'You awright, Dave?' The most appropriate thing for me to have done would be to prostrate myself at his feet.

We sneaked in past the box office to the stalls and hid quietly behind a pillar. Unfortunately, the door then opened behind us and a couple of skinheads walked in, telling us they couldn't believe their eyes when they saw us just stroll in. They then opened cans of beer, lit cigarettes and talked loudly, so it was no surprise when a guy walked up the aisle and told us to get out, on the promoter's orders.

PARADISO

4 MAY 2020, AMSTERDAM, THE NETHERLANDS

AJAY SAGGAR

Oh man. I was so sad to hear of Dave Greenfield's passing. Anyone who knows me will know how much the Stranglers mean to me... first single, first album, first gig, first love! And Dave lifted the Stranglers' sound into a different cerebral musical universe.

Ajay Saggar with Dave Greenfield and JJ Burnel at the Paradiso, Amsterdam, and his signed original copy of Black and White

His prog-meets-space jazz keyboard attack was the perfect tonic to the bass thunder of JJ and spikey guitar of Hugh. He was technically on the spot, but what made him special was his musical imagination, lifting the songs high above the punk clatter and filling your ears and senses with adventure. I was truly a 'fan' when I got to meet him and JJ in December 2019 when they played in Amsterdam. It was hard telling them how much they meant to me, as I'm sure they get that a lot. But Dave sensed my happiness in that short time and took the time to have a chat and was genuinely interested in me for that short amount of time. And that meant a lot. Safe travels, Dave. No more heroes!

ENGLAND

JULY 2020

DANIEL STEARN

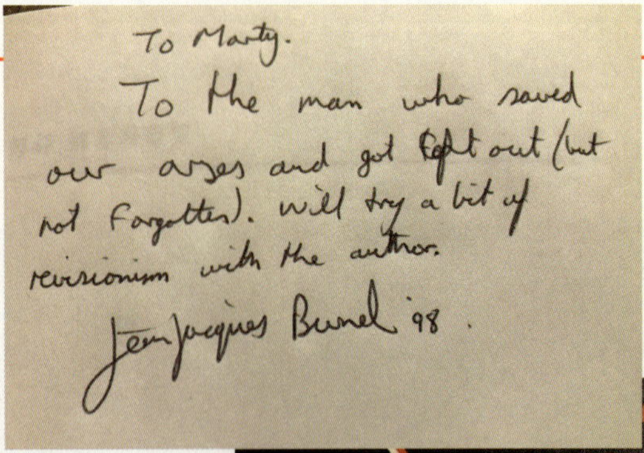
To Marty.
To the man who saved our arses and got left out (but not forgotten). Will try a bit of revisionism with the author.
Jean-Jacques Burnel '98.

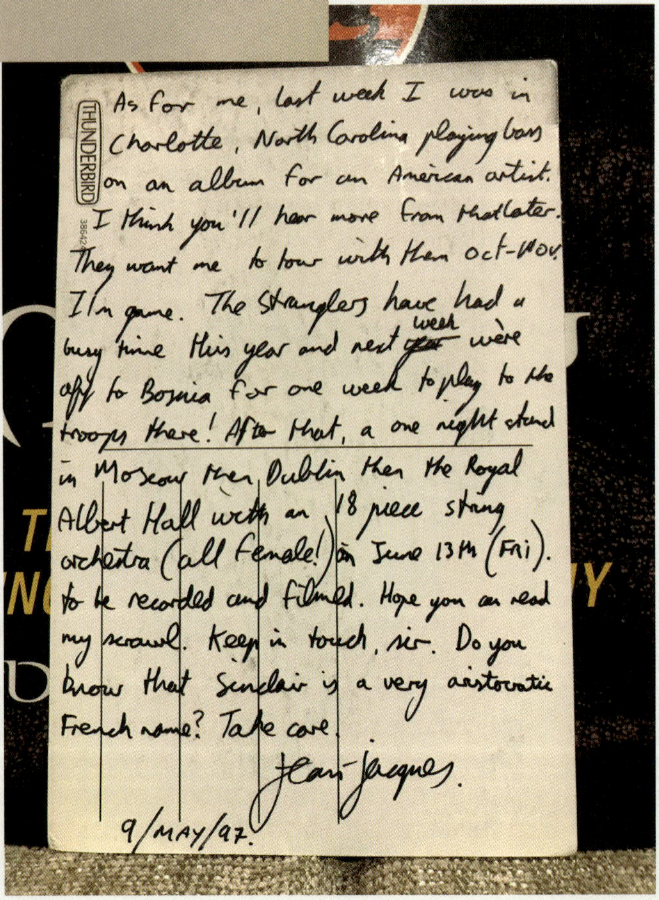
THUNDERBIRD 38642

As for me, last week I was in Charlotte, North Carolina playing bass on an album for an American artist. I think you'll hear more from that later. They want me to tour with them Oct-Nov. I'm game. The Stranglers have had a busy time this year and next week we're off to Bosnia for one week to play to the troops there! After that, a one night stand in Moscow then Dublin then the Royal Albert Hall with an 18 piece string orchestra (all female!) on June 13th (Fri). To be recorded and filmed. Hope you can read my scrawl. Keep in touch, sir. Do you know that Sinclair is a very aristocratic French name? Take care.
Jean-Jacques.
9/MAY/97.

Daniel Stearn got a secondhand copy of No Mercy and a pleasant surprise

I've been a Stranglers fan man and boy. I grew up with my father listening to classical music, my mother indulging in Trojan label reggae and disco, and my sister who was into T.Rex, Alice Cooper, etc. The Stranglers were the first music I heard that was *my* music, and I'll never forget the excitement of seeing that red logo on a new release or poster. Indeed, for many years I would not be seen without my leather neck thong or monkey boots!

A stand out moment in 1998 was the announcement of the forthcoming Stranglers biography, *No Mercy*, by David Buckley. This was of course a hugely exciting prospect and I looked forward to acquiring a copy. But... the universe had other ideas and for many reasons I never got my copy. Over the years, I searched bookshops wherever I went in the hope of finding this now out-of-print book.

In 2020 I found a hardback copy of the book on Amazon. It was coming from Dallas, Texas so I expected it would be a few days... Come the end of July, no book had arrived. Amazon were suggesting it had been lost in transit and I should seek a refund. I didn't want a bloody refund – I wanted my book.

It arrived the next day. And inside was a handwritten inscription from JJ 'To Marty', two Triumph postcards from JJ to Marty and handwritten margin notes by JJ! A unique item, and well worth waiting 22 years for!

GUILDFORD

15 AUGUST 2020, GUILDFORD, UK

STEVE WORRALL

Steve Worrall went on a pilgrimage around the Guildford area – photo Steve Worrall

I was devastated by the terrible news about Dave Greenfield. After all, the band have been in my life for over 40 years now. I vividly remember 'No More Heroes' being part of the soundtrack to my youth and when I was old enough to really get into buying records, 'Duchess' and 'Nuclear Device' were among the first on my list. I decided it was time to pay homage to one of my all-time favourite bands and in a little tribute to Dave, I finally got round to doing a DIY tour of Stranglers-related locations in and around the town of Guildford - where the Stranglers were formed back in 1974, which gave them their original name (the Guildford Stranglers) and which is perhaps their spiritual home, despite none of the members actually coming from the town.

It was something I'd been meaning to do for ages, and despite the band's fearsome reputation I was surprised to discover most locations involved were surprisingly posh. Guildford itself boasts an attractive High Street that thankfully still retains a bit of character, rare in most of England's generic town centres these days. Then there's Chiddingfold, Bramley, Shalford and Godalming - even the names conjure up images of cricket on the village green and afternoon tea, hardly the high-rise council flats along The Clash's Westway or riot-hit Notting Hill and Ladbroke Grove. It's certainly a far cry from the working-class streets of Joy Division's Macclesfield or Salford and the polar opposite to the 1970s Lower East Side of New York's legendary CBGBs scene.

But I guess that suits the Stranglers down to the ground. I mean, they were always outsiders - unfairly derided in the music press as being too old, too clever or too musical to be 'real' punks, often airbrushed out of trendy punk retrospectives and exhibitions. However, despite the leafy suburban commuter belt area that saw the band's formation, the Stranglers always had far more menace, danger and genuine punk attitude than the majority of their safety-pinned, dyed-hair contemporaries. And music journalists, fellow musicians, record companies and sometimes even their own audiences felt the wrath of that seething anger and distr ust.

DARK MATTERS

RELEASED 10 SEPTEMBER 2021

CRAIG WOOD

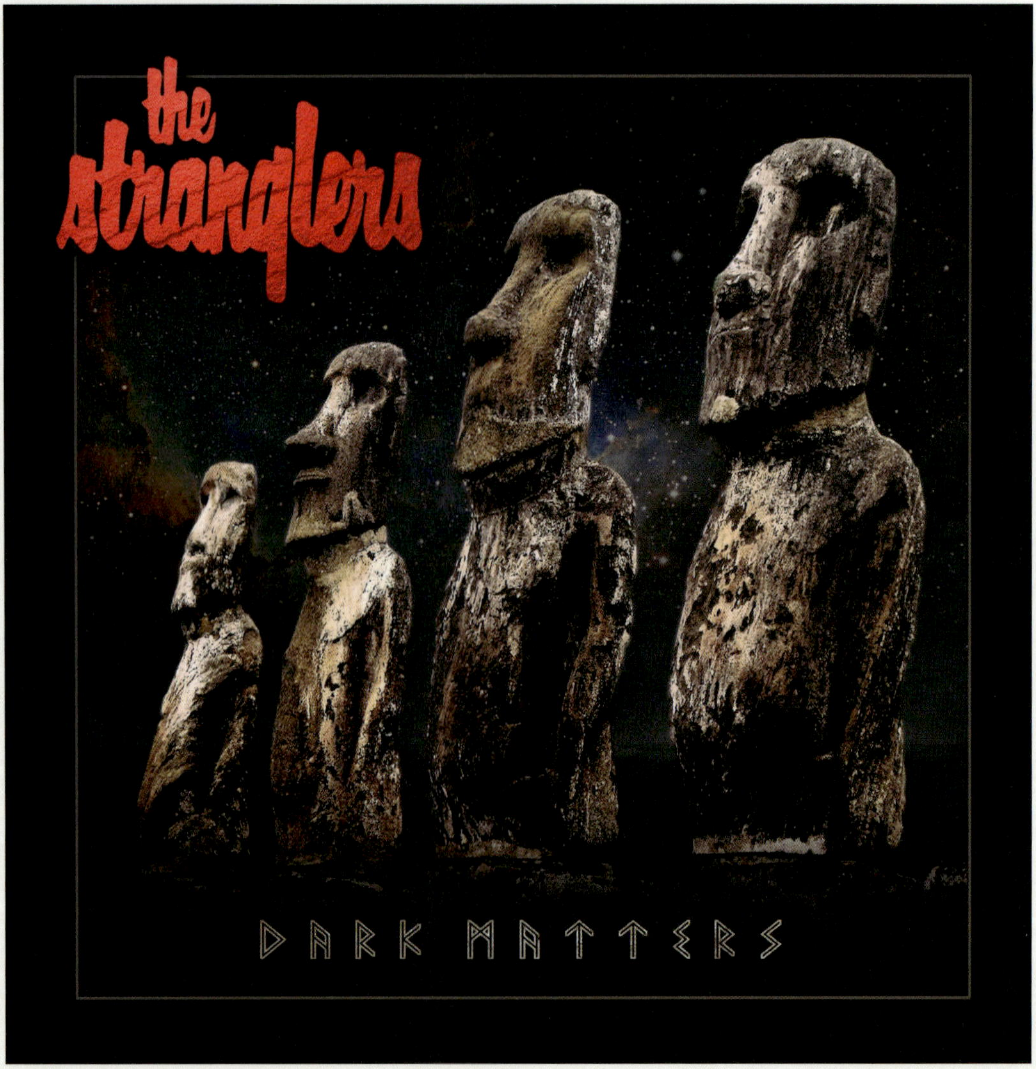

The release of *Dark Matters* became a very poignant moment for me. I did not expect a great deal from it, but as release day approached, I started to count the days. Come the Friday, I was up early and waiting for the postman to deliver the album. I watched him approach from a distance and witnessed with absolute dismay as he walked on by. But 24 hours later it arrived, and it impressed. 'No Man's Land' is my favourite track, with Dave's solid chords and his bubbling, glistening, sparkling piano on the chorus, and JJ's bass, quirky at the start and malevolent through the middle eight. This is closely followed by 'Water', where Dave's magnificent sweeping, swirling intro is augmented by every little touch throughout. 'This Song' has wonderful arpeggios accelerating off a fast pace, while 'Last Men on The Moon' has another big sweeping intro from Dave's piano and 'Breathe' is beautifully melodic throughout.

I was apprehensive about the gig on the following year's tour, initially thinking that they would play as a three piece and have a guest (or guests) stand in for the irreplaceable. When I eventually read about Toby, I was not best pleased, until I read the letter from Pam giving Toby's recruitment to the band her blessing. Dave was my absolute hero – no one could replace him - but I certainly don't bear the guy any form of grudge. But the gig was absolutely magnificent, and Toby did really well. Very much a case of 'Vive the Stranglers!' Bring on *Suite XIX*!

DECEMBER 2021

JUDITH WRIGHT

My brother-in-law John Burke was a huge Stranglers fan all his life. John sadly passed away on 17th December 2021, aged 59, so missed his last two gigs he had tickets for - Manchester (where he was from) and Newcastle (where we are from). Some of the family went to both gigs with a heavy heart. John and my sister were married to 'Always the Sun' and he was carried out of the church at his funeral to the same song. John loved *The Raven* and we have all got a raven tattoo in his memory. Going to see the Stranglers were some of the best nights of our lives.

John Burke (right) and his brother-in-law Stephen Wright

O2 ACADEMY

28 JANUARY 2022, GLASGOW, UK

SUE MACLEOD

I've been a fan of the Stranglers since 1977 when I heard them on John Peel's Radio 1 show. I was 15 at the time. I saw them many times in small venues including the Red Cow in Hammersmith and the Nashville in West Kensington. I think they also played at the Winning Post in Whitton, a great pub to see bands and you didn't need ID in those days! I saw them regularly up until Hugh left, but I fell in love with them again in the last ten years or so and Baz (who I still think of as the new boy) is doing a great job. I last saw them in Glasgow in 2022 and loved their tribute to Dave.

GAVIN REID

As a kid I was always aware of the Stranglers. My dad played them a lot around our small house in Dennistoun, Glasgow as he played music while he cooked and the Stranglers would be his usual choice. The music would seep through the kitchen door, in the living room and I would become a fan via osmosis. Time is recorded by such terms as B.C, A.D., Stone Age, Bronze Age, years, months, seasons, decades, weeks, minutes and seconds. My dad chronicles time by the Stranglers. 'I met your mum around the time they toured *Dreamtime*,' and, 'It was around the time of *The Raven* that I moved house.'

When, at nursery, the teachers said we could bring in a CD for the end of term party and when I got asked, I apparently said 'Stranglers'. My parents decided to ignore my request. I spent a lot of my childhood watching VHS tapes and I watched *The Video Collection 1977–1992* a lot. I was a big fan of Hugh Cornwell climbing out a giant ear, the band pulling their face skin off, the Battersea Park strippers and a girl having her head shaved.

I was 14 when I decided to properly listen to the Stranglers. My bus commute to secondary school was noisy and a dangerous experience. I went to school in a rough and tumble working class area of Glasgow full of Neds. The bus would be crammed to overcapacity every day and nobody sat nicely. If you wanted to get on the bus, it was pointless getting on the one across the street from the school because of the number of people trying to get on the bus after school. You had to walk to four bus stops away. It was a sensory overload where people shouted, spat, pulled and prodded at each other. The hooligans would fight each other and rip up the seats, all this happening without shame, out in the open next to wee old ladies with their shopping bags. It was a stress to get a bus that sometimes didn't get to its destination as the police were called because all the windows were kicked out or the bus was set on fire. I got so fed up with the ordeal every day that I began walking to school.

I enjoyed the downtime, loaded everything onto iTunes and began to listen to the Stranglers albums in chronological order, including the live albums. It was a delight to walk to school in all weathers and begin to be fanatical, filling in the blanks and hearing what Hugh Cornwell barked at the crowd during live recordings. There are streets that lead to my school where I remember listening to particular songs, miming the drums and charging along the street. Listening to 'Time to Die' for the first time, I remember going up a steep hill and with every step I punctuated every word. Someday. I'm. Gonna. Smack. Your. Face.

I took to researching their history by watching clips of them on *YouTube* and reading articles. I have dyslexia and I've never read a book before but I was determined to read Hugh's book, *Song by Song*, the biography *No Mercy* and Hugh's autobiography, *Multitude of Sins*, which came out just about the time my walking to school started. I read them all with success as I was desperate to know all the details. My dyslexia made me fidget, and when I read laying on my bed, I would read the left page, laying on my left side and then the right page lying on my right side. I was accustomed to the Paul Roberts era, while my dad wasn't that complimentary about that time as he had lost interest in them then.

One afternoon I asked my dad, 'What happened to your original records?' He said, 'Broken or probably binned, because they warp in the heat. The paper sleeves get bashed up over time and we played them so much they became unlistenable. Some of the later ones, *Aural Sculpture* and *Dreamtime*, might actually be in my mum's loft.' He was going to visit my gran that day and I went along too.

I asked my gran if I could go up in the loft. She insisted that my dad sort it out first because they hadn't been up there for ten years or more. The ladders weren't attached, the light bulbs only flickered and my dad got covered in dust. The trip up into the loft was abandoned for another time. My dad said, 'That's a quarter of an hour of my life faffing about with a ladder I won't get back. You could probably get those LPs off eBay for 50p.'

Every non-school uniform day, in amongst tracksuits and ripped jeans, I would wear a Stranglers t-shirt. When I learnt what embroidery was, I would take a plain shirt or polo shirt to clothes menders store to embroider a little red rat on it.

One of my first successes with a woman was because of the Stranglers. I went on a date with a hobbyist burlesque dancer who dressed like she was from the Fifties. I was out of my depth with her on the date, I felt shy, and I stumbled over my words because she was so sexually imposing. I was losing her, but I said my favourite band was the Stranglers. She sprang to life; it was her favourite band too. The Stranglers sparked a conversation that seemed to last forever about music, horror films, holidays, sex, alcohol, conspiracy theories - and the Stranglers.

I went on a couple of dates with a Swedish girl called Fanny. I had to tell her about 'Sverige' and got her opinion on Hugh's Swedish, she said it needed work. I was also in love with a girl at art school who resembled Dave Greenfield. She had a cute black bob haircut like Dave and wore a green painting jumpsuit. I put her off when I tried to encourage her to stick on a false moustache. I could've gotten a second kiss if I had stayed quiet about Dave.

I remember my dad coming to life when he was listening to 'Spectre of Love' and being impressed by the album, *Suite XVI*. I remember him shaving in the bathroom mirror singing 'I hate you' and cheekily pointing at me during different parts of the song. There were many times when heading to a wedding or a day out with the family and Dad would be playing a Stranglers DVD. He would be open-shirted and mid-deodorant spray, playing along to an invisible bass while my mum flapped around him, 'We are going to be late!'

After years of harassing my dad to buy posters and take pictures at gigs, fuming that I couldn't go with him to see the Stranglers in action and see 'he who shall not be named', I finally got a ticket as a birthday present to see the Stranglers in November 2008.

It was such a memorable night. There were so many people there, a big choice of t-shirts to buy and the support act was Starbase 109. I remember screaming with delight when 'Waltizinblack' played, and the four figures appeared and started to play. After the first few seconds, my dad would say into my ear what the song was: 'This one is 'Tank'.' I sang confidently along to the songs I knew and mumbled along to the ones I didn't. A man climbed up the wall next to the stage while they played 'No Mercy'. A woman also flashed her boobs at the band. It was a belter of a first gig.

Other special moments were when I went to two gigs on the same tour for the first time. I saw them in Glasgow on the Thursday and, after school on the Friday, my dad handed me an envelope with tickets for the Stranglers gig in Edinburgh that night. 'You'd better get changed out your uniform.' My uncle who came with us gave us a lift to Edinburgh.

Now my dad and I know how to get to Edinburgh and navigate around with no problems these days. Many years later on a family trip to Edinburgh, my dad kept looking around, inspecting the streets wide-eyed, saying, 'I wonder where we saw the Stranglers?' We then went to Wetherspoons. As we walked in my dad was telling me that we'd seen them at the HMV Picture House. He looked up at the big room we entered and said, 'Oh! It's here, this was the place.'

I took a religious pilgrimage to the Hope and Anchor pub in London. It was a sleepy Monday afternoon. The bar staff were chatting to each other and I said, 'Is the downstairs open?' They said, 'No, it's closed.' They went back to talking to each other. I interrupted the conversation again and asked, 'Well, could I possibly go down and see it because I'm a Stranglers fan and – '. I was cut short. I was told, 'It's only opened for gigs.' I didn't get a chance to say, 'I've come from Glasgow to see downstairs.'

Jet Black appearing on BBC Breakfast was memorable. He was eccentrically wrapped up in a black hat, scarf and sunglasses. I remember him pontificating that the Stranglers weren't punks. This weird appearance got the Stranglers trending on Twitter. There were tweets asking, 'Why's Jet Black so wrapped up? Did BBC Breakfast forget to put the heating on?'

There was a comedy sketch show in Scotland called *Burnistoun*. They had a sketch about old men watching their favourite bands on *YouTube* because the band wasn't active anymore. The band in the sketch were obviously based on the Stranglers. The bass player was pouting with a leather jacket on. The lead singer had wavy hair, a choker and a long coat. The keyboard player had a big black moustache, and the fake band was called The Murderers. One of the comedians in the sketch was Robert Florence. I cornered him at the Glasgow Film Festival. I could tell by the look in his eye, he was thinking, 'This wee guy is going to ask for a photograph,' but I asked him, 'The sketch that is based on the Stranglers; why didn't you get a big fat guy for the drummer?', and he said, 'Just didn't have the staff.'

The Kelvingrove Bandstand was the last time I saw the Stranglers with Dave. It was my dad who told me Dave had died, while I was lying in bed dejected by life. I was so gutted. Life had been so crap during the pandemic. It was an absolute kicker that the pandemic that had taken away my plans had now taken away my favourite band.

I've seen the Stranglers 17 times since 2008. I have loved all the gigs as I'm always eager to get to the venue. Along the way maybe they should've dusted off songs that don't get a chance to be played live, but the 2022 Glasgow gig made me cry. There was so much emotion: were they going to disband?; gigs got rescheduled; will they ever get to play the *Dark Matters* tour?

I got teary-eyed at 'Relentless' as it spoke about nostalgia. I lost touch with friends and would-be lovers in the pandemic, and I aged too. Dare I say grew up. The line, 'She's lookin' old, but so am I' was the tear-jerker. 'Never to Look Back' did its work on me again as all my pandemic anger, confusion and frustration came out. Toby Houndsham fitted in straight away, and I'm so glad they're still doing it with no sign of stopping. The Stranglers will go on forever!

ROBERT MARSHALL

From when I was a ten-year-old primary school kid growing up in Glasgow until November 1990, when I was married and old enough to know better, I kept a note of my favourite song/single/album-track at the time – my own personal number one, you might say. It began with 'The Pushbike Song' by The Mixtures and ended with Julee Cruise's 'Falling' – the theme song from TV series *Twin Peaks*.

Robert Marshall has seen the Stranglers a few times and owes his musical tastes to his brother

Straight in at number one in September 1977 was 'No More Heroes', which in my charts was sandwiched between 'Yes Sir, I Can Boogie' by Baccara and 'Belfast' by Boney M. Further Stranglers 'chart-toppers' followed in the shape of '5 Minutes', 'Tits', 'Nubiles (cocktail version)', 'Nuclear Device', 'Bear Cage' and finally, 'Let Me Down Easy' in February 1985.

Only The Beatles, Rolling Stones, Donna Summer and Slade had an aggregate numero uno score greater than my Stranglers' 'Super-Seven' in my charts. If I'd continued with this admittedly questionable practice post-1990, the Meninblack would be way out in front by now. When you are a supporter of both Partick Thistle FC and Scotland's national football team, you need some decent music to help you deal with life's disappointments. The music of the Stranglers also served as an antidote against the likes of Thatcherism, mullet hairstyles and ubiquitous American soaps.

Incidentally, some of the aforementioned hits 'did it for me' sometime after their original release date and are as a direct result of the influence of my younger brother Allan, the real Stranglers fan in our family, who did his damnedest to save me from the twin evils of disco music and commercial shallowness. Unlike me, Allan is able to watch footage of the 1978 Battersea Park version of 'Nice 'n' Sleazy' ignoring the strippers and concentrating fully on the musical talents of Black, Burnel, Cornwell and Greenfield.

ROUNDHOUSE
SJM Concerts present
The Stranglers
Plus Special Guests The Popes
Friday Evening
09 March 2012 Doors 7:00 PM
Level 1, Main Space, STANDING | 32 60
Unreserved
The Roundhouse is a Grade II listed building. Original features include 24 pillars in the Main Space which, depending on the configuration of the stage, mean there may be an impaired view from some seats.
£26.00 Standard 1332572
2013275 7

In terms of my attendance at actual live gigs, the Stranglers are the runaway winners. Gigs at the sadly now demolished Glasgow Apollo Theatre in November 1981 and London's Roundhouse in March 2012 are possibly my favourites.

Post-Lockdown and it was an emotional return to the Glasgow O2 Academy in January 2022, some twelve years after my then-teenage son Robbie had accompanied me there for his first Stranglers gig, to see Baz and the boys kickstart this renaissance. Meanwhile, my brother, as usual, helped me out with the lyrics, in addition to the titles of the lesser known (to me, anyway) album tracks. Thanks guys.

TIM KING

Tim King and Sheron Hambly had their first date at a Stranglers gig

The Stranglers brought us together. My wife and I had our first date at a Stranglers gig in Rock City, Nottingham in March 2004. In our 40th year, we were both long-term Stranglers fans, and were both determined to get the most from our new life together. The odd pandemic aside, we've been back to re-live our first date at Stranglers gigs every year since. The 2022 gig in Glasgow was an emotional affair, particularly JJ's tribute to Dave, but it also marked the end of an era for us. Thanks, lads, for the entertainment and joy. Stranglers for ever.

G LIVE

3 FEBRUARY 2022, GUILDFORD, UK

ANDREW ROWE

Andrew Rowe and his wife Natasha at G Live

I was 11 years old and tasked with sorting out the camping gear and ropes for the scouts' next big adventure. As I approached the scout hut, I could hear this loud din of music. It sounded like a crashing of drums as I peered through a crack in the door. Little did I know this was the future of the Stranglers. I was heading to the big school of Bishop Reindorp. I was no longer a small kid and eager to impress. The school teacher asked me in front of the class what music I listened to. I blurted out, 'The Stranglers!', not even knowing one of their records at the time.

From then on, I was considered a rebel and a punk and I spiked my hair and even had it dyed blue at one point. (I have no hair now.) My first album was *Rattus Norvegicus*, which I played non-stop each evening after school.

I've count of how many concerts I've been to over the years but my very first was at Guildford Civic Hall in 1980. I was asked to remove my boot laces for ''elf and safety' and ended losing one of my DMs, which my mum beat me for as they were the only shoes I had for school.

The last concert I went to was back at the Civic Hall, now renamed G Live, in 2022. This was my first chance to take my new wife to see the Stranglers so she could see what it was all about. Now she understands why I chose 'Golden Brown' for our wedding. God bless you, DG and the Stranglers, for writing a song that has so much meaning for us.

IVAN HANCOCK

Billed as the 'final full UK tour', this Covid-delayed gig is something I had looked forward to for... well, years. As soon as it was announced I wanted to return to the

Ivan Hancock took several photos

town where I first saw a gig – Penetration at Guildford Civic Hall in 1979 – and see the Stranglers in the town where they started out. If there's one band I associate with throughout my gig-going life more than any other, it's the Stranglers. Six decadesinblack from the Seventies to the Twenties… for them and for me.

For me it all started with 'No More Heroes' on the weekly Radio 1 chart show in 1977. I remember discussing my potential purchase of the single with school (and lifelong) friend, Big Gra. I was concerned it was a bit of a short track and I was skint. Big Gra pointed out that they cut them short on the charts, and as a respected spikey-topped, Doc Marten-wearing punk of the class, I took his nod of approval and bought the single, with picture cover, from Squeeze Inn record shop in Ashford Common. Weeks later, I returned to buy the *No More Heroes* album and that was it. A lifetimeinblack had started.

My first giginblack wasn't until July 1980 at London Rainbow. Old tickets, handwritten lists and scrapbook bits have helped me piece together my decadesinblack. Guildford in 2022 was at least my 28th Stranglers gig. The 28inblack include appearances supporting Simple Minds and Alice Cooper and a Hyde Park Green Day out. There are festival performances at Guildford, Reading and Ross-on-Wye. A trip to Wolverhampton in the Paul Roberts era in the early Nineties stands out. Me and my mate Chrisinblack were stood outside trying to sell a spare ticket and, to kill time, started spotting lookalikes. 'This bloke looks a bit like Stuart Pearce,' I muttered, thinking the bloke who had rocked up bore more than a passing resemblance to the England full back and massive Stranglers fan. 'Hang on, it *is* Stuart Pearce!' I got him to sign the spare ticket and kept it. It was top gig, fuelled by beer. I remember 'Walk on By' and Dave Greenfield doing his 'downing a pint while playing a solo' thing.

2022. By the time I made it back in from the everlasting wait at the bar, the 'Waltzinblack' walk-on music was over and the place was heaving with tall mature blokesinblack. 'Toiler on the Sea', 'Something Better Change' and 'Sometimes' started things off brilliantly - songs to spit words out to. New boy Toby was introduced on keyboards to a supportive cheer.

We got 'Skin Deep' and 'Nice 'n' Sleazy' and a couple of selections from the new *Dark Matters* album, which is a strong memorial to Dave Greenfield. 'Water' and a cover of the Disciples of Spess song, 'This Song Will Get Me Over You', follow. There were five songs from the new album in all, including later on, 'The Lines', an acknowledgement of aging and experience, and the inevitably emotional 'And If You Should See Dave'.

It was a big and appreciative crowd without being wild. We are all getting oldinblack, I guess. In 'Nuclear Device', the shouts of, 'Bruce... She-ila' were a little muted – perhaps there's a lot of 'Golden Brownies' in. It did get a huge cheer. A track that made it into the set from one of the Baz Warne-sung albums, *Suite XVI*, was the modern classic, 'Relentless'.

'Walk on By' was as magnificent as ever, the fourinblack meandering down their focussed paths that each of their instruments took. The set built to my favourite section – 'Straighten Out', 'Duchess' and then 'Hanging Around'.

A few bottles of Corona lager were cracked open as a nod to the pandemic, and JJ mentioned how they couldn't get a gig in Guildford back in the early pub gig days.

There then followed a pub rock in the form of 'Go Buddy Go'. To end, JJ ascended the sparkly-lit steps to the drum and keyboard platform. He then descended, bass slung at the ready, for a mock 'My Way' finale and they launched into the song that started it all for me in 1977, 'No More Heroes'. Still a beauty.

STEVE WORRALL

It was such a thrill to be able to witness the Stranglers' emotional Guildford homecoming, and for once I wasn't down the front but up on the balcony, so I could fully appreciate the great lighting and sound at G Live. When the farewell tour was announced, I guess like many fans I was intrigued... Maybe I was even in two minds about the decision to go ahead after the sad passing of Dave Greenfield. I didn't know how they were going to do it - would it be an acoustic tour, or would they incorporate backing tapes of Dave's recorded organ parts? Who knew what was in store?

The announcement that the band had recruited someone to play keyboards was interesting. After all, Dave was a musical genius and a much-loved original member. In the end, they certainly made the right decision, as the number of dates marked as sold out undoubtedly proved. And new keyboard player Toby Hounsham excelled in what must have been a very daunting task; I mean, it's not as if he can take a back seat given that Dave's iconic trademark keyboard sound was so integral to the very core of the Stranglers.

However, Toby did a fantastic job, the highlight of which was probably the extended instrumental on 'Walk on By', which was faultless. I didn't hear one negative comment about his performance from fans either at the show or online, and what with such a positive reaction and the band proving to be on such good form, I think they would be silly to call it a day completely.

From the opening bars of 'Toiler on the Sea', it was apparent that the Stranglers sound had certainly not been compromised and neither had their energy or seething aggression. 'Something Better Change' and 'Sometimes' were as vicious as when I first heard them. The band were on top form and the chemistry and friendship between JJ and Baz shone through, their on-stage banter always a joy. Toby was introduced and it was all handled perfectly, with the right balance of respect and determination to pay tribute to Dave in the best possible way - to fully enjoy the music.

They treated us to all the hits and favourites, such as 'Peaches' and 'Nice 'n' Sleazy', but it's always interesting to discover what curveballs the Stranglers will throw at us and that night we got one of my favourites, 'Curfew', which was amazing, and 'Baroque Bordello', slightly less so. The band's commercial peak was nicely covered by 'Skin Deep', 'Always the Sun', 'Golden Brown' and 'Strange Little Girl', although there was a bit of a lull, as 'Don't Bring Harry' doesn't quite do it for me.

‘Water’ and ‘The Last Men on The Moon’ from new album *Dark Matters* were both cinematic and atmospheric slow-burning numbers with strains of Ennio Morricone’s Spaghetti Western soundtracks. The over-the-top disco beat of ‘White Stallion’, with its pulsing sequencers and operatic recorded backing vocals, reminds me of Sparks and was a bit out of place, but ‘This Song’ is a real modern-day Stranglers classic that captures all the aggression and energy we love. And strangely enough, I was sat next to football legend Stuart Pearce, star of the ‘This Song’ video and a huge Stranglers fan.

‘Nuclear Device’ was ear-splittingly powerful and the three-song salvo of ‘Straighten Out’, ‘Duchess’ and ‘Hanging Around’ that closed the main set cranked up the excitement to fever pitch. But then it was all over. JJ and Baz came back on for an acoustic interlude of ‘The Lines’ and an emotional ‘And If You Should See Dave’, during which the stage lights were dimmed, leaving the keyboards bathed in blue light as Baz sang, ‘This is where your solo should be...’ It was a moving moment, no doubt about it. Then Jim and Toby returned for the final encore, ‘Go Buddy Go’ and ‘No More Heroes’, JJ climbing onto the drum and keyboard riser to deliver that iconic bass intro. What a show, what a performance.

The Stranglers never cease to amaze me with their resilience in the face of so many trials and tribulations, and long may that continue. The good news is that it probably will. Although this was billed as the farewell tour, I don’t think it marked the end of the Stranglers.

O2 APOLLO

11 FEBRUARY 2022, MANCHESTER, UK

STERLING-ROSE KELLY

Sterling-Rose Kelly saw the Stranglers in 2022

I fell in love (and that’s the exact word for it, it was a dizzying, instant kind of love) with the Stranglers when I was 17 years old. They were the kind of band teenage girls didn’t listen to in 2017: angry, grotesque, ethereal, beautiful. I played the first four albums on repeat, my headphones turned to maximum volume, drowning out the world with *The Raven*, *Rattus Norvegicus*, *Black and White*, *No More Heroes*.

I’d listen on the bus, staring out at the grey nothingness of town, watching the rain on the windows. I’d hide my headphones in my hair and listen in boring lessons, escaping into daydreams of tiny pub gigs and hissing amps and bands driving round in ice-cream vans, a world I’d never seen but ached to be part of. They'd play through my dreams, too: every word, every crunch of the bass, every swirl of the keyboard keeping the shadows out.

JJ Burnel's basslines were magnetic. I'd come home from college, pick up my bashed-up second-hand bass with the dodgy frets, try to work out every note of 'Nice 'n' Sleazy' or 'Peaches' or 'Down in the Sewer' by ear. I'd copy the sound as carefully as I could from the tinny phone speaker, thrashing through each song without a pick, snapping the strings violently, not caring if my fingers bled or blistered. That's how I learned to play bass. My technique was messy, my translations rough and sharp-edged. But with each note, my love for both bass and for the Stranglers became something powerful, something obsessive. It held me together even on the days it felt like all the stars in the sky were burning out.

That was five years ago. I'm 21 twenty-one now, still picking at a bass, still daydreaming, still in love with the Stranglers. I've seen them play live three times: Rock City in March 2018 and Manchester Apollo in 2019 and 2022. That last gig tasted so bittersweet. It was a freezing cold Friday and me and my boyfriend had queued in the rain (me freezing in my leather jacket and a homemade Stranglers cropped-vest top) to get a good spot.

The hypothermia risk was worth it: I was crushed up right at the front, hanging onto the barrier. Nothing, nothing on earth could sweep me away from that spot right by the bass amps. Someone sloshed their overpriced pint down my back, someone else tried to squash down my spiky hairdo. I didn't shift. I was home.

I watched JJ Burnel like a hawk, every note, every movement, every snarl, every smile, memorising it all. My boyfriend laughed at me after, 'You didn't take your eyes off him once, Sterl!' And I didn't. Just stared and stared, and smiled and danced and stuck my tongue out like a thing possessed. Singing, shouting, sweat drenching my arms, beer drenching my hair. I revelled in the cheeky disgustingness of 'Peaches', felt my blood heat up at the gritty fury of 'Nice 'n' Sleazy' and 'Straighten Out'. I had tears ruin my makeup at 'Always the Sun' and 'Strange Little Girl'. Part joy, part sadness. Those two strobe-lit hours went by in seconds and a lifetime.

There was a crowd at the front of the stage when the lights snapped on; carrion crows scrapping over the drumsticks. I hovered by the barrier too, wondering if I had a chance in hell, arms outstretched, waiting, barely breathing. I reached out and JJ Burnel threw his bass pick right to me. Someone twice my size shoved me in the back. I ended up half-skewered across the barrier, where my steel-toe boots collided with a few scrabbling hands – but the pick vanished.

A shout from the stage, a Guildford voice, 'Did you get it?' I shrugged my shoulders, still hanging over the barrier. 'Nah, man... it's gone, like, fuck knows where.' JJ reached in his pocket and fished out another pick and I knew this was it, this one was meant for me, and it flew straight and perfect into my hands. I shoved it in the pocket of my leather jacket quick as anything, held it safe, feeling the edges bite into my palm. Second time lucky.

It lives a good life now, that pick. I can't hide it away in a dusty frame. It comes with me to my gigs, thrashes at the steel strings of my own bass in murky basements and pubs of Manchester. A little piece of luck.

There's so many more things I could write about. Digging in boxes of records and CDs in Rob's Records and Rough Trade Nottingham with my dad and my brother on Saturday afternoons, looking for the physical copies of the songs I knew off my heart already. Smiling at one of the tour crew (who must have taken pity on me) because he threw me a paper setlist at the first Stranglers gig I went to, duct tape and all.

Me and my best friend shouting and singing ridiculously to 'Peaches' (especially the bit about liberation for women, we thought it was the funniest thing ever) whenever we heard it played in the basement punk clubs in Manchester. So many beautiful memories.

So thank you, Stranglers. Thank you for the beautiful, snarling, ugly chaos. For the fury, the joy, the filth, the love. Thank you for the basslines, the rhythms, every note, every word. Thank you for being the sun after a storm. And thanks for the bass pick.

All the love, Sterling-Rose.

GUILDHALL

14 FEBRUARY 2022, PORTSMOUTH, UK

ANDY PERCY

At nine years old I heard 'Peaches' and was blown away. I went to secondary school in 1979 and I bleached the arm of my school blazer and all the black jumpers my mum had brought for my school term which... fell apart! I still want a white-sleeved black jumper. I finally got to see the Stranglers live at the Hammersmith Odeon. I don't remember the date but it was the night all the security was sent out before the band carried on playing. Oh, and Hugh spanked some lad on stage - that hit the news. Next day at school, my form tutor said the Stranglers were old news so I did the old bucket filled with water over the door gag and it worked a dream!

I was gutted at the passing of Dave and went to the gig in Portsmouth to say a goodbye. Thing is, I left saying hello to a great line up and can't wait to see you live again. I love you all. You're the best fucking band ever!

JON BEGS

An old school mate, Gary Greenwood, was playing an album his older brother Kenny had just bought. This was the summer of 1977. I heard the sax in the background as 'Grip' rang out from the record player in his bedroom. I was entranced by the musical melody of Dave's keyboards lilting away. Gary and I chuckled like the 12-year-old kids we were when we played 'Peaches' and heard the S word – heady days indeed. And so began my lifelong love of all things Stranglers. I saw them first in 1978 as a spotty 14-year-old, at Southampton Gaumont, and then again in 1980 at the same venue.

I met them at Poole Arts Centre in 1982 and got *Rattus* signed by JJ, Jet and Hugh – Dave was not with the band when they arrived for the soundcheck. However, we sneaked in and watched from the back of the hall as they tested the kit for the sound. The gig was awesome – packed, hot, sweaty and absolutely jumping. I have seen the band many times since, mainly in the south of England.

Throughout my life I have immersed myself in their music. They kept me going during my teenage years when things were rock bottom at home. My room was a shrine to the band with *NME* clippings, posters and cuttings from floor to ceiling. Mum had a really bad drink problem and would take this out on Dad most nights. Without being able to put my headphones on and switch off, I don't know what I would have done. I lost count of the number of times I went through *Rattus*, *Heroes*, *Black and White*, *Live (X-Cert)* and *The Raven* just to drown out what was going on downstairs. This helped me cope and survive. For that, I can't than the band enough - they were the soundtrack of my youth in so many ways and they helped me keep my sanity, and helped me discover music at its very best along the way.

Aged 15, I got a *Rattus* tattoo on my right arm. I got rotten drunk on cheap cider with my best mate at school at the time, Piggy Miles, and we staggered our way to Ray's Tattoo Parlour in Palmerston Road, Boscombe in Bournemouth one sunny afternoon. Clutching my large *Rattus* badge, Ray agreed to don us both with the rat and the rising sun. My allegiance to the band was firmly cemented for everyone to see from this point in time. The tattoo has been noticed all over the world and provoked some brilliant conversation. There seems to be Stranglers fans all over the place.

Due to work I dropped off grid until the early 2000s, when they came to Salisbury. I met Jet doing a gig promo in the Old George Mall and had a great chat with him. The gig that night was fantastic. JJ was my idol as a teenager and I was up by the stage and to the left, mesmerised as I watched him play bass. I saw them again in Salisbury in 2013 and then for the *Black and White* tour. The final song that night was 'No More Heroes' and JJ walloped his bass at the beginning. The resonance of that bass sound caused the ceiling of the Salisbury City Hall to vibrate so much, I swear that the dust and muck stuck to that ceiling for the last 20-odd years started to fall down. I've never heard a bass note like it!

Like all fans I was absolutely devastated by Dave's passing. I wanted to pay my respects to him and the band on their final tour. Obviously Covid delayed things for two years but as the date for the rearranged Portsmouth gig got closer, I was transported back to those heady days of being a teenager and seeing the band for the first time again.

From the start the band were absolutely at it, drum tight and rocking like the best band in the world that they absolutely are. And this is where I come full circle to the best Stranglers song. When those first four synthesised notes at the start of 'Grip' sounded out in the Guildhall, I was gone, bouncing up and down like a bloody pogo stick, absolutely lost in this anthemic song which I first heard 44 years ago. The band absolutely nailed it and I have to say if that was the last time that I ever see them play live, then when I go, I will leave this mortal coil one very happy Stranglers fan.

Thanks for everything, guys.

TRACEY HAMMOND

I've always been a stranglers fan ever since I was 14 and heard the first few intro notes of JJ's bass on 'Peaches'. I had posters of him on my bedroom wall as a teen, replacing David and Donny as I transitioned from 'boy next door' to 'bad boy'. I've seen the band live many times over the years but have never had the bottle to go close to the stage until the last few tours. As soon as the tickets came out for their 'last UK Tour' I bagged myself tickets for Portsmouth and Reading.

I realised that JJ was about to have a 'special' birthday around that time. The Pompey gig was on Valentine's Day and Reading the 22nd, the day after his birthday, so I thought I'd get him a card and try and give it to him on the 14th. I went on the Moonpig site and designed a card for him, the headline being 'Barracuda Bassist Turns 70'! I was quite proud of my efforts.

Tracey Hammond's birthday card for JJ was bigger than she expected

Two days before the gig, the card arrived. I. Was. Mortified. I must have ticked the wrong box, because it was a *lot* bigger than I thought it was going to be. It was mahoosive, like a bloody table top! I had a dilemma. Do I give him this one, or scrap it and buy a normal 70th birthday card, with an old man with a pipe and slippers on it? I decided to stick with Plan A. Be brave, woman!

My gig buddy Gary couldn't stop laughing when he saw the size of it, but he walked with me round to the stage door at the Guildhall as I tried to deliver it. Sadly the 'Covid police' (Guildhall staff) wouldn't accept it on the door (as if I had enough spit contaminated or otherwise to lick an envelope that bloody big...) so I had to leave it at the box office. Hopefully it gave JJ a smile anyway, if he got it.

We got into the venue early and were in the front row, centre, and what a great experience. I met some lovely folk and had a good laugh. The worst part of the night was forgetting to press 'record' during the instrumental on 'Nice 'n' Sleazy - epic fail!

At Reading the following week (the day after JJ's birthday) I managed to get in the front row centre again, along with several of the folk I'd met the week before. This time I remembered to press record. JJ and Baz came so close to the edge of the stage, I had to zoom out! I was also lucky enough to get JJ's set list (which was dated 21st February, Bristol, the night of his birthday) so I was over the moon.

At the end of the gig, my mate Heather started talking to an older guy and I (being Welsh) picked up on his Welsh accent. It turned out he was originally from North Wales, just up the road from where I was born and raised. We chatted for a while and I left them to it as I wanted to get some merch. When Heather caught up with me, she said, 'I thought you'd have tapped him up to try and get backstage for an intro to JJ'? And then it dawned on me. We'd been chatting to the lead singer from the Ruts DC and I hadn't recognised him, even though I'd stared up at him for 40 minutes earlier on that evening... Another epic fail. It's hilarious to think I've spent 30 years as a cop and couldn't pick him out in a line up, and it looks like I missed my last chance to meet my hero!

DOME

17 FEBRUARY 2022, BRIGHTON, UK

PAMELA EARL

My old boyfriend introduced me to the Stranglers in the autumn of 1982; it was just before my 18th birthday. My first record was *The Collection*. I was in the States and wanted to get to know their work. My first proper record was *Feline*. In my freshman year at uni, I bought *The Meninblack*, *Black and White* and *La Folie* all in the same day on import. My roommate loved them too.

My first Stranglers gig was at the Metro in Boston in 1987. I nearly missed the concert because I was studying Interior and Environmental Design and had to give a presentation. I had to take a taxi to the Metro with my portfolio. I had a glass of bad white wine. So much so, I didn't touch it again until '96.

The venue was intimate. I'm from Houston and used to the Astrodome which holds 60,000 people. The audience was much older than me, which made me feel like an intruder. Then the Meninblack appeared, in black and looking very grumpy. I was so close to the stage I could've touched JJ's Doc Marten's. They were raw, tight, full-bodied and commanding. It's the best concert I've ever attended, and 35 years later, I still think about it.

My favourite song is 'Tramp'. It's an exhilarating, atmospheric, passionate work. Jet's in the driver's seat. Hugh's voice is gorgeous, evocative. JJ's bass is throaty and assured. Dave's keyboards are urgent and heady. 'Tramp' is European with lashings of jazz. One day I will be in a convertible and play this song very, very loudly. Or on a very, very fast bike.

My first Stranglers' songs were 'Grip' and 'London Lady': 'Tell-me-whatcha-got-to-look-so-pleased-about!'

They were my muses at art school. I used their lyrics to 'Midnight Summer Dream' in my Calligraphy final; portraits in pastels, etc. When I immigrated to London, I was very much alone; the relationship with said boyfriend was over. Seeing them on stage was a bit like seeing mates. I was 25 years old. When I had to turn 30, I went to Paris. I listened to their music on my Walkman. Again, they were reassuring and comforting; just damn brilliant.

Dave's death inspired me to create found assemblage box art. They're based on Joseph Cornell's 'romantic museums'. The exhibition had over twenty works. Three are of the MiB. I dedicated the exhibition to Dave Greenfield. I hope Dave knew just how significant and inspiring his work was, is; what he meant to all of us. It's still quite upsetting. I still cry. He was bloody brilliant.

When I saw them at Brixton Academy in early 1990, they seemed a bit lack lustre. Now we know why. I momentarily had a panic attack when I remembered seeing how their fans behaved in the Seventies. Nevertheless, the show was fab. I carried the Brixton ticket in my wallet as a talisman. Alas, the wallet was stolen. It's a miracle I still have the Boston ticket stub.

I recently saw the MiB at the Brighton Dome. They were so good, so strong. The lighting was super. The glitter ball for 'Golden Brown' was unexpected and magical, such a deliciously dark song, but not as dark as 'La Folie'. It's the only time I've wept at a concert, when JJ and Baz played 'And If You Should See Dave'. I can't imagine many dry eyes at that moment.

As with the first concert, I took a taxi, this time home to Lewes. There I toasted the Stranglers including Hugh, with sparkling wine and crisps. This time the white wine was delicious. Hand-over-heart, if JJ, Baz and Jim Macaulay want to continue with Toby Hounsham, that's fine by me.

O2 ACADEMY

19 FEBRUARY 2022, BIRMINGHAM, UK

ANNA WOODCOCK

Anna Woodcock got a very special birthday present – Baz's sweaty towel

I have been a fan since I was seven; the first song I heard was 'Ugly' because my dad kept on telling me about the swear words in the song. I remember saying that the Stranglers were too loud so he would play 'Waltzinblack' the whole time on repeat. I saw the Stranglers for the first time at Grillstock in Bristol 2016, then in Devizes in 2018, on the *Dark Matters* tour in Birmingham, Bristol and Cardiff, and then in Birmingham in 2022, my favourite.

My dad booked the tickets in 2020. Covid pushed it back two years and the rearranged date for the gig landed on my birthday. When I found out, I was extremely happy but also worried, because if I get too happy, I overwhelm myself and make bad choices.

When the day came, I was so excited that I was having panic attacks on the way there, but the thing that kept me calm was knowing I was going to meet my dad's Stranglers friends which is what I've always wanted to do! When I got to the venue, I was on the balcony at the front on the side, right next to Baz (and the speaker).

When I heard 'Waltzinblack' come on, I felt myself having another panic attack but as soon as I saw the band come on stage – boom! - my whole body changed and I was so calm and happy. When they had finished, they all got together and bowed and they were about to walk off stage. Baz got his towel and started wiping all the sweat off his head and turned around and started walking towards me. He threw his towel up at me and I got it and nearly every one of my dad's Stranglers friends were looking at me and they were happy for me.

Lots of people said it was gross, lots of people told me to wash it and lots of people asked me if it stank... but all I was thinking was, 'This was the best 16th birthday I've had in my life, and Baz has just made it even better!' I got noticed by JJ, Jim and Baz throughout the whole show. It made me feel worth it and happy, and I haven't felt like that in years... so thank you, Baz and everyone. I have new friends, a new big crush (Baz), happiness and something to hold onto when I feel like shit.

The Stranglers live in Birmingham, Cardiff, Sheffield, Cambridge, Warrington, Leeds and Guildford in 2011

THE HEXAGON

22 FEBRUARY 2022, READING, UK

HOWARD WINCHCOMBE

With great excitement the day came after a long wait to see the Stranglers once again. I have followed them since 1976 to present day. They did not disappoint! Gritty, professional and a great sound. My nephew and son and a good friend enjoyed every second of it. It's strange, I feel like an 18-year-old when I'm there, and then realise I am an old guy! Thank you, all of the Stranglers. Thank you for my teenage, middle age and old age memories.

JOHN CAITHNESS

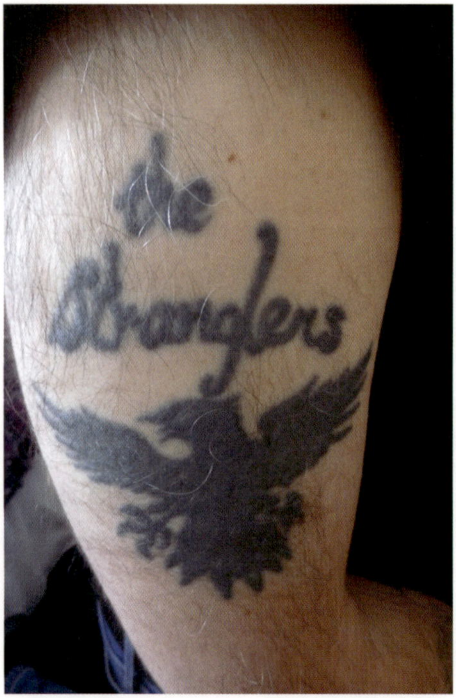

John Caithness had his copy of Rattus confiscated

I first discovered the Stranglers back in '77 when an older friend did a punk tape for me and it included 'Peaches', 'Something Better Change' and 'No More Heroes'. I was hooked and from then on was committed to the band, and punk in general, which was greatly aided by the late John Peel. By the time I turned 13 in November 1978, I had *Black and White* and all of the singles and then I bought *Rattus*. My father, who hated punk, heard 'Ugly' and confiscated the album on account of the swearing, which was rich coming from parents who used the word 'fuck' as punctuation. He finally returned the album to me with strict instructions not to let my mother hear it, who herself was an Olympic standard swearer. This was my first lesson in authoritative hypocrisy.

Still, the band have been part of my life since I was 12 and I have loads of albums, been to loads of gigs, and have loads of t-shirts and memories. My 25th birthday was marked with a tattoo. My wife Julie and I saw the Stranglers in Reading in 2022 and... what a gig! It's one of the best I have been to of any band over my 41 years of gig going. Thank you to the Stranglers for being a major part of my life.

Y PLAS, UNIVERSITY OF CARDIFF

25 MARCH 2022, CARDIFF, UK

SAMMY MARTYR

Sammy Martyr with JJ, Baz and Dave

I find myself something of an anomaly amongst the younger Stranglers familyinblack members. My parents weren't particularly Stranglers fans, besides knowing the odd song; most of the other young 'uns I've met seem to have been raised by Stranglers-fanatic parents. Sometime in 2006, at the age of 12, I bought a *Best of Punk* compilation and one song in particular stood out by miles. It was called '(Get a) Grip (on Yourself)' by the Stranglers. I had never heard anything like the keyboards and instantly knew I wanted to start playing the piano.

By the age of 15, I was more into the rock and metal bands of the early Noughties but my listening habits shifted with the advent of streaming services as I discovered the treasure trove of music from the past. I had a few playlists with the odd Stranglers song on, but decided delve into their albums, each one with a striking album cover, strong conceptual feel, intellectual lyrical content and genius musical performances from each of the four members. Thus started a continuing obsession.

I had neglected keyboards for a few years but the complexities of Dave Greenfield's playing inspired me on a deep and meaningful level. His melodies have a calculated genius which always seems to be exactly what the song needs. His ever-evolving arsenal from one album to another got me deeply interested in synths and I dropped all my other A-Levels to take up music production and form my own band, Martyrials.

My first gig was in 2010. At this point I wasn't au fait with the line up changes and when I first laid eyes on Baz, I remember thinking, 'Wow, Hugh's changed a lot!' Since then, I have been to many, many shows and met all of the current line up and most of the previous members including Dave, where I told him he was the reason I played keyboards. I'm grateful to all the members new and old that have kept the band going for this long, so that someone born in 1993 could see their favourite band live so many times.

The Stranglers have been the soundtrack to my life and have been involved in many poignant moments. Their songs seeming to take on a new meaning with each listen and I seem to hear new things all the time: 'Was that synth line always there?'

They have been the soundtrack to my descent into drink and drug usage. The *Meninblack* album in particular is one that made a lot more sense when you're 'on another level' shall we say (though the accompanying paranoia of *Meninblack* conspiracy theory binge-reading is certainly not fun). I never met 'Harry', but I understood what they meant when they said, 'If once there was life there, now there's compromise' in relation to alcohol. Dark moments, *Dark Matters* indeed... But they also soundtracked my recovery and continued sobriety – two and a half years at time of writing, one day at a time.

I am sad that I never got to meet Dave when I was sober - I was recently reminded of the first time I met him with my friend Louise after a Birmingham show as I have no memory of it - a memory I can never get back. Their *Rebellion* 2019 show is also particularly important to me as it was one of the last times I saw my good friend Lucy Reynolds alive, as she sadly took her own life a few months after. She loved the Stranglers.

The band were, and continue to be, one of the most pioneering, original and creative groups on the planet, unafraid to take massive creative risks and ditch everything they had done on the previous album to go in a radical new direction. I went to four gigs on the final full UK tour. I hope I get to see them more times and that there's more music on the horizon. But whatever happens, the Stranglers aren't going anywhere and interest in them doesn't look it's stopping any time soon!

STACY SCHULMEYER

My best friend Penny and I booked tickets to see the Stranglers at the *Reading Festival* in 1983 to celebrate finishing our A levels. Our results weren't exactly as good as our parents had hoped, and Pen couldn't go so I headed off with her then boyfriend and his mates. This was my first time seeing the band and what an introduction. Down at the front, with the masses, having the time of my life.

Pen and I saw the band many, many times over the years, even getting to go backstage for drink with JJ and Baz after a gig in Oxford in 2010. Jet was in his room eating Chinese so we didn't see him, unfortunately, but Dave came over to ask for a light. I felt like all my Christmases had come at once.

Stacy Schulmeyer was at Cardiff in '22

In 2011, Pen called me to see if I wanted to go to the Convention in Camden. Hell yeah! We booked a hotel and off we went. Once inside, we had a little wander around and who should we bump into but Pen's ex-boyfriend from our school days and his mate who I had met at Reading. We had fabulous weekend reminiscing and catching up on the last almost 30 years. Since then, Andrew and I have met up every year (apart from Covid times) to see the Stranglers a couple of times each tour. When the last tour was announced, we booked Guildford and Brixton (which was originally the last date) but when Covid hit and the dates were rescheduled, I was gutted that he and I wouldn't be together for the final gig of the full final tour as there were no tickets left for Cambridge.

Then all of a sudden, Cardiff was rescheduled - and there were tickets! The icing on the cake was seeing JJ and Baz in their car after the sound check and having a chat with JJ just before the gig.

My first Stranglers gig and last gig of the full final tour with Andrew - the circle closed... or did it?

BRIXTON ACADEMY

5 MAY 2022, LONDON, UK

MARK DAVIES

Mark Davies at the 2019 Tokyo 'Meet and Greet'

The Stranglers have just always been the soundtrack to my life. Never a day goes by without something by them coming up on my playlist. My first gig? I don't recall the date but it was at Hammersmith Odeon. I just remember as a young teenager the frightening aura of the band dominating the stage. The crowd bouncing all as one, the sweat, the bruises, the lost voice. This memory was vividly recreated at Brixton 2022, especially the bruises.

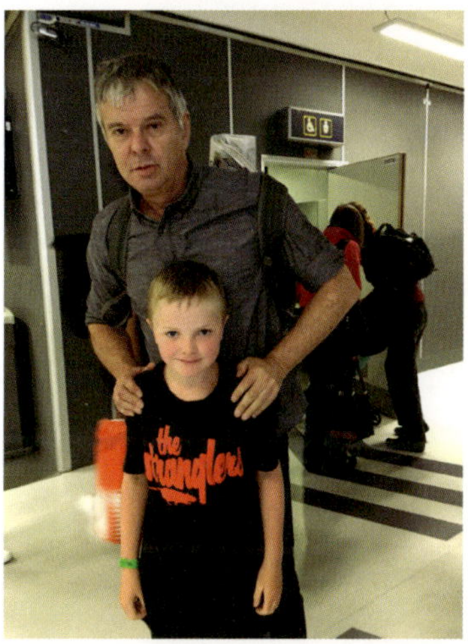

Mark Davies' son Nick with Dave and JJ

My favourite live track? Oddly, 'Waltzinblack'. Once the lights dim, the 'Waltz' plays over the PA and the hairs on my neck rise in pure anticipation of the next 90 minutes of sheer exhilaration and excitement. I have seen many, many gigs over the years whilst living in the UK, all of which are now but distant memories.

I left the UK in 1997, shortly after the *Friday the Thirteenth* gig at the Royal Albert Hall. This was the first gig I took

Mark Davies' son Nick with Dave

my newly married wife to. I recall travelling home on the train, clutching a black balloon, thinking, 'Could that possibly be my last ever Stranglers gig?' But roll on several decades and I have been fortunate to continue seeing them around the globe, especially making the effort when they come to my newly adopted country, Australia.

In February 2016 I completed my first (complete) eight date tour around New Zealand and Australia; many thousands of miles were flown. In July 2017, I was so proud to take my wife and my boys, Ben (10) and Nick (8), to the Bands in the Sands gig at Perranporth. I was even more proud that Nick was determined to join his dad on the rail for the entire gig. The highlight for him, or maybe for me, was that Baz personally handed him his set list and his plectrum. To cap it all off, we flew back with Dave and JJ on the plane to Stansted, where they both happily chatted and posed with Nick. A very proud dad moment.

In April 2018, I completed another full New Zealand and Australia tour and November 2019 saw me in Tokyo. The three gigs were so good and the Japanese so meticulous in the entry to the venues. We had to queue up in the order of the ticket number. Luckily for our small group from Australia and New Zealand, we had low number tickets. The Japanese crowd was very exuberant and we got to go to three soundchecks and have one meet and greet with the whole band, with Baz mouthing off the whole time.

February 2020 saw another complete Australia and New Zealand tour completed. But COVID-19 was bubbling around and less than two weeks after the tour, Australia's borders closed and the world as we knew it ended. Little did I know that Saturday 15th February 2020 at Auckland Town Hall was the last live gig with Dave Greenfield I would witness.

February 2022 and Australia reopened its borders. Perfect timing as I had six gigs on a *Final Full* tour to attend in the UK, with a new line up. I seriously have no idea if I will get a chance to see the Stranglers again, but it has been one hell of a ride and the final tour will have ended it on a high for me. And, yes, 'Waltzinblack' still made the hairs on my neck rise.

MALCOLM WYATT

The Stranglers at the PRS for Music Heritage award plaque unveiling. Photo Barry Cain

I so wanted to get down to my old manor for the PRS for Music Heritage award plaque unveiling and invite-only short set at The Star in Guildford on the last day of January 2019. But it wasn't to be. Geography, family circumstances and commitments and a lack of cash defeated me. The closest I got was a brief feature on the ITV's *News at Ten* and a trawl through social media. Ah well, maybe another time.

But then the world changed forever that following year, the coronavirus pandemic affecting us and the way we lived, immeasurably. And then on 3 May 2020 the lights went out good and proper as word came through that Dave Greenfield had left us.

Three years after that Star date with a difference, I'd have loved to have made it when JJ and Co. returned to the site of my first Stranglers show in late January 1982 at Guildford Civic Hall, where hopefully the spitting from the more moronic elements up front had finally stopped. But, again, I failed to show up. I could blame geography and finances again, but while there was a feeling that coronavirus had hit us hard and while it was so good to be back out there again, there was still that nagging feeling that Dave would no longer be there (in body at least), and maybe it would all just be a tad too emotional.

I've managed to catch Hugh's band in fine form either side of the lockdowns in Clitheroe then Manchester, and they continue to impress (with no element of competition when it comes to comparison with Mr Cornwell's former band), but somehow this was different. Stupid, I know, because if JJ, Baz and Jim – along with new recruit Toby Hounsham – could get back out there, surely I could too. Yet the pandemic still wasn't truly over, and perhaps I was happy enough just clinging on to that picture in my mind's eye of Dave supping his pint, mid-solo, on my last sighting in 2014, that wonderful grin there for all to see.

Besides, by then I had a new LP to wallow in, the rightly acclaimed *Dark Matters* – landing nine and a half years after Jet Black's last studio contributions on *Giants* – proving to be the most wonderful of tributes to an iconic keyboard player's memory that his bandmates could deliver. That introductory swirl of the organ on 'Water' is just the first moment that brings a lump to the throat. Then I'm proper gone when the keys come in on 'This Song'. And that's before we even get to 'And If You Should See Dave'. Three songs in, and I'm a mess.

In the words of 'The Raven', 'Fly straight with perfection; find me a new direction.' The Stranglers have nothing to prove. They go on, and they remain vital. And even if they throw it all in just around the corner, what a legacy they've left us. Thanks, fellas.

TIM BAGNALL

Tim Bagnall's son Alex is now a fan

I could go on and on about memorable gigs - there's loads of them: Exeter 2007, when my kids came to see them for the first time; numerous times at Manchester Academy bumping into old mates on the barge-march down to the front; losing my brother mid-gig at The Forum in Kentish Town in 1993, to later find him fast asleep in the disabled section; my brother (again) having a piss down the front at the open air Maine Road gig supporting Simple Minds in 1991 – the bog was too far away so he sparked a near fight with some Simple Minds fans before a group of Stranglers fans backed us up (I can't blame the Minds fans, to be fair, but it was a brilliant familyinblack moment); and loads of gigs with my missus, who gives me plenty of grief for spending a fortune on the band but doesn't like to miss anything!

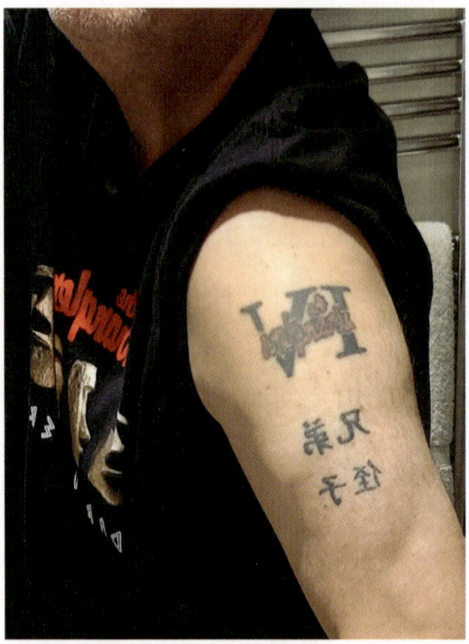
Tim Bagnall's badge of honour

Probably the most gratifying thing is seeing my son Alex singing along at gigs as he's a regular now too. To know he is feeling some of that attitude that I did so many years ago and that the music - old and new - is stirring his soul is just the best!

Like it is for a lot of people, it's been a long journey with the band but they really have been some of the best times of my life. Being a Stranglers fan is a badge of honour. Long live the Stranglers!

ROB OCKFORD

Rob Ockford wanted his Stranglers tattoo left alone

I first got into the Stranglers when I was 11 years old. My sister's boyfriend had purchased *No More Heroes* but decided he didn't like it and gave it to me because he knew I really liked the title track. I first got to see them live in the mid-Eighties and have lost count of the number of times I have seen them.

I decided to have the band's name and a rat tattooed on my right arm, and some years later when I met them at HMV in Birmingham, all the members signed their autograph around the tattoo in pen. The next day, I had all the signatures tattooed over and it looked superb.

Some years later, I was unlucky enough to be involved in a major accident where I was badly burnt and taken to hospital. I was then transferred to the specialist burns unit in Birmingham. On entering the A and E department, I was met by various doctors and nurses who bombarded with questions about my beliefs and things they could or could not do. As I was totally off my face on a cocktail of drugs, I apparently told them they could do anything they wanted apart from touching my Stranglers tattoo. This was to have a major bearing on my treatment, as I had suffered a 50 per cent burn that was mostly third and fourth degree and I was given an eight per cent chance of survival.

I required loads of skin grafts. As I had told them my tattoo was off limits, they could not use the skin from that area and this made their job so much harder. I then spent the next two weeks in a coma, so there was no chance of me changing my mind about my decision.

Whilst in hospital, a lot of the staff would come into my room and comment that I was the crazy bloke that was fighting for my life when I entered the hospital, but all I was worried about was my tattoo. I spent the next three months in hospital recovering. That was a long and painful time, but at least I had loads of time to listen to music! I also had a signed CD and picture of the band sent to me by the fan club, and that took pride of place on the wall of my room.

Some months after my accident, JJ Burnel sent me an email wishing me well and a speedy recovery, and a copy of it still hangs on my wall along with some of my other Stranglers memorabilia. I was amazed that he had taken the time to contact me, and it was a fantastic gesture that I will never forget.

Thankfully I have made a fairly good recovery, and have since had my right arm covered in tattoos that are Stranglers related, but I decided not to have my original tattoo re-inked even though parts of it are scarred and burnt.

MATTHEW ELVIS BROWN

During the first part of lockdown, Jim Radley devised The Raven Inn - a socially distanced pub night for Stranglers fans... Very soon, Paul Cooklin and me were drafted in to assist with hosting, planning and running, and for 14 months or so during the pandemic the three of us did a Raven Inn Zoom meeting every Saturday – keeping our love of the Meninblack alive and opening our virtual doors to fellow fans and friends from all over the world. We still host these Saturday sessions on a monthly basis.

After the crap the planet has been through with the pandemic, and losing Dave and the best part of two years, it was a real shot in the arm to see the band again on their Final Full tour this yea. They were as tight as ever and the energy that Jim and Toby bring to the band is brilliant...

God bless The Stranglers and the Familyinblack.

STUART PEARCE

Stuart Pearce, Toby Hounsham, Jim Macaulay, Baz Warne, JJ and Kenny Jackett

Ten years ago, when Carol and I first became a couple (we are now married), she was aware that I was a fan of the Stranglers, this punk band from the Seventies, and that I was a regular gig-goer over the years. Being a music fan but not of the punk genre, she was intrigued to come along but a little worried by the band's reputation and that of the punk and new wave music scene. I found a summer festival somewhere in Surrey that the Meninblack were headlining and, with a little nervousness, she set off with me to experience her first meeting with a so-called punk band. As we arrived in our car, we parked up backstage and got out of the car to be greeted by JJ and Baz, who were charm personified. They offered Carol a cup of tea, which they made themselves, and having had a 15 minute chat they said, 'Well, now you're here we'll get started.' Carol looked at me in amazement and asked, 'Are all gigs like this?!' To which I replied, 'No, only the Stranglers ones, as they look after their fans.'

Photo Darren Rochell

ACKNOWLEDGEMENTS

Richard Houghton would like to thank: Neil Cossar; Liz Sanchez; Gabriel Smith; Owen Carne; Antoine Lukaszewski & David Boni for the photos; Ivan Hancock; Graeme (Mully) Mullan & his blog Alternative Mullster; Rory Fiztgerald; Steve Worrall & his Retro Man blog; Malcolm Wyatt & his blog writewyattuk.com; *The Independent* & James McNair.

And the womaninskyblue, Kate Sullivan.

L'Olympia in Paris, Wednesday 27 November 2019. Photo by David Boni

Photo Antoine Lukaszewski

SJM CONCERTS PRESENT
THE
STRANGLERS
RATTUS AT THE ROUNDHOUSE
30 YEAR ANNIVERSARY
PLUS
JOHN COOPER
CLARKE
PLUS DJ
ANDY DUNKLEY
(THE LIVIN' JUKE BOX)
SUNDAY 4TH NOVEMBER
LONDON ROUNDHOUSE
0870 389 1846 / WWW.ROUNDHOUSE.ORG.UK

the stranglers
MAMA Concerts
THE CONCERT COMPANY
VORVERKAUF: MÜNCHEN: Pressehaus Bayerstrasse, Tel. 5306351 · Discocenter Citta 2000, Tel. 344759 · Radio Rim, Theatinerstr., Tel. 226503 · Hieber am Dom, Kaufinger Str. 23, Tel. 227045 · Abendzeitung, Sendlinger Straße, Tel. 2377223 · ABR, Karlsplatz 12, Tel. 5904334 · ABR, Sendlinger Straße, Tel. 240439 · ABR, Hauptbahnhof, Tel. 5904234 · Kasse Circus Krone, Tel. 558166 · Pavillon Schallplatte-Shop, Tel. 597336 · Asta, Amelienstraße
Freitag, 23. Juni '78 · 20.00 Uhr · München – Schwabingerbräu

Interteam Tour Promotion presents
the stranglers on tour
Ratus Norwegious
1C 064-99458
No more Heroes
1C 064-99560
ELECTROLA
Freitag 20 Uhr
23. November '79
Saarbrücken
Aula der Universität
23. Nov. '79

ΡΟΔΟΝ-LIVE!
ΜΑΡΝΗ 24, ΑΘΗΝΑ, ΤΗΛ. 5247427
the stranglers
Special Guests NO MAN'S LAND
ΠΑΡΑΣΚΕΥΗ 22 ΦΕΒΡΟΥΑΡΙΟΥ
ΣΑΒΒΑΤΟ 23 ΦΕΒΡΟΥΑΡΙΟΥ
10 Μ.Μ.
MY MUSIC
ΕΙΣΙΤΗΡΙΑ ΠΡΟΠΩΛΟΥΝΤΑΙ:
ΣΤΑ ΚΕΝΤΡΙΚΑ ΔΙΣΚΟΠΩΛΕΙΑ & ΣΤΟ ΡΟΔΟΝ
ΠΛΗΡΟΦΟΡΙΕΣ: 52.47.427
ΠΡΟΠΩΛΗΣΗ 3.000 ΔΡΧ
ΤΑΜΕΙΟ 3.500 ΔΡΧ

the stranglers
HOT
Hljómle
Póker
HALLI &
Laugardalshöll
Forsala aðg
FÁLKINN V

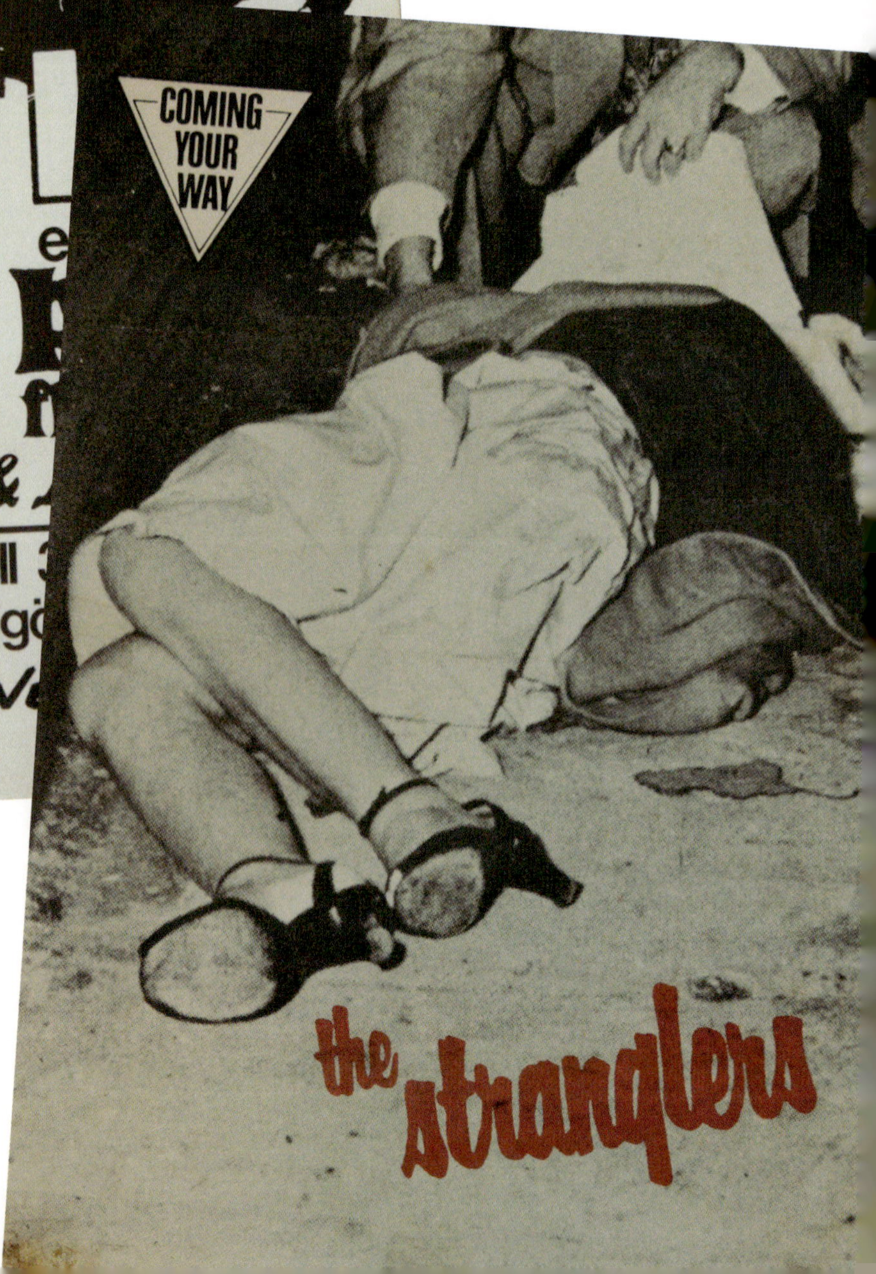
COMING YOUR WAY
the stranglers